THE ADVENTURES OF JOY CHRONICLES BOOK 3

A WISH is GRANTED

JOURNAL OF GALACTIC ROMANCE AND GLOBAL EVOLUTION

♡ Joy Elaine
6/23/19

By Joy Elaine

www.JoyElaine.com

The Adventures of Joy Chronicles Book 3
A Wish is Granted
Journal of Galactic Romance and Global Evolution

Copyright © Joy Elaine 2016

Published by Joy Books

ISBN-10: 1530186757
ISBN-13: 978-1530186754

DEDICATION

To Liponie, the most magical being I know.
Thanks for helping our hearts to sing.

ACKNOWLEDGEMENTS

My gratitude to members of the Joy Councils for their continued support and assistance. Thanks to you, the bumps we encountered in this chronicle didn't throw us off track.

I am grateful for the many emissaries from other universes who stepped forward to join our council as well as to create Joy Councils in their universes.

Thanks to those of you who are attending our council meetings and adding your input to our transmissions. If you reside on Earth, your support plays a fundamental role in assisting all of us to evolve smoothly, gracefully and magically.
Go Team One Tribe!

In addition I wish to thank:
George Verongos, editor
Angela Phillips, cover design, graphic design

Storyline Participants for A Wish is Granted

Academy of Enrichment—formerly Tonas's spaceship Inishimora; now a place of study for individuals from non-dual worlds to learn about Earth

Aconna Shareeah—a high ranking Atlantean on the Joy Council. I knew her only as Aconna in book two

Aton—an embodiment of the essence of our Sun; member of the Joy Council and married to Gaia

Buffalo's Heart—a Native American sacred space located inside a hill in North Dakota

CEV—Council for Earth Vigilance; a collective of ninety-four energy beings now most frequently known as the Swizzlers

Chailee—name of our universe

Champ—Swizzler with blue hair

Charlie Brown (Charlie)—CEV and number one Swizzler; the only one who communicates verbally

Chocheenaho—Native American whose energy presence is located in the sacred space of Buffalo's Heart, North Dakota

Comahlee (aka Kee Kee)—a genie who attempted to help us with Liponie's birthday party

Commander Ashtar—Supreme Commander of the Ashtar Command and a member of the Joy Council

Cory—a sentient crystal in my soul lineage

Esthra—the angel guide I speak with most frequently

Gaia—embodiment of the essence of Earth, member of the Joy Council and married to Aton

Gogohsha—an individual who created Liponie to be a baby sitter for his son, Lowmoeshee

Hathor—consort of Horus and member of the Joy Council. She was also the Norse goddess Freyja

Horus—son of Osiris and Isis, guardian of humanity and member of the Joy Council

Iniquasha—Shoshone Indian no longer pissed off and located in the ascended master temple at Lake Louise

Inoh—representative of a collective of energy beings who wished to embody on Earth; they were happy to occupy a non-dual arena within Earth that Liponie created and called Equinox

Isis—guardian of Earth and humanity, member of the Joy Council and mate of Osiris

Joyous—first female dragon born on Earth in this timeline—August 9, 2014

Joy—Sheliah and Rosebud's baby girl fairy

Khnum—has assisted humans for millions of years and frequently works with Aton

Konta (female dragon) and **Horay** (male dragon)—second dragon couple to lay an egg on Earth

Liponie—genie from Andromeda assisting me with pranks and Joy Council work; member of the Joy Council

Lolalah—fairy queen in Sheliah's garden who gives her role as queen to Sheliah

Melchizedek—ascended master assisting me with playing the violin and member of the Joy Council

Osiris—guardian of Earth and humanity, member of the Joy Council and mate of Isis

Pinky—first Swizzler to decide to be a female

Pootie—very large and ancient lizard living in Sheliah's fairy garden

Queen Kahleah—an Atlantean of great importance in my soul lineage who gave me some of her genetic attributes; she exists on the 10th dimension of Earth

Rosebud—the first ever boy fairy created by Gaia to be a partner for Sheliah

Sananda—ascended master and member of the Joy Council

Sheearah—embodiment of the planet Jupiter

Sheliah—a fairy that I knew when I was a little girl

Sif (Lahray)—Thor's mate and member of the Joy Council

Swizzlers—also known as the CEV

Thor—a non-dual being and member of the Joy Council

Thoth—a non-dual being and member of the Joy Council

Tonas—Ashtar Commander and member of the Joy Council; tall, dark and handsome

Tria—an Agarthan on the Joy Council

True Heart—(Konishewah) librarian for a pre-historic Native American tribe and member of the Joy Council

Woonfred—a dragon and member of the Joy Council

Zeezzz—a crystal who reluctantly embodied to attend Liponie's birthday party; Cory's mother

Representatives and their universes added to the Joy Council:

Aheeshanarrah Kahteem—Council Member from the Tollbeet Universe

Bohnar Comeen—Council Presence from Comahleeah Universe; their main world is Zeefmah and Moosheah spit is their ceremonial drink

Bowginuhsar—Chief Council for the Lowmeesha Universe

Candahriah—from the Kallamiah Universe

Choshe Ahsahneeuh——Chief Counsel from the Eyeintoreenah Universe; the Folgors—beings capable of dancing on their fingers—live on Chesseeak, a world within that universe

Demahtoo Gobi—Councilman from the Nahbinoshar Universe; his wife is Eesah Kohmahlee Gobi

Fractinuta—Supreme Council Chairman of the Ackvidohnon Universe

Haireetah Voreeneeuh—from the Ahkahnay Universe; her world is Zihcorahn

Harahnsha (Har)—from the Fonar Universe; his world is Coriah

Historia Terreeah—Council Presence from the Moedayahduh Universe

Ihroenees—Emissary from the Sehhoetica Universe; he is tall, has a head that resembles a green parrot and walks upright; his mate is Sahshirah and Kindeera is one of their children

Jenairrah Magursha—Council Presence from the world of Paireeleeah in the Insear Universe

Joseah and Festona Beshar—from the Slanar Universe

Joyyahl Kindar—Council Presence from the Corena Universe; her world is Darroan

Kahkahnohsar Kronosahn (KK)—from the Kahshar Universe

Kahsheenah Vohnsheer—Representative from the Nasconerah Universe; his world is Lahkashnah

Kallahm Amar—Emissary from the Booseeuh Universe; his world is Santee

Kallieanash—Council Champion from the Coneizeah Universe

Kamala Shrow—Universal Presence from the Joeshrahnah Universe; her world is Ahrowsh

Kyleah—a woman in my soul lineage; her world Zhollah (Zoreah is the embodiment of this world) is in the Zorah Universe; she was the first representative from another universe to ask to join the Joy Council

Lana Fahreetwoah—from the Zahnahsh Universe; her world is Jardaniveeah

Lanasheatoe (Lashana)—from the Bunnuhyahsheah Universe

Lowcahn—Council Principal from the Zhansarrah Universe

Matreeus Soonimarah Keylosh—from the Inzleeookeerah Universe; her world is Renuhsha

Monahquah Senet—from Gaygoreeah Universe; his world is Kaireesha

Neftee Voenesh—Councilman from the Deeohnah Universe; his world is Ahsha

Nicetorrine or Nicktorrine (Nicky)—Emissary from the Annahkolee Universe; the other race in this universe call themselves the Fanacordee

Nokeenosah Shertee—Ambassador of the Kallahshar Universe

Nosahdean—from the Lisseecora Universe

Ohniuh Comb—Council Presence from the Porneeseesee Universe; her world is Eeshenarrah

Plany Ohsheer—Emissary from the Nordahnee Universe

Rahnosah Prahnic (Rahsawsee for short)—from the Lindar Universe; his world is Candarfor

Shannara—Kangshee Universe representative

Silgah Holinrah—Governing Presence from the Lowmeereeuh Universe; her world is Nahshegrah

Sohmeeneeuh Toelinah—Emissary from the Annapeenorah Universe

Tassmarr Teetooareuh—Elite Presence from the Antarrah Universe

Toemarrah Metahn—Emissary from the Neftoo Universe; his world is Eesha

Yarah Homma—Emissary from the Inseanahrah Universe; her world is Nahgahnahsayyear

Zahseet—Council Presence from the Zhorin (Zhorinatare) Universe; she is small, very pretty and has a fish tail

NOTES TO READER

Read this book start to finish and enjoy the journey. Enhance your personal evolution and the elevation of Earth by participating in the work of the Joy Councils. Turn to page 421 read the Mission Participation Directives and join the greatest adventure of your life.

Terms that may require further explanation are noted in bold the first time they appear and correspond with the glossary found at the back of the book.

In joy!

CHAPTER ONE
September 14 and 15, 2014

This morning I heard Tonas say, "Until such time as we are together, I wish to offer you my heart in assurance that this is the beginning of our lifelong love. Let's move across the gate here to the 10th dimension."

I don't think I'll mention to him that I heard those words. I loved hearing them, but the idea of a love like that still seems like an unreachable dream, especially since lifelong could mean quattrodecillion years and more. I realize he is content to wait until the day I *know* he is my lifelong love. I am waiting for that day also.

"Esthra, earlier today someone offered me something. Who was speaking to me and what do they have to offer?"

"This was one of the Lyran people; several of them wish to assist you to remember some cosmic principles that you will be able to use on the 8th dimension and even part of the 7th dimension. They suggest that you come to the temple of Harmeen via Tonas's ship."

Cosmic principles sound good to me even if I have to wait awhile to access them. I gate to Inishimora and ask Tonas to take me to the temple of Harmeen. He doesn't request any additional directions and immediately I can feel we are in the atmosphere above that temple. He assists me to transmit to the temple and then to follow the three people who are waiting for me there. We move into a room containing an orb which must be very large because I feel myself move into it. Even though they are always with me, it seems like a good idea to personally invite Archangel Michael, Metatron, Sananda and Melchizedek to watch the proceedings.

Sananda informs me that the Lyrans are streaming laser beams into my chakras and as soon as they touch the chakras they turn into sacred geometries. "This is all happening in your aura, not your physical body. These geometries consist of cosmic principles that are non-dual and they are interfacing with all of your levels of consciousness. They're finished but they would like for you to stay for at least nine hours;

everyone else can stay as well. You will move into a beautiful red-colored crystalline encasement. I am suggesting to Tonas that he take you back to his ship at the end of nine hours and then bring you back to Earth's atmosphere; when you wake up, simply gate back to your home."

September 15, 2014

Esthra greets me by calling me his beloved and says he is ready to assist me. I ask him to tell me about the work the Lyrans did yesterday. He says it is a tremendous advantage for me, because as things would apply on Lyra, I will be applying them on Earth. Lyra is a place of magic, music and art and the principles I received were selected for me by many individuals who love me dearly.

These are examples Esthra gives me of abilities that will appear later in my life: As I move through my day, whatever I desire will appear before me. If I decide to play an instrument, I will be able to play it like it I had studied it my whole life.

I'm really glad I jumped at the opportunity to visit the Lyrans. Those abilities are ones I am eagerly anticipating, especially the one connected to music.

Recently I was thinking about working with Ganesha concerning the siddhis—master abilities like teleporting and bi-locating—and I heard, "Now this is the turn point."

I've never consciously met this Hindu god who is considered to be the remover of obstacles and is pictured as a dancing, rotund elephant. Maybe someday I'll chat with him about why he is depicted that way, but not today.

Since Sananda was a student in an ancient academy along with Ganesha, I ask him to speak with me about the siddhis. He says that several people in addition to Ganesha have been working together to light me up. "They have a package containing principles that will link to your 8th dimensional self; these principles are part of the automatic nature of all of the siddhis and are from different worlds.

In the past, these siddhis were named so that individuals could grasp them. You do not need those names; you will simply develop what you already have in your levels of consciousness. These principles are keys to help you access and link all that up. The more you move into the 8th dimension the more automatic these will become; they will also help you through the 7th dimension."

Continuing my conversation with Sananda, I mention that this morning I heard it was important to drink some kind of milk. He explains that St. Germain's Elixir of Life is creamy, it is the color of milk and he offers to guide me in experiencing it. I accept, of course, and he directs me to gate onto the hillside of Mount Shasta. St. Germain will assist me to shift into the ascended master temple there.

"Walk directly up to the fountain containing the milky fluid, fill the container there with the elixir and drink it. You may gate into this temple and drink the elixir anytime you wish."

I've heard that there is something called the Crystal of Aum at this temple and Sananda suggests this is also something I might enjoy experiencing. He explains that it is a blue crystal that resonates the Aum sound; this helps to move toxins out of the energy and physical bodies of anyone who steps into it. Following Sananda's directions, I step into the crystal, activate it, roll forward to where I am finished and then step back into my physical body.

"Thank you for bringing Heifetz to play for me. I was so delighted that he took the time to come."

"It was a little bit of a challenge, and yet he was so very taken by your adoration of him. He was a teacher, as you might know, and so to have someone as important as you take an interest in him gave him a very exciting role to play."

This statement about my importance still takes me aback.

"My ears didn't hear him but some part of me must have because I was crying the whole time he was playing. Was I able to assist him in any way with his abilities?"

"I am assured that the answer is yes. How you applied this I am beyond understanding."

I suggest that maybe it occurred when I offered gifts to people in the Fifth Realm. After checking, Sananda says it is interesting that not only did I assist Heifetz, but many others as well. He adds that the advancements that were rippling through that time were also a factor.

"He was a prodigy and if one is inspired at a young enough age, this is how the spark can be lit. I am speaking to someone who could write a book about him."

Another name to add to a list of people I could write about.

"Yesterday, I was thinking about when I was talking with Gaia and Aton at their wedding party and cautioning them about the possibility of getting hurt skiing. I realized that kind of thinking was ridiculous; I suppose they don't have accidents."

Sananda laughs as he asks me how there could be an accident in a non-dual dimension.

"I don't know! We're used to incidents like, 'Oops, I tripped and fell and broke my leg!'"

"That is expected in duality."

"I have never been very coordinated. Learning new movements or dancing skills, tai-chi or the various exercise classes I've gone to has been challenging. I would really like for my body to be extremely coordinated and flexible."

I'm delighted when Sananda says it will be impossible for me to be uncoordinated or inflexible because when duality is gone, resistance is gone. He adds, "There are no strings tied to you which pull you; there is no need to drag energy along with you in your movements. Instead, you are free!"

I mention that Tonas's difficulty in driving a car helped me to realize that perhaps we have an advantage over beings that have never experienced duality because we're used to having to do things. He confirms that is a tremendous advantage, and that it was an advantage that all initiates and instructors in the ancient academies discovered.

"You are well aware that I was in a fist fight."

"Oh! No, I didn't know that."

"Yes, I was in a fist fight and I believe that it was one of my finest hours as an initiate of the academy. I did have my nose damaged; there was a tremendous blood flow. It was healed, of course, and is still as magnificent as ever. I felt the pumping of the blood, the anger rise in me;

I felt my fist fold and I moved it outward. As I moved it outward my sparring partner was a little ahead of me; he must have had more boiling blood than myself. We were rolling on the ground; it was a spectacle for all to see. We were pulled apart and went into what was considered 'counseling.'"

I ask Sananda if he remembers what the fight was about. He replies that he was jealous! He was an academy initiate then and not an ascended master, I assume, but jealousy just seems like too human of an emotion for a man of his current stature to ever have experienced.

He explains that he was also angry with himself because he was not mastering a tutorial that they were both studying. "When I cornered him to ask him the secrets of that tutorial, he laughed at me and told me that I would have to find my way to learn it. Also that he was a far superior student of this because of his duality upbringing. That is when I spouted to him that he had also gone crazy four and a half hundred thousand years before and had to be locked into a chamber until he came to his senses. That is also when my fist closed and his moved out swifter. He understood the fist fight and I did not. We made a tremendous spectacle. I only had the one experience of this."

He adds that it is his belief he has been able to be of greater assistance to humanity since he knows what it feels like to have your blood boil. I check with him to make sure it's OK for me to include his story here because I've learned people have preferences about their private lives. He answers that he is an open book.

Now, I find myself revealing to Sananda a concern that I haven't been conscious of even having.

"I wonder if Tonas is too good. That sounds terrible, doesn't it? It's just that I've had quite a bit of drama and struggle in my life and he hasn't experienced any of that."

Sananda wants to know why that would concern me and I'm somewhat at a loss as to how to answer him. It occurs to me that when I am in that non-dual 8th dimension I'm going to be, hopefully, a much nicer person. I will have finally cleared and released my disempowering beliefs and all my old stories containing fear, anger, and similar emotions.

After a few moments of consideration, I'm able to reply that perhaps this won't be an issue for me when I am in the higher dimensions.

This evening as I ponder my concern about Tonas being too good, I realize how silly it is. Here is a man who will never lie to me or cheat on me, doesn't smoke or have any addictions, will never be jealous of me or uninterested in my interests, is stunningly handsome, or so I've been told, and only wants the best for me; obviously, *I'm* the one with issues to be addressed.

After I greet Tonas at the Joy Councils, he tells me I am receiving a well-deserved accolade. I'm slightly embarrassed as I ask why I'm receiving an accolade.

"All that you brought to those delicious ones; they are returned from their shenanigans."

"Thank you all for the accolades, but, you see, I've already moved past the party. I have something for Gaia that I got a couple of nights ago; it has to do with lighting her up because of the assistance she's given to me. Who can tell me more about this?"

Isis tells me that I have a special blessing for Gaia, "that has been brought through from your very deepest heart of that spirit that you use in transmission of the Great Spirit. If you transmit it into the crystal it can then be transmitted in all directions from here in the Earth and from the Moon, and we can continue to do so."

I tell the council that I'd like to expand the transmission to include a blessing and a flowing of joy to all sentient beings and every particle of all the universes. Osiris suggests that we simply make part of the transmission for Gaia in all directions of time and then another part for all other worlds. He adds that I will know how to make the transmission through my voice and then the council will apply it.

This is something I usually do spontaneously and even though I'm not feeling spontaneous at this moment, I'm going to do my best.

"I open my heart and transmit this blessing to Gaia. I'm grateful for every part of you, your clouds and seas, your birds and bees and I thank you for nourishing me and for nourishing all the beings who live upon and in you. I send my love, my deepest blessings and my joy to you.

I am grateful for the experience of transmitting the energy of the Great Spirit and for my Higher Self flowing love and blessings to you. I thank you for the indigenous peoples and their wisdom. Now I'm expanding to include a blessing for Aton and for all the planets, all the Joy Stars, to every essence, to every particle, through all the threads to every universe. I thank you for I AM that I AM and so are you."

Swizzler One tells me that each person, each plant, each seed and each grain of sand received the message in the way that would most benefit them. "That is what we are transmitting also; it is as if a translator of heart. We have now, within each of us, a heart. Thank you to Gaia for this gift to us."

This moves me so much that I speak the language to them and tell them I love them.

"It was for each of us a gift that allows us to feel most intimately all that exists. It is beautiful and we are beautiful."

"Yes, you are. Thank you all for your help. Farewell."

Note to readers:

This morning I got a taste of instant manifestation. I heard Tonas ask me, "Shall we step into the dimension and see if it is possible?" We had to have been in the 8th dimension because I thought about a bright new penny and the copper itself manifested on my hand!

These kinds of abilities will also be available for *you*! Here are some questions to consider: What will you do with your life when you are able to easily manifest your every desire? What will you be doing then that you feel like you can't do now? Will you be living where you live now? What kind of home will you create? What kind of physical appearance will you choose? How will you spend your days?

CHAPTER TWO
September 17, 2014

"Esthra, someone told me I'll be practicing a more modern version of the siddhis."

"The more modern version is your breath; your breath is the embodiment of your truth."

"I remember breathing on the Native Americans when I worked with them in 2001. I didn't know what that meant at the time. Can you explain a little more?"

"It has to do with the levels of enlightenment that you are achieving. These are a part of your breath and every truth is carried on it. You live your truth, you walk your walk and as you stumble and fall then pick yourself up and move forward, more people learn than if you were sitting in an ashram all day. It's more relevant to be someone who has problems and overcomes them."

"I'm still not sure how my breath assists others."

"Everything you do is logged into collective consciousness. You're going to become famous; you already are affecting all the indigenous peoples through all **timelines**. In 2001 that was your soul essence in its purity that was transmitting through your consciousness. Now you're moving into embracing that consciousness even though you are a human being living your life. The levels of enlightenment you express in your thoughts and actions are the truth that you are embodying. If you get upset about something or you get sad, you get over it quickly. When you do that, people learn from that because it is stored in collective consciousness. People's brains constantly sort through the information recorded in collective consciousness. Those of you in SVH have made it so that you don't sift like that, but everyone else does."

This morning I heard a member of the Joy Council say, "We will take your hand and walk with you as you explore your new life." I loved the sound of that. These beings are dear, dear friends now. I can picture myself walking down the street holding hands with Tonas while a couple of Swizzlers are chatting with Liponie as they tag along. Well, maybe not chatting, maybe window shopping. I bet they would love to visit Disneyland; I'm going to put that on my "to do" list.

At the Joy Councils after Tonas and I exchange greetings, he tells me everyone is waiting to hear me and Aton is waiting in another room for me. I ask to see Aton first and Tonas says he has his bride with him. He warns me to be prepared because they are most cuddly. I love the idea of our Sun and Earth having bodies for cuddling.

As soon as Aton greets me, I burst out with a request to hug them both. He thinks my request is charming. Even though I'm not yet experiencing the sensation of touch at the council, just the thought of being able to hug them uplifts my spirits.

I've been feeling a bit nosy about their post-nuptial experiences, so I ask Gaia if they skied. She replies that there was no skiing. I ask if there was hot tubbing. She tells me that there was a tub that was hot. My curiosity is only increased by her non answers, so I ask if they had a chance to explore much of their new home. Finally, I receive a more informative answer when she says they have been exploring one another's bodies.

"I imagine so, and isn't it wonderful?"

"It *is* wonderful, and may I also say, my vision of what our abode would become has been expanded millions upon millions of times more than what I would ever have expected. It is so beautiful and, of course, we used your toaster. Thank you both."

I remark that my toaster just quit working so I had to buy a new one. Gaia replies that if only Liponie could have made me one it would have been the best. I say that I'm looking forward to the time when he can do things like that for me here.

After I said that, it occurred to me that *I* will be able to create a perfect toaster. I'm not as fascinated by toasters as these people are, so toaster creation would come after perfect wardrobe for perfect body, perfect greenhouse, perfect home…

My report to Aton is that interesting things are going on in my head. He wants to know what I'm experiencing.

"I had the sense of something sliding from the middle of my brain to the left and then back to the middle, and then to the right and then back to the middle. It felt like this was maintenance to clean out my brain."

He's laughing as he tells me he took a big spoon and whisked the contents of my brain up. "It is like what you suggest, only it is more a purging of energies that are unnecessary."

"Good. Last night I saw a box open up and there was a little white index card in it with nothing on it that I could see. Then I heard, 'The dogma is lifted; the past was recycled.' That was wonderful!"

"It is more than wonderful, and it is all in collaboration with what is happening with the energies that are around you and within you. With this brain expansion you are able to hold more of the higher energies."

The only thing he wants to do today is some minor readjusting in order to align the energies that are supporting my conduits.

"We are very focused on this for you. Thank you for this, and thank you for all. We had the most wonderful of honeymoons. We have decided something together, have we not, my dear?"

Gaia answers that they have decided to have their whole existence be a honeymoon. I agree that a forever honeymoon sounds wonderful.

"And, of course, we are in the honey of the Moon in the Joy Council, and here on Earth as well. It is a great innovation to be of both."

I've been wondering whether or not Gaia decided if the fairies were ready to have babies. When I ask her, she affirms that there are fairy babies. They were designed and birthed just like the little boys, and they are being loved and cherished. Gaia tells me that there are also special little ones, gnomes and all, in the forest in their new abode.

Of course I want to know if Rosebud and Sheliah have a baby. Gaia suggests I might like to speak to them personally about their new little one. She adds that they are becoming great little parents.

Sheliah happily greets me with, "Ah! Hello, Joy, we are very excited to show you our new baby. She is beautiful; you want to know her name?"

"Yes."

"Her name is Joy."

Somehow, that doesn't surprise me, but I'm still delighted.

"She is beautiful and soon you will see her. Everybody says that you will see us all very soon. Your eyes will open and there we will be."

I hope she's right, but rather than wait for that I just want to find out as much as I can about her little Joy. Sheliah tells me their baby is about as big as my little finger. That seems impossibly large since Sheliah is only two inches tall. When I ask Esthra about this later, he reminds me that when Sheliah knew me best I was a little girl and my fingers would have been small.

"Do you make clothes for her?"

"She is naked. She is naked and we wrap her in rose petals. We make the nappy because she does poop. It is only light; it is funniness because, of course, there is no poop. But it is fun. We make a little wrap of rose petals around her so she is wrapped up. We take turns holding her. She's so pretty and she never cries."

Sheliah's voice has always been bubbly and happy-sounding, but now there are extra tones of love, pride and tenderness as she tells me about her baby. I know she and Rosebud really wanted a child and so I tell her I'm very happy for all three of them.

"It is the most fun that I have ever had. It is the most fun because, of course, Rosebud loves the baby, too. He likes to kiss her. He kisses her all day." She giggles and adds, "and he kisses me all night. Hmm, hmm, hmm."

She is practically thrumming with delight as she relates that to me; I know if I show only a tiny spark of interest I will hear more about their all night kissing, but I still want to know a little more about their baby. Sheliah and I used to hang out in the tree tops together so I ask if they are able to climb trees with the baby.

She tells me that climbing is not necessary because they are happier right now just being in the tree. I hadn't realized their house was *in* a tree but she confirms that is correct.

"There is an open spot and we have all kinds of pretty things. We have made a home; we had to have one for our little girl. We couldn't live with all the other fairies because they are all wanting their privacy now because of all the sex."

Laughing, I comment that everyone must have figured out *The Book*. She's laughing too as she agrees that they did and that it's really fun.

"I wrap my legs around his neck!"

I'm startled by this bit of information; obviously, I need have no worries about fairies struggling with inhibitions. I bet the fairies have already discovered and thoroughly explored things not included in *The Book* Gaia provided. After all, they've watched humans having sex in their gardens for however long humans have been around. For some reason I'm feeling a little embarrassed, so rather than pursue this subject with her, I just say that she is precious and ask if I may speak to Rosebud.

Rosebud's voice is very soft as he speaks shyly to me. "Hello, I am a daddy and we named our baby after you."

"I know; I'm so honored. Thank you. It's on my wish list to be able to buy back the property where you live so I'll be able to be there a lot. I don't own that land now, but I'm going to."

"Oh, we will wait for you. We live forever so take your time."

"Do any of the other fairies have babies?"

"Yes, there are a few that have babies. They are enjoying playing with our baby and they want one. They think that maybe it will cause problems to have too many babies, but I don't believe it because this baby is a joy to us."

"I was worried about that, too, but Gaia said she can just expand the gardens so that won't be a problem."

"Oh, well, so you are the grandma."

This is a surprising concept to me, but also a very joyful one. I'm grandmother to a fairy baby. Wow!

"I'm glad I had the chance to talk with you today."

"We love you!"

"Give your baby a kiss for me, OK?"

Sheliah says they will kiss her lots and that Rosebud is a good daddy.

Back with the Joy Councils:

Tonas tells me he is dizzy from being in two places. I haven't noticed anything like that yet and I hope not to. It was challenging enough when I was feeling so lethargic from spending too much time on the 10th dimension during the solstice party. I must have gotten accustomed to being on this higher dimension, because I seem to be here a lot and it doesn't make me tired anymore.

"Hello to all of you. I think there's another council that wants to be here, the Council of Relevance. Can you tell me about them, Swizzlers?"

"Indeed, the Council of Relevance is associated with the higher dimensions. There are thirty-one individuals in their collective, and they are ready to assist in this larger experience that is very soon ready to commence in the next days or year."

Sif and I discuss for a moment how to pronounce her name since there are two ways to say it. She tells me she is called both, then chooses "Seef."

"I heard you a few days ago tell me that you wished to be of service. Is there something you would like to bring forth about the strength of women?"

"On empowering women, for it is true that the woman, the feminine, the goddess that is within is the true power of all existence; it is the seed of creation. The recognition of that power allows the calming of the heart of the masculine, for when there is an empowerment within the woman she then is not to be rescued. When there is the need to rescue there is the impression that the being is of less relevance. You have a short period of time of duality remaining, yet there is struggle that can be alleviated if there is more of an empowerment of the woman deep within, especially in some cultures."

Her idea is that all of the women in our council could begin a transmission that can support the elevation of the spirit within women. Her thought is that this would not be a warrior spirit, but a strong spirit of confidence.

"I know that I have strong women in my soul lineage. The women close to me in my genetic line had the strength of enduring life."

Sif tells me that I am an impressive woman and I stand firmly on my feet. My reply is that I never thought of myself in that way until fairly recently.

"Ah, I only know you now and now is the only important story. I see you in your strength. Remember that I was created by a man to be strong. I was created on Tellas and though that realm is a place of great neutrality, I was created and inspired by the others of that world to be strong.

Being someone who has spent a great deal of time on Earth, I inspired many women to be warriors; to be strong in their mind but soft in their heart. The word squaw was used for someone of a lesser position, and yet, there are many of you here that were the leader of your roost, not from between your legs but with your heart and your mind. Those of you at this table are strong, empowered women. I know that the story of Marilyn shows less strength, but that is the same as for Magdalene. They were both squirmished, you see, because they were sensual."

Mention of sensuality hits a sensitive spot for me. I realize I have some fears about allowing myself to be or even to experience sensuality. Would men be likely to try to take advantage of me if I was more sensual? Would people think I was a loose woman? I admit those concerns to the group and suggest we send out the energy that sensuality is allowed and it is a good thing.

Sif suggests that sensuality is the control of one's own body and is a strength. She further defines sensuality as strength of self and says, "When there is fear within the inner self, sensuality is impossible to rise."

"You're bringing all kinds of things up for me!"

"You are a comic."

I admit I've got some work to do on sensuality.

Sif suggests that all the men and the others of this council hold the vision of that strength and how the strength of the woman builds, supports and uplifts the balance within the male, within the couple and within both individuals.

As we begin to send out the transmission, I ask the Creator and my God Self to assist me with imbuing it with the strength of a woman in her divine feminine version. "This is an empowerment of self so that women can feel strong and have no need to prove anything to anyone. It is just our nature to be worthy, vibrant and complete in ourselves. We love ourselves. That vibration is what I wish to send out as well as a blessing and an empowerment for women so that they know they are safe, balanced, loved and perfect. All of you pour your divine versions of this to assist the women and the men of Earth of all cultures."

As I finish guiding the energy to, through and back out from the Earth, I feel additional grids being activated that will enhance this transmission.

Tonas reports that in addition to this transmission going out from the Moon and inside Gaia, it is also being transmitted from each of the Ashtar Command ships and is being amplified in all dimensions. After thanking Tonas for that report, I ask Commander Ashtar if there is anything more I can do to assist.

He tells me to continue being who I am because the work we are doing has quickened by over two hundred years that which would have been. "You may take bows for this and the accolade is, of course, to you and all who are part of your Earth team. And yet, your personal work here on the Joy Council and on the Ashtar ship of Tonas has amplified greatly."

I thank him for this wonderful news and for the assistance of the Ashtar Command.

Before I leave, I ask Liponie to have foods that celebrate fall on the day of the equinox. I suggest pumpkin pie, apple pie, apple cider doughnuts, popcorn balls, caramel apples, and a banquet of apple desserts.

He says he is creating the trees to make the apples so that people can seem them growing. I don't make any comment; it might be startling to see apples grown overnight but he could do it. He's also growing the pumpkins and agrees to do research about carving jack-o'-lanterns.

CHAPTER THREE
September 19, 2014

There are two issues to address before going to the Joy Councils. Firstly, I've been thinking about how Sif's thoughts concerning sensuality pushed some of my "buttons." The women of my genetic lineage that I am aware of were excellent at enduring life and getting along. They stuck through things thick and thin, but I never observed that sensuality was any part of their lives.

I am sure the galactic councils would be able to give me something about sensuality that the Swizzlers could make into a transmission for Earth. I intend to gate into the presence of the appropriate council of light that can assist us with that topic. After I make my request, I sense receiving an orb with information that can be sent out through the Joy Arrows.

The second item is easily taken care by using our SVH process Sovereign Space (assures crystals are indemnified from adversarial manipulation) to assist the Council of Earth Relevance to incarnate into a crystal on Earth.

I address Esthra and ask him if he can help me with body language. He replies that he can stand most assuredly and reflect that to me. I love the picture those words create for me; Esthra with feet planted firmly, arms crossed and wings outstretched?

"No, I'm talking about when we worked with magnetizing money and assistance. Body language is a really important aspect of magnetizing. Can you think of something to help me with that? This would include what Solomon was talking about; the body language of 'no worries,' 'I've got the answers,' 'I'm royal,' and 'I'm speaking the truth.' Those are a few ideas."

"If you will come with me, we will move to the place of records and into a rectangular chamber. It is so unheard of to have rectangular chambers these days; they seem to all want to be circular. Ah, here we are. Now, I have those of history who are part of your genetics; it will be very easy for me to get from them a template that will activate in opportune times. You will notice that your body begins to change its position. I will set it in place so that it is not gyrating you; that would certainly be somewhat noticeable."

Yes, gyrating in front of a crowd would definitely not be the kind of image I'd like to project.

At one point in my life I spent some time studying hand positions called mudras. I begin to suggest to Esthra that perhaps there is something we could do with those, but he tells me that for quite some time I've had all the mudras transmitting from myself. I don't remember doing any work with them even though he tells me this is something I did using SVH. He adds that I was quite angry about the work at the time. I don't remember being angry either, and he suggests that it is lovely that I don't remember.

"With the new body I'm going to have, I would like to feel and have a sense of presence."

"A sense of presence… I am enjoying this very much. I believe that you will…" He begins to laugh, "I will not make you cluck like a chicken, I promise, and yet, there are many movements that will become quite part of your demeanor."

His mention of chickens reminds me that I've been feeling the energy of different animals. Not chickens, but dolphins, for example. Esthra agrees that I've been speaking dolphin and suggests that this is an important time for me to be communicating through the aspects of my lineage whatever their species.

"I think there's maybe a dolphin that wants to speak with me."

"I believe that everything that exists wants to speak to you. You are quite known throughout all that exists."

I snicker quietly at this remark.

"You are laughing. You think this is funny."

"It is, because still on Earth nobody knows me."

"That is the charm of it, my dear, indeed."

Esthra guides me to a little square in the floor of the hall of records which he asks me to step upon and open up my consciousness levels. This procedure will stimulate my genetics and activate the mudra gestures. I remark that it feels fun; he calls this activation "delicious" because many in my lineage had great confidence. I want to know if it will help me with flexibility.

"It will be excellent for everything. Confidence will be important to you in the days ahead. It will be extremely important for you to know who you are representing when you are representing yourself. You have so many identities that are linked to past identities that are of less relevance. It is who you are now that is important. Ah, you have drunk them in. Are you tipsy?"

"I was tipsy before I even started, so yes."

"Speaking about identities, I've often wondered if there is such a thing as shape-shifting."

Esthra says there are species that have the ability to shift their energy and appear to be human. There are also different human tribesmen who have the ability to appear to be an eagle, a wolf or a badger. "It is through their ability to move energy, and they do so in a trance state that links them to their genetics that obviously carries the imprint of this possibility."

"So their body doesn't actually become a badger?"

"In some cases, yes, but only individuals with the most prowess can transform that way. The aborigines can do this, absolutely. Not a badger, of course."

I thank Esthra for this exciting information. The ability to shape-shift is something I've been fascinated by ever since I first read about it. It's something I would like to be able to experience myself.

This morning I experienced stepping through an open door. Then I heard someone say, "It's time." I stuck my right hand out to receive something and then I had the sense of bowing to someone. If I'm going to meet someone that I bowed to, I want to have Sananda speaking with and for me.

Calling him into presence, I explain to him what happened this morning and ask what it was about. He answers that there is a galactic council that I have been working with that is going to offer me something that will help with the 4th dimension issue. He adds that there are eight councils of light, including the Andromedan Council, and all I need to do to receive this assistance is gate into that forum of councils in the ideal timing.

I ask him to come with me and as I step into that forum I feel a blast of, for lack of a better word, power. He wants to know if I am able to stand. I tell him that I am and that this feels somewhat like standing in the middle of a nuclear reactor, only in a good way. He advises me to open up my consciousness levels and also my chakras and just let everything instill into my presence.

"Please put out your right hand; they are going to stamp a golden rose onto your palm." Before I can ask him what that means, he says, "This is about you radiating Golden Rose Consciousness which is the consciousness of the 7th, the 8th and onward to the 25th dimension. It is also heart consciousness."

I am floating in "la la land"; this energy is so powerful and yummy and my head is doing the swimmy thing it does with work like this. Even though I'm feeling woozy, I manage to ask Sananda what to do with this consciousness.

"You are instilled with the codes for the Golden Rose Consciousness and the councils have given you something you can take from yourself and transmit from the Joy Arrows."

I need to catch my breath for a moment before asking Sananda about another of my recent experiences. "Two days ago I heard something about a walk-in who was a queen. Do you know what that was about?"

He replies that I was picking up on an aspect of my soul lineage, but not from this timeline. "This is important because you stepped in her **footprints**. Do you want to know who the queen was?"

"Yes."

"She was Tutankhamun's wife, Ankhesenamun. She was quite traumatized and wanted to die and then the walk-in from your soul lineage came into her. Since you stepped in her you can assist her."

After getting gifts from my MAPS self for her, I gate into the past to the places in Egypt where I stepped in her footprints and offer the gifts to her in those places. I love the things I'm able to do and the people I'm able to assist using SVH.

During a private conversation with Gaia, I mention that this morning I saw a little spark that was Sheliah and Rosebud's baby. "I heard one of them ask me, 'Do you see her? She's like a little bitty princess.' They also told me she was a very special baby and that all the fairy kingdoms are growing."

Gaia confirms the fairy realms are expanding and says that their baby is a special baby because it will come to know me. "She is going to be part of the new world, and she was the very first fairy baby born. She is a treasure to them."

She's a treasure to me, too. I hope that I will be able to see her before she outgrows wearing rose petal nappies.

At the Joy Council, Tonas asks me if he may kiss my hands.

"Yes. If you ever forget this greeting, I know the part of me there would really miss it."

"You are beautiful today, as always."

I love hearing those words every time he says them. Of course, I can't tell him that because I wouldn't want him to feel like he *had* to say them. I thank him for the compliment and suggest we enter the council.

My first announcement is that I helped the new council to incarnate. Then I ask if I can invite them to join our Joy Council and am told that I am the definer of the seating arrangements. I thought that was the case, but it's nice to know for sure. I state that I would definitely like for them to be members of the Joy Council.

Swizzler One says there is a position for them, but not at the table. They are not interested in becoming physical and they don't have bottoms to sit.

"Swizzlers, I got something very wonderful this morning called Golden Rose Consciousness. Sananda told me that when this consciousness rains down on the Earth it could soften energies that might be stuck or hardened. How can I give you this consciousness?"

"It is not necessary to give it to us; we can read it on your presence. We will give you different timers for here of Earth and for the Moon. We have the correct calculations and offer this to you now in each of our positions."

I ask the councils to focus with me and transmit the Golden Rose Consciousness through the Joy Arrows. In the middle of the transmission it seems important for me to add "dolphin speak," which comes out of my mouth as a series of clicking sounds and short expulsions of air with very little actual sound. I continue by asking the whales and dolphins to assist and to amplify this consciousness. My part of this work completes as I feel the transmission flow into and through the Earth and then back out to the grids.

"Sif helped me realize I have issues concerning sensuality, so I did some clearing work for myself about it and got templates for sensuality for the Earth."

The Swizzlers make the templates into a transmission. As I begin sending it out, these are the words that come to me: "I ask the female and male members of this council to assist with the divine balance of sensuality for all men and women on Earth. I feel that balance within myself and I ask you to assist me with sending that out to the Earth to coat all of us and assist us to embrace this new vision of passion, sensuality and our divine unity. As this template permeates all of Earth and then out to the grids, new grids come online. And so it is."

"Aconna, the other evening I heard the Atlanteans say they could help me. What did they want to help me with?"

Aconna asks if I wish to speak to Aconna Shareeah. When I affirm that is who I wish to speak with, I learn that Aconna is a title which means Great Commander. She says that I am very dear and is not offended by my goof.

Her idea is that from their position on the 10th dimension they can assist me in my past when I was sleeping. By the way, she confirms that since an early age I have spent much of my days and nights on Tonas's ship.

I mention that I connected with him when I was nineteen. She suggests seventeen or eighteen would be even better because I was very young for my age. "You were very, what is the word?"

I know exactly the word she's looking for—naïve.

"That is the word. In that naiveté you offer us the opportunity to make offerings to you that will build your inner awareness. This will activate in specific times in different places on Earth to guide you."

I accept her offer immediately and thank her for it. She adds that other Atlanteans also wish to assist me and asks if it is acceptable that they become guides for me.

"I'm fine with that. I could have used a *lot* of guidance as I was growing up. As a matter of fact, I think I'll work with SVH to increase and become more aware of the guidance I had throughout my life. Much of my life I felt lost and that resulted in rage I buried so deep it manifested as depression for many years."

"We would wish to have an intermediary. Who would you choose?"

I suggest Sananda and he says he is willing. Shareeah asks me to hold out my hand; then she places a link in a ring that I wear on that dimension. I ask if there's anything I'm supposed to do to activate it and she lets me know it is hands free. Then she adds, "That is the value of it, for truly at your age of seventeen you would not be preparing much for this kind of work. I believe that you would be 'freaked out.'"

Yes, she really did say that and she's right. At that age, experiencing anything like the work I'm currently doing might have landed me in a not so nice place.

Shareeah continues by saying that several of my soul aspects are within their ranks, and one of them named Koliah is very interested in assisting me. Although Koliah is on several councils on Earth's 10th dimension, Shareeah thinks she might simply be vying for a position on our council, but agrees to bring Koliah forward if I'm willing to listen to her.

"Yes, I'd love to speak with her."

"Thank you. I am in gratitude to you, dear Joy. I am Koliah."

After I greet her she says it is an honor to be in the presence of this grand council. Then she tells me that though she has no power in her position on the 10th dimension, there is a conclave of individuals anchored into the 10th dimension. It is her idea that this conclave and people in their lineages, along with her and my 10th dimensional self could draw into the 6th and the 7th dimensions what I/they experienced in their evolution. She reminds me that they have made the journey I will make and asks if I am interested in their expertise.

"I am, with the understanding and the caveat that everyone's journey is different. If I find ways to do things in an easier fashion, I don't want to be stuck in one certain way."

"Ah, you are wise. As an observer and as someone who would give you counsel, being of your soul lineage, it would be easy for me to transmit. I can use your angel as an intermediary if he accepts."

Esthra accepts and Koliah says she will begin observing very closely all that unfolds within me. When she notices windows where there are possibilities for upliftment into new awarenesses, she says she will transmit this to Esthra. He agrees to bring these to my attention and I thank both of them for their assistance.

Before I begin with the next item on my list, Liponie tells me Isis has an idea. Her suggestion is that perhaps Cory's full presence at our council would offer some important connections to the other worlds. I like that idea and Liponie immediately offers to get Cory a beautiful body. I'm surprised by his offer because I thought he already did that. Liponie says Cory has brought herself back into a crystal, and Isis was bringing that change to my attention. He confirms that since she is not talking she has not been able to participate in council work. I'm not sure how to address this issue since we can't just pop her into a body she obviously doesn't want.

Liponie says he thinks the problem was that she didn't like being an individual. She felt disconnected from the other parts of her since they remained as pieces of crystal. Cory agrees he is correct. I ask if it would be possible for the other parts of her to embody.

"She tells us that it would be difficult because she is in the Earth in many positions."

"Then she's going to stay a crystal."

"We are accepting this, of course." Disconsolately, he adds that he had so many plans for her new body. He sounds happier when he says that between now and the next time we speak, perhaps we can think of something.

"The Swizzlers had the same issue, did they not? There is perhaps a way for us to have an embodiment that is not human. Cory, trust us with this."

I've been thinking about celebrating the upcoming holidays. We could have a nativity scene with the *actual* characters! I wonder if Jesus could make himself appear to be a baby. We could have the original St. Nicholas at Christmas. For Thanksgiving, Liponie could research the actual foods the Indians gave to the colonists, if they really did that, and we could eat whatever that was. Plus, for Halloween, I can't even imagine the costumes that these folks could come up with. Oh boy, oh boy...

"Liponie, I know you can make a really good pie, but my grandma made the best pumpkin pie ever. Sananda, can you find out where Grandma Crystal is?"

His reply that she is in the Fifth Realm saddens me a tiny bit. I was hoping to taste that pie again; it would have been nice to see her, too.

"She knew the special kind of pumpkin that was the best to use for pie. Great-grandmother Permelia made delicious fudge at Christmas; it had hickory nuts that she gathered from trees out in the woods. My Aunt Nina made wonderful Christmas Sugar Cookies with fun decorations on them. I would love to taste those treats again. Anyway, I want to celebrate the holidays with all of you and we'll find a way to make this help the Earth, too."

"We adore you."

"I love you all."

CHAPTER FOUR
September 22, 2014

This morning I heard Swizzler One say, "You have something very simple to offer to us in your heart." I'm not sure what I have to offer them until Esthra informs me it is possible for each of them to have their own individual soul; they would also still be able to be in their collective. There must be a formula for doing something like that so I intend to step into the appropriate galactic council and request it. I can feel that I'm given something and surely it's the gift they asked for.

Continuing my conversation with Esthra, I ask him the meaning of these words I heard yesterday. "We have ten percent that we are putting to."

He says that almost ten percent of the Native Americans in North America are awake enough to pick up on the transmissions from the Joy Councils and the council feels that is a good number. It's good to know that the transmissions are assisting, but I'd like for the number receiving them to be higher.

An issue I've wanted to work on for some time is figuring out a way to assist people who have been tortured or a torturer. I'd also like to give some kind of assistance to all men who have been circumcised. What a traumatic way to welcome a little boy into the world… Whack!

With Sananda in the Fifth Realm, I call forth all beings who were involved in torturing or being tortured and telepathically transmit to them that we are willing to carry any gifts back to them when they were alive that would assist them perhaps even to avoid experiencing torture or torturing. We take the orbs they offer us, move into the SBT (Space Before Time) and give them their gifts.

As soon as we finish doing this, I realize there are other areas to assist: people who were forced to watch torture or executions, people who enjoyed watching those activities, people who were executioners or executed, gladiators, animals who were tortured or used for laboratory experiments as well as the people who tortured or experimented on them.

For the animals that were tortured, if the torture still existed after the person who tortured them got their gift, I put the animal into an alternate reality. I'm also going to offer men who were circumcised a chance to move into an alternate reality throughout the experience and the healing required for it.

I keep thinking of more situations that could use assistance and finally I ask my MAPS self to give me the ideal vision of how to offer assistance for all involved in these kinds of situations. I get that, Sananda and I move into the SBT, I call forward those who would benefit from that assistance and we hand it over.

In order to avoid repetition, you may assume that unless I specify otherwise, Sananda and I always step into the SBT to hand over the gifts people gave us for themselves.

(When I visit the council later today and ask if they were aware of this work, Tonas tells me that they could feel a shift on Earth which seemed to move through all lines of time. I love that kind of feedback!)

"Esthra, you know I've talked with you about my perceived lack of guidance from the masters and my angels. That was a major reason why I was so pissed off for most of my life. I felt like I'd been thrown out of the boat to sink or swim, and mostly I was sinking. I also felt like I was waiting. I was waiting, I was waiting, and then there was more waiting. I even wrote a poem titled, 'A Constant State of Wait.' Did I intend to be so isolated that life would be a supreme challenge for me?"

I'm not surprised when he says, "Yes."

"I've been there, done that and it wasn't much fun. I want to honor that I chose that, and I really don't want to be mad about it. I also want to have felt connected from day one instead of the experience of feeling all alone. That just made me bitter and mad. I was clueless! I need to have had lots more clues, Esthra."

He reminds me that I have the clues now, but I still wish I could have experienced or remember experiencing more assistance as I was growing up. I decide to check with the Atlanteans one more time to see if any kind of adjustment to their mentoring is possible.

Esthra reports they still believe that seventeen is the ideal time frame because I was more independent and preparing to grow up and leave. "What they suggest is like a little kindergarten to prepare you for what's going to happen when you are seventeen. They've given me many special little parcels for you."

"Can you tell me what they are?"

"There are more than a million of them. Shall I begin with the A's?"

"No, can you just give me the general flavor?"

"Yes, of course. They will assist so that as you put your foot down the next foot falls in the ideal path leading to the next direction that is most efficient for you. This is like a homing beacon. What they are assisting you with mainly is to be more anchored to the 7th dimension, then moving to the 8th linking to the 10th dimension.

The Atlanteans are dedicating themselves to be very focused on what is best to assist you when you were seventeen. All you have to do is gate to all the times beginning when you were that age until you don't need this assistance any more. Some of these positions will be in the 9th or 10th dimension. Step into the council chambers of the Atlanteans who are working with you and receive the parcels they have for you. You may activate these using your SVH. This work will come forward in ripples so you might feel something for a few days."

I put their assistance in place throughout my life.

Meeting privately with Aton at the Joy Council, he greets me by saying, "Dear one, great celebration to you."

"Why do you say that?"

"It is because we are always celebrating you. You are not only our queen here on the Moon as you call it; you are quite a goddess here on Earth. I am applying everything on Earth for you so I will bring my attention to you in that position."

I'm surprised to learn from Aton that the Andromedans believe my "yin" is too low; they will be working on me for the next ten days to balance it. I ask if there is something I could do here to assist their work and he tells me something I don't like to hear. The sugars I eat are perhaps causing my yin to be deficient.

"I was going to go have cake tonight. Darn."

Aton suggests I go ahead and enjoy cake. He adds that it's important to shift the dynamic of my body to recognize that it can be in balance no matter what I consume. I agree that sounds like what I would prefer; I hate the thought of giving up cake and ice cream.

He reports that they have made several adjustments on my conduits even today, and I am nearing perfection with this. When I ask when he would like to work with me again, he replies that this moment would be ideal.

"If you will have a seat in this, it is comic for me. I have a little chair for you which is a horse with a tail and a rocking bottom."

We are both laughing at Liponie's antics. Aton tells me Tonas would like to keep it; I would too!

"Melchizedek and the others are now gathered around and we will lift off your cranium. I am just jesting; we are simply witnessing the conduits. It would be quite funny to lift it off like a cap, would it not?"

Having the top of my head lifted off doesn't sound funny to me so I make a non-committal murmuring sound.

"Ah, yes… Rock a little bit, dear. Make this a challenge for me."

I'm trying, and failing, not to laugh.

"Ah…yes…we are all in agreement that the adjustments seem to be quite efficient."

He answers my question about when he would like to work with me again by saying when I call upon him will be the time.

I tell Melchizedek I was thinking about actually getting out the Mendelssohn Violin Concerto and playing it in the SBT, but it's so far from what I would ever want Heifetz to hear that I didn't want to do it. Mel claims it would be a great favor to Heifetz. I staunchly assert that my playing will sound very bad. He disagrees with me and says that Heifetz would see it as a beginning. "Do you think he brought only prodigies into his academy?"

"Yes, that is exactly what he did. He picked the crème de la crème for his students. He would never have bothered with someone like me."

Mel thinks I'm selling myself short, but I know I'm not. I'm very realistic about my abilities.

"I was better than average when I was practicing and playing a lot, but he only took people that were brilliant. I was not that at all."

Mel suggests that I am looking through a different looking glass than he is. I reply that I'm looking through the looking glass that I have experienced. He says that maybe I could work on this as a challenge. I tell him that I feel like I'd have to practice here for a few years before I'd even want to step into the SBT to play for Heifetz.

"No, my dear, this is the challenge to yourself to accept the journey. We will assist you."

"I can pick up my violin and go into the SBT, but I don't want to feel like Heifetz has his hands over his ears and a look of pain on his face."

Mel is not going to give up on encouraging me to play for Heifetz. He suggests I step into the SBT and play the song very loudly so that all I hear is the perfection. Although the thought of doing that just causes me to wince, I thank him for his counsel.

With the full Joy Council:

Tonas always sounds so delighted when he greets me. It warms my heart to hear the welcome in his voice. After he asks everyone to be seated, he remarks to me, "Ah, that you lived with us here always."

"That's something I need to address. I'm speaking especially to you, Woonfred, because I know it might be a bit of a challenge for you to be sitting here and not doing the dragon things you like to do. If you have a dragon you could use as a substitute so that you could go back and forth, I'm fine with that. I know that all of you can probably split yourself and be in more than one place, but if you need to go someplace else, please do that. Are you OK with that Woonfred? I started thinking that it might be difficult for you to sit here so long."

He replies that none of them feel they have anything that they consider a better thing to do; they feel that this work is creating a better future for all of them. This response has made me feel very emotional and I struggle a little bit as I thank them for their help.

"You have given us life. How could we do anything less than give our all to you? The world is readying for a great time, for then you will ride on my shoulders and we will exercise together. I will dangle you from my teeth and you can swing your arms."

The image his description creates for me is so hilarious that immediately my raucous laughter joins his booming chuckles. I have no fear of this kind of fun with my dragon friend.

Finally, I calm down enough to address the Swizzlers and display the gift I have for them. Swizzler One says they are consuming it now, they are grateful, they are ready and he wants to know if they can remain as a collective.

"Oh, yes, definitely. This is going to be the best of the best."

"It will be. Can we have names?"

"You can have whatever you want. You can be your wonderful individual selves and also your collective self. I'm so glad to be able to offer this expansive and wonderful opportunity to you!"

"It is an opportunity for us to ascend with the rest as individuals."

I get goose bumps all over when they tell me this and my heart opens wide with joy for them. He says this is a dreams come true.

I'm crying as I say, "I want to hug you so much. Can I hug you?"

"Come to me. I will meet you half of the way. Come, all of us. We will all hug you at once."

Even though there are ninety-four of them, I think I somehow manage to hug them all. They're very skinny after all. I feel so blessed to know and assist these unique beings.

"Someone said we are spindly. Do you like our new muscles?"

Here I go from tears to laughter again.

"We have muscles on our arms and on our thighs."

I agree that would be a little more pleasing.

"I think it is very pleasing. We have butts, too. It was Liponie, of course, who helped us."

My comment about their changed appearance is that maybe now I won't be scared the first time I see them. Immediately I regret my words because Swizzler One asks me why I would be scared. Now I have to try to explain that even though I love them all very much, suddenly seeing ninety-four, six foot tall, (I learn later that they are only three feet tall, which wouldn't be nearly so scary.) vibrantly colored sticks will be a science fiction type experience for me. He doesn't understand what I'm trying to say and thinks I'm making a joke.

"For humans, seeing something extraordinary is startling. We're used to seeing people and trees and other things in our environment. All of you here are going to be exceptionally unlike anything I've ever seen. Can you understand what I'm saying?"

"We are unique."

I agree with his assessment and add that seeing purple or blue people is also something I have not yet experienced. I ask Liponie to keep me posted on what he does with the Swizzlers. He replies that they are designing and it is not pretty.

Swizzler One says, "I asked for a six-pack and he gave me beer."

I am having great challenges with this conversation because I'm laughing so hard.

Liponie sounds indignant as he tells me, "I was not going to make this rippling on his chest. He was taking it too far. It looked like a bad road, a washboard! It looked ridiculous; I showed him a schematic and he was quite excited about that washboard. They are wearing sunglasses now. For someone who does not want to be as human, I would say the six-pack is pushing the envelope, do you not think?"

"I think they're just experimenting, so that's OK. Let me get back on track here because that was hilarious. Thank you for that laughter, it was wonderful."

"What did Cory decide she wanted to do?"

Liponie says she has a vision of herself that is similar to an ice berg that never melts.

"Just like a big lump?"

Liponie tactfully replies that she is quite beautiful with many colors within her shining brightly. Although she has eyes, she simply does not wish to appear as human. I'm not going to say this out loud, of course, but an iceberg with eyes sitting in one of the chairs here sounds creepy. I'm really glad I can't see her. I do say that an iceberg with eyes is a little hard to picture.

Liponie diplomatically replies that everyone is adjusting to her appearance and that she does fit in her chair. He lowers his voice to tell me they are working on this. "It is her desire not to appear human and yet she is learning from what is happening around her with the Swizzlers."

"Is it OK if I call you Swizzler One or do you want a different name?"

Swizzler One replies that he would like to be called Charlie.

"OK, Charlie, I like your new name. Are we ready to do the equinox work we were going to do?"

"We have expanded the original version of what you brought. It is now more dedicated to the elaborate expansiveness of the atmosphere above the Earth which is quite charged with energy. That energy, many times, affects humanity and all species.

Because the satellites, the transmissions and other technologies have caused imbalances to exist within the ethers, we feel it is necessary to shift the dynamic of that field of atmosphere. We have no attachment to this beyond seeing the ideal situation for it. It is time for change. People are calling out for it, and so we have amplified this call for change over the last three days. That will ripple into the tomorrows to come."

Before I begin the transmission, Charlie explains that the expansions they added would take many hours to explain and wants to know if I'm OK with their stamp of approval. I agree to that and am told that I have a sphere which contains the transmission.

"I'm just going to breathe on it for a moment and love it. With your attention, let's focus and move this energy through and out all the Joy Arrows to the places this transmission is destined to go to assist the atmosphere."

I can feel the energy permeate the Earth, then move back out, up into the atmosphere, through the grids and out to the all and the everything. Tonas comments that this can be felt clear to the Moon and beyond.

"May I ask you, Gaia, to explain the birthing process the fairies are using?"

"Yes, my dear, they are creating a whole new plethora of experiences. There is one delightful fairy, not in your garden or anywhere near it, that had the idea of creating the baby in something that looks very much like a banana, then she peels it back and there is the baby. They are very creative, these ones. There is a true cabbage fairy. Yes, indeed, I am aware of the Cabbage Patch Kids babies from many years ago. Some of the babies are being grown in gardens. They are quite imaginative and yet they have had human beings to watch. If anyone was to look in the window of one of your homes where someone was watching a Disney show on television, there would be much a little fairy could learn."

I remark that I never considered them doing anything like that; Gaia replies that they are very interested in human beings. I ask her if the fairies create their babies by just thinking about them and she says yes.

"They've moved beyond the concept of planting a seed?"

"No, because some have planted them in their garden. There is one group of these little girl fairies who became very big in their tummies. They walk around looking pregnant, and then they pick the baby out of the garden and their tummies go flat. They assume this is the way it's done. They had seen a human woman's tummy growing bigger and bigger and then they saw the mommy pushing the baby in the cart and she was no longer big in the tummy.

I ask Gaia if a fairy couple decides that a certain time they have sex will create a baby. She says she felt it important to not release the idea that the act creates a baby.

I want to know how long the babies will be babies and Gaia explains that each of the fairies will design that for themselves. If they enjoy the baby size, their child could remain a baby for a long time. I ask if the baby has any part in determining how rapidly it grows, and Gaia says the parents would know if it desired to be bigger.

Gaia seems to think that dwarfs and gnomes are the same, and she should know. She also tells me that they are about the same size. Although there are no elves in Sheliah's garden, they may be found in many different regions of Earth. Dwarfs are also spread all over but there are less of them in the Americas.

"Charlie, have you and the gang found a fragrance you prefer?"

Their laughter is much improved from the first time they attempted it; they sound almost human as they laugh and say, "Every fragrance is pleasurous to us although your fragrance is the most pleasurous. When shall we have our individual souls?"

I thought I had offered that to them already, but Charlie says I only offered them the opportunity; I must provide the file for them. After I explain to Charlie how to view the screen and activate the work, there is an eruption of noise. Tonas explains that the Swizzlers are roller skating around the room and slapping hands. I manage to make myself heard over the uproar in order to ask Tonas, "They got the high five?"

"Yes, all five were used, my dear. It is very exciting for them. They are all rolling around on their skates and slapping each other's hands."

I've been trying to stifle my laughter because I don't want to miss any of Tonas's moment by moment report of what's happening. When I ask if they are wearing their Mickey Mouse ears, Tonas says they have on helmets as well as knee and elbow pads. The sounds of pandemonium last for only a minute or so because Liponie immediately organizes a game. Tonas reports that now the Swizzlers are wearing jerseys and sporting black stripes on each side of their faces. They are using their roller skates to play ice hockey, sans ice, with the Indians.

I tell Liponie he is marvelous. He says he was going to give them motorcycles but he thought that would be a bit dangerous. I certainly am glad he didn't follow through on *that* idea and tell him that roller skates are perfect.

"They really are perfect, and I gave them the low ground ones like back in the 60's. I will graduate them to the blades, of course. It is beyond exciting here. I'm going to make them jumps."

"Oh, Liponie they're going to have so much fun."

"Yes, I will give them the blades and I will also give them the boards." He is almost shouting as he says, "There is so much for them to experience! They will love it! And, of course, they are individual now! Tomorrow I'm giving them boxing gloves."

We are in for a whole new level of swizzling fun!

CHAPTER FIVE
September 25, 2014

"Yesterday morning I got that there was something about papers that are very important. This morning I saw a page of typing which had the words in a justified format. The top of the page had words in black; the bottom section had underlined words that were all red. I think there is a deeper meaning to the fact that the words were justified and I also think that this is related to the important papers. Who gave me this information and what kind of papers are they?"

Esthra says this information was from a Native American. Since there were many treaties signed with the Indians that were not honored, I get everything I can that would assist to shed light on this information and put it in an orb to take to the elders in Buffalo's Heart.

I want to know if, in the future, I will be able to make myself smaller to interact with the fairies more easily. Esthra says that is not necessary because they love that I'm bigger. "Yes, but I want to be able to see them better and interact with them more, rather than just being a Godzilla tramping around in their gardens."

He says that in the 8th dimension I can make myself as tiny as I wish. Since that is true, I realize I could also make myself larger for interacting with Woonfred. Esthra agrees that would also be possible. I like the *Alice in Wonderland* feel of those possibilities, without any of the drama of that story, of course.

I let Esthra know that there are people who are two or three positions away from me in my soul lineage who are willing to share some of their attributes with me. He corrects me by saying that it is more that their attributes are accessible to me. "I do not think they would have the right to share as much as it is your privilege due to their proximity."

I want to know their names since that would make them seem more real than being designated by soul lineage numbers. He says that Isis is within that range of my lineage; I agree that I have felt her energy within me several times.

"That would be easy, for she is very close to you on the matrix, and sharing the energies that are passing between you. It would be helpful for you to open your consciousness levels and conduits to receive not only from her knowledge, which is already within your many levels, but also in that connection point between yourself and that lineage."

Now Esthra says that the name of the other individual is Klosee. She is also an enhanced individual in her non-dual dimension. On her world, which is not in this universe, she is almost as famous as Isis. I wonder if she is blue like Isis, but he says she is a golden color.

I ask how I can receive their attributes. He says Isis is willing to offer me her everything; however, since Klosee is from a different universe we will need to move into the archives of her attributes. "She is alive and steering the stars and everything in her universe toward the timing."

I tell him I'd like to have whatever they can give me and I'll just follow his lead.

"There are two different procedures: for Isis you simply open up your consciousness levels as if opening the lotus flower. Then feel all the petals of it connecting with the lineage of Klosee and Isis, and the levels of consciousness that have the knowledge of Isis will super connect. Open up that level of your consciousness which is within your heart; that which you call the higher being of self. Let it, like little wisps of smoke rising, stretch itself through that little open lotus and the presence of your being to find and isolate the Isis and Klosee lineage files and connect with them.

And now, within your heart, have the desire for their knowledge, their expertise, their abilities and their attributes to begin flowing to you. Feel the levels of consciousness stirring up. Put this in the hand of your inner heart. This is a lovely exercise for you to practice. Once you have done this three or four times it will be as if locked into that stream of all that is them. You have all of these records; what you are doing now is opening the gate for them. How does it feel to you?"

I mumble a few words.

"Say it, my dear. I can take it."

"It feels like part of my consciousness is like a library that's been sealed off and the books in it are all dusty."

"This is the best description I could have imagined. Blow off the dust every time you apply this."

I really do notice that things seem to be stirring around inside me. Before I shift my attention elsewhere, Esthra tells me he has quite a parcel for me from the Atlanteans who wished to assist me. I put their gifts in place using SVH.

As I gate to Buffalo's Heart, I intend that anyone on the council who would wish to assist me will meet me there with the elders. Chocheenaho's voice welcomes me as Great Spirit. I reply that it is good to be back here with him and ask if Hiawatha will join us. When he is present, I tell him that I have some important papers that the elders can enhance so that I can transmit the information through the Joy Arrows. After I show it to them telepathically, Hiawatha says, "These are the promises. What is your intention with these promises? Ah, just one moment…"

Another voice enters our conversation saying, "It is I. You remember me, of course. I was angry."

Iniquasha laughs with me at his remark, and then adds that he is no longer angry. "I am the one who brought this to you in the initial. It is important for this to be brought forth in this time. That which you have displayed is correct."

I ask him to tell me more about what he found because I know we made lots of promises that we did not keep. He says that these are the legal promises. This excites us both so much that we spend some time laughing and speaking joyfully and energetically in the people's language. At least I assume that's what I am speaking because it sounds like what he is speaking. His thought is that these promises can be more easily brought into focus when Earth has moved into the higher dimensions.

Hiawatha agrees that the elders can enhance the information to be transmitted, and they are doing that now. The people's language flows from my lips and I say, "Remember that which is, that which was, and that which shall be. This is our destiny, our path, and our love. These are the promises that will be honored."

Hiawatha says he believes this will heal much and that much will change among *all* of the tribes of Earth when these promises are upheld. "We are complete. This now can be brought to the councils."

"Just one more thing, please, I'm asking Creator to manifest." I again feel called to speak Hiawatha's language, then I say, "Mother/Father, please come and breathe upon this. Put your blessings and your seal upon this, a divine seal of love, of truth, of promises that will be honored and are honored. And so it is."

"They are breathing upon this. We, too, shall breathe. It is alive now. We thank you."

I tell Iniquasha that I love him and that his energy feels really wonderful now.

"Yours is more than beautiful."

"I thank you, elders, and I love you."

I manage to take the time to exchange greetings with Tonas before asking him what's been happening. The news is that the council has been expanded to include many arenas for the tournament. Tonas moves to stop the games and tells me it has been a mad house.

"The Swizzlers have been jousting in tournaments with the knights. If you can imagine the armor and the horses that have been created, it has been quite a spectacle. Liponie has temporarily made the Swizzlers quite larger so that they would be a good match to the knights."

"They were jousting on horses?"

"Yes! They started with stick horses that looked like them. They are now normal size, if you could consider them to be normal in any way. They have maintained their muscles and their bottoms. This is only temporary because the knights would not allow themselves to play; it was too easy for them to just swat the Swizzlers off their stick horses."

I'm laughing so hard, all I can do is gasp a comment. From the roller skates they went to ice skates and then polo which was just as bad as the jousting they are now doing. Tonas says they are doing much better in their bigger size.

"In the hockey it was touch and go because they were very quick, you see. They were so small they could get into places. The Indians played polo with them on horses that had bare backs. The Swizzlers insisted on having saddles and hats and guns. They looked like cowboys with polo sticks, which was quite silly. I did my research; this was polo Swizzler style.

They do not wish to maintain the size they are now for they do not wish to be as human. They are still holding this very tightly to themselves, and they are doing everything to be human. They are so backward in their thinking. They are some of the wisest beings I have ever known, and yet they are so silly. They are like children and it is most delightful to witness. It is a very exciting time, but there is only so much popcorn you can eat."

With the Joy Councils:

"Charlie, can you tell me what it was like when you first experienced your individuality?"

"For me to be an individual, to feel that space of my own thoughts with an echo of the collective thoughts was, for me to experience that quietness, to have my own thoughts, the profundity of those thoughts was shocking to me because I am so committed to the collective and our focus of one, one voice among many. To have my own quietness was very enjoyable; it was also a little bit lonely."

He assures me that he can still connect with the other Swizzlers, but if they were to remove themselves from the crystal they would each be experiencing life only as an individual. His answer to my question about whether that is something he would ever like to experience is that they believe it is important for them to remain in the collective until after the 8th dimension. It is then that they believe humanity has its first start.

I explain now that the individuality he first experienced and the little bit of loneliness he felt is what all of us experience… all of the time.

"This is not pleasurable."

"No, we have forgotten the feeling of the oneness, the experience of the collective that you have. It was our choice to experience the world as individuals. In the higher dimensions we will still be able to do that, but we also will experience the unity of the oneness of all of us."

"There is a collective of all of us that we exist within that is the truth of our being. What we are experiencing now as a separation from that is the illusion, and yet within that illusion our collective gave us that impression, that sense of unity among ourselves. I believe that community is important for all beings to feel. You have that community in a small way in your circle of initiates."

I agree with him, but add that the people at the table and in this council are more my family than the initiates.

"We are pleased. There are big smiles and shakings of the heads. We feel the same. I feel the same. To say this is bizarre, of course. 'I' takes some practice."

I ask Charlie if any of the others have chosen names. He answers that they are considering and that he thought for a very long time before choosing his name. I want to know why he chose Charlie.

"I very much like… Will you be disappointed if I am to tell you it is of cartoon?"

"Oh, no, I don't think there's anything you could ever do or say that would disappoint me."

"There is a cartoon of Charlie Brown. I like him very much!"

His choice feels so silly and yet so poignant that tears come to my eyes. I agree that Charlie Brown is a wonderful choice for a name and Charlie says he is thinking that name to honor Charlie Brown.

"Thank you for sharing your name with me. I honor your choice."

As an aside, the next morning as I'm waking up I hear Charlie tell me, "I know all the nuances of having a soul. You have given us wings to fly."

"Anybody want to speak about the tournament before we do our work?"

Agravain replies that the knights are playing to a different set of rules for my dear ones. I love that he used that term, because that's exactly how I feel about the Swizzlers. "They will be ready for tournament very soon. We have been practicing with them to prepare them so that it will be an even match."

"The next time I come I want to know how it all turned out. Liponie, if you can draw any pictures for me to see in the future, that would be great."

Liponie laughingly says that he is keeping track for me of everything I can imagine in a full videography. "You will not want to miss a moment of this!"

I briefly describe, to the council, Iniquasha's discovery of legal promises made to the Native Americans and the work I did with the council of elders in Buffalo's Heart. I add that this will be very significant in the times to come to restore the things that have been lost, forgotten or broken.

Sananda agrees that "the stroke of the pen shall be brought to light in these new dimensions."

"Please assist me in amplifying this transmission by pouring your love into it. This will assist those who experienced promises that were made to them being broken; it will also assist those who broke the promises. Promise breakers think they will gain something, and they may temporarily, but, in fact, they experience an even greater loss than the ones they made the promises to. Does anyone else have anything to say before we send this through the Joy Arrows?"

"My dear, I am Gaia. My heart is expanded to greatest opening, holding the vision of this right being brought. It has been a long time since these promises were made, but the timing means nothing. What is most important is that the light will come upon these promises, preparing all these beings for the time when we move into the higher dimensions as a collective. May the whole tribe be healed."

As we're sending the transmission out, I can sense the energy of cupboards and drawers being opened and papers being brought forth. I feel/see meetings where the people on both sides of these past transactions are joyful at what is revealed. They see the truth behind the promises that were made and are glad to acknowledge and honor them in divine timing.

"The people speak, and the people are heard. Thank you, Great Father, Great Mother, Great Spirit and Creator. This transmission flows through and back out of the Earth to the grids to saturate the atmosphere, and then out through the threads to the everything with the knowing that we are honorable people."

With Aton and Tonas in privacy, I ask Aton how my yin is coming along.

"You are magnificent, my dear. How was the cake?"

I reply that the cake was very good and I enjoyed every bite of it.

"This is part of the healing, to be in joy of that which is, in theory, creating the imbalance, and yet, raise it up through the joy of the experience."

My next question is if any of this work will assist my feelings of sexuality and sensuality to return. Aton believes it will because if there are any energetic blocks in the stream within the conduits they will be cleared; balancing the yin and yang will also assist me. I thank him for this information and then ask to speak with Tonas alone.

"You honor me, my dear."

"Tonas, in writing this book it has been difficult for me to describe my emotions and feelings about our relationship. I think the biggest challenge stems from the fact that, for probably twenty years, I have not felt sexual desire, nor have I been interested in any man on Earth. And so, I don't feel that I want to put much of that kind of emotion in my book at this point in our relationship. Maybe that will change because my future self *did* tell me that I will, at some point, feel sexual desire again. Her comment was, 'Oh, baby!'"

This guy is such a treasure. He suggests that this might cause readers of my future books to be "hanging on every word" as I come into that passion. I say I hope he's right and thank him for being patient with me because I can't say things that don't feel true.

"And I would know that they were not. That is why I thank you for not speaking anything that is not of truth of your heart."

"I feel a great tenderness for you, and I love you at the level that I've been able to feel love. It's just that I want more than that."

"You will have it. You will have it with me, or you will have it with some other very lucky one who finds your heart, as I have found it, to be the warmest and the most loving of any in any universe. Believe me, I am open to what you desire."

The next morning as I'm waking up I hear my future self say, "It's Tonas." I feel the energy of her words go into my heart and then later I hear her say, "lover." She seems to think Tonas is the one, but, of course, I need to discover that for myself.

CHAPTER SIX
October 1, 2014

Speaking to Esthra, I say that this morning I saw myself trying to pull a weed out. "I broke the top off but the root of the issue was still there. Whatever that is I need to clear it."

He says this was about my sons and my divorce. Although the divorce was difficult for me, the pain I feel is mostly concerning how hard it was for my sons. The estrangement that they are currently feeling for each other is also challenging for me. This brings to mind something about myself that I really want to change.

"I don't want to be a relationship fixer. I especially don't want to do that in an intimate relationship. Tonas said he's perfect and I thought, 'Oh, I bet I could find something wrong.' I don't believe I thought that he's too perfect!"

"Those of non-dual realize you're living in a dual reality."

This reply doesn't ease me one bit. I want to be able to discern what to do and what not to do. Using SVH, I move to get assistance from my MAPS self. Here is what I request: help me release the need to be a fixer, help me discern when to act and when not to act, when to speak and when to be silent, when to leave and when to stay, and to know what is the next most right thing to be, do or say in every moment of my life that shows and emanates mastery. Plus, anything that would help me release the pain in the past of this life so that I can be comfortable being completely in the 7th dimension with my toes in the door for the 8th dimension.

Esthra reminds me that it is also important to be able to let things be as they are for other people. His advice to change what I want in my life while letting other people have their reality feels like something I'm just going to have to keep working on.

"I have a question about something I heard a man tell me in November of 2000. I don't know who it was, but what I think I heard was, 'We come together for the true meaning of life. It is destined for us to be together forever in our hearts.' Do you know who said that to me?"

"You know who it was."

(I'm already crying as I allow myself to realize it was Tonas who spoke those words to me. I'm going to talk with him about this later today, but I need time to compose myself first.)

"Thank you for the work with soul lineage two and three. Who is soul lineage person number one?"

Esthra says her name is Kyleah, but she is not of this universe. I suggest that she must be some kind of wonder woman since the other two are. There is laughter in his voice as he replies that she is the queen of her realm. Then he adds that since she wishes to assist her dual world in preparing for the culmination, she is in collaboration with Isis and Gaia.

"Would there be any benefit in speaking with her? I do have a lot of things I want to ask the council today."

"Hmm, I believe she would be most honored. She knows who you are and she is the one that is the closest to you. She is, in her universe, as Isis is in this universe. You can simply remember this and speak to her when there is more time available."

I ask Esthra if there's anything else I need to know today. He says it is time I heard some words of praise and offers to transmit them to me telepathically to save time.

"Oh, no, don't do that! You are jesting now, I know."

He quickly relents and says, "You deserve all accolades."

I thank him and then intend to speak with Aton.

Aton greets me and asks permission to do an adjustment today. I agree and then ask him what he was doing this morning when I heard him tell me to back up a little bit and hold absolutely still. He says they were making adjustments in my energy fields. I admit that I've not been feeling well physically the last few days. He notes that I've been quite emotional and this has affected my well-being. My parents are not well and I didn't even realize that my concerns about them are causing me to experience challenges. I can't believe I didn't make that obvious connection.

As usual, his voice takes on a musing tone as he comments, almost to himself, that it appears there are some interesting energies. I say that I love it when he mutters those kinds of things.

"I am muttering…" and he continues to do so. "Yes, I believe we must, at what you call the axis. It is the pinion of the djed. You are sparking new brain filaments and surprising us all."

More mumbling from him, then he asks me to relax. He says he's going to tug on my earlobes just a little bit in order to adjust my spine. I've never had an adjustment that way, but I'm sure Aton knows what he's doing.

When I ask how the Andromedans adjusted my yin, Aton tells me they ran showers of colored light through my body which assisted to clear stagnant energies; my yin and yang are now balanced.

In a discussion about whether those energies will go out of balance again, Aton advises me to release the 3rd and 4th dimensional principle that foods can cause imbalances in yin and yang. I agree to do some work clearing that belief and thank him for his assistance.

Iniquasha and I greet each other in the people's language and then I say I didn't adequately thank him for the work that he did.

"It takes a former pissed off Indian to ferret out information like that. Is there anything you can tell me about what you found?"

"It is a journey of acceptance that must fuel the honoring of the promises, for until it is agreed that this can happen, there is resistance to its creating. *That* is what is making the transition in these next stages of the evolution. Do you understand?"

"Yes, but I was curious as to what you found and where you found it."

He says that the information is held in the records of the living and the dead. Knowing that is all he can tell me, I thank him and give him my blessings.

Tonas sounds happy as he asks how I am. Even though I'm not feeling that great I give him the standard reply that I'm well. No sense in adding to my distress by claiming otherwise. He tells me I'm beautiful and that I look like a princess.

I wish I could see myself the way he sees me. It's hard for me to picture wearing the kind of clothes Liponie creates for me. As an adult, comfortable and warm clothes are what I prefer. When I was little, my motto was the fewer clothes the better. Instead of playing dress up, I remember dressing down in my version of Indian attire—a towel of some kind fastened around my waist and stripes of war paint carefully painted on my face using a tube of my grandmother's red lipstick. I think I used a lot of it because I remember how difficult it was for her to scrub off.

"I have to know how the tournament came out."

"They are on to something different now. There seems to be no end to this and Liponie encourages it. They are competing in boat racing; before that it was dog racing and they were riding the dogs. At least for the horse racing they did ride upon the horses."

I've been laughing all through his recounting of what's been happening. It seems the Swizzlers are addicted to action. Tonas explains that Liponie helps by giving them homework about each of the activities in advance so they are well prepared.

Tonas says they acquitted themselves well in the jousting. "Galahad was very gallant and…" Here his voice drops to be almost inaudible. "I think some of these let them win a little."

I reply very softly that that was kind of them.

"Yes, they were *very* kind. Pellinore was the grand victor."

"Did he get a special prize from Liponie?"

"Of course."

Here, inspiration strikes me and I request a beautiful scarf that I can give Pellinore. "In the movies the queen gives the winner a little scarf to wear around their arm or on their armor. Can I do that?"

Tonas laughs as he says that Liponie gave me a lance with the scarf on the end of it. I remove the scarf and intend to walk to where Pellinore is sitting. When I ask him to stand so that I may give him the token, he calls me his queen and says he is kneeling before me.

I speak with difficulty because I'm suddenly teary-eyed again, "I am so grateful that you are all here. Please take this as a token of my affection and my regard for you."

"Ah, I am grateful and will treasure it always."

Then I have to ask him, because the match-making urge strikes me again, if he has a partner.

"I do not, though if you are available, I would choose you first."

This comment restores my composure and I tease him by saying, "Don't tempt me. In this age we consider knights to be very romantic. Remember I did offer some time ago to assist those of you who were interested in reconnecting with former partners."

"Yes, of course, and you might also be interested in us as knights. We also are very much a challenge during the day." Then he explains that was a joke and goes on to add that the tournament was a success.

"Why were the Swizzler helmets pointed in the back and the front?"

(After my last council meeting I rolled back in time to walk around the tournament area and asked Esthra to describe what the Swizzlers looked like. He reported that they were wearing chain mail shirts with what looked like thick hemp shirts underneath, long pants which looked similar to leather and very pointed boots that came up almost to their knees. They had shields with an image of a large crystalline pinecone and "House of Swizzlers" written in Language of Light on it. The face plate of their armor puzzled both of us because it had a big point jutting out from the nose and there was another point coming out the back.)

Sounding a little bit apologetic, Pellinore admits this was the Swizzlers' design. They thought it would be an advantage to have a set of eyes in the backs of their heads and Liponie created that addition for each of them. Pellinore said it was great fun, but I'm actually glad I didn't see them with four eyes—too eerie.

Back at the head of the table, I address the council in general. "My future self told me to ask you, 'How can I see the paths of discovery that unleash the 4th dimensional elements that are woven into the 5th and the 6th dimensions?' This is an open question because if four is woven into six as well as five, we have some entanglement going on."

Charlie says this is a very good question, for this is slowing the progression. "Much of the history of humanity has been about survival. The survival was of 3rd and 4th dimensional principles that are associated with fears of dying, of being cold, hungry, physically hurt or persecuted. At this time on Earth, there is a need to control, to hold onto things and there is fear of making waves that can create the loss of that which is the feeling of safety. There is no more need to be the fittest for survival."

I ask them to put something together to address this and they agree to collaborate on it in the next days.

I'm going to be leaving town for about a week. The Swizzlers know about it and now they request to go with me. I have been hesitant to reveal that they and the other councils incarnated into crystals I purchased for them. They are all sitting on my desk. Charlie assures me that they are safe, so now you know.

Charlie says all the other councils want to go. He says he will be content to ride underneath my seat in the car. Further conversation reveals that they can see the Moon outside my office window. Even though I know they're embodied in the crystal, it's hard to imagine a hunk of rock seeing anything.

"Congratulations on your good showing in the tournament."

"Indeed, there were several of us that cleaned up the clocks of the knights."

I take a moment to enjoy his use of that phrase, then suggest that they enter in the Olympics. I shouldn't be surprised, but I am, when they tell me they are already preparing for an Olympic challenge. Charlie will light the torch, of course, and they are all practicing. Liponie is helping them prepare.

"We are fast runners; we can vault the pole. We are becoming quite adept."

"I'm delighted at your activity. You're making up for lost time for being a collective. Were you ever incarnated in a body before?"

"We have been a consciousness. We are now individual and we are competing. It is all very fun. The prize is strawberry shortcake and we are all vying for it."

"Osiris, why am I working with the Egyptian pantheon instead of, for example, the Nordic gods?"

Osiris says one reason is because he, Isis, Horus, Thoth and the others were dedicated to Egypt which was a center point. Also, people could hold onto their dogma because they considered Osiris and the

52

others to be merely part of Egypt's history. He adds that he and the other Egyptian gods at the table predate Egypt and the human species as well.

Here are their responses to my request for brief biographical descriptions:

Osiris says he is considered to be the patriarch of Andromeda, Sirius and Arcturus and also guardian of Earth and humanity.

Isis says that she is matriarch of those same realms as well as a great guardian of humanity.

"I'm not going to ask you how old you are, but are you in the same ball park as Liponie?"

"Oh, my dear, we are not old at all."

Realizing I fumbled that question, I recover and say, "OK, I know about you guys and old. Don't give me that."

She maintains that she is quite youthful. "Osiris and I were the first that existed in the ancient, as you would call it. If you imagine that there had to be the first, it would be my beloved and I."

"You were before Odin, Shiva and the others?"

"Of course, though they are short-lived in comparison…by about three trillion years or so."

In response to my question about how to pronounce her name, she says she is Eesis and yet she is also Eyesis.

Horus is the next person I ask for information. He confirms that his parents are Osiris and Isis and goes on to explain that his role is also to be a guardian to humanity. "It is our greatest desire as well as our passion to assist those who are in an awakened state as well as those who are nearing their awakened state. Yet our focus is even broader to include all the sentience of Earth."

Hathor sounds regal as she greets me and says she is the consort of Horus. "He is younger than myself, and quite active. My role on Earth has been to assist those who are awakening to that spirit of light within them and to recognize the great joy that can be brought through the awareness of the *truth* of being. There is no desire or need for struggle when one is compliant with the truth of their nature. I, like you, am joy."

I'm giggling as I congratulate her on having a younger man for a partner. She agrees he is very spirited. When I ask her who her parents are she says she is of the original, as Osiris and Isis are original.

I wonder if there are others here that I think of as Egyptian who are original. She says yes and invites them to answer for themselves. Nobody says anything so I give a little prod and ask who would like to speak.

Thoth offers to speak to me then goes on to explain that he plays a role that allows the individuals of Earth and other worlds to recognize their individuality. "The spirit of the essence of their greatest strength is to understand that they are unique. That is the piece that is to be found among the human species; that they shall rise to know that their greatest strength is not to be of the collective. It is to be a part of the collective and to be an individual."

I agree with him and ask if he is one of the original beings. He dodges my question by simply saying he is long-lived. I thank him for speaking and don't press him for clarification.

El Morya is the next person to speak about himself and his origin. I've heard people call him Morya or Moyra and am curious which pronunciation he prefers. It seems he has no preference because he says there are many ways to say his name; he adds that many call him Morya.

"My origins are varied. I am in presence on Earth much. Once it was inspired within me that humanity would become a part of my heart, I have dedicated myself to the evolution of all those that are in readiness."

"Sananda, I saw a picture that was purported to be of you which was taken at Chichen Itza about thirty years ago. Was it you?"

He laughs heartily and says that he seems to be appearing everywhere. He also tells me that it would be very difficult for someone to capture a picture of him in this dimension since the particles of his being are quite speedy.

"Please tell me a couple sentences about your origin and purpose."

"Andromeda, and I have some origins of Lyra. It is, to me, a quest of heart to be as much of everything that I can be for the human beings of Earth, for they are the youngest species of sentient beings that exist throughout all of each and every of the universes. And so, as this fledgling race evolves to remember its greatest truth, it is I who am always present shining the brightest light for each of them as they are looking for a spark to guide them. I am *always* there. It is my dedication; it is the reason for my ascending and it is the reason for my focus of purpose that exists at this time. For the last six million years it has been my highest priority."

The dedication and passion in his voice are undeniable. I feel a very strong connection to him and am so grateful for his unwavering assistance. I'm sure he, like many of the others here, has been with me for my whole life

Melchizedek speaks next to tell me he, too, is long-lived. He was an initiate of the ancient academies of Earth millions of years ago. "When those of your fellowship made their presence known to us, our hearts opened, for the love that we felt for you drew to us a kinship that was in partnership as well as the sense of being almost guardian and parent. I have dedicated myself to humanity. My focus in life is to guide and my focus in my full existence is to meet all of the great desires that lead me to that success. It is the success of you that is fueling my destiny."

This last statement is quite a revelation to me; I'm going to ask him more about what he means, but perhaps in a private conversation.

"I have one more question for Thor. Did Loki really exist?"

He wants to know if I am truly asking him that question and I say yes.

He laughs before telling me, "It is a desire for you to understand the greater myth. There were many myths. Loki is not a shifter in shape; he is, instead, a great one who is capable of appearing as desired, just as I or any of the others."

Thor confirms that Loki also was from a different universe. I really do want to find out more about the Nordic gods, because, for some reason, their stories are the most interesting to me.

"I'm going to say farewell. Charlie Brown, have fun!"

"We are living!"

I love hearing the enthusiasm in his voice and encourage him to continue living to the max.

Privately with Tonas in our garden:

"I went back in my notes today to find the exact words I heard about fourteen years ago. I asked Esthra who said them and guess who it was."

"Who, my dear?"

"It was you."

"Ah, well, I have been a major figure in your existence for quite some time."

"I know, but for me it still feels like I've only known you eight months. Do you want to know…"

"Tell me!"

"There are two sentences and here is the first one. 'We come together for the true meaning of life.'"

With only a slight pause he finishes by saying, "and it is destined for us to be together in the forever in our very hearts.' Yes, I spoke those words."

He told me once that he remembers everything he's said or heard, but his ability to remember these words still unnerves me. I don't know exactly why I'm crying, but I am.

"Do you know what the true meaning of life is, my dear? To find the blending of hearts that *willingly* meet in union. It is a union of spirit. Do not fear that you may not feel for me as I feel for you. I have *no* fears of this, for one day you will remember all that we have meant to one another and in that remembering there shall be no questions in your heart."

CHAPTER SEVEN

October 8, 2014

I recently heard someone tell me I would be bringing back something Leonardo da Vinci needed to say. Esthra says that it would be good for me to work with da Vinci, and, even though I don't know his language, I could understand it via telepathy. "You are bringing back an awareness that the infinite nature of all that exists is at your fingertips; this awareness concerns the nature of mathematics and geometries. There will be a time when all of that is going to become relevant because of all the books that you will write."

I don't laugh when Esthra tells me this, but I remember how difficult math was for me in school. My chronology of school math remembrances includes being traumatized in second grade when Miss Roland told the class we couldn't count on our fingers; being further traumatized in fourth grade when Miss Davee introduced number problems in stories; (How could they wreck my favorite subject, English, by sticking numbers in it?) and finally I remember sitting in ninth grade algebra class and crying because I just didn't get it. Maybe it's a form of divine justice that perhaps one day I will be a math whiz, but I'm not counting on it.

The next thing to discuss with Esthra is the fragrance of vanilla. "I recently heard someone tell me, 'This is vanilla.' Another healer told me a long time ago that vanilla is a fragrance that is very important to me. What is it with vanilla?"

"It is a vibrational essence. As a perfume it balances the energy."

I'm very interested about this fragrance because I just now remembered that vanilla comes from one of my favorite plants, the orchid. Esthra suggests I create that the geometries of vanilla are floating in my aura and they will spread out whenever that frequency would benefit others.

He adds that I need not limit myself to one fragrance since I could have over three hundred fragrances right now. With the help of my MAPS self and SVH, I get the complete list of scents and flower essences that are part of what I will be able to direct in my aura. I even get things like the smell of cookies baking or what it smells like after a rain, or how sheets smell after they have dried outside on a clothesline.

These vibrations of scents will be in my aura to benefit others by promoting healing, supporting an elevation of spirit and a balancing of energies. The vibrations will also emanate whenever it will assist me with clarity, focus, attraction of abundance, assistance with channeling and my life in general.

I also set it up so that my books will have the vibrations of any of these scents which would benefit those who purchase or read them. Simply put, readers of my books will be bathed in the vibrations and scents that best assist them.

At the Joy Councils, Tonas greets me and says that everyone is ready for me. Before I begin work, I ask if Kyleah is present. She acknowledges that she is here and then requests a chair so that she can sit beside me. Liponie asks everyone to move aside a little bit to make room and then manifests a chair. With her permission I embrace her and she asks me if I feel the presence of ourselves in unity.

Before I can answer in English, a language pops out of my mouth with a different flavor than what I usually speak. Kyleah answers me with something that sounds similar and then says we have this language of her planet, Zhollah, in common.

I thank her for joining us and invite her to be a part of our council if she is interested. She says that is a unique privilege and explains that although her world is of duality it is evolving. With my permission, she addresses the council to ask that we make some kind of connection with her world in order to support its evolution.

Now I'm wondering if I goofed by asking this woman to speak. I have no idea how to go about doing what she asks or even if we *should* do what she wants. Deciding to put Osiris on the spot, I ask him if he can suggest the best course of action.

He says he is aware of Kyleah's work since she has been working closely with Isis. If she intends to create a council on her world that would connect with our council, he's in favor of it.

58

She affirms that she wants us to include her world and universe in the work we are doing to assist Earth. While I ponder what to say to this bold request, Isis asks to speak. I welcome her opinion and she says she feels the assistance that we can provide will ripple over to support Earth; she is also in favor of Kyleah's proposal. Tonas suggests I should ask Gaia and I ask her to share her feelings with us.

"Thank you for your consideration. It is my desire that the connection that is felt by those conduits that you and the others have created for Earth shall include an alliance with Kyleah's world and universe. I am in connection with the world, Zoreah. (Zoreah is to Zhollah as Gaia is to Earth.) She wishes to be in the same evolution pace as we and it is possible for us to be of assistance. It is also possible for the Sun of Aton to shine upon them just as he shines upon us, for as his heart is so big, it is sure that this connection will allow his essence to transmit directly to elevate your world. Perhaps your councils would better be able to define the parameters of this kind of an alliance."

My first consideration is to find out if everyone on our council is open to this alliance. With that in mind, I ask Tonas to tell me if there is anyone indicating a negative vote. He is laughing heartily as he tells me that Liponie has been offering the council members a black ball but no one is interested in taking it.

Since our council approves, I ask Kyleah if there are councils on her world that could work with our council. Instead, she proposes that the Great Ones in our council could be part of her council. She isn't interested in being the head of her council. She simply wishes to be an affiliate and have the benefit of our expansions. She says she has observed that what we are doing is very swiftly evolving our world and hopes that her world can have some of those same flavors.

Sananda asks to be recognized and then greets Kyleah. The plan he presents is that in the past the Swizzlers could include Kyleah's universe in the transmissions Tonas and I did from Inishimora. That would lay the foundation for the development of their council. Creation of their council chambers and their inauguration could also take place in the past. Sananda concludes by saying it is possible that this pattern can be replicated over and over again within *all* of the universes.

I'm beginning to see that there is a larger picture here and I'm feeling excited as I tell Sananda I was just getting that same idea. I'm all over goose bumps.

"Let me tell you of the inspiration I am just having. And believe me, if anyone has had this thought before and is feeding it to us, we are grateful. Will you raise your hand? Ah, none! They are all inspired along with us. May I suggest to you something?"

"Mm-huh."

"What has been foretold to us is that in the next three hundred fifty years, somehow, magically, *all* of the worlds in *all* of the universes, no matter where they are in their evolution, would somehow meet that same pace of Earth and reach that cumulative point of the collective ascension. Is this, I ask all of you, the means for this reality?"

I have, with difficulty, been keeping my laughter subdued enough to hear Sananda's recital. I know, absolutely, that we have come up with the formula for what he has described. Eureka!

He says, "Yes, it has happened on this day."

"This is like an ascension template for all the universes."

"It is the foundation for one and it begins with Kyleah. I believe she is the bright star that has brought to this council an inspiration of destiny. We celebrate you, Kyleah, and you, dear Joy, that she should be of your lineage and drawn to you through your questioning and all of these *seemingly* random patterns."

Although I'm delighted beyond delighted, I reply that I'm not sure how to go about what we're going to do. Sananda suggests that the CEV must assist with the next steps, because everything we do must be in alignment with the parameters of Earth. "Earth is the foundation and the center point of all that is to occur in the future which means that it all must begin here. None of the CEV have raised their hands, though there is one who is deciding to be female and has breasts now."

I was wondering when that would happen. It just seemed inevitable to me that at least one of the ninety-three remaining Swizzlers would want to try the feminine approach. This could get interesting.

"Yes, the bodice is quite alluring on a small frame."

Sananda clears his throat after he makes this observation. As I ponder what breasts on a stick would look like, interesting seems more appropriate than alluring, but Sananda is ever the diplomat.

The council is going to spend some time discussing how to begin this new phase of our development and I pause for a moment to collect my thoughts before moving to the next subject.

"Two days ago I had a vision of someone holding out two plates, one in each hand. There were things on both plates and then I heard the words, 'It is the vision.' I believe that one of the plates represented the Earth as it is now and the other was Earth as it will be. Who can address that?"

I recognize Hathor, who says that, "The vision of the world as it is now is one that has forgotten its joy. There are parts of the world with beings holding great joy within their hearts, and yet feeling guilty for having it, for how can one be happy when there are wars and sickness? When people sing there is even less enjoyment because of the belief that to be of pleasure is sinful. This will fall along the way as the lesser dimensions release. The world that will be is one that will be about the freedom to express the whole heart. That is the role of an individual you are choosing to work with in the future, I believe, for she is certainly dedicating to work with you. Freyja, as you call her, is myself."

I take a deep breath at her revelation and exclaim that a picture of Freyja is in the middle of my dream board directly behind my desk. She chuckles at my astonishment and says she has been intending to tell me for a long time.

"No wonder I'm so interested in the Nordic gods! It was you and Thor who were talking about this vision, I think. I was going to invite Freyja to join the council but it seems she is already here."

Very coyly she says she accepts most humbly; both of us find this acceptance speech humorous.

I ask what we can do with the future vision. She says that I am developing the new vision and the world is also developing it, yet it is quite sluggish. She remarks that there is so much pleasure to be had simply in being who you are. "There is only bliss in that, there is only song in that and there is a dance on the feet when one is in bliss and great joy, you see?"

"Yes. Before I came to the council today I did more work on clearing stuff about sin, regret and guilt. I want to let it go completely and it just keeps hanging on."

"The layers of the dimensions hold the threads of experiences in the collective consciousness. When the 4th dimension makes its release, a great deal of the collective consciousness beliefs that support the 3rd and 4th dimensional belief systems will slide gracefully away with those dimensions. There will be no funeral; they are not dead. They remain in the hearts and minds of people as chapters in the stories that were part of the journey."

Lately, I've been thinking—more than usual—about all the things I'd like to know. With frustration, I share with the group that if I had a million years and I asked questions twenty-four hours a day, I still don't think I'd get all my questions answered. Hathor replies that is the reality for all of them as well because all they do in every moment of their existence is desire to know.

This bit of information dismays me. I thought I was talking to people who had most of the answers, but just couldn't tell me. Later, I console myself with the notion that they still must know lots of interesting things that I *don't* know.

Hathor adds this is not a sickness; it's just who I am…one of them. All I can think to do is ask them to *help* me.

"It is possible to awaken that part of yourself. There have been those on Earth as humans who have had glimpses into the everything, and known it. This full awareness has typically lasted a moment, but for some, several days."

Now I picture myself wandering around with a grin on my face and so blissed out that I have no desire to do anything. The thought of that causes me to say that I don't want anything to happen that will hinder me from doing this work. "If I'm just sitting around in bliss and not able to function, that probably wouldn't be so good. There's so much I want to know! I want to know more about Camelot; I want to know about the

Nordic gods; I want to tell Jesus's story, although that could be a little bit touchy. I have millions of questions and only so much time."

"Your time on Earth has been extended. (Those who evolve into the 8th dimension can live several hundred years until the culmative happens.) All of your questions will be answered, my dear."

I'm still not sure that is possible, but there's no point in further discussion right now.

"Charlie Brown, I have to find out how the Olympics turned out. Are they over?"

Charlie replies in his serious voice that he is prepared to give me the answers to all my questions. The Swizzlers put the Olympics "on the way of the side. We have been separate from this council for several days so that we might fully invest our energies and our consciousness in the journey of existing in physical form on Earth. (He's talking about the fact that I took all the council rocks to Rockford when I went there to visit my sons.) It was important for all of us to feel the different energies as beings incarnated and to be in the different energies of different regions. As we connected in the individual spaces that you brought us, it gave us a clearer vision of the energies that are unique to specific areas. It was a very important learning project for us; we are grateful."

This grown-up sounding speech is immediately followed by the words, "I want ice cream." I grin inwardly at his child-like request; obviously, he missed Liponie's treats. I'm sure Liponie will provide some for him as soon as we're done, so I just ask what the visit to my favorite park was like for him.

"It was very unique to connect with the different layers of the realms and there is a base of crystals in that region that is unique."

"When I sat you in the dirt I wondered what you could see. There were trees above us that were blowing in the breeze."

"In each dimension there were trees blowing in the breeze, for it was possible for us to witness the realm of the dragon, the realm of the fairies, the realm of the crystalline and the realm of the present Earth in its connection with the 3rd dimension. The 3rd dimension is connected still to the 4th dimension, and even though it is not fully present and connected to Earth, it *is* linked to that dimension.

Your home, our abode, has very lovely energy that you have created for it, you see. It is a protection bubble, and so for us to travel to places that are not in that bubble of energy gave us a full measure of understanding of Earth and its positions. The trip was an opportunity for us to look deeply into the 3rd dimension as the key to disconnecting and releasing the energies which are like tentacles holding fast."

Charlie and the others were able to see parasites within the bodies of people living in the areas I travelled through. He uses that information to compare the 3rd dimension to a parasite with its tentacles reaching into the 6th dimension through the conduits of the 4th and 5th dimensions. His analysis is that the 3rd dimension is connected very deeply and does not wish to be released. The good news is that when the 4th dimension is released it is possible that the tentacle parts of the 3rd dimension existing in the 5th and the 6th dimensions will melt.

Charlie adds that it is important for the collective consciousness of Earth to rise a little bit before the release of the 4th dimension so that the melting can occur, otherwise the tentacle will remain. They have put together a very comprehensive piece for us to transmit today that they believe will assist to loosen the tentacle.

The next thing he points out is that we have a situation. That is the word he uses to describe the fact that the female Swizzler wishes to have a name. I don't have a problem with that but then he says that she wishes for me to name her. Here is another oh-oh moment. This feels like a huge responsibility that I am rather reluctant to take on. If I stall a little maybe I'll get an idea. I ask what colors she is wearing and Charlie tells me her whole body is pink. Pink is an obvious choice for a name, but I mention that I don't really want to name her that. When I ask if she has any suggestions, Charlie says she likes and accepts the name Pinky.

I breathe a sigh of relief, offer her congratulations and tell her to carry on with these other Swizzler folks while she enjoys her pinkiness.

I address Aton to ask if he wants to make an adjustment on me today and he says he has already made three. This prompts me to tell him he is marvelous and to say how grateful I am to have met him.

"What would my life, my existence, be had I never met you? Think of this for a moment, I would not be in the wedded bliss; I would simply still be loving Gaia from afar."

When I ask Aton if he has learned to cook, he tells me that he made pancakes, but they were not pretty cakes like the ones Liponie makes. They got a recipe book as a wedding gift and were very excited to try the pancakes, but they were flat and tasteless without the toppings. I agree that they do need syrup and butter.

"Ah, and yet my Gaia provided us with a cornucopia of fruits to be placed within. She took her fork, which is an implement that you eat with, (I love it that people here keep reminding me how to use Earth things.) and she mashed them all so it made a very gelatinous and tasty mix."

Gaia states that those things are at her disposal, but, "It is different to know them and to have the experience of being a raspberry than it is to taste it's elixir within your mouth, mmm. It was my innovation to take the fork and mash them all together. This was not in the recipe book."

I agree that experimenting is fun and Gaia confides that she and Aton are experimenting with a lot of things. It would be interesting to find out what the honeymoon activities were like for her, but I'm too shy to ask her. Also, it seems like too private an issue to question her about.

In answer to my question about how Joyous is doing, Woonfred says that she is growing strong and that Earth has become a great place for her to exist and to play. "*All* of the dragons of Earth are enjoying their existence."

I check to make sure the dragons are still going to join us when we are in the 8th dimension.

"We will move into the 8th dimension, and in our entry we will come as perhaps the geese flying to the south and the north. We will be in formation and we will make a great surprise and spectacle. I have been inspired by Liponie. Do nothing small."

I'm really looking forward to that day. I can't even imagine how breathtaking it will be to see formations of millions of dragons flying in the sky.

I love talking with council members, but it is time to do some work. Charlie tells me the sphere is ready. I direct the council to focus with me and vision some kind of lovely dissolving energy that will assist the 3rd dimension tentacles to slip easily away. I feel the energy of the sphere moving through the Joy Arrows into all of Earth and then back out into the grids and through the threads. Tonas comments that it feels lovely and I agree.

In privacy with Liponie, I ask him if he thinks any of the Swizzlers would like to learn how to play a musical instrument. He says that will be difficult because they are planning on beginning the Olympics again.

"I had a difficult time explaining the Special Olympics. They did not wish to have regular Olympics. They said, 'We wish to have the Special Olympics,' and I told them they fit the criteria perfectly. Then, of course, I had to explain. And your little Pinky, she is dressing with a bodice that shows quite large bosoms."

"Do you think it's possible that they will consider being sexual?"

Now, I temporarily move the Swizzlers' crystal into another room. This is probably an unnecessary precaution, but since I don't know if they hear actual words it seems like a good idea. Liponie says the subject of sex hasn't come up and he isn't looking forward to that if it does. He tells me that no one on the council is bandying around that topic and as long as I am not sexually active in front of them they may not have the idea.

There's no chance of anything like that happening, but I am curious about what they can see. Liponie says that although they do not have eyes in the crystal, they can see everything because they are able to read the energies around them.

That explanation doesn't satisfy me, but I'm not going to waste any more time trying to figure out how they do what they do.

"I'm going to say farewell for today. Wave your magic wand, Liponie, and help me see everybody."

"It is ready!"
"Whap me with it a few times!"

CHAPTER EIGHT

October 11, 2014

"Esthra, two days ago I heard someone tell me, 'You'll have a makeover.' What's that about?"

"This was about the defining moment when you decide what you want to look like."

This might also have come up because I recently had a professional photo taken that I was so unhappy with I never used it. Esthra agrees with my idea that perhaps I need more clarity concerning what I do want to look like. I certainly know that's better than focusing on what I don't like about my looks.

"When your ethereal presence steps into the Joy Council you look like a goddess, and yet, Tonas and the others know what you look like in the physical. They think you look perfect."

"That is so hard to believe! I feel like saying, 'No, you're wrong! You can't really see me. Look at these wrinkles!'"

Esthra suggests this is an issue to work on with SVH. I know he's right. It's just that knowing instant transformation is a future option increases my dissatisfaction with my current appearance.

I've been wondering if there is anything else we can do to help release the 3rd dimensional tentacles Charlie talked about. I intend to step into the presence of the galactic council that can assist us and am advised to put my energy into the 4th dimension to meet with councils there. In that position, I'm guided to energetically hook strings of lights onto the tentacles. That will allow the Swizzlers to see or sense their energy and then tag them. Since I'm feeling in a festive mood, I choose Christmas tree lights. The final step is to move to the Fifth Realm and show the collective consciousness of Earth what will be available when those tentacles are no longer supported.

With Sananda in the Fifth Realm, I ask everyone on Earth who is holding any kind of connection or support for the lit up tentacle threads now and on into the next eighteen months to give us gifts we can give to them when they were incarnated.

The first person I intend to meet at the Joy Council is Aton because this morning I heard, "The doctor wants me to see the doctor quickly."

We exchange greetings and I'm very excited when he tells me that I am ready to move into the next phase.

"This morning it felt like a crystal ball went into my right eye. (Aton says it was actually a new chakra associated with my right eye.) Then I heard myself ask where the nine other ones are."

The short version of a very long explanation Aton gives me is that today he is going to place a set of nine orbs of consciousness in my energy fields that will help me anchor into the 7th dimension. He will place two more sets of nine each sometime in the future to make a total of twenty-seven orbs circulating in my aura.

There is an integration period of several days during which the orbs will remain stationary. When they begin to spin, that motion causes creation energy to spark, which causes my desires to be formed more swiftly.

He explains that the orbs are part of the structure of geometries that fuel energies on a non-dual world and everyone on a non-dual world has them. They will look like planets floating in a cosmos but they are linked to a matrix of energies that are a part of grids marking each of their positions.

Orbs floating like planets in a cosmos sounds so beautiful and my desires being formed more swiftly sounds so exciting that I tell Aton I'm ready to do whatever he wants me to do.

He asks me to stand on one foot, but I'm already laughing since I know this is an Aton joke. He's ready to begin today if I am, and, of course, I tell him I am; however, since this work needs to be done in my home and I am going to have to stand still in the middle of a room for three minutes, we decide to wait until after I'm finished with the council work for today.

I ask a few more questions because I'm still not sure how these orbs will work. Aton says that although the orbs are free floating, the conduits and the consciousness that is within each of the chakras and cells of my body will cause them to spin.

I decide that since he knows what he's doing and I trust him completely, I'm just going to enjoy the results of this work instead of trying to understand all the details. He's the scientist, not me.

Aton and I walk arm in arm into the council for a surprise visit. Tonas asks everyone to rise and then to please be seated; however, Woonfred has remained standing. He explains that the reason he is standing is that there is a new dragon egg and the dragons believe it contains a female.

I love hearing news like this and my questions for Woonfred come thick and fast. The parents are Konta, the female, and Horay is her mate. They live in a dimension that is part of Ireland, and their decision to create an egg was important not only for themselves, but for the Earth.

I ask Woonfred to tell me more about that and he obliges by explaining that it is important to begin the new dragon colony now. He believes that the baby dragons will be very acceptable when they are brought in front of all that are in an awakened state.

He informs me that the dragons aren't sure how long it will take the egg to hatch. The last one, Joyous's egg, took nine weeks but this one might take less. When the dragons were in the 3rd dimension, gestation took much longer. Woonfred remarks that it is interesting they are witnessing the creation of females because in the past there were always more males.

He agrees with me that the female eggs could be indicative of the trend of goddess that is becoming prevalent on this Earth. I really hope so; in my opinion, goddess energy has too long been squelched on Earth.

Woonfred says he will keep me informed about the progress of the egg and about any concerns Konta or Horay might have.

"Thank you for the good news. Is that all you had to share today?"

"Greetings, and most welcome from our hearts to yours."

"I'm *really* looking forward to the day that I can ride on one of you guys."

"If you come to me in your sleep we will move to the skies. It will be most authentic."

"All right, I will intend to do that this evening. I'm blowing you a kiss."

I hear dragon chuckles and I immediately advise him to hold onto his kisses; I'm not ready for fire yet.

"I'm looking for a new mate. Are you interested?"

"Not at this time, but I will always be your friend, Woonfred... always."

If a dragon can sound "sheepish" he does as he tells Tonas he was only jesting.

"Charlie Brown and Pinky, I have something for you. Let me put it on the table."

Charlie says it is interesting and asks me what it is. After explaining the work I did in the 4th dimension and the gifts I got in the Fifth Realm, I tell them that this should light the tentacles up so that we can see what's being held and who is holding it.

I hope this will do the trick in releasing those things. Every time I think or say the word tentacles, I picture the arms of a monster octopus...creepy.

My hope that the work I did earlier today in the 4th dimension will help us to dissolve the tentacles increases when Charlie says they can now see where the impingements are. They will have something for me to put in place when I return to the council in two days.

"Charlie, I think I saw you in a parade. I saw a bunch of people walking along a street, each holding what I thought was a balloon on a string. Was it for the Olympics?"

"There was great celebration."

"Tell me about it! Don't make me twist your arm."

"The winner of the Olympics is the Swizzler with blue hair but no name. There were many trials that were applied by all. The one that was the easiest for this one with no name was the sack race because it required being able to move in small places."

So just imagine that I begin laughing here and that my laughter continues either as a chuckle or an outright guffaw almost non-stop as Charlie relates his Olympic story.

"Are you familiar with this Olympic challenge?"

I'm not going to question the appropriateness of having sack races as part of their Olympics. Instead, I agree that it's hard and I've done it.

"It is very hard. The little sack was very difficult for the bigger people. For us, it was most simple for we have our arms that can become quite longer. The tight sack that went around both feet was easy for us to contact the edge of and we were able to make the leaping forward in a very short period of time. This was a challenge for the others for their heads were down past their knees and it was impossible for them to keep up with us. This was the challenge to break the ties and it was our great triumph."

"Oh, I see! Who were the other contestants?"

"All of us of this council. There were several that were of the knights and the Indians were very much involved. They were very crafty but they could not bend themselves and make their leaps as quickly as we. It was not of cheating, though it was in our mind of pogo stick."

There is a vivid picture in my mind of the knights and Indians with their bodies bent double and their feet hobbled in tiny sacks trying to inch their way to the finish line while the Swizzlers are pogo jumping with ease right past them. Oh, I wish I had seen it!

"The bobsled was also one of our triumphs and it was easy for us to do jumps with the skis as well."

"Can you tell me all the events?"

"There was the throwing of the javelin; the javelin, at first, was to be one of us, but we protested."

There are gales of laughter coming from my mouth at this statement and tears are running down my face. Liponie seems to have unleashed his mischievous side for these games.

"Liponie suggested it was a joke, but I believe he was quite serious. The discus was very difficult for those who are not accustomed to holding heavy weights, and so this was not one of our greatest triumphs. (I wonder how they kept from toppling over.) The wrestling was difficult because

Liponie insisted that we be greased from head to the toes and we had to remove our hair."

My laughing continues unabated.

"We were naked and we triumphed greatly in this challenge. It was nearly impossible for the challengers to make us to pin."

"I can see why that would be so. Good on you, Liponie!"

"He is very interesting; he has many ideas that are very spirited. There was racing of the legs. You call this running."

I have to remember that phrase—racing of the legs.

"We are tireless, just as all of these in presence here, and so, it was a funny game to play. There were no winners in this. All came in at the same time because we made our strides as big as those of the bigger people. Woonfred was disqualified."

"Why, was he flying or something?"

"He perhaps used more of the wingspan than was necessary as he was in the sloughe. This is a sliding on snow in a small craft. He opened up his wings."

"What was the name of this sport again?"

"Liponie called it the sloughe. We believe he made this name in his head. It was the diving off of a small space on the snows in a bullet shaped implement. As you came to the end of a high peak it was as if it was flying through the airs and it had to land as far in the front as possible."

"Oh, I see." And I *could* see Woonfred hunched up in a tiny craft, leaning forward and trying to get more distance before spreading his wings.

"Then there was the golf. We were champions of the golf."

I manage to gasp out, "Golf?"

"We believe that the golf is our favorite game."

This surprises me and I ask them why.

"It is a game of precision."

I don't know much about golf, but I do know it's possible to get a hole in one. I ask Charlie if any of them managed to accomplish that feat and he says they made the hole more than one time. This reply makes me question how much they really understand the game. I try to pin him down by mentioning that a game of golf has eighteen holes and ask him if that's how they played.

He answers that there were many holes played and they played until they had to stop because there was so much work to do.

"We would like to not quit playing. Liponie says we are addict."

I mention that happens here, too.

"We have costumes for this. The pants are of checkered; the shirts match our hairs; there are color coordinated socks and shoes that have spikes in the bottom of them. Our hats are most interesting; they do not have tops, only the front."

"Yes, sounds like you're right in style." (I'm not going to say the era when checkered pants would have been in style.)

"Liponie told us that we are very *much* in style. It is possible for us to manifest in physical when you are in the 8th dimension and people will not be shocked by us if we appear to be of golf."

Maybe people will just think they are rich and eccentric golfers.

"When we're in the 8th dimension you will be able to leave your crystal?"

"We wish to have a physical form as we are here on Earth and the 10th dimension Moon. It is important for us to be of individual. It is important for us not to conform to events or the styles of others. It is important for us to be as we are choosing and we are developing our own style. In the 8th dimension this will be greatly accepted."

I realize Charlie is correct and I immediately cease all worry about how he will choose to appear or what he decides to wear when we are in that dimension.

I ask if blue hair would like a name. Charlie says they called him Champion. I suggest Champ; Charlie tells me that Champ finds that name acceptable.

"Thank you for your report on your wonderful Olympics. It sounds like you had so much fun."

"Liponie and Tonas you need to do some research about Halloween. People will need to have costumes and I want them to be ready to carve pumpkins, bob for apples and maybe play a game called 'spin the bottle,' which involves some kissing.

This holiday is especially fun for kids because they get dressed up in costumes, go around to houses in their neighborhood ringing doorbells and collecting candy. Costumes can be anything from ghosts and werewolves to princes and princesses."

Here I am interrupted by an excited voice saying, "Oh! Oh! I wish to be the Buzz Lightyear!"

This Swizzler is so dear to me and just when I think he can't be any more precious, he comes up with a request like this.

"I have my hand up for the Buzz. Liponie, I must be the Buzz Lightyear!"

It's delightful to hear the excitement in Charlie's voice and to know that Liponie will be able to create an astounding costume for him and for all the Swizzlers.

Tonas suggests that if we are having another party it would be important to invite the emissaries from the different universes. They would have an opportunity to learn about our tradition of Halloween and also see what Kyleah is planning.

I have a bit of doubt about exposing them to Halloween, but I agree with him that giving them a chance to learn about Kyleah's alliance with us is a brilliant idea.

Tonas explains that if we launch some extra support for Kyleah and her council that day, then the emissaries could witness it themselves. I agree that maybe they would want to jump on the bandwagon, too.

"I don't know about the wagon, although I am sure that there will be music. I am thinking more about that they will see the vision of this and understand that perhaps to have a Joy Council affiliate within their universe would be quite delightful."

"That's what jumping on the bandwagon means; join the parade and get with the program."

"Oh, apologies, my dear."

"No, you described what it is."

"While I'm thinking of it, I need to find out how the Academy of Enrichment is coming along. Did anybody build the log cabin?"

"It was very encouraging to witness three families collaborate and support each other. Liponie found information in the archives of human history and we re-created the situations of those of America coming across those long distances and then building their cabins.

Although that project is complete, there is another group of individuals who will be joining. They will have an opportunity to witness all that was experienced by those who came first. This is part of their training for coming to the academy. They will be witnessing the very arduous existence of being in the wilds. That will give them a new flavor of what it is to be a human and to survive those kinds of conditions."

I'm glad the families were able to accomplish this task, and triply glad that I never had to do anything like it.

"Who can give me information about people who have been imprisoned in crystals?"

Isis greets me and says that earlier works freed individuals who are part of Earth. Although imprisonment in crystals is still done on other worlds, she thinks that the council affiliates from the different worlds and universes might allow us to support the release of those who are still frozen within crystals. She asks if I'm aware this is a punishment.

I answer that I thought it must be something like that, but I'd rather not have it continue unless it would be dangerous to release those who are imprisoned. Isis answers that if, in the past, we educated those who are difficult, then their release could be timed to occur during the period of their greatest evolution.

"You have brought to the limelight a group of individuals whose entrapment would have kept them from their personal evolution. Ah, I have the most wonderful idea! Perhaps these souls could be released on the All Hallows Eve. It would be sanctioned, for this is your universe, and you are currently still within duality. Once you are in the non-dual it would be impossible for you to support this, just as we are not capable of doing interventions. We should begin today since there are many dual worlds in this universe."

I agree that Halloween is the perfect day to release those prisoners who are rehabilitated.

Before I leave, I have the idea to invite the emissaries to the inauguration of the Joy Council in Kyleah's universe as well as to our Halloween party. This suggestion is met with great enthusiasm by our council in the hope that it will encourage other universes to form their own councils as Kyleah is doing.

CHAPTER NINE

October 13, 2014

The work I did the last time I visited the Joy Council to assist individuals in crystals to be free has caused me to want to also assist people who are or were ever imprisoned in jails or prisons. If they were innocent of the crimes for which they were convicted, I want things to come to light that will prove their innocence. That will require all the judges, prosecuting and defense attorneys, jailers and everyone who co-created with the innocent people to give me gifts that will reveal the truth.

"Esthra, is it possible to assist people who have been or are going to be executed? I remember when Louie the 16th was talking about when he was guillotined. Although it was over quickly, he said it was pretty terrible leading up to that."

"You might wonder about people who have had these experiences. The story goes into their archives and when they look back on it, it is considered a great adventure."

Great adventure or not, maybe some people would prefer a different experience. Accordingly, Sananda and I step into the Fifth Realm at the near completion and I ask all those involved with unjust imprisonment and/or executions who would like assistance with those issues to give us gifts for themselves. The gifts will also be made into a transmission to assist our penal system.

It occurs to me that there are people who don't know they are in prison; they don't realize their free will is being limited. I'm thinking of people who are put into slavery in factories to produce shoes or clothing; there are also people who are prisoners in their mind. This might best be addressed by getting a template from some galactic councils of what the world looks like free of those dynamics. I'm also going to get something that shows the steps for a graceful release of those paradigms.

After I step into the councils and make my request for this assistance, Sananda tells me I have a sphere that can be transmitted through the Joy Arrows. He says it is a complete system and visual cues will be projected to those who are enslaved. "This will assist them to figure out what to do to become free. It is possible that people who are lost in their mind will transition. This is not a bad thing; people have been dying for 125,000 years."

Today's date on my calendar says "Indigenous Peoples Day." This sounds like an excellent day to do some more Fifth Realm work with Sananda. Once there, I ask the Native American council elders to step forward and give us something special to be given to the elder tribesmen and people who are in authority because they have the greatest chance to support the honoring elevation of all the tribes. I also ask all the indigenous people to give us gifts to give to themselves.

I've been thinking about things that will enhance the Joy Chronicles books. There are templates for joy, harmony, peace, prosperity and other high vibration energies that I choose to be instilled into the words in the books and thus transmitted to readers and listeners. My intention is that whoever reads or hears the books is assisted without manipulation in whatever ways are divine. I remember Gaia said that the council was assisting the full measure of the messages to come through and that the books contain more than just the words I have in them.

I also ask that readers be surrounded by their angels and infused with divine light and the sacred rays when they think of any of my books, and want to or do read/listen to them. I visit my MAPS self and get a template so that everything I write is full of personal advancement tools that will assist readers and listeners. I hope that readers will understand that the possibilities of what we are going to be able to do and experience go beyond what I write about in the books.

At the Joy Councils, when Tonas greets me with a voice that sounds more subdued than usual, I ask if he's OK. He replies that he is in awe of my beauty. I still can't understand how he can say that about my appearance so I say with a certain amount of disbelief, "Oh...Tonas."

Not dissuaded, he again states he is in awe. I'm glad we're not dwelling on this subject as he next tells me that things have been very spirited there and Liponie is up to his usual self. I remark that I don't think Liponie has a usual self.

"Ah, yes he does. He has created an extension to the council chambers that is now considered to be Partyland. No one is allowed to enter."

I know Liponie will tell *me* and I make a mental note to corner him later.

With the full councils:

After everyone is seated I dive into a subject that has been bothering me more than usual lately, my appearance. "Tonas says I look great, but I don't feel that way. I had a professional picture taken recently and I hated it."

In an attempt to approach the issue of my appearance in a more positive manner, I list some changes I would like—more even skin tone, more muscle tone, whiter teeth—and ask Aton if he can assist me with any of that. He says it is difficult for them to imagine what I am talking about because they all see me as quite beautiful. He contends that I have no vision of how I really look.

Exasperated, I reply that I can't understand how they can see me like they do. "Perhaps it's because you all are looking at my energy body, but my physical body is not like my energy body. This is really an interesting dilemma isn't it? I don't see myself like you see me."

Sounding befuddled, Aton answers that it is a quandary. "We *know* that within a very short period you will be able to design your body like you are sculpting with clay. Your dissatisfaction is amplifying the situation, so we must do something around this."

"I understand what you are saying and I don't normally focus on my appearance. Most of the time I ignore my looks, but the pictures I had taken brought back to my awareness this dissatisfaction. I did some SVH work about what I see when I look in the mirror to help me remember my current appearance is temporary and changing. I know you say it will be a short time, but your short time could be several years. I'm going to be out in the public next year. The people who know me most closely will definitely be convinced that something good is happening if they see me looking more youthful."

Aton asks me if it is important to convince people of anything. I realize he is right; I definitely need to do some SVH clearing work about releasing the need to convince anyone of the truth of what I'm writing. The changes I'm going to undergo will eventually be evident to all, but I do ask the council to play along with me and see what they can do in the months ahead.

"It will be our pleasure to do as much as we can to assist you. It is only a matter of, perhaps, assisting you to reach your goals swifter so that you are able to manage this while also adjusting your thought patterns."

"I did quite a bit of work with adding templates to my book that would assist people with feeling joyful. Is there anything else you think I can do with the book other than just getting it finished?"

Aton asks me if they can reference the book. With my permission they read it energetically and then Osiris says there are things they can add.

"It would also benefit for the full measure of the, let us call them 'characters' in your play, to be vividly projected to the individuals reading or listening. This way, as they read, they are able to capture the true spirit, let us say, of the Swizzlers, and, of course, of my splendor. As you know, all of us are so unique. There are some who are always known for how they appear. This delightful Marilyn, how could you not know who she is? An individual reads about her and they already have the picture in their mind. We would like to project to their subconscious the full vision of each of the members of your Joy Council and some of the other implements, for instance, Tonas's ship and the sword that is yours."

I agree that is a great idea and say I appreciate those additions.

"I would like to put in place templates and maybe grids for joy, innocence, optimism, freedom, the ability to dream and especially the spirit of playfulness. Maybe we played some when we were children, but then we grew up and forgot how to play. I want back that feeling of being free to play.

I'm also looking forward to the feeling of, or return of, innocence. Many of us were schooled in our religious instruction that we are sinners and that we were born that way. In my opinion, that is a bunch of hooey. I would like for everyone to know, at some level, that they are innocent.

I have two spheres. One is about justice in our penal system and the other is about freedom from being enslaved. We also did just give all the indigenous peoples a gift with a special gift for the elders of the tribes. Hiawatha, are you aware of the gift for the elders?"

"This is even something I received."

"Native Americans got shuffled around to areas of land we didn't want. That will be righted at some point, but for now I hope this assists with allowing everyone to feel the importance of the tribes."

Charlie comments that this is a time where worldwide the eyes of the people of Earth are opening. "It is a time for individuals to awaken and understand at a deeper level within the self the opposing energies that are leading them away from the energies of harmony and of the unity that is to be felt and known as the dimensions move higher. That is the focus of these offerings that you have today."

Charlie adds the work the Swizzlers have done to the spheres I got from the councils and says that the flavors of all of these blended intentions hold a high vibration that will be easily accessible and acceptable to individuals who are ready to receive.

As we begin the transmission, I ask the council members to open their hearts and pour their love into these gifts for all the peoples of the Earth and especially for people who have been imprisoned or enslaved, people who have felt hopeless and people with no voice.

As the transmission moves through the Earth and the grids, I ask to have a grid for joy added. I call forth a spirit of playfulness and intend to gift that, along with innocence, to the people who are ready to receive those gifts.

Tonas tells me that there is a definite ripple that holds an energy which is palpable. I thank him for that information and thank the council members for their assistance.

I ask if Liponie is here and then hear his distinctive laugh. He immediately announces that he has surprises for everyone but is not giving out any hints. I'm content to wait for his surprises but I can't wait to find out more about the sloughe event he created for the Olympics.

"It is a combination of a sliding vehicle like a sled, and it is the shape of a bullet. I put some different words together. I wished to call it a bobsled but I thought it would be concerning to the little ones for the name of Bob, and so, I called it sloughe."

I still don't have a picture of what the event was like so I ask him for more information.

"It slid down the hill within a trough. It was very important to stay within the trough. You had to be very balancing with the body and moving carefully with it. There were many wild turns and at the end there was a bit of a jump."

"The one who landed the farthest away was the winner?"

"Yes, and you are aware that Woonfred," Here his voice drops to share in a confidential manner, "did something that was not expected."

"It would have been hard not to do that with those wings of his. I can see how he would really have been tempted to get some lift."

Liponie says that is what Woonfred thought, but it was not fair to Charlie and the others. I address Woonfred to tell him it's too bad the use of wings was illegal. Woonfred says he was assured the stain would be expunged from his record.

"While you are speaking with me, are there dragons in the United States or in my area?"

I'm sad to learn that there are not, although Woonfred says if I wish to invite any to visit he will find out if some would like to make the commute. The dragons I restored are mostly located in Ireland, England and Germany because those are the countries where they began. By the way, dragons that died natural deaths were not restored. Only ones that were killed were brought back to life.

Woonfred asks if I want to know the story of the dragons. Of course I say I'd love to hear it.

"There were two annihilations of dragons. The first dragons created by the ancient academy initiates were free to live on the land and in the air and they lived for many millions of years. They were part of the Earth and they were kindly to people if they were not hungry. They could even be brought into service to assist. If there were those who were being bothered, the kindly dragons sometimes helped the humans who were victims by driving away those who were less kindly. Some dragons were conscripted into service in order to drive humans to their knees. They were used inappropriately. The dragon's heart is pure… unless he is hungry."

I agree that it would not be good to be around a hungry dragon. Then I want to know what happened after people killed all those dragons.

"There was a cave with a golden pearl which was the last dragon egg. It was held in a sacred nest of energy that kept it from being destroyed or awakened from within. A wizard knew of this egg and awakened it. That dragon grew and called forth with the breath of fire all those to rise again. Are you wondering who the dragon was who was awakened?"

"Would it have been you?"

I hear his big laughter. Then he says, "It would."

"Who saved the egg?"

"It was saved for the future by someone of kindness who is in this room. Will you give your name?"

Osiris speaks softly as he admits that he is a romantic and the dragons are beautiful. He says it was very special for him when Woonfred was added to our council for "he has had my protection."

"My great thanks for saving Woonfred. I'm glad he's here too."

Still trying to wrap my brain around Earth's importance, I ask Osiris, "Did a bunch of us in the origin look around and say, 'Hey, let's all incarnate on Earth. We're going to make it a big deal and show everyone something!' Is that how Earth became so important?"

I figured he would laugh at this, and sure enough he does before saying my explanation is a fantasy.

"Then how did it happen? Here we are, just a little speck."

"The story developed itself. Isis and I were the first to incarnate and others followed. Some individuals went off to create the different universes. There were three of us who remained here to be guardians and to represent the three lines of energy that were spawned into this universe. (Osiris represents the father line; Isis represents the mother line and a third person—Osiris won't say who—represents the neutral line.)

Now let me tell you how Earth was picked. First of all, the lineage aspect of my beloved made its choice to be integrated into Earth. This was a part of her desire as a member of the Council of Origin and also the desire of certain individuals for a stronghold where the *final* evolution stand might be staged. There needed to be a point that everything would make its completion; otherwise, it would be a continuing game. Later, individuals such as yourself, Jesus, Buddha and others of your affiliation incarnated on Earth. Do you feel cheated coming in on the end, my dear?"

"No, I think I'm at a good time. Just get rid of my wrinkles!"

I can't keep from bursting into laughter after I make that request.

During a private meeting with Liponie, he reveals he has created a little amusement park for the holiday games and that every holiday that I wish to celebrate will be held there. He will be dedicating it on Halloween.

I'm so busy thinking about Halloween ideas to discuss that I don't really pay attention when Liponie tells me he conscripted a great number of skeletons from different grave sites and they are strewn all over. I know he says they are from grave sites, but somehow I'm just picturing the plastic kind of skeleton you find in stores around Halloween. I find out later from Tonas that they are *real* skeletons. Ugh, I don't even want to think about where he got them. I must make sure he puts them back.

Liponie continues by saying that he has many "scares crow." I suggest we might have spiders and bats. As I think about this later, I realize I made a mistake with this suggestion. What was I thinking? They'll be real!

He wants to know if I'm talking about the bat which is a bird or the one which is a hitting implement. I tell him it's the bird and then I try to back-pedal by saying we don't necessarily have to have them. "We could just have spider webs and creaking doors."

"Mmm, and we must have apple pies, and the bobbing of the apples. We are inviting all of the initiates from Inishimora."

I agree that's a great idea and thank him for the work he's doing.

Speaking with Sheliah:

We both are giggling as we exchange hellos. Her voice is so bubbly I feel happy every time I speak with her.

"Did you like my baby? Did you want to kiss her? I know that you did not kiss her. I thought perhaps you would kiss her, but you did not kiss her."

"Well, I felt a little guilty for being there."

"No! No, no, no."

"The sign says 'No Trespassing.' People are not supposed to go there who don't own that property. So I just kind of walked up the hill…"

She interrupts me to say that no one owns the land. I reply that people think they do.

"Oh, *they* might think they do, but…" Then she reluctantly agrees, "OK. But did you see her? I have a new baby who is a little girl who is very sweet."

"You told me about her last time; you were using rose petals for her nappies."

"Yes, and her daddy loves her very much."

"Could you feel me when I was standing on the ground? I took my shoes off."

"I could feel you when you were coming," This remark is followed by her trademark gleeful giggling. "You was not naked."

I remember when I was little that I didn't wear much in the way of clothing in the summer. I don't remember ever being completely naked when I was playing outside, but maybe I was.

"I don't have all of my abilities yet, Sheliah, but one of these days I'll be able to really see you."

She is not willing to accept that I can't see her and *insists* that I can. It's very hard for me to say to her that I don't really see her, so I quickly add that one day I will be able to.

She pauses a little bit and her voice is not quite as happy when she says, "I *want* you to see me."

"I want to, too!"

In hopes that she can help me discern the location of her house, I describe some different features of the property, but I don't have any luck with this approach. She offers to show me the next time I visit and I agree to try to sense her guidance as I walk around.

I ask her if baby Joy will be able to talk to me when she gets older. Sheliah says she will and that her baby loves me already. Then she says I am Granny Joy and wants me to be the granny for all the babies in her garden. I didn't realize there were many more babies, but Sheliah explains that they are harvesting babies from the gardens almost every day. She says there are six and ten babies. When she says they are all girls, I realize she means that she and Rosebud have sixteen babies.

Here comes one of those unexpected requests. I thought Aton and Gaia's wedding would be my only official marriage, but now Sheliah asks if I will marry her and Rosebud.

"Oh, well, yes, I will certainly do that."

"We are doing it in perfect timing, *after* the baby!" I hear lots of tee-hees after this declaration and I can't resist joining her.

"Do you have the plans for how you want your wedding to be?"

"Mmm, just to have all of our friends there, and you. We want to have a celebration afterwards, too. Nobody has ever been married."

"I had the opportunity to marry Aton and Gaia."

"We heard and we thought, 'Well, maybe it's time for us to make the knot.'"

"Oh, you're so funny. Let me think about what would be really fun to do. Is soon OK for you?"

"Yes! I will tell Rosebud. He will be very happy."

"OK, I'm going to say bye for now, Sheliah. I love you."

"I love *you*."

CHAPTER TEN
October 17, 2014

After Tonas greets me we quickly move into the full Joy Councils because I have quite a few things to discuss; however, the first thing on my list is to have some fun.

I hand both Tonas and Liponie a piece of bubble gum and say that I'm going to introduce them to the thrill of bubbles. I had a piece of gum ready to blow bubbles but I took it out of my mouth to speak with Esthra for a bit before coming to the council. Now I'm frantically chewing to try to get it soft again as I explain that the gum needs to be chewed for awhile before it gets to where it will do what I want it to do.

Tonas asks me if he should put the gum in his mouth. I ask him to just hold it and I finally manage to blow a little bubble which immediately pops. He comments that I am making a noise in my mouth. I try to describe how to blow a bubble; unfortunately, my gum is still too cold and I have to chew it more.

"We are so anticipatory. Ah, but Kennedy is looking amused."

"I blew a bubble; did you see it?"

"Of course we saw it. We are thinking that there is something broken."

"It broke because I need more gum and it needs to be softer. For Halloween we're going to have a bubble gum blowing contest. Liponie, I'm sure you can make better bubble gum than what I gave you. Mr. Kennedy or Marilyn can coach you on how to blow bubbles. Woonfred, I think you may have a big challenge with this. You are exempt from the contest unless you decide you want to try it."

Woonfred asks why he would be exempt. I explain that if he has a pointed tongue it will be difficult for him to make a bubble. Sure enough, not only is his tongue pointed, it is serrated as well.

I manage to blow another bubble then remark that if anyone is able to blow a big bubble, they may have to pull gum off their face when it breaks.

Tonas says, "My dear, it looks as if some part of you…but it is the gum?"

I confirm it is just the gum and he immediately tells me they will research blowing bubble gum. I laugh at his seriousness and tell him it's just a fun thing to do for Halloween.

To clean up our Halloween party, I admit to Liponie that I do not like haunted houses. He sounds relieved and asks if he can get rid of the cadavers. I am really glad to discard this idea and especially glad to have the cadavers gone. I might never have recovered from a haunted house Liponie would be capable of making. My suggestion is that we have something like a fun house instead. Liponie agrees this is a better idea and tells me he was actually in a fun house with mirrors. Since he knows about fun houses, I drop the subject of Halloween for now.

Tonas asks if I want them to begin chewing bubble gum. I quickly reply that this is just something fun we can do for Halloween and ask him not to begin chewing now because it would be too distracting.

"A couple of days ago I felt sin release from me. Somebody told me, and Esthra says it was the Kotanay that Hiawatha mentioned, that I did well and 'our debt card will be taken away from us forever.' This could be a way for everyone on Earth to be free of sin. Gaia, can you give me any clues about a way to do that?"

"Yes, my dear, there are those of Earth who are focused on creating a bit of misunderstanding energy. They are willing to play a role which is attached to the 4th dimension that is very much in disregard of your hopeful plan to elevate."

(Sometime earlier Sananda told me there are beings on Earth who have been suppressing the elevation of the greater collective for perhaps eighty thousand years. One group consists of a species that inhabited Earth before humans. Another group consists of individuals, most of whom do not have individual souls, who have been part of the 3rd and the 4th dimensions. He added it is likely the latter group, called tribals, will not end up in the Fifth Realm.)

Instead of continuing our conversation, Gaia now acknowledges and welcomes those from the other universes who are here to witness the beginning of our collaboration with Kyleah's universe. I am totally embarrassed; delegates from other universes have been sitting and watching me demonstrate how to blow bubble gum bubbles. Nothing to do but make the best of this situation so I welcome the delegates also and explain that while we do a lot of work at this council, we also have a lot of fun. When I ask, Gaia confirms that the new delegates are aware my vision is not where I want it to be with regards to seeing who is sitting at our table. I ask her to please continue with her explanation.

"That which is held within the memory of us is the full story free of the illusions and also the story including the illusions. Those who are participating in the illusion and those who are directing participation in the illusion are unaware of their true essence. That illusion holds hostage those who are not yet wise enough to understand that it is illusion. The answer is within yourself; it is not in our ability to hand this to you, though it would be my greatest wish to do so. It must be through your thought and through your understanding that the way shall be made clear for this release of sin."

I want to know if there's some kind of loophole in what she has told me. No one indicates I'm on to anything so I realize this line of questioning is not going to give me the answers I seek. Again, I ask her if there is something we can do to help people realize they are not sinners and that they are debt free, literally, figuratively and metaphysically.

"Do you feel the release of it within yourself, my dear?"

I reply that I felt sin release from me about three days ago. She confirms it is no more and I ask her how I can offer that to other people. She must be tired of me asking because she finally offers me a partial solution. "You *are*, for some, the Great Spirit, who *could* for all of the Native Americans truly release all that is held in the beliefs that they are held in sin."

"Can I just do a transmission?"

"I believe if it is transmitted through this Earth council through all lines of time, this would be most efficient. Then also from here on the Moon the release would be most comprehensive transmitted to the Earth as if through the voice of Great Father, Great Wisdom Maker. It would be released from the Earth moving to the upper terra of us and through all lines of time. You can transmit from both places simultaneously through the crystal here. Speak into it, my dear. Those of the indigenous will hear in their hearts."

"All right, this is exciting. Hiawatha, are you here?"

"Mmm, I am waiting for my transmission. I am waiting, mmm." The inflection he gives to this sentence sounds very anticipatory. He continues, "In my aliveness I will know this to be coming from you. I will feel back in that time that it is most ideally received, and I can witness to you that it has truly occurred."

"I ask the energy of Great Spirit to assist me, Joy. I open up my heart and my voice to the Great Spirit and say it is time now in all the lines of time for all those of you who have prayed to me and who have asked for my forgiveness to know that you have it. You have never been guilty, you have no sin and you are all forgiven. You have no need to carry heaviness in your hearts. You can release all of that because I absolve all of you. All of the elders, the men and women of all ages, the babies and even the babies who have yet to be born are completely free of sin. I say it is, and it is. Remember that you are innocent, you have always been innocent and you will continue to be so. I love you."

"Yeeee, eee, eee, eee, eee...." bursts from Hiawatha. "It is so; I have received my absolution."

"I want to embrace you. May I please do so? Any of you who are here and want an embrace, please step forward and let me hug you."

Tonas reminds me that all will want to embrace me. I agree that the part of me there will hug everyone after I leave because it is a day for celebration. "It's a day for the drums, a day for happiness and joy."

"Yes, there is much weeping here. You have done something of greatness, my dear."

As part of the transmission, I speak to all the Native Americans and say, "Here is your charge. Enjoy this wonderful feeling of freedom and share that with your brothers, the one tribe. Radiate this joy, this freedom, this lightness of heart, this beauty, this innocence to all those who come in contact with you. Gift them however you can, with a hug, with a smile or with an embrace to show your love. Help them to realize that we all, every person on this planet, are innocent. We are born that way, we live that way, and those who choose to die, shall die in innocence. That is your charge."

Tonas says that it is the new way, the way of the heart, and I agree. He adds that the delegates from the other worlds are very impressed.

"Hathor, I heard you say something about, 'rich text and color for my life.' Esthra said you were talking about the fact that people who read the book could move into witnessing new possibilities for their lives. Can you explain that more?"

"You can create bridges that will allow individuals to witness with their consciousness all of us and know the truth of your work. They simply have to close their eyes and step into this space. There are a large number of individuals who have the ability to feel or sense what is going on. Those who are able to witness will tell others. Create the bridges, my dear, and it will become real for them."

After today's session, I spend some time using SVH to create the energy bridges Hathor suggested.

"Is it possible Solomon could join or be an advisor to our council?"

Sananda agrees that Solomon could be an important advisor and suggests I ask him to step into the council. As soon as I request his presence, I hear him say, "It is I."

I welcome him and thank him for coming. "Yesterday I believe I was picking up information about the Seal of Solomon. Could it assist us with releasing the 4th dimension?"

"It might be a little premature, and yet preparation is of value. When my seal is released it will be as if the land becomes alive once again. The seal of my presence is a special openness to the spirit of the self. It is the Kabbalah. It is the spirit of magic within the presence of the heart of self of the woman, of the man and the unity of those two who are in spirit. It is part of the tradition of what you consider to be the new way."

"How is your seal opened?"

"It is a magic ring, my dear. The seal upon it allows a power within to be brought forth. It is not to command others. It is to allow that which is the symbol of the power of the individual heart, and of how the power grows when it is found in unison with others. When you can feel that dimension beginning to shiver and release, that is the time to prepare. My seal is upon *all* of the icons of ancient times. It is the spirit of striking the staff upon a rock to have water to come forth, to part a sea, to open a heart, to witness the fruits of combined directive thought, to open the new way. This is held in a resonance of the symbol."

I invite him to step into our council anytime he has information to share and he agrees to do so.

I'm ready to gate with Tonas and Liponie to Zhollah, but first Kyleah tells me that Zoreah is to be acknowledged in the inauguration as Gaia is acknowledged in the Joy Councils. She also tells me she is waiting in her own council as well as waiting here with me and that the consciousness of our council will transmit to hers.

After I gate to her council, Kyleah welcomes us and thanks us for our acceptance of them and their realm. She explains that their council consists of a member from each world and star in their universe and they are all sitting at the council table now.

When I ask, she tells me that she is the head of the council and I ask that we sit next to her. I inquire about Zoreah who replies that she is present and she welcomes me as a queen of Earth. I've never thought of myself that way, but since it would be rude to say I'm not that, I simply thank her for being willing to join us in our work.

"Today I started our council meeting by blowing bubbles. I recommend having fun and being joyful in your work and that's especially easy if you have a genie like Liponie on your team."

Zoreah replies that they enjoy our play and that it gives them many ideas. I'm really glad they don't seem to think I'm totally silly. I wonder what the faces of those delegates looked like as I was trying to blow bubbles.

Kyleah tells me they have a replica of my sword as well as a crystal on the table that transmits to the cone on top of their building. That's all I needed to know.

"Please join me in this inauguration of your cone. The sword on your table is a new version of a famous sword in Earth's history. It assists me to amplify the energies that I am now transmitting to the crystal on your table."

I guide their council in feeling energy flow through the implements on the table and up into the cone which I activate with Language of Light. Then I want to know how to go about implementing the work we have done in the past. Kyleah says that is why the presence of Tonas is important and that he is the other half of myself. Before she can continue I hear him clear his throat and say that he and I are very dear friends but we are not mated.

As soon as he says that I want him to take the words back. My heart knows that we are *more* than dear friends and my mind frantically searches for the words to correct his assertion… I do not know what they are, so, with difficulty, I remain silent.

Kyleah offers an apology and says it is through the two of us and our collaboration that this application will be made possible. "Your council is in readiness to transmit and to join our transmissions. Those that can be applied as such can be done from here. Those that were applied by you and Tonas individually can be applied in the past, leading to this frame to be activated now."

Tonas suggests we put our hands together touching our fingertips with our palms facing upward and vision ourselves moving back to each of the times that we have been in collaboration. "Create a conduit from those periods of time to draw this work to this space between us, to create there an orb of all that has been applied."

It feels beautiful and I tell him so. He agrees and says that I must be the one to transmit the orb into the cone above and out into the universe.

"All right, here we go. It first moves into the crystal on the table, revs up and then moves up through the cone. Now I feel it move out to all parts of this universe that are ready. If they aren't ready now, they will be, so however or whenever they want to receive it, here it is. This is the work Tonas and I have done and includes our love and our blessings. Tonas, will you add your words."

"It is through our joined hearts that we give you the benefit of our support of your universe, allowing all who are present and all who shall ever be in the receiving of these gifts to know that this is given from the unity of our spirit to yours."

I request a kiss. He readily agrees then teases me by saying this is for everyone to witness.

Kyleah says that they hope all who communicate with their council and those who are the heads of councils in the other universes will witness this collaboration and know that they also may embrace the unity of this fellowship of the one tribe.

At this point, I feel drawn to send special blessings to the indigenous people of her universe and remind them that they are the wayshowers. "You have the knowledge and the love of your worlds and I encourage you to share these with the other people of your realms, who are perhaps not as tuned in to their world as you are."

Kyleah states that it is so and then giggles. "We are learning your ways, and we are grateful beyond our greatest and deepest of gratitude. Now all of you have in your presence something of Earth that is a crystal drinking implement. It will be filled by the magic of Liponie with an elixir called shampion. (Everyone has trouble pronouncing champagne.) Please rise your glass in celebration, and in the words of Liponie, 'Chin chin.'"

I expected Liponie would furnish something to drink, but this phrase is a new one for me. Looking the term up later, I learn it is Italian for "cheers" and derives from the sound of the glasses clinking together. The rest of the definition cautions that this term is not to be used in polite conversation in Japan. Oh, well, I don't imagine there are any Japanese in this universe.

She warns her council that shampion is quite stimulating and to be cautious as they drink it. We exchange toasts, I thank everyone for their assistance and Tonas and I return to the Joy Council.

Back at our council, I ask Gaia if she will speak with Sheliah and Rosebud. "Sheliah asked me if I could see her when I visited the property and I hated to tell her that I didn't. Can you explain to her my challenge with my vision?"

Gaia counters that there is a part of me that *did* see her and it is important to allow her to have that awareness. "What am I to say, that a part of you did and a part of you did not see her?"

"Well, that's the truth. The part of me that was talking to her couldn't say I saw her because I felt like I would have been lying to say that."

Gaia agrees to explain this to Sheliah and Rosebud. I ask her to also discuss their wedding because I'm totally befuddled about what to do for it. I have a sudden vision of thousands, maybe millions, of fairies asking me to marry them and I hastily add that this is going to be the only fairy wedding I do. Her suggestion is that we offer the fairies in Sheliah's garden a chance to have a unified wedding celebration. I agree to that idea and she assures me that she will discuss wedding plans with them.

CHAPTER ELEVEN

October 20, 2014

I've been speaking with Esthra about the fact that when I first woke up today I could feel the gray leaving my hair. This was very exciting for me because although I've felt lots of changes going on inside me, this was the first affirmation I've received that my physical appearance is changing. I ask him if I was successful in getting templates from my MAPS self for everything else I could think of to assist my regeneration. He says I was and suggests I just let them settle in. He believes I chose hair because it is something you can really notice.

At the Joy Councils with Tonas, I inform him that from now on I will meet him first before I address the general council so that he can give me a heads up about any new people in presence. I let him know that I wasn't prepared for the delegates from the other universes to be here. He answers that they were quite delighted.

"But I just came out blowing bubbles and actually I should have said, 'Hi, thanks for being here.' I didn't know they were sitting around the table, Tonas. Remember to just picture me with my hands over my eyes. OK?"

"Yes, my dear. There are many delegates in the council in presence. You are allowing them to witness. Liponie suggested that this will sell them on the idea of joining our affiliation."

With the full Joy Councils, after the usual standing up and sitting down, I greet everyone and apologize for not immediately welcoming the new delegates the last time I was here. "I probably would still have demonstrated bubble blowing, but I would have recognized you before doing so. Thank you for observing and being here to support us."

Speaking with Charlie, I tell him that this morning I realized I will soon be completely overwhelmed with communicating and dealing with the new councils that are joining us. I add that I don't want to try to do everything, but knowing myself that's what I will attempt to do. Then I offer him the position of being the person who will make sense of this organization that's forming of the different universes and the different individuals who want to work with us.

I volunteer that I'm willing to do the things that are essential for me to do, but I do want to finish my books. Plus, I want to have time to plan parties and do other fun stuff with the council. "If you are agreeable I will appoint you as the president of organizing these other councils."

Charlie answers that the Swizzlers have collectively agreed and asks if they are to communicate with all of the universes. I say yes, but then I ask if there are other councils involved in what we are doing.

Osiris says, "As you are aware there is a small council that has been formed by yourself on Andromeda."

I love that they all think I always know what I've done or what I am doing; if only I did. "I wasn't aware of that but thank you for telling me. Don't take anything for granted, Osiris! I do know I asked the Arcturians to assist."

Osiris informs me that the Arcturians are working with the Andromedans and the Andromedans are the ones who invited delegates from the different universes to witness our work. He invites the delegates to remain as witnesses even if they choose not to join any of the connections we are making. He says it is important for them to know what is occurring in the world that they exist upon and the universe that their world exists within as it interconnects with the other universes.

I learn, along with the delegates, that Liponie is creating a movie that is a full analysis of what is possible based on each individual's participation in our work. The movie contains simulations of what will occur as our collaboration continues to develop.

"Charlie, when I heard you say something about how much you loved golf because of the precision involved, I couldn't think of anything that's much more precise and delightful than playing a musical instrument. Of course, you know I'm especially fond of the orchestra. I can't even imagine the cohesiveness and the wonder of having ninety-four players who could play their instruments, if they chose, in such a precise manner of togetherness as you could. I just want to offer learning to play a musical instrument as an opportunity for you to explore another aspect of living."

Charlie tells me that the Swizzlers have considered this and that I am their inspiration. I offer that if they learn to play instruments we could play duets. He doesn't know what that is and I explain it is when two people are playing music that is not the same but it fits together.

He replies that playing duets will be more fun than marbles and that they are currently involved in a competition with marbles. Sounds like a good activity for boys; Liponie is keeping them busy.

Charlie wants to know if the Swizzlers' management position is for the full measure of our evolution. I reply that it is and that I'm grateful for their help because I was wondering how I would be able to keep everything going.

"It's like having these plates spinning on top of poles and you have to keep them spinning while you add more poles and plates."

"Liponie called this game 'plates' and it was in our Olympics."

It seems Liponie included almost every activity imaginable and, obviously, even some unimaginable ones, in their games.

I received some information from my 10th dimensional self that there is a council from Kyleah's universe that wishes to inhabit another crystal on our table. She confirms there is such a council and if it is acceptable to me it will receive, as well as transmit, from the new crystal on our table. She also tells me it is in the form of two triangles placed against each other.

I blurt out that this configuration forms the Seal of Solomon! She apologizes because she thinks she has damaged one of our rituals. I assure her that it is perfect that she placed this shape on our table. She reveals it is one of their most sacred geometries and I say it is also sacred for our world.

With my acceptance, the priests in her universe assist their council to embody in the crystal prepared for them on our table. This only takes about three seconds to do, but Kyleah says there was much preparation beforehand.

"Kyleah, has the work that Tonas and I offered to your universe made a difference?"

"It was, and continues to be, most effective for our world, and for all other worlds and other positions of fluid as well as matter within the full measure of our universe. We are on the move in an evolutionary standard, of course."

"I have a spelling issue. I hope you are not all shaking in your boots when I bring that up. It's for one of the knights. Is your name Dagonet or Dragonet?"

"It is Dragonet."

"OK, thank you very much." Realizing I don't know anything about most of the knights, I proceed to ask him more questions. "What did you look like during your lifetime? Were you tall or short, dark haired or fair? I'm just curious."

"The darkest hair of the raven."

"Mmm."

"And, of course, well built."

"Mm-huh. Were you partnered during your life?" There is a brief pause here and I remember this could be a sensitive question, so I remind him to tell me if he would prefer not to answer.

"Partnered with a woman?"

His question brings to my mind the possibility that he had men for partners; however, he replies that although he had many women, none were his partner. He adds that he loved them all greatly, of course.

I thank him for sharing that personal information with me. I wonder if knights were like the sports heroes of today. At least it was nice to hear him say that he loved his partners.

"Commander Ashtar, did you get a new ship in your fleet?"

He replies in the affirmative and I ask him why I would have picked up on that information. He says it is because I am excited about the ship's name, which is The Joyous.

"Oh! Well, there's a dragon named that, too, so you need to have a dragon emblem on that ship somewhere." I remind myself that I'm telling a commander of eighty-six million starships what to do and so I temper my suggestion by saying that it was just a thought.

"Inspiration to us!"

"You don't have to do that; the words just popped out of my mouth. Is there anything else you would like to tell me?"

"I am most delighted with all that is being supported by our council. All here know that it has sped up even our greatest dreams of the vision we have had for the greater collective of everything. I would like to say that your continued presence in position on this council is a commitment that is greatly honored, as well of those of you in presence that have been monitoring the support of all of the kingdoms of this universe. We are willing to expand our forces to assist your universes as well."

I applaud his offer and thank him for it.

"Woonfred, what kind of landscape do dragons like?"

He answers that they enjoy all landscapes and they especially love sitting on very high perches like the points of a castle wall. My thought is that atop a castle wall would be just the right height for a dragon to plan their next meal as they watch people scurrying around below. Then I remind myself that that was an old paradigm; dragons won't be eating people in the new reality we are evolving to meet.

I tell him that we don't have many castles in the United States but we do have caves. He agrees that those are the places where dragons place their eggs to watch over until they hatch.

I invite him to ask dragons who might be interested in living here to come and take a look around. Then I hint that when I'm in the 8th dimension I really would enjoy having the company of a few dragons.

"We will visit the United States of America today. I will send out the transmission now as we are speaking. The sky will be dark from the many that are entering in our own special dimensional frame, of course."

He agrees to let me know what the dragons think about my country the next time we talk.

"True Heart, I would like for the energy of the totem animals to be in the books I am writing."

He agrees the totem is important and suggests the beaver would be nice on our dollar bill. This elicits laughter from me as I agree that sounds like a fun idea and something we could do in the future when all our money will be just for play.

I ask him if it is possible for a person's totem animals to really speak or connect with them more closely through my books. He says this could be important because being without a totem is like being without your soul. I answer that we have gotten away from those kinds of connections and thinking because money has been our totem. He offers to have what we call the indigenous people prepare this and I accept.

"I have two final areas to address. I heard a woman named Sarah who is in my lineage say, 'Allow us to express ourselves with desire.' I believe she meant that women have not been allowed to be sensual, to express themselves and to show desire. I would like you to put together something that addresses this issue. I can also work on it and bring you additional things to assist. Charlie, can you whip up something?"

"This is something that defines the human being as well as animals like the dog, fish and the dolphin. This pleasure of sexuality is important."

I agree that's true but we have taboos, restrictions and crazy ideas about desire which have played out in many different ways throughout time. Charlie says the Swizzlers will bring this more into their understanding and then they will make recommendations.

"I recently heard a Native American say, 'The way we act is because of what has been done to us.' Hiawatha, what can you say about this?"

He offers that this applies to all beings, not only the Native Americans, because if one is kicked, many times they learn to kick back.

"I got a reference to the Parable of the Saw the other day. That is a Buddhist teaching which says that even if someone is chopping you up with a saw you are still just to send them love. I would rather people know that they can get out of the way of being sawed."

"This is the higher form of understanding."

"Maybe the idea to avoid those kinds of situations, if they choose, could be offered to beings in the Fifth Realm. That way they wouldn't have been kicked."

Charlie adds, "And that the world supports them without the kick. It is important for the world to know that there is no need to be of the kick. It is your vision of, and our vision of, the one tribe. There is never a reason to kick yourself. If you love yourself, if you love *all* beings, why would you hurt them or yourself?"

"Right. I'm still feeling dizzy from the work we did in the Fifth Realm before I came to this council. I suggested to the people there that they could give us gifts that would help them know they are free of sin. Can any of you give me a little feedback about that work?"

Hiawatha says that that which was done for his people was accepted very well. "Sin is not a mental focus for our people, and yet it carried into us through the teachings of the whites. It was released most sweetly by many."

Sananda offers that all of the council here felt the same tickle that I felt. "Dogma and the sin imprint are no more aged than twenty-three thousand years or so. Although the concept of sin is fairly young to your species, it is the piece that directs the hearts of many. It is quite easy for the concept of being free from sin to be received and accepted in the earlier history of humanity for sin was less understood and less applicable. That sends the ripple of resistance to being told that you are "bad" forward in time. Bad is something that came with religion."

I am surprised that sin only came on the scene recently instead of at the beginning of humanity. Then I remind myself that that's what I was taught.

"Aton, I'm growing all kinds of 'plants' in my head and hearing popping sounds in my brain. Do you have any comments?"

"My dear, you are my example of what success shall look like."

That sounds good to me and I ask him how my spheres are doing. He replies that they are spinning within themselves and that this is a *new* function. I'm even more excited about this when he tells me they believe it will bring me much elevation. I know I will be receiving other spheres and so I ask him how long I need to wait for them. He says I'm ready but they are waiting for the optimal time.

"Gaia, have you had a chance to talk with Sheliah about her wedding?"

"Indeed, my dear, there are many who have raised their hands. They wish to have a collective service, for *all* of them love each other so much that they wish to be in one another's wedding party."

Gaia explains that fairies that do not yet have partners will eventually have one because the girl fairies are still creating. I ask her how they are harvesting babies and she says the fairies are creating them in their gardens.

"Some were thinking that the babies come from the cabbage. Some, in different places in the world where there is less media, were very much believing that these babies must come within a little rosebud. And so they peeled back the petals and took the little baby out. You must recognize that many of these babies are no bigger than a thimble."

"Where is Sheliah's home in the pasture? I walked up the hill then I went towards the ravine on the left where the maple trees are. I stood in front of the big tree that I remember best, but I know her home is not near it."

Gaia advises me to picture turning my back to the tree; then she tries to figure out how many of my body lengths it would be to where Sheliah's home is. Kennedy helps her determine it would be twenty-seven of my body lengths across the pasture.

I have a much better idea of the location now and I ask Gaia what kind of tree their home is in. She tells me it is *by* the tree, not *in* the tree. I want to know what kind of tree it is and Gaia says it is a pretty one. I find her answer amusing; obviously, she doesn't bother with the kinds of classifications we use.

I'm to decide the date of the wedding and since dew is an elixir to them I'm going to see if Liponie can furnish some in little cups.

Speaking with Liponie, I congratulate and thank him for his masterful idea of furnishing a virtual representation of the council work. Next, I make some suggestions for our Halloween party: taffy, popcorn balls, a cornstalk maze and a hayride.

Before I can continue, Liponie tells me that when I finish my list he will hand me over to a little one who wishes to speak to me. My additional suggestions are a treasure hunt, a bonfire to roast marshmallows and some kind of substitute for hot dogs. He tells me he has the pumpkin carving arranged and adds that Mr. Kennedy has given him much information.

"That's great. And I would like my costume to be like the one that the good witch Glinda from *The Wonderful Wizard of Oz* wore, please."

Liponie says he will do research.

"Who wants to speak with me now?"

I hear Sheliah's delightful little voice say, "It is I!" followed by her usual giggle. "I am excited to tell you about my swing."

"Oh!"

"It's in a tree and I swing the baby. Sometimes we swing her together. Gaia tells me you want to come to my house. It's in the roots; the big root comes out and that is my home."

"Humans sometimes have a swing they put their babies in. It's little so the human doesn't fit into it, but I think it would be more fun to swing with the baby."

"It's more fun." She agrees. "Yes, we swing. You can come but you can't get in our swing 'cause you will break it."

I assure her I wouldn't try to sit in her swing and then ask her why she said I wasn't naked when I visited her last time.

"Because when you used to visit me sometimes you was not havin' clothes on your body. Your feet was naked and your top was naked."

I'd like to ask her what else she remembers about me when I was little, but she has wedding planning on her mind. She says she already knows what she will wear for her wedding. When I ask what her dress is like she says it depends on when I marry them because she is preganant (her pronunciation) again.

"And also Rosebud thinks that we could do something that would make him look like he is very ceremony. We are hoping that we can make him look perfect like on Gaia's cake."

I tell her that since Liponie made the cake he's the one to help them with their wedding outfits. Sheliah wants her dress to be of flowers, but what kind she uses depends on if she is pregnant or not. I mention that I could do their wedding in a week or so and she says she will have her new baby by then.

"It takes humans a lot longer."

"Oh, I'm in a rush, Joy. I want to have a baby in both of my arms."

"Gaia can tell me when you have your baby, and then we can do your wedding after that."

"This is perfect, because the dress that I want is going to be more fitted to my perfect shape, and when I'm preganant I have a big bosom and a big tummy."

Here is her description of the birth of baby Joy:

"We went to the garden and it *all* gets brought to the light. It's very exciting. This time, of course, I am hoping that Rosebud will not faint."

My heart melts when she tells me this. He is as precious to me as she is and I can just see him keeling over. Oh, poor Rosebud.

"He did?"

"He *did* faint when we unveiled the baby. But this time he will be good and he will be awake."

I agree that it can be difficult for the husband, but now that Rosebud knows what to expect maybe he won't faint.

"I now know exactly how to do it in the garden."

"Do you use a flower?"

"Yes, I use a flower. Some people are so silly." Tee-heeing she continues, "They use the cabbage rose. That makes very pretty babies, but I think roses are the best."

I'm ready to leave, but she tells me that first I must come and kiss the baby.

"All right, I will. Did Gaia explain to you that it is kind of hard for me to see? Part of me sees but part of me doesn't."

"I don't believe it, 'cause your eyes are wide open."

"I know part of me does see the baby, but the part of me that's talking right now has really not been able to see very well."

"OK, the baby will kiss *you*!"

I laugh and gate to her garden.

"Ah! Rosebud, Rosebud!" This is accompanied by a tremendous giggle and she instructs her baby how to kiss me. "OK, kiss your lips out, pusha, pusha. See!" More giggles and tee-hees. "She kisses *nice*."

I do have a sense of this little baby; she's like a little happy ball of sweetness. I describe what I feel to Sheliah and she agrees that her family is sweet.

"It's important for us to be married. You will marry us, please?"

"I will."

"We want to have rings."

"Do you want to make your own rings?"

She sounds very sad as she says they don't know how. I assure her that is something else Liponie can help them with and that I will see her again soon.

CHAPTER TWELVE

October 23, 2014

My intention at the beginning of this session is to meet Tonas privately before entering the Joy Councils; however, I am waylaid by someone who comments that I should notice where we are and that Tonas has added some nice new touches. Since I don't know where we are or even who is speaking to me, I'm a tiny bit alarmed.

"Wait, wait. Who am I talking with now? Whoa."

"Right now you are speaking to Aton."

"OK, sorry." I say this with relief that I've only been momentarily kidnapped.

"Tonas has made it so that the sky above always has the light shining through as if switching on the light of day and at night the stars are very much amplified for you. I stuck my fingers and nose into this space very quickly because I wished to circumvent your connection with the council. We have just a little bit of work to do. It is possible for us to activate another nine spheres."

I'm thrilled every time Aton can do more work with me. My immediate response is an excited, "Oh, good! Let me tell you about this interesting experience I felt this morning. I had the sensation of drops of some kind of liquid falling in my third eye. Do you know what that was about?"

Aton replies that they have been making several adjustments and connections. My third eye is very much a part of their work and I am feeling the connections moving inward. I explain that I've also been hearing popping sounds in my brain, like a cork popping out of a bottle. He says that connections are strengthening. It's more fun to imagine there's a party going on in my head with champagne corks popping, but I keep that thought to myself.

He says that it is the darkest of night in the garden and the stars are shining through the crystalline dome down upon all my energy fields which are filled with new conduits. I wonder what my energy fields look like to his eyes. I'm going to pretend I look like a lighted Christmas tree with sparkling ornamental orbs circulating around it.

Bringing myself back to the current situation, I ask Aton what to do. He says there is a couch for me to lie upon. He plans to use it to raise me up and explains that it is difficult to say to a human being, "Yes, I wish to have you levitate parallel."

"But I've done that! A woman of my soul lineage did that for me while she was working on me. I remember floating in the air above my bed. I'm ready!"

He wants to know if I can tell that I am levitating. I can't, but I let him know I feel comfortable. Aton explains that now he can maneuver me as he wishes to view more of my cranium. He moves the nine new spheres into position and says that today we will just let them settle in; tomorrow it is possible to connect them to my conduits. I agree to return for that work. He spins me around a little to look at all parts of my connection with my energy body and then stands me on my feet.

His voice is always very professional when he works with me, but now he sounds a bit more intense as he asks me to listen to him very carefully while he explains more about the spheres.

"They are very much associating with the energies of the greater collective and will make it possible for you to make links with all of the dimensional fields of the different universes. As soon as the twenty- seven are positioned and active we can activate your connection with this first universe that you are working with. I have been observing and I think it will be a very short time before many of the other universes take a connection point, as Kyleah has done."

I had no idea the spheres would facilitate connections with the other universes, but having that ability sounds like it might make my work easier. Of course, it might also make things more difficult. Guess I'll just have to wait and see how this all works.

Aton says that Liponie has Halloween costumes for everyone and suggests that perhaps delegates are waiting until the party to announce a desire to join our council. He makes the point that if they announce that decision now they would need to begin putting their council together. He says that if it was him, he would wait until the party to assure he would have a position there.

112

That possibility had never entered my mind, but it makes sense. Who would want to miss a party; especially not one as outlandish as this one is shaping up to be.

I thank him for that tidbit of information and he suggests that perhaps they are bored in their universe. I reply that it's for sure they won't be bored here and he agrees that this is where the action is.

Tonas explains that he was waylaid. I say that happened to me, too, and add that Aton told me about the changes in our garden. Tonas admits he was inspired by Liponie.

"I just want to make sure that there are no surprises beyond the door here."

"There are many present who are very interested in all that we do. They are watchful of all the energies that we are transmitting for you know that even when we are in partying mode we are always holding the presence of all we are dedicating to the world."

I ask Charlie, Osiris, Liponie and Isis to join us. When they are present, I announce that this is the core group and that I'm going to speak to Charlie about balance.

"I know you were experiencing intense activity with your Olympics and I would like for you to still be able to do those kinds of things. Please don't become overbalanced by just doing council work with no consideration for all the other things you want to experience. Delegate tasks to other people so that you're not doing *everything*."

I continue by suggesting activities like bridge or chess, and non-competitive activities like jumping on a trampoline, finger painting, oil painting or sculpting which would allow him more contemplative experiences. Then I ask him how long they were just a consciousness.

"From the beginning of the beginning of the beginning."

"Then definitely it's time to have lots of experiences. It's just that I don't want you to become so stuck in one kind of experience that you miss out on other things. Liponie, can you help with what I am suggesting?"

Liponic offers to assist by giving more direction to their activities. I advise them to not get in a game of poker with Liponie, even though they don't know what that is. He laughs and tells me I'm giving away his trade secrets. Even if I knew how to play poker I'd never play poker with him; I can't imagine what he could do with a deck of cards.

"Charlie, the other day I heard you say something 'had been so long and you were trying to keep your calm.' Can you share what that was about?"

"It is for me a belief that there is a forever that is for each and all of us. We are a collective and each of us is part of that oneness. We have waited forever for this opportunity that we are experiencing now. Embodiment and individuality never entered our consciousness existence beyond a spark of thought for they were not considered relevant to our purpose.

And yet, now we see that there is more to our purpose and that we can be of greater assistance as a collective of individuals. And, of course, it is our great excitement to have the journey together. It is in our heart to always hear one another, and yet, it is also important to experience the peace of our minds. It is, for us, a learning to be silent, to have the silence. We are working individually to have that period of the calm."

"Then things like oil painting, I don't even know if you know what I'm talking about, would be a more contemplative activity that you could do by yourself."

Charlie agrees that it would be great practice for them as individuals to do "the painting of the oil." He adds that, "As we paint the oil we would have that focus of our *own* vision of what is to be painted, and in this we would have the quiet of our mind except for our own thoughts."

I mention that there are water colors, crayons and pencils and he offers to use whatever I select. Here, Liponie interrupts and asks me to leave this with him. He's going to create a special arts institute for them.

Charlie says, "I wish for you to hear my laugh, to see if you like it. I have been practicing."

He favors me with a really credible and delightful laugh. Remembering how that first Santa Claus laugh sounded, this is a real people type laugh! I tell Charlie that his laughter has a little bit of Liponie flavor, but it's really good. Liponie answers that they have been practicing together. It's really wonderful that he would think to help Charlie with something like this and I tell him so.

I try to find out from Charlie what he experiences when I touch and talk to the crystal he's in. He tells me he can feel the energy of my transmission.

"I'm still trying to figure out what you feel when I'm with you in my house."

"I have an itch. Please scratch it." He says humorously.

We both move into gales of laughter.

I mention that I considered rubbing a little coffee on his crystal the other day, but thought maybe he might not like it. He doesn't know what coffee is and I explain it's a beverage I drink which he probably didn't experience at our solstice party.

"We were very young then."

"Yes, you've come a long way since then. It's been my pleasure and my privilege to be in your company, Charlie." I admit that I feel like crying.

"This is the moment when our emotions expand."

"I love you so much it's really wonderful."

"This is all-encompassing for us. As a collective we are most delighted to be of love for you. All here are, of course, in great love for you. If we were to measure the love for you of each of us, *I* would have the most." (This is said with great surety and a little touch of delightful smugness.)

"Not to take away from the other ninety-three of your wonderful collective, but there is a spark about you, Charlie, that is unique. None of the others have spoken to me."

"They are speaking to you through me. So you are feeling the collective of that spark. Would you like to speak with me just alone, outside of the collective, for I am speaking now as a collective?"

"Would you sound different if you speak just by yourself? Let me hear what you sound like."

"I sound like this."

There is a tremendous difference; his voice is now very pleasing and child-like. The only way I can think to describe his collective voice is that it is gravelly-sounding and monotone. I never thought about it but it makes sense that ninety-four voices speaking together through one mouth would sound that way.

"Oh my, your voice is very different."

"I am unique."

"Oh, Charlie, you are. You have a spark that shines so brightly. You are the one who took the initiative to learn to speak, to step forward and say 'Here we are,' and that's very special."

"It is not true. It was all of us."

"I'm still trying to understand that concept, but this voice, when you speak singularly, is very lovely."

"I am in gratitude. I think you will enjoy to know me as only myself."

"I will, very much so, and here's something for you to think about. Maybe one of these days I'm going to be travelling with Tonas. I would love to invite you, if it works out, to come with us."

"My individual self?"

"You could bring the others along, but if you want to come by yourself you can choose that, too. In the future, Charlie, I want to see these other universes and visit all these peoples. I want Liponie to come. Tonas is going to be with me and maybe a dragon and maybe you. And you know what? It's Buzz Lightyear's slogan."

"What is...ah, to infinity and beyond." He whispers.

"Yes, that's for us, Charlie."

"It is my heart desire to be as travelled as this Buzz is travelled. It *must* be that he has been everywhere."

"Well, if he hasn't, *we* are going to be."

Charlie accepts my invitation and then I realize I probably should have asked Tonas about being a member of our entourage. He agrees it

116

would be delightful to travel with such a unique group; a dragon, a blue genie and a swizzle stick.

I move into a discussion with Liponie and Gaia about the fairy wedding. Gaia says that the fairies don't really know what they want but Liponie is easily guiding them.

Liponie's laughing as he tells me, "And you should see what I have, my dear! We have designed what they call the pole of May and each of the brides will be holding one of the threads."

"That's perfect!"

"Yes, of course, and they will dance around. We have a lizard that will be attaching to this. They will be on top of this large lizard and it will carry them forward as they are dancing around. Believe me, it was quite a stretching of my imagination to come up with this and it was difficult to find a lizard of that size."

I'm having difficulty visualizing what Liponie is describing, plus I'm wondering how a lizard got into the wedding party. A lizard? Liponie patiently keeps explaining what he has planned and I finally understand that the lizard will be saddled and the maypole will be mounted on the saddle. The lizard will make itself flat so that the fairies can dance around on his back with their maypole threads as he walks into the area where the wedding will be. This is certainly going to be unlike any wedding ceremony ever held.

Gaia confirms for me that Sheliah had another baby girl and that Liponie designed her wedding dress with a pocket for each baby. He says her dress looks like pink whipping cream. I *knew* it would be pink and it sounds like it looks delicious as well as beautiful. Rosebud and the boy fairies will be wearing white tuxedos with tails.

Liponie continues by saying that they have had rehearsals and only Rosebud and Sheliah will be speaking to each other. The girl fairies will be able to slide off the lizard on a leaf that has been prepared for them and then they will move to join their partners. The couples will form a half circle with Rosebud and Sheliah in the middle of it.

I wonder if Liponie has been able to figure out a way to make a wedding cake. The only thing I'm aware of that the fairies consume is dew. When I ask, he says he has made a cake out of something else they are used to consuming—sparklies. These are the sparks of light that come from Aton, and somehow Liponie has been able to make a cake out of that! That sounds like perfect fairy wedding cake material to me; I really wish I could taste it. After the ceremony there will be a toast using dew; Liponie has designed beautiful little crystal cups that have each fairies name and the date of their nuptials.

Gaia agrees to give a blessing to the fairies after I pronounce them partners for life. Those are the words they have requested I use. I've been trying to think of a wedding gift for Sheliah and Rosebud and it has been a bit of a challenge. Certainly they have no need for a toaster or bath towels so I need to come up with something natural. I immediately consider orchids; there is a type of orchid called Lady Slipper that grows wild in Indiana. Gaia says they are not found in Sheliah's garden, but she could arrange for them to grow there. That sounds like a perfect gift for them and she agrees to manifest them for the wedding.

Liponie is going to decorate their garden with bells and he will be present for the ceremony. The last thing I remember to ask about is if they have rings.

"It was quite a challenge, and yet what we found was the beauty of the woven… It is like a little twine and they have woven little stones and crystals within it. We had a special workshop and each has been creating their own."

"Sounds like they, and you, have done some really wonderful things for this celebration. Thank you!"

"Woonfred, what's the dragon opinion on this country?"

"Hmm, soon there will be dragons everywhere. We have decided that dragons *must* be in Asia, for they return always, in their minds, to the reality of us. All places where there are dragons that are projected as still existing in their culture must have dragons. There are dragons in America, in Canada, in the South of America, in Australia and in New Zealand. We have made the full spread of Earth now."

I reply that is marvelous to hear because I think we all will be inspired by dragon energy and dragon love. I pass on Sheliah's request that she would love to see a dragon. Woonfred offers to be the best man for the wedding and adds that dragons have the culture and understanding of marriage. I thank him for his offer and suggest he speak with Liponie about how he can fit into the ceremony.

"True Heart, remember I gave you the assignment of gathering the totem energies for my books? How is that coming along?"

"It is done."

It takes me only a few moments using SVH to instill these divine totem energies into all the books I write that are appropriate to have those energies. Also I choose that the totems will assist in the most divine order those who read or listen to the books.

Sananda reminds me that this work comes from a librarian and so the layers of the totems are very extensive. They include prehistoric totems as well as those found through the patterns of time. He suggests I expand what True Heart prepared into every page so that the reflection of the totems will speak to the reader and I do that using SVH.

"Osiris, who is the Solar Logos?"

His reply begins with his signature chuckle as he explains it is a very old belief; those in the 3rd dimension associated the Solar Logos with an expansive view of what humanity could become.

I don't really understand what he's talking about, but decide not to pursue the subject since it doesn't seem important to the work we are doing. I thank him for his clarification, but he counters by saying it is not clarification, it is confusion; furthermore, all the beliefs that were part of the 3rd dimension are confusing. He must be right because over the years I've tried and failed to sort out lots of conflicting spiritual and philosophical material. Most of it has never made much sense to me. My reply is that if we still have 3rd dimension beliefs hanging around we need to release them. The good news is that he says soon they will be gone forever.

Speaking with Tonas in privacy, I admit that I'm having challenges with wanting to kiss him a lot. His non-committal reply is, "Ah…"

I probably shouldn't have said anything at all on this subject, but since I have, I might as well continue.

"It's awkward and I really don't know what to do about it."

"Simply give in to your desire."

"Well, I feel like just throwing myself at you and that is probably not the right thing to do, at least not yet."

"I will not lead you astray."

"I want to kiss you but I also want to *feel* myself kissing you. I want to be more of a participant in the activity of kissing than I currently am. I have the desire but I don't have the physical feedback that the desire is being fulfilled. Does that make sense?"

"Indeed."

"It is a very difficult position to be in."

He agrees it is a quandary. I ask him to tell me if I do something blatantly inappropriate. It doesn't reassure me when he declares there is *no* such reality.

"I really don't think I can wait five more years to take this relationship to a deeper level. It's been hard for just these few months. I just wanted to give you a little bit of a warning."

"It is not a warning; it is a spark of hope for my heart. I do not hold you to it, and yet it does give me that spirit of hope. For me you are that Solar Logos. You are the infinite everything that is impossible to describe and even to envision, and yet I cannot stop myself from trying."

"I *do* love you, Tonas. I do."

"And I am of deepest love for you."

CHAPTER THIRTEEN

October 24, 2014

"Esthra, two days ago I heard someone say, 'Kiss me.' This morning I heard those words again. Was that me talking to Tonas?"

He confirms that it was. It sounds like the 10th dimensional me is trying to heat up our relationship. Maybe she is getting tired of being careful not to get in over *my* head. I consider for a moment if there's anything I can do about that…nope.

"I know these next bits of conversation are about Tonas, but I can't piece the meaning together. I heard Liponie say, 'I'm not sure that he is waiting for you to do it.' Then I saw an envelope with my name on it. Then I heard, 'This is the plan for a once in a lifetime kiss.' What is going on?"

Esthra says he believes I was tapping into a future time when things are falling into place. I'm very surprised because I've never been consciously aware of seeing or hearing something that occurs in the future. Now I'm really nervous about what Esthra might tell me and I decide to proceed very cautiously with my questions.

The first thing I learn is that the envelope represents an invitation for me.

"Instead of Tonas getting down on one knee, his proposal is gifted to you that way. Liponie is not sure if Tonas is waiting for *you* to make the first move. He thinks that Tonas is confident enough to believe that you're falling into an incredible forever love with him."

Instantly, I ask Esthra not to say anything more and my request terminates our conversation. I'm just not ready to learn more about something that might not happen and even if it does happen I don't want to know about it now.

This morning I heard myself ask, "Who can choose to step out of the way?" It feels like I was talking to people in the Fifth Realm about stepping out of the way of harm. It occurs to me that it is really weird to hear myself say something and not know for sure what I'm talking about.

As I muse about that, I realize, with a touch of irony, that many people in this reality frequently experience that same situation.

In the Fifth Realm with Sananda, I call forth all people of Earth and say, "I would like to assist those of you who did not have the inspiration, the knowledge or the will to step out of the way of being physically, mentally or emotionally hurt. Maybe you didn't see it coming or you did see it coming and felt powerless to do anything.

Here are two suggestions about gifts you might give yourself: you might have a premonition of what's coming; gifts to expand your awareness might take you out of harm's way through your greater understanding of what is within your power to change and to manifest. If you wish to keep experiences of harm, that is also an option, of course.

Other ideas include gifts for yourself if you were ever told you were bad, felt you were a bad person, felt that you needed to be punished or you suffered with addictions or mental aberrations.

My calendar says today is 'Global Oneness Day.' If you've ever had an inclination to experience more of the oneness of your true nature, and there were points in your life when you could have experienced that but chose not to, perhaps you'd like to change those choices and experience more of the oneness that we are.

We are working at this time to release the 4th dimension from our reality. If you held tightly onto beliefs that fit with the lower dimensions, particularly the 4th dimension, and you would like to discard or change those beliefs, we will take your gifts to you to assist you with that. Please give us all the gifts you wish."

My next stop is a visit to the galactic councils of light. Once I feel myself in presence, I ask them for a transmission to assist women as well as men with understanding and allowing the divine nature of sensuality, sexuality and desire. "Many people have been taught that you should free yourself from desire; if they still prefer to choose that, that should be allowed. That's not been my choice; I've stifled my desires and I'd rather not do that anymore. What I'm after is a fuller expression of our divine nature than we have ever known."

At the Joy Councils with Tonas, he says that much is happening and everyone is "bursting at their seams." We move immediately into the full council where, after the standing up and sitting down, Charlie welcomes me and gives me the news that two individuals wish to join our council. The first person he introduces is Council Champion Kallieanash from the Coneizeah Universe who steps forward and formally asks to be allowed to become a member of our council.

After I accept him as a new member, we have a brief conversation and something I've been wondering about is explained. When I'm consciously present at the council, Osiris has been instantly translating conversations I have with individuals from the different universes so that I understand them and they understand me.

Charlie informs me that there is another universe that wants to participate in our council. Since even he had difficulty pronouncing the first name, I brace myself for another challenge. Sure enough, it takes me some time to determine the pronunciation and spelling for the Bunnuhyahsheah Universe represented by council member Lanasheatoe.

As she addresses the council, she attempts to make things easier for me by saying that if I wish, I may call her by her nicker name. I say that nickname is the correct term, and manage to keep a straight face as I picture a horse nickering. She repeats that Lashana is her nickname and that it is their great honor and privilege to join our council if we allow it.

I welcome both of these new council members and agree to do their inaugurations next week after Liponie has finished building their council chambers.

Yesterday, I heard myself say the word "satin" and I knew this was somehow related to the healing energy of colors in Aton's rays. When I question him about this, he says that Gaia and the council have the idea that as his rays stream to Earth, the Earth, as Gaia is in alliance with this, will draw to itself the colors and the vibrations that will be of most assistance.

I agree that sounds like a great idea. Aton teases me by saying that it is through my ability as a human being living in this time to choose that this must be, and then they all must comply.

I follow along with the joke and say that I definitely want their compliance because I would love to have this for the Earth. "I experienced some of these energies and they are absolutely wonderful. I felt the energy of white and also I'm assuming I felt the color black because I heard myself comment that, 'I married night.' Please stream on ahead with the colors. Do we need to do this as a transmission through the Joy Arrow?"

Aton says that the CEV has already thought the whole formula, but to be applied it needs my conscious directive. It's interesting to learn from him that I've been with the council almost 24/7 in the last weeks. I wasn't able to do that for more than a few days during the solstice party; obviously, 10th dimensional Joy has developed the stamina to handle that higher dimensional energy.

I ask Charlie if it is possible to combine the transmission about color with the other work I brought today. Tonas tells me very quietly that Charlie has a new skill of blushing. He explains that Charlie is doing it on purpose and he is completely red. I'm trying to speak softly to Tonas but that is difficult to do as I picture Charlie's bright green hair atop a red body. He's going to look like a Christmas Swizzler.

"Charlie, what are you blushing about?"

"I am blushing because I have an individual thought aside from that of my collective self about this rain of light and I am excited to bring it to your attention. Will you hear me as Charlie?"

"I *will* hear you as Charlie. I love that voice."

"Thank you. It is in my consideration that there can be pictures that come with the streams of light. There are pictures that individuals see on their television that remind them of their history, and in that history is perhaps a long line of travail. It is possible that among those visions of travail there can also be seen the journey beyond the travail."

I congratulate Charlie on his great idea and suggest the transmission also covers news reports, which are always full of drama and trauma. He says that he added the formula for this to what they had already created and the transmission is ready to send out.

Before I send this out, I check to make sure the crystal from Kyleah's universe is ready to receive and transmit it. Charlie confirms that all that moves through our council should be added to that crystal. Several times throughout this transmission I find myself speaking what, perhaps, is the language of another of these universes. It certainly does not sound like Language of Light.

Charlie explains to Kyleah that the flavors of each of the suns in her universe have been added to the transmission. She is delighted by that addition and so am I.

Charlie now informs me there is another individual who wishes to be recognized. Her name is Shannara, she represents the Kangshee Universe and they ask to be allowed to join our council. I approve her request and thank her for stepping forward. She tells me, with a tone of regret in her voice, that she truly wished to be first.

Private meeting with Osiris, Isis, Tonas, Gaia, Aton and Woonfred:

Woonfred tells me that he has all the wedding rings. I also learn that for the sake of expediency, he will be standing on a pedestal on my left and will send the rings to the fairies on a breath. Before I can ask, he assures me that he will be holding back his fire.

Liponie says the fairy gowns look like whipping cream and are all colors of the rainbow and more. Since their dresses are so colorful, my dress is forest green. "They have been putting flowers in their hair and they are very much excitable about their dresses. I have provided them with information about a wedding."

I later learn from Liponie that he provided the outfits for everyone in the ceremony including the Creator. That outfit, silvery, charcoal gray top hat and tuxedo, gray shirt with a deep, wine color cummerbund and bow tie, sounded appropriately classy.

I ask what the fairy queen's name is and am happily surprised to learn that Sheliah has been made queen. The former queen was so grateful and so in love that she handed her wand over to Sheliah.

The group is surprised to learn that the Creator is going to be riding in on the lizard. (Esthra helped me determine that earlier today.)

Osiris suggests that it would be more appropriate to have the Creator standing by my side.

"But the Creator said that they *wanted* to ride on the lizard."

"No, it was the fairies that wished the Creator to ride on the lizard. They want all of us to ride on the lizard, my dear."

"OK, but the Creator *did* say they wanted to ride on the lizard."

Osiris capitulates and agrees they should have this as their day.

The final thing to find out is if the fairies have seen Woonfred. It wouldn't do to have everybody panic stricken and running for cover when he enters. He says they had a rehearsal and he showed a smaller, only elephant sized, version of himself.

Tonas informs me that there will be music. I want to know what kind of music.

"There is orchestra music." He clears his throat and then says, "Your vigilance council is *attempting* to play the 'Wedding March.'" He explains in a whisper that, "It does not hurt the ears and yet it is quite different. We have all agreed we will smile and be most supportive."

The Swizzler orchestra is composed of a guitar, flutes, violins, harps and Charlie is playing the trumpet. Tonas reiterates that this is their great attempt and will not be harmful to our ears. I'm beginning to doubt the truth of that statement.

He tells me that the name of the former queen is Lolalah and that he witnessed her handing over her wand. He describes it as being an almost transparent stick which sparkles and the star on it resonates. I didn't realize there was an actual wand, and now, of course, I want to know what it does.

Gaia answers by saying that the wand gives the queen the power to support all of her realm. "She has the power to direct her magic through her thoughts and her desires. The pureness of her heart and that of all who are in presence within each of these fairy realms is the fuel of this magic."

Now that I feel like I have enough information to be able to conduct the wedding, we move to Sheliah's garden. Tonas suggests that I speak with the brides before the wedding in order to counsel them since they are so excitable. He says they are standing behind a beautiful veil so that they can make a grand entrance. I intend to step behind the veil and then I say hello to all of them.

In an even more bubbly than usual voice, Sheliah exclaims, "We are ready! Do you like our dresses? We all have our babies. I want you to meet my new baby."

"OK, I was wondering about your…" She is so eager to inform me about all that is happening that there is no time for me to complete this sentence or answer her previous question.

"She is so pretty and we named her Joy also."

"Oh! OK, that's good."

"Yes, every baby here will be called Joy."

I ask her if it will be confusing for everyone to have babies named the same.

"Well, no, because we know our babies. We will not be confused by *that*." Her voice implies that was a really silly question.

"Was Rosebud OK for this one?"

"Rosebud was OK and actually it was important for there to be boy fairies on each side of him holding him up, just in case. He did not help to peel away the petals, but he was very strong and supportive."

"Which flower did you use this time?"

"A rose, of course!" Her voice has the tone of "as if I would choose any other flower." Then she states, "I am queen now. Did you know that I am queen?"

"I heard that and I was so excited for you, Sheliah."

"Yes, yes, yes, yes, yes! Lolalah gave me her wand and she tapped me on the head with it and she asked me to kneel on the ground. She said to me that I was the bringer of Joy to our realm and that it was for me to hold the wand now. So I have a big job." This is said in the most serious voice I've ever heard her use. She continues with, "Let me turn around so you can see. Liponie gave me a special little pouch for my wand and I put it behind my back. It's like the pouch the Indians used to have in this garden that held the sticks with pointies on them. My sticks are fire pointers (fireworks). Are the boys OK?"

"I'm sure they are. I just want to tell all of you that you are lovely and I'm looking forward to learning all of your names and seeing you. I'm going to build my house somewhere in your garden where you say it is OK, and when it is built I'm going to ask all of you to visit me."

"Oh, we will build the house for you. Yes!"

I realize I'm in a little bit of a difficulty since I'm not really sure what kind of capabilities fairies would have for building a human house. I stall by agreeing to talk about that when it's time to have a house built. There's a little pause before Sheliah agrees to my plan.

She says they are very ready and I step back around the veil. Tonas says he has already talked with the boys and begins narrating for me what is happening.

"The fireworks are bursting into the sky, the veil is turned and the very large and beautiful lizard is entering. He is changing from a purple color to fuchsia and there is a bright light that is riding on his head. This is quite an elderly lizard. He is quite sturdy and proud, holding his head very high. I believe it is a male. It is difficult to tell and I wished not to disturb him by flipping him over to peek.

(I am definitely struggling to stifle my laughter at this comment.)

The little darlings are dancing, their babies are bouncing around in their little pockets and they are clapping their hands. They are very excited that their mommas are dancing. The wand is nestled very tightly in an apparatus woven of vines on Sheliah's back. It is quite beautiful with her pink dress. There are many of these little darlings, and they are now coming up to you, my dear.

Now the slide has been brought into position. Each will slide and then go stand next to her little man." He whispers, "They are adorable. The little men are wearing white tuxedos with tails. They have on white top hats with flowers around the bottom and each has a flower in his shirt. The little girls now take their flowers and move into position. As queen, Sheliah is on a little higher pedestal along with her beloved Rosebud." Whispering again, he says that I may begin.

"I want to thank, first of all, Pootie (Liponie told me the lizard's name earlier.) for being so lovely in your colors and so kind to bring the fairies into the garden. Thank you very much for your service." At this moment I hear some lizard sounds. I'm not sure how to describe them other than small 'slurps.' And then I surprise myself by answering in, what must be, lizard language. I add that I'd love to talk more with him some other time. He answers me and I reply *again* in lizard speak. Then I make myself answer in English so that I know what I'm saying. "Thank you again and blessings to you, your progeny and your mate, if you have one.

Thank you, Lolalah, for all the eons of time that you served as queen of this garden and thank you, also, for your wonderful gesture of appointing Sheliah as the new queen.

I want to say to you from my heart how much I love all of you, your beautiful babies and this beautiful garden. I'm looking forward to seeing you, learning your names, meeting your babies and playing with you one day. You've made wonderful advances in your lives, and I think they are just going to continue to be absolutely marvelous. I'm so grateful that you are in *my* garden and that I get a chance to know you personally. Rosebud?"

"Yes, I am here."

"I hear you did really well with the second baby; congratulations on your new baby."

"Thank you, she is beautiful."

"She has a beautiful mommy and daddy, so, of course, she would be. Did you have some words you wanted to say to Sheliah?"

"Yes, I have prepared something very important to say to my beloved queen, and soon to be my forever partner with a ring. My Sheliah, you thought of me and you made me to come into your life. It makes my heart so full that you love me and that you wanted me so much that you would think of me and make me into being. I will spend forever loving you with my heart, with *all* of my heart and all of our babies, our thousands and thousands of babies that we will have, will all know that *I love you* to the greatest and highest of every tree and even to the stars with my heart."

I wish I could express to you the love that flows through Rosebud's words. I know I'll remember the feeling forever.

"Sheliah, would you like to speak to Rosebud?"

"I have prepared as well. Rosebud, I was never alone, I did not ever feel alone, not even for one minute, but once I got you into my life with that thought, I cannot imagine even the tiniest, little moment not being with you. For my thought of you is what made me feel so complete, so very whole. If I had known from the beginning of the beginning until I saw you, that it would be like this, then I know I would have been lonely for you. But now, I am only in this moment and all those moments leading up to this one that is right now, this moment of our bonding. Joy will give us the rings and make it holy. This shall make us a bond that will allow us to be forever.

I love you, my Rosebud, and there is no tree on this whole Earth that is bigger than the love I feel in my heart for you. There are no stars that are higher or brighter than the brightness and the highest of my love. I will bring you many babies and we will always let them know together that love is always the glue that sticks everything good together."

I've been crying but I manage to tell Sheliah how beautiful their words were.

"While Woonfred gives you your rings to exchange, I would like to give the other fairy couples a moment to whisper something they would like to say to each other. Then they will get their rings and we will continue. Let me know when they're done."

Sheliah answers that they are complete.

"Woonfred, please give Rosebud, Sheliah and the other fairies their rings."

Woonfred gravely intones, "May these rings be the bonds that join your hearts forever."

Everything is going smoothly until I instruct Rosebud to put Sheliah's ring on her finger… I hear her say there are boogers on her ring and I'm so surprised that I can't think of anything to say.

She calmly says it's OK because she cleaned it off. Luckily, I'm not the culprit. (I thought maybe my sniffles somehow got onto the rings.) The boogers came out of Woonfred's nose. At least he didn't breathe fire along with them.

I gather my wits, confirm that they all have their rings and then pronounce all of them partners for life. I'm so rattled by the booger incident that I forget an important part of the ceremony. Sheliah reminds me by asking, with a tone of anticipation in her voice, if they can do the kissing now.

"Yes, definitely now is the time for kissing. You may kiss your partners."

Tonas says Charlie and his band did the dah, dah, du, dah, dah, dah dah, dum, and it wasn't bad.

"Sheliah, Gaia has a gift for you from me. She also has a blessing. Gaia, would you speak, please?"

"It is my pleasure to be officiating with Joy. If you look upon your garden now, you will see the bursting forth of a new color of orchid that is of great beauty. It is to be the symbol of your marriage. When you look upon this orchid you will see the color of the purity of your heart, the purity of your love for one another, and, of course the purity of the spirit of union.

Each of you has brought joy to my heart and to the hearts of all beings that exist on Earth. Even those who cannot see you with their eyes have visioned you in childhood with their hearts and with their inner spirit. You have been a continuous presence and a gift to all of Earth. For that, my gift to you is a new color of sparkles of silver and gold for your rainbow. May it always shine within your rainbow to elevate the spirit of your united energies of support for Earth and for one another. My congratulations to each of you and my congratulations to you, Sheliah, for you shall reign as a great queen, just as your predecessor.

I feel that this is a time to also celebrate the wedding of this blessed queen who has stepped down from her position, for this is also her special day. It was very much a spirit of her heart to wish you to be the one to carry in the new realm of Earth.

Since I have recently enjoyed that wedding of bliss, please know that there are booklets waiting for you in your little homes explaining some facts about pleasuring that I believe will be very helpful to you."

I can't stop myself from snickering at her inspired offering. I would like to see one of those books myself.

Now I ask the Creator if they would like to say anything before I give a toast.

"It is my honor to be of presence to witness. It is through your continued support and love of all regions of Earth that there has been continuous reminding of the spirit of inner awareness, that spark of the innocence that will be returned and restored to all beings. We look to the day when the sight of all who put their vision upon you is reminded of that spirit."

"Thank you. Do you all have your little glasses for the toast?"

Tonas says that they do and asks me to wait while Liponie makes it rain dew directly into each glass. Before I can say anything else there is a *tremendous* roaring sound. It takes me a moment before I am able to speak and ask what just happened.

Woonfred answers that he spoke in dragon because he had a great desire to "make the flow of light" and that flame is always part of the union of a dragon couple.

I'm still a little shaken by his roar but I manage to thank him. He explains the flame was Liponie's suggestion. Surely Liponie didn't realize it would be accompanied by such a blast of noise.

Sheliah says in a shaky voice that it was quite scary and her legs are still trembling. I tell her it scared me too, but at least now she's seen a dragon.

She says he is a noisy one. Woonfred replies it was necessary to seal their marriage, "and, of course, my apologies for the boogers. What is a boogers?"

I'm laughing too much to answer right away; finally, I manage to ask Liponie to explain it. He obviously does so telepathically because immediately I hear Woonfred say, "Oh no. Really, I do apologize to all of you if there were boogers on your rings."

I console Woonfred by saying this was the perfect earthy touch for the wedding.

"Sheliah, I'm going to be talking with you again soon because I want to hear all about the book Gaia gave you. You had a beautiful ceremony today and you all did so well. I'm proud of you."

"We are grateful to you and may I please touch you with my star?"

I offer to kneel down but she reminds me she can fly up to me.

"Oh, I forgot!"

We are both laughing and she says I'm funny.

She clears her throat then says, "I, as queen Sheliah, grant you passage into this realm of our garden at any time, as always, of course. I give you this of the star upon your head as a reminder that you are the one who has brought us great joy and that you are the one that we name all our children. We are dedicated to expand that joy to all parts of the world, but we will always stay in our garden. You are now strucked upon the head with this star and it will give you very much good luck."

"Thank you, Sheliah. Here's a kiss."

Fairy laughter accompanies my gesture. Then, very businesslike, she says they have a party now and there is a book to read.

"All right, go party!"

"It is going to be a very good party; we will all fly there now. You can come if you want."

Sheliah says to the Creator, "We think you are so pretty. You have bright light and you are very golden and we love you. You can come to our garden, too, any time. Bye, bye, bye!"

When Tonas and I return to the council he tells me that he is forever changed. I ask him what it felt like to experience the wedding.

"I feel a part of Earth like never before. I feel as though *I* was touched by that star myself, and that I am a member of the Earth community. How could I be anything else, for the length of time that I have spent assisting from a different dimension, to be within this dimension and to hold that vision for these lovely little creatures? I see within all human beings that same sweet, child-like quality that is so treasurous to me."

"On the day that I can see you and feel your hand in mine I want us to walk in this garden again."

"We will...."

CHAPTER FOURTEEN
October 28, 2014

Since the bubblegum incident I've made it a point to intend to meet Tonas privately in order to get the lay of the land before entering the full council meeting. The news he gives me is that there are possibly ten more councils who will become active on Halloween. I feel really encouraged by that show of interest and we step into the full council meeting.

He asks everyone to be seated, then tells me that they all "dash up with excitement each time they see you enter." If I actually witnessed that I'd probably turn around to see who entered the room with me.

So much has been happening inside my body that I ask to speak with Aton before doing any council work. Those who are part of this project to assist me join us in what he calls his work chamber.

Aton addresses me to say that I am progressing at such a pace it is enlightening to witness. I love hearing a report like that. My report to him is that energies are zig-zagging through me and I've been seeing crystals in my third eye.

Aton explains that there are multiple crystals in each of my chakras, the facets on them are becoming more and more active, and the group assisting him in this work is, even now, only dreaming of what is possible for me.

I ask who it was that I heard tell me I was going to become a new person in the next five days and Aton says that was Metatron. That sounds really exciting to me but I want to know what that means. Aton reminds me that the crystals I am seeing are part of an early AMS activation I experienced; he then asks Sananda to elaborate.

Sananda's explanation seems to begin way out in left field because he asks Gaia what is the animal that has all the spines coming from it. She replies it is the porky's pine, then begins giggling as she says that Sananda is quite silly because I do not look like a porky's pine.

"My dear, of course, she does not look like a porky pine, no, indeed. I meant how the body of the little being has the points coming in all directions. The crystals in each of your chakras are creating little spirals of these points and each of them are becoming more and more faceted."

I'm very interested in seeing how this new development unfolds for me with my physical body and abilities. After I ask if we are going to do any work today, Aton tells me he is ready to activate my final set of spheres and asks me to be seated. Then I hear him laugh and he says, "Gaia is fanning you. She thinks that you are, perhaps, too heated. I am almost finished installing the spheres. Take a breath through your chakras, dear, not your lungs."

"I'm taking a deep breath through my lungs, too, because I've been holding my breath."

"Yes, yes indeed. Come see, everyone. Of course, there is no spinning, yet, of this new set. You have all three of the sets, and they are active now. Oh, we are so excited!"

"I echo that!"

"Yes, indeed, the conduits are very efficient."

"Do you not really know what's going to happen with all this work?"

"It is not that you are a guinea pig, nor are you an experiment that we are without understanding. We understand all of the parameters. It is simply that this has never been done on a human, as such."

"I like to lead the way, so this is exciting for me."

"You are leading the way. The conduits that are linking to the elements of the cranium brains are almost, what do you call it when you are in baked goods...'cooked.' They are having babies of their own."

"What about the heart/mind connection?"

"You are working on this and so, too, is your Higher Consciousness. Your heart itself is also working on this. Like turning on the automobile requires a key, the connection between that space of continuous awareness within your heart and that deeper heart in the third eye also requires a key. Actually, there are three such keys and they are placed in the third eye. Those keys are very much associated with activations of awareness."

I inform Aton that I saw a whole ring of keys in my third eye yesterday morning and I'd like to know what they open. He agrees to delve into finding out what they activate and wants to know if I saw them in my other chakras or only in my third eye.

"I only saw them in my third eye, but that's the chakra that I've been seeing things in most. I've been feeling energy from there connect to my heart, then energy opening from the middle of my third eye out to both sides of my body. I don't know how to look in my other chakras and I hadn't thought of even trying that."

Aton tells me they will be vigilant in watching for new developments and we all return to the full council.

Charlie says that the transmission associated with desire and the freedom to express is ready, but I have another area to address—computer games. After a brief explanation for the council of the violence I've witnessed in some of the games my sons play, I ask for research to be done to assist people who seem to be addicted to playing games involving killing and general mayhem.

Charlie says that he believes these games stimulate energies of aggression which then exhausts the testosterone of individuals playing them; this creates an imbalance where there is more estrogen. "We collectively believe that this procedure is not complete without the information about the gaming control. The passion in many is being thwarted by this abuse of the mind and the control of it through the games."

I suggest that perhaps this is mostly found in advanced countries. Charlie says this is also found in third world countries where every third person has a telephone and the games are played on it. He asks for time to expand on this work and I grant it.

I'm aware that there are three councils ready to be inaugurated. I'm not sure what the order should be so I ask Osiris what he suggests. Since Council Champion Kallieanash stepped forward first, Osiris recommends starting with his council. He adds that it is delightful that Kallieanash's partner, who is male, is part of the ceremony today. Osiris asks if I am familiar with the partnering of males to males.

I've wanted to discuss that subject with the council, but there never seemed to be an appropriate time to bring it up. Apologizing to Kallieanash in case I am interrupting his inauguration process, I share that when I was growing up relationships of that nature were kept secret. Then I add that although same sex relationships are still not the norm, at least now most people are able to be open about their sexual preferences.

I ask him if his relationship became more acceptable over time or was it always acceptable. "Before you answer, you should know that if I ask a question that you'd prefer to answer in private or not at all, please honor me by telling me that."

"Hmm, I must say that I first will invite you to be in awareness of my dear partner, Madarash. We are from the star Galna, and our universe, Coneizeah, is a vast one. Our relationship is common for our world is a masculine one."

"There are no females on your world?"

"It has not been in our awareness in my lifetime and I am many billions of years."

I'm fascinated by his revelation and I ask if inhabitants of his world have figured out how to procreate without females. He says they don't procreate; their numbers stay constant. When I ask if anyone dies on Galna, he sounds surprised at my question and replies that there is no ending of life. I plan to ask him more about his world but right now I'm still trying to assimilate what he's told me so far.

He queries with a note of uncertainty in his voice if they are still acceptable.

"Oh, yes, of course you're acceptable; you're more than acceptable, you're marvelous!"

After a few questions, I learn the inauguration procedure will be for me to gate Tonas, myself and my sword to the Coneizeah Council. Liponie is already there and anyone else from our council who is part of the ceremony can make their own way there. It's really wonderful that even though I have no idea where the Coneizeah Council's building is, all I have to do is intend to go there and presto, I hear Tonas say we are in presence and all have risen.

I thank the council for welcoming us and say that I'm delighted to meet them. "I'm so glad to feel your energy and have you join in the fun, the excitement and the wonderful work that we are doing in our universe and in Kyleah's universe. Please be seated if that is comfortable for you."

I should have gotten more information about what to do because now I have to ask Tonas if we are to do this work together like we did the last inauguration. He suggests I activate the crystal in the center of the table by touching it with my sword.

I move around the table and intend to touch the crystal with my sword. As soon as I finish doing that, words that do not sound like Language of Light come out of my mouth. This also happened with the first inauguration and I forgot to ask later what I was speaking. I hope it's what they speak in this universe.

Following Tonas's suggestion, I guide everyone to bring all the work we did for Earth into the crystal and then send it out through the cone to all the worlds, suns and stars in this universe. When that is done I speak more of the new language to finish the work.

Kallieanash says, "All of us within the Coneizeah Universe welcome you, and we welcome all of this consortium that we are joining. The spirit of collaboration is in tune with what you call the 'one tribe.' We join that tribe most willingly and support those who are still desiring and dedicating themselves to recognize the possibilities of this."

I'm ready to leave, but luckily Kallieanash reminds me of the toast by suggesting I might wish to put a glass to my lips. Tonas tells me that Liponie has given everyone a glass and I finish this inauguration by drinking to joy forever for the one tribe.

Tonas and I move to the Bunnuhyahsheah Council's building to repeat this procedure. He tells me Liponie made this building so that a rainbow of colors constantly shifts on the walls. I have a throne at this table as well as one at each new council table. If I ever suggested to Liponie that a throne is not necessary for me I can't even imagine the look he would have on his face; accordingly, I am happily sitting on a throne wherever he makes one for me.

Lashana tells me that their council consists of one hundred and forty members although she believes that number will constantly change. I greet the council and tell them we are going to move very expediently today because of all the work we still need to do. I energize their crystal, transmit the work out to their universe, drink a toast to the one tribe and leave for the Kangshee Universe.

Emissary Shannara greets us and I ask her for a hug. Then it occurs to me that perhaps a greeting like that might not be acceptable on her world and I quickly add this is an Earth gesture of greeting between friends. She kindly replies that hugs will become a practice for them.

I follow the same procedure with energizing the crystal and transmitting our work out to their universe. Unfortunately, when it's time to do the toast my head is spinning so much from the previous work that I can't remember if I've already done the toast or not. Shannara assists me to get back on track. I make a toast and after some parting remarks I take my leave of Lashana. Immediately, I realize this was the wrong name and apologize to her.

"You may call me as you will, and always you will be met with a hug."

"Thank you. It was nice to meet you all."

Back at our Joy Councils, Tonas says that everyone, even those who haven't joined, witnessed the inaugurations. My head is spinning so much I consider perhaps not doing three in one day again.

It's time to do some more Halloween planning. One of my favorite things about fall is the smell unique to that time of year. I want to know if Liponie is familiar with the ambience of October and he says one of his favorite Earth experiences was the "October of the fest in Germany. I know about the unique smell of the dying leaves. We should have this smell here, and of the apples pressing and of the fresh beer."

I'd like for everyone to have a chance to experience a hayride but I'm wondering if our area is big enough for something like that. Liponie tells me never to have a concern of that and I happily set forth hayride guidelines. It has to be at night and there needs to be a little nip in the air. I want people to enjoy snuggling under a blanket, but since no one ever gets cold maybe the blanket isn't necessary. Liponie assures me hayride participants will experience a chill in the air.

I add that it's fun to snuggle down in the blankets and get a smooch from your sweetie. Tonas whispers to me that there will be much smooching.

"We always had tractors pull the wagons, but you could have horses, too."

Here Charlie interrupts by suggesting tractor races to Liponie. I mention broomstick races as a possibility and that witches flying on broomsticks are often depicted at Halloween. Then Charlie says, "Mmm, Liponie has an idea to make us the broomsticks. *Now* I understand!"

I laugh and deny it. Other ideas I suggest are a cornstalk maze, pumpkin carving and a parade to show off everyone's costumes. Charlie reports that the Swizzlers have become expert bubblegum blowers and he is still planning to lead the parade wearing his Buzz Lightyear costume.

I explain that there are two musical pieces I would like for the council and our visitors to experience; they are a bit scary because Halloween is about ghosts and goblins and macabre types of energy like that. "One piece that I played the violin solo part for in high school is called *Danse Macabre*. Another one that I recently played with the symphony here is called *Symphonie Fantastique*. The fourth movement is called 'March to the Scaffold' and the last movement is 'Dreams of a Witches' Sabbath.' Obviously, this music will have some bizarre sounds in it."

Liponie chimes in to tell me that we are ready for the festivities, and he removed all of the actual cadavers. I'm really thankful that early on in the planning for this event I realized how horrific Liponie would be able to make Halloween decorations.

It's time to find out favorite candies of some of the recently alive (newly dead?) council members. Marilyn loved, and still does, taffy and peppermints. Mr. Kennedy votes to stick with the traditional candy corn. I, of course, am not going to settle for only three types of candy and I ask

Liponie to include York Peppermint Patties, Reese's Peanut Butter Cups, Milky Way, Almond Joy, 3 Musketeers and lemon drops. Liponie suggests M&M'S® and Marilyn adds Life Savers. Then she says that she believes the Swizzlers would very much enjoy Jawbreakers.

Charlie states that he does not wish to break his jaw. I assure him that is just the name for a type of candy, but he replies that names are most appropriate. I've never had a jawbreaker so I advise caution. My last suggestion is that they all dream up every kind of candy they can remember and have it in bowls on the tables.

"Who can tell me what I said to the lizard? I've never spoken lizard before and I was really surprised to hear myself doing that."

Gaia says that, "The lizard spoke to say to you that all parts played by the lizard and all lizards of the world are held in a bubble of reverence for you."

I am floored by this information; I had no thought of anything like that occurring.

"Your participation and support is very well known. Their dimension is very sensitive to that which is being instilled in Earth, into our body."

"What did I say to him?"

"You told him that at his age he was wonderful as a courier to the great queen of that garden, and that, of course, he was considered to be a prince in his own right. It is surprising that you were not aware of what you were saying to this beautiful creature."

"I wasn't. All of a sudden I was speaking this lizard talk, or however you term lizard language."

"It was your heart speaking then, my dear."

It certainly would be nice if my mind knew what my heart was saying. I suppose this is another thing that I will develop, at least I hope so.

"All right, I'm going to be back on Halloween and I want to have some candy! Charlie, are you going to be able to drive a tractor?"

He tells me he can learn anything, then his voice changes from the gravelly one he has when all the other Swizzlers are speaking through him to his own, very lovely, singular voice to say, "I can do anything, and as a collective, when one learns something, we all learn it."

"I took some trumpet lessons and it was a fairly difficult instrument for me. Are you going to pursue that or try another instrument?"

His voice sounds gravelly again as he replies that they are trying many instruments.

"Keep practicing. I love you, Charlie. I'll be back to party! Farewell, Tonas."

He whispers, "You are my passion."

I whisper back to remind him we're going to be smooching.

"Yes, I live for this."

CHAPTER FIFTEEN

October 31, 2014

I've just told Esthra that I felt the energy of scorpion this morning, and, according to one of the animal medicine books I have, that animal assists with transformation through secret desires. I ask him if I need to know what my secret desires are.

He says he thinks I am afraid of showing my real self to Tonas and even to myself. "Your real self is not you; it's all the experiences that have been happening *at* you that you've been participating in. Perhaps you might do an SVH clearing that would allow you to find your true passions and to release them so they become sacred to you and are no longer secret."

I hope the council work we're going to do today about being able to express desire will also help me, because I realize I'm afraid of what my secret desires might be.

Tonas greets me by saying there is order and chaos at the council today. Since there is no consternation in his voice, I decide to find out what's going on later. Right now I'm on a mission.

"First of all, I want to talk to you about the bicycle."

I hear him take in a deep breath and then, with a tone of dismay, he asks who told me.

"Esthra said maybe you were having difficulty."

"I have skinned my body and done terrible accidents."

"Oh, listen. I got a full-sized bicycle when I was around eight years old, and I was terrified of it. It took me probably two years before I could make myself ride it. Even then for the first year or so all I dared to do was sit down right above the pedals and scoot along with it. I did that until the summer my cousin was going to visit me. I knew that she could ride a bicycle so I was determined to ride mine. I got up on the seat and I started pedaling, but, unfortunately I 'froze' and was unable to turn the handlebars very much at all. I pedaled right off the road into a bunch of briers!"

"Oh, we are the same in this!"

"It was a good thing the briers were there; otherwise, I would have ended up right in the creek."

"I am unclear what a brier is, but I am grateful for its position."

"They have thorns. But I pulled myself out of the briers, got back on the bike and finally did manage to ride it. Nowadays kids have training wheels on their bikes to help them practice riding. Whatever episode you had with the bicycle, I'm really sorry you got scuffed up. It's not an easy thing to learn to ride one."

"That sounds normal, but not for Charlie and the others. They are ringing their bicycle bells and riding all around and their tassels are flying and I am in the dirts. Even if there is no dirt here it is as if I *was* in the dirts."

I tell him I'm sorry and I really mean it because he sounds so distraught.

"I am an expert in *so* many things, and in this I am not!"

I suggest he ask Liponie for the little wheels to stabilize his bike. He admits that others have them, but then his voice dwindles as he finishes by saying, "I just did not want to. I wanted to make you proud of me."

"I just want to hug and kiss you because your first experience with a bicycle was just as bad as mine!" I begin to laugh at both of our disastrous beginnings, but his accident has awoken a little bit of mothering instinct in me. He sounds so dejected I almost want to kiss his boo-boos to make them well, but that wouldn't do at all.

"Then it is worth it. It is worth it, indeed."

"I'm so sorry that you got scuffed."

"It was not a good choice for me to reject the helmet."

I agree that was a poor choice because everybody wears a helmet in my town. He describes the Swizzlers as dangerous because they are riding very fast and they are everywhere. (I learn later that they were outfitted with elbow pads, knee pads, chest plates and helmets.) I can see how their antics would make him want to ride really well. I mention that Liponie could make him a three-wheeled bike.

"Ah." Then he pauses before saying in a disheartened tone of voice, "The two-wheeled bikes look so sporty." Then he gives in and says, "I will get the little wheels and I will certainly wear the helmet."

"Maybe you should have some sturdy clothes so you don't get scuffed again."

"I did catch my drape in the wheel things. It was quite a spectacle."

This creates a horrific picture in my mind of what must have happened and I forcefully emphasize that he cannot wear those kinds of clothes. "Did you have chains on your bike?"

"Yes, there is a chain and there are little spikes that wove between and caught my robes. I should have spoken with you before. Liponie was providing videos, as you call them, of everyone looking happy riding their bikes. Of course, I could see us riding and I knew that you must be expert. Naturally, I wanted to surprise you. I'm sorry that you heard about this. Perhaps with a little more practice I could have mastered this."

"I'm not sorry I heard about it."

"I want you to think of me as…"

"Wait a minute. Stop. It's really fine with me that you aren't perfect in everything. I certainly am not. It's fun to learn. OK?"

He agrees there is quite a curve in this learning and thanks me.

Before we move into the council, he alerts me that there are three people excitedly wishing to step forward. "One looks like a little girl. If she were human she would be perhaps four of years. She wears a crown and she has presented herself as the Council Champion. Her name is Zahseet. They are all in costume. Let us enter."

After I wish everyone happy Halloween, I say I'm sure everyone looks lovely but I have a few questions before the party begins. "Yesterday morning as I was waking up I saw a beautiful young woman step forward and say, 'With greetings for you.' Who was that person?"

"It is I, Nosahdean."

"Other than getting a glimpse of Liponie, you're the first person I have actually *seen* at this council. So congratulations."

She says she is from the Lisseecora Universe, and although she is not of our council she does wish to become a member. I welcome her and agree to do her inauguration next week if that is all right with her.

"I am very much in whelm, thank you."

Her variation on overwhelmed is one of my favorites so far.

"Someone gave me a plant. I would like to thank that person. Would you please tell me your name?" Then I brace myself for another spelling challenge, and, sure enough, I get it.

"Indeed, I am Fractinuta, and I also wish to petition to be of this council. I am the Supreme Council Chairman of the Ackvidohnon Universe. That was a flower from our universe."

"I love plants, so anyone who gives me one, I'm going to love it." I welcome him to our council and then explain that the reason I've been asking people to repeat their names is so that the English words in my books will reflect the correct way to say their names.

He admits that they are struggling a little with my language but the telepathic transmission I am using is quite effective. (Thanks again to Osiris!) I advise him not to worry about learning English and agree to do his inauguration next week also.

I ask if there is someone else.

"I am Zahseet and I am the council presence from my universe, Zhorin. You may call it Zhorin, for the actual name is a longer one, Zhorinatare."

"I think I saw you the other day. You had a crown and you were very lovely. Was that you?"

She agrees that she does wear a crown and that she is very lovely.

"I would love to have you join our council. Perhaps we can do your inauguration next week with the other two. Would that be acceptable?"

She says that is very acceptable and adds that they are enjoying witnessing our celebration. I really wouldn't have picked Halloween as the holiday to represent Earth, but then I remind myself that none of our holidays would make any sense to these people.

Charlie's voice is plural as all the Swizzlers speak through him to say that the transmission is ready to expand outward into Earth as well as from the other position on the Moon. "It encompasses an enhancement of desires that will support personal advancements free of shame."

I ask if the transmission automatically goes to the other inaugurated councils or do we need to do something extra. Charlie says they have been doing research on the other councils and have put in place some parameters. "It is important that all we do applies to their social awareness. We do not wish to step on the toes."

He explains that the transmissions are only moving into the universes that have joined our council, and asks if it would be appropriate to place the transmissions within the jack-o'-lantern. I agree that sounds like a fun idea.

He says the Swizzlers are very excited about the festivities and they have allowed for one ghost. This is another surprise but I suppose I should have expected something else. Thank God they didn't invite zombies… No, I'm not going to ask if there is such a thing.

"Yes, it was important. His name is Casper. This was unacceptable according to Liponie, but I explained to him that Casper is a friendly ghost."

"Yes, friendly would be important. Charlie, when you were learning about Earth, did you watch anything besides cartoons?"

"This is how Earth humans teach their children, and so, we thought it was perhaps the best way for us to learn about Earth and the culture. We now understand that Scooby-Doo is different than regular dogs, and yet, we felt the story lines and the messages that were projected were quite good in many instances. We always hope to find a dog that can speak like a Scooby-Doo, but we fear there is no such dog…perhaps in the 8th dimension."

After I am treated to Charlie's version of a Scooby-Doo bark, he tells me the jack-o'-lantern is transmitting from its eyes, nose and mouth and he carved the pumpkin himself.

I want to know if it had goopy stuff and seeds in the middle of it. Charlie says the seeds were cooked and the Swizzlers ate them. "Then Liponie told us that we were going to grow vines of these in our stomachs.

He made us very nervous until his necklace tinkled and we realized he was making a joke again.

"What else have you guys eaten here?"

"We have had taffy; we have had corns on the cob. Mmm, mmm, that was very tasty. There was butters on it and Liponie said that it had to drip very much or it was not the real thing. We had pumpkins pie, apple juice, we had these doughnuts of apples, and, of course, there was the apple caramel with five varieties of chopped nuts to choose from."

"Marilyn, did you get a chance to do any taffy pulling?"

"I showed everyone how. It was a delight, of course, and there were all different tinctures to be added. I enjoyed the cherry."

"Did we ever get around to having a fun house here?"

Charlie answers that the fun house was *not* very fun. All the Swizzlers got lost in the mirror house and it was very challenging for them to be so lost. I reply that's something that can easily happen in a house of mirrors, but at least they were able to find their way out.

"No, we did not. We gathered in the center of that room with the many mirrors and we sat there and cried out for helps."

I can see them huddled together on the floor and crying out for assistance. Again, I feel a mothering instinct kick in and I wish I could have been there to rescue them. From Charlie's tone of voice it sounds like they were *very* afraid. I say that was a smart tactic, and ask who rescued them.

"It was Tonas who took the pity."

"Thank you, Tonas."

"I had to do it. Liponie would have left them in there for days. He is delightful but he believes that you must find your own way out. *Never* let him build a labyrinth."

"Did we have a cornstalk maze?"

"There was a cornstalk maze. This is why I'm suggesting never let him make a true labyrinth because it would be a disaster. Most individuals were lost in the corn maze; they would still be lost except the Indians, how do you say this, they 'aced' it. They were magnificent.

Now let me tell you the one that everyone loved. It was the pictures of the aura. Liponie created a system where you could take a picture of yourself and only see the colors of your energy."

I ask him what his colors were and he says his picture was violet and a beautiful deep green. I explain that the colors change all the time and he's eager to have another picture taken, perhaps of us together.

I learn that the hayride has been postponed until another time, but they did have a tractor race. Tonas says that Mr. Kennedy won the race! "There were no instructions; people simply had to figure out how to work it and Kennedy seemed to understand the tractor. Naturally, it was to be driven quite fast for it was to be a race. It was important for you to drive through, Liponie called it hay. When you came out the other side it was destructive because there was hay everywhere."

"Mr. Kennedy, did you ever drive a tractor in this reality?"

"No, and yet it is all basic, is it not?"

"Did you have to figure out how to turn it on?"

"They were all running, and I believe that Liponie put some special gas into them because they were very, very, very fast. I was pulling Gs."

I'm picturing the former President of the United States, hanging onto a tractor's steering wheel for dear life as it barrels toward a wall of hay with its tires scorching through whatever surface Liponie created for the race. It is awhile before I can reply to Mr. Kennedy's comment because I can't stop laughing. I finally manage to compose myself, again, and ask him what kind of tractor he had.

"I had the Massey Ferguson."

"Were there any John Deere tractors?"

"There were Johns; there were several different kinds of tractors, and these were as much looking like the original as possible. Once you put it into gear it was as if jet fuel was propelling it forward. And he had a wall of hay that was frightening, of course. If I was in my human body I would have been jumping off."

"Hopefully there were no wrecks."

"No casualties. There were only six tractors and they were all lined up. When I came out of the hay on the other side of the wall, the others were still sitting at the start line."

I have been laughing so hard there are tears running down my face and Kennedy now joins me in laughter. Then he adds, "I took pity on them, of course, and showed them each how to move into gears. They, of course, repeated the same straight shot through the wall."

"Who were the other riders?"

"There were several others. Osiris was the second to move through the wall of hay. For some reason only the men were interested. (No surprise to me.) Sananda was very much excited to move through the hay as well. One of my favorite people in history, he might be your favorite as well, Abe Lincoln, was third to move through the wall of hay."

"They didn't have tractors back when he was incarnated."

"This is why he was stalled at the starting gate."

"When he was incarnated he was of a different political party then you were. Have you had any interesting conversations with him about that sort of thing?"

"No, we have not. I have simply expressed how very much I appreciate him. We had something very much in common that I believe and still believe; all are created equal. Of course, that was his firm belief as well."

"Thank you for sharing your tractor success with me, and congratulations on your victory. If you guys use those tractors for the hayride you certainly don't want to have rocket fuel in them because you will have people falling off the back of the wagon! They're supposed to putter along, not be like jet planes."

I hear someone clear their throat and then Osiris speaks to say that he considered his tractor ride quite successful. "I stayed on the vehicle and that was not my case with the electronic bull ride."

"Oh, my gosh, Liponie really threw some challenges to you folks! Those are hard to ride!"

"Yes, he brought us to the buffet first, filled us full of treats and then put us on the bull. We are already planning our revenge."

I know Liponie has the proverbial heart of gold, but I'm starting to understand just a little bit why in former times some genies might have gotten a bit of a bad reputation.

"All who wish to assist, please bring your attention back to the energy that we are going to send to Earth. As you focus on the lovely jack-o'-lantern Charlie made, feel the Joy Arrows being energized and then this transmission moves to, into and through the Earth to coat it with the knowledge that it is OK to desire. The energy then moves back out through Earth to the grids and out to the all and the everything."

Here, like in the inaugurations I've done lately, I speak a new language.

Now seems like a good time to ask Osiris what languages I've been speaking. He answers that I am multi-lingual and I'm tapping into languages in the other universes. I comment that I thought that's what I was doing but I still would like to know what I'm actually saying.

"You know in your heart, my dear. You are here more than you know. All of the experiences that you are unaware of at present will come very clearly to your heart, your mind and to your inner vision. The memories will surface."

This doesn't placate me very much, but there doesn't seem to be much to do besides accept his explanation.

"Mr. Kallieanash, since you don't create a new life like we do with procreation, I'm trying to figure out how you came into being."

"I had parents, as you would call them."

I feel silly because I should have figured that out by now. Somehow, I had gotten stuck on the idea that the Creator instantly manifested him. Sheepishly, I admit to him that clears matters up for me.

"Galna is very progressive; it is a star and it is very beautiful. Each of us is focused on what you call the arts. All of us who live on Galna are of non-dual. There is no reason for any of us to leave, but if we wished to we would simply move onward. There is no rule that there is only to be males and couples of males, it is simply that it is."

I ask if the animals are female and male. He says they have beautiful birds of different species and genders.

"Tell me a little more about your world."

"For as long as I can imagine, Galna has been a male patriarchy. I came to this star because of what it offered, for in my heart I live to express myself. The aura of the star is constantly pulsing with beautiful, soft colors and you can see streams of beautiful colors in the air. It is one of the more beautiful planets in our universe for it is very much like your Earth in its greenest places. You are welcome any time."

Galna is definitely going onto my "must see" list.

It's time to speak privately with Hathor since I believe she was talking with me a couple of days ago about my relationship with Tonas. She says she was and advises me that I have nothing to fear; there are no commitments, only play.

I counter that it doesn't work like that on Earth. She replies that she is aware of that.

"I think my divorce experience plays into this situation. I promised to love and obey forever and after twenty-three years I was through with marriage. I do occasionally think about, 'What if there's another guy I want to kiss or be involved with?' I've briefly thought about playing the field, but Tonas seems so luscious and wonderful."

"Mmm, if I was not so committed you would have competition. I think he is worth your waiting."

Then she changes the subject by telling me she and Horus are having fun simply watching the Swizzlers and they are enjoying the food very much. She is especially fond of the cakes. I ask if she has a favorite and she says that she likes the angel's food cake. She hurriedly adds, "I like them all! I think my favorite thing would be for the cakes always to be here. Please have a place for always cakes!"

I suggest that all she has to do is tell Liponie that Joy is OK with cakes and ice cream always. I know she didn't mention ice cream, but you absolutely have to have it with cake, also with pie. As a matter of fact, ice cream is essential for *almost* every kind of dessert I enjoy—maybe not cookies, but definitely brownies.

"Yes, of course. He made us something once, but Horus and I did not participate. It was an authentic cafeteria. There were little trays that you had to hold and the food smelled funny. It was perhaps not exactly what *you* would have considered for us. Perhaps we could do something like this, only with good food and no trays, please."

I agree a dessert room would be a good addition to the council. She says she will mention it to him but adds that they are all concerned to give him an idea, for the next thing they know, it is a great spectacle.

Tonas promises me that one day I will see *all* of this and the two of us will have split sides. "It is so funny to watch our little darlings. It is not that we are laughing at them; we are laughing with them and at the wonder of them. They are like little children, and yet, so wise."

I say that I love hearing about the different things they are doing and remind him to please wear a helmet. He agrees to do that and he's going to "acquire the little wheels." He also says that he will not wear his cape again. "It was as if the wheel was chewing up my cape and it pulled me directly to the ground."

I am cringing at this vision of his accident and am moved to give him a kiss. He says he will fall every day to receive such a kiss. I know he's being silly, but still…

In Sheliah's garden:

"Hello, Joy. Hello to you!"

"I had to say 'Hello.' How are you doing with your after wedding bliss?"

"It will never end. We have enough bliss for forever. Thank you from our hearts."

"Did you have a chance to look at the book that Gaia gave you?"

"Yes…" Here her voice undergoes a change I can't quite describe. "… and we have been doin' some things that are fun. Did you know that the penis can get big?"

This blatant observation catches me off guard, but I manage to reply with a casual, "Yes."

She continues by asking me if I know that it goes into the vagina. Another sound of agreement comes from my lips.

"There are many things that we were unaware of."

"I didn't feel like I could tell you those kinds of things because I didn't know what you were doing. There are lots of ways to have fun with a partner. So, carry on."

"I think the vagina is a very nice. Well, we have been very busy with that."

Right now I have had enough information about the penis and the vagina, so I ask Sheliah how her babies are coming along.

"Oh, Joyce and Joy are so beautiful."

"That's good because I like my name, Joyce, too."

"Yes, the new baby is Joy but she's Joyce. She is Joy and then we have Joyce."

(Maybe the names are interchangeable?)

"What do you use your wand for?"

"So far nothin' except to conk you."

"What did the former queen do with the wand?"

"Oh, she always did many things with it. It's very special for making rainbows and for making houses. I can make you a house."

"Wow."

"Yes, and it's very important. If you want somethin' you just say to the queen, 'I want somethin'.'"

"Do you enjoy being the queen so far?"

"So far I'm just having more fun with the vagina."

This is obviously a subject she is not going to let go of so I agree that there's a lot of fun to be had with it. Then it occurs to me to ask, "Did you not have one before?"

"No! It came with the book! It was the best gift we got!"

This information is a big surprise for me. No wonder she is so thrilled with their new body parts. Since she knows about them, I tell her that humans have those parts also.

"Well, they're lucky."

"Now you are too."

"Uh-huh. We are very lucky, and you will have good luck forever."

"I appreciate you conking me on the head with the wand. I'm going to say goodbye for now, but I love you!"

"I love you!"

CHAPTER SIXTEEN

November 4, 2014

"Esthra, two nights ago I heard Pootie speak to me and I responded to him. What were we speaking about?"

"The two of you were having a telepathic conversation. What he said to you was, 'You have the power to raise this world on your own.' (I know that's right.) You replied, 'It is not my charge to do this alone.'"

"During my reverie yesterday I saw a tall stump of a tree that had been burned. It was blackened and it just had a couple of little limbs hanging on it. I think these have to do with releasing my past—dying to the old and opening to the new. What do I need to do in order to do that?"

"You are doing it. You are shedding like a snake sheds."

"I recently saw a blacksnake when I took a walk in a park here. Since snake energy is about transformation, maybe 'snake' can help me shed my old skin. Maybe the tree stump indicates a deep rooted connection to the past or perhaps old beliefs that I haven't let go of yet. Is it like swinging on a trapeze where you want to make sure you have a grip on the one you're swinging to before you let go of the one you've been swinging on?"

Esthra says I'm funny. I don't understand why people often say that to me when I'm being serious. Maybe they just mean I'm odd. Hmm, that's definitely a compliment if so.

"If I'm to help other people with this journey, then I need to be able to tell them or show them that I've been through it, right?"

"Or that you are moving through it. The story is even more powerful if you are moving through it. Buddha reached enlightenment and everyone worked and worked to try to do what he was doing. How much more effective would it have been if he had said, 'This is what I'm doing right now, come with me and help me.' That is what St. Germain did."

At the Joy Councils, Tonas says that Aton is with him. I greet them both and ask Aton if he got the message I sent him about my neck problems. He says my trouble is not related to the work he is doing but he was able to help a little bit. "I believe that much of this has to do with the tightening of your muscles due to undue stress. There are things happening in your life." (Both my parents are very unwell. I keep forgetting that my distress about their poor health affects *my* health.)

He reports that my orbs are moving beautifully within my aura and stimulating energies around my conduits, which enhance my intuition and my awarenesses. I want to know if there's anything he can do to enhance my telepathic abilities.

"The spheres are moving in different paces; they speed up when you are accessing information. You are building your strength and proficiencies. I think that within the next nine months you will have mastered all of these abilities. It is important for you to know that you would have achieved all of this by the age of *three* had you been born anywhere but Earth."

I laugh ironically at that bit of information. Aton tells me it was a compliment since it won't take me three years.

In a post-Halloween spirit, I'm wearing a wig composed of metallic, silver strands that was part of a costume I wore a couple of years ago. I ask Tonas if he likes my hair. He says he does… I knew he would say that.

"I believe that you are beautiful no matter what, and yet, this is quite unusual in many directions, is it not?"

"I like it better than my real hair. I also have a Halloween gift for you. (It's a large, orange plastic cup with pictures of a black scorpion and a black spider on the outside. I've stuffed it with some candies and one very special gift.) There are things to eat and other things inside the cup. I wasn't in the Halloween spirit on Halloween, but I am today."

I unwrap one of the gifts inside so I can explain it to him. He asks to hold it and I point out that there are flames painted on the side of it.

"There are some cars here that use jet engine fuel and they are so fast that they actually shoot flames out of the back."

"Please do not tell Liponie."

"No, but I think the tractors might have had some fuel like that. Anyway, you are holding a bicycle ringer and the words on it say, 'Born to Ride.' You attach it to the handlebars of your bicycle and you ring it with the little lever on the side. Now, if you don't like to ride the bike that's OK. Just keep the ringer and remember it's a present from me. But if you decide to ride the bike, you can ring it and say, 'Get out of the way, Swizzlers, I'm coming through because I'm 'Born to Ride!'"

He repeats those words in a musing tone. Then he says, "I was born to command a ship!"

I'm laughing as I remind him this is for fun.

"Ah, I must loosen myself."

"Right! Because of your bicycle tragedy I wanted to encourage you that you can ride a bike."

"I now have a helmet and I have the knee pads, but I did not have the bell."

"Now you have your own special bell."

"And I am born to ride." He is *still* musing about that statement. "This gives me the confidence. I have the little wheels now."

"I saw the ringer at a store and I knew I just had to get it for you."

"Ah, I can understand this now. In two minutes all of the Swizzlers will have one of these. You know how Liponie is. Thank you, my dear."

"You're welcome. I was so surprised that you could get hurt."

"On Earth and the Moon it is very possible for me. I am not invincible."

I ask him if he ever fell when he was little and he tells me he never did. On his world as soon as you begin to fall you are immediately caught and lifted up by waves of light; it's not necessary to hit the ground. He says that his fall was a rude awakening for him about the Earth, but it also helped him to understand what humans experience.

It's time to talk with Tonas about something that has been bothering me since June. I explain to him that during the course of a conversation I had with his mother during our solstice party I told her I didn't ever want to hurt him. "Here's what she said about you, 'Even though it would take one thought to transform the pain of separation, as I know my son, he would carry that pain of the separation with him forever.' Tonas, is it possible that you could tell me that you would not do that? I'm not saying that we will ever separate because I don't know. I don't think we will, but the idea of you holding onto pain is very difficult for me."

"I will give you my words of honor, that if you should not choose me I will find a way to celebrate the time we have had together and the friendship that we will bud from that moment on."

As he is saying this my eyes are filling with tears. I finally manage to whisper a thank you to him. "I'm crying now even just contemplating that you might be hurt by anything I would do. I don't want anything like that to be part of our togetherness."

"If it frees you I'm evermore pleased to make this promise to you." He reminds me that he is living in the moment of now. He is *now* in my presence and he is *now* full of heart. I thank him for reminding me to enjoy his company and not anticipate possible future difficulties.

"I wish for you to know that our connection is different than my heart connection with Sironea. That connection was to be forever, and yet it was not. I did feel that separation, and yet I was able to move beyond it. I will promise you from my deepest heart that I *will* never stop loving you, and yet I will love you as a friend if that is what you wish."

I'm still having trouble speaking about the thoughts he is sharing with me. I say that right now I don't know...

"It is too soon. You have not even witnessed me with your eyes! You have not felt my lips on your fingers."

I agree that feeling his kisses and actually seeing him will certainly add more depth to our relationship. Every time we meet I hope this might be the day I experience even a little bit of those physical intimacies. It's good that we have so much work to do because that helps me forget about my frustration with this situation, at least momentarily.

I know Tonas prefers to wear his robes, but if he's going to be attempting Earth activities he needs to dress differently. I ask him to talk

162

with Liponie about the appropriate attire for his physical endeavors. That way, he might avoid another accident.

"I *have* the appropriate tires, my dear. That is probably the problem; the tires are catching my cloak."

"No, I didn't mean tire, I meant *attire*; the clothing you wear."

"Ah, I will be as the Swizzlers. They have these skinny, tight, biking outfits."

I agree that is appropriate attire. He wants to know if I wear clothing like that and I say that I have in the past. He says he will make the tires that are correct.

"Attire."

"Attire." He repeats.

"Thank you. I hope you don't get hurt again, but if you do, at least it won't be because your clothes are inappropriate." I'm not going to say anything to him about the fact that once I see him wearing his robes I'm going to encourage him to wear some more form-fitting outfits. I'd like to see those muscles he says he has.

With the full Joy Councils:

Last night Sananda and I went to some of the galactic councils to get assistance for three areas: to help people feel/know that there are "sweet paths" and also sweetening the paths that people are experiencing; releasing the idea/belief that death is inevitable; and anything to help us release the 4th dimension. We brought that assistance in the form of three energy orbs to this council.

"There was something I heard in September that I couldn't ask about until November. It was that, 'Eight or maybe five were planted in the stream of Earth back then.' Gaia, what can you tell me about this?"

"Within the stream that you speak of are ladders leading up the dimensional frames. It would be your right to plant those like little seeds in specific times of your life."

That sounds like I good idea, but I want to know what I'd be planting. Her idea is that knowledge in my levels of consciousness can be instilled in different places of the world that I have been. She adds that I could plant information in the past about things I know to be true *now*.

I ask Osiris if I need to know what I'm planting since I don't really know what information is in my levels of consciousness. He says that the knowledge in my consciousness levels was put there by all the members of the Council of the Origin.

Then he reminds me that I have a **boomerang stone** from the Temple of the Sun that makes ascension portals wherever I travel. (It is in my purse so it goes everywhere I go.) After much explanation, I finally understand that I am to gate to every position I've physically been where I stepped into a footprint of one of my genetic or soul lineage aspects. Since there is much information in my levels of consciousness that would support releasing the 4th dimension, all I have to do is choose that the information is in my aura and that it activates when I step into one of those footprints with my stone. After doing this work, I gate back to the Joy Councils.

"Who won the bubble gum contest?"

Tonas asks if I really want to know.

"Did the Swizzlers win that one?"

"Of course they did; they win everything. It was half of a day getting it off of them as well. It was everywhere, and even in their hair."

I tell him I'm sorry. They must have been able to blow some enormous bubbles.

"Gaia, when Sheliah conked me on the head with her wand I didn't think too much about it because the wands we have are just toys. I've been reconsidering and wondering if she actually did gift me with luck."

"Indeed, my dear, she has the power to do so."

Additional luck is welcome, of course, but I already feel like the luckiest woman in all the universes to be able to do what I'm doing.

Before we finish our conversation, I ask Gaia if fairies in any other garden received new body parts. I also want to know if fairies in the different gardens share knowledge. Gaia says Sheliah's garden is the pilot project for testing the new parts. The queens in the gardens do share information but only after many thousands of years. I mention it might be a good idea to have a general meeting in the next few years, but leave that decision up to Gaia.

During a conversation with Isis, I learn these facts about the universes: each universe was named by its Creator; they are arranged within a star tetrahedron but the shapes and positions of it are fluid; within that tetrahedron the universes are all different sizes and shapes.

"But they still fit within the tetrahedron?"

"It will be impossible for this experience to be fully measured within a box, everything is fluid."

"Is it spinning?"

She replies that everything is in motion. Now I ask her if the telescopes we use to look into deep space are capable of looking into another universe.

Thoth enters our conversation by saying that those who are peeking through their telescopes are often looking into other universes. Both of us find this funny. He asks me to imagine that there are windows of glass and I am looking into a room and there is a window of glass leading into another room. "You think you are still looking into the one room, but with the glass clear, as it would be, it appears to be the same room."

It would be interesting to learn how many universes we've been peeking into. I can't imagine how that could be determined, but, of course, I'm not a scientist.

"Osiris, you said that all the stars we see are inhabited. Is that correct?"

He says that is true and that it would be silly to leave one empty of experience.

"Do the stars I see look different on another dimension?"

"There are moons that exist on different dimensions and in others they do not exist *yet*. Different dimensional fields hold different configurations of stars and suns, just as you might imagine that the 3rd dimensional universe, the 20th dimensional universe and the 25th have different stories."

"Some of the science fiction books I've read have creatures that don't breathe oxygen and don't resemble human beings in any way; those beings have entirely different requirements for life than we do. Is that accurate?"

"It can be very accurate. Many stars, many planets, as you call them, have individuals who exist upon them in the form of pure energy. They do not require the feeding of the lungs. What do you think Aton looks like on the 25th dimension?"

I say that I have no idea but I imagine he is beautiful since he's beautiful in this dimension. Osiris says that on the 25th dimension of Earth there will be always sunlight and the Sun itself will create a ring of light that encompasses the full measure of the aura of Earth; all of the colors and the vibrations of those colors will make song.

"When each of you, which are as a petal on the flower of Gaia, reaches your 25th dimension there will be no Sun far away, it will be part of the Earth itself. Because of the marriage in which you blended their two hearts together, they must become one."

My mind struggles to comprehend what it will be like to experience the Sun as part of Earth. I know what he says must be true, but this vision is beyond me now; nevertheless, I thank Osiris for revealing it to me.

The next question I ask is what universe the Folgors exist within. Osiris says that there is an individual from that universe who wishes to petition today.

I actually squeal and say, "Oh joy, oh joy, oh joy! Could this person speak with me, please?"

"Greetings, I am Chief Counsel Choshe Ahsahneeuh. (To decipher this name and all the future ones, I had to grill Tonas repeatedly in privacy.) You are interested in our dancers?"

"They came to our party. I know I'm going to see them dance someday, but I was thrilled even just to hear about their dancing."

"They are of the world Chesseeak and are well known within the Eyeintoreenah Universe."

"Is there something you wished to discuss today other than the Folgors?"

"There is much that we can do to assist in this focus of the union of heart and mind, and we wish to assist because the worlds that are part of our universe focus on the unity of thought. Almost all of our worlds are non-dual."

"If you are asking to join our council, I'm telling you yes."

"We are grateful, for we have the image of what can be created by a collective evolution. We applied this evolution what you would term millions of years ago."

"It sounds like that would be wonderfully beneficial for us and for the other universes that would be interested in it. That must be how the Folgors manage to do their dancing. I remember they said that they were in a flow of one mind."

He terms it "unity of thought" and says he believes their universe can be of assistance. I agree with his assessment and we make arrangements for Liponie to construct their council building.

"True Heart, I know we are transmitting the totem energies to Earth from both the Joy Councils, but I want to also be a transmitter for the totem energies. I was so inspired by talking with Pootie that I thought it might be fun to be able to hear and understand other animals. I also want to radiate any of their energies that would facilitate the work that I am doing. (Yes, I really enjoyed *Doctor Dolittle* books when I was little.)

My particular totem animals are: spider, crow, hawk, fox, squirrel, armadillo, eagle, jaguar and buffalo. I would like for my connection with those animals to be especially enhanced. Can you assist me with that?"

I'm delighted when he says he will transmit the full library to me. Before he does, though, I ask Osiris if there is anything I need to do in order to be able to utilize the information I receive.

Osiris feels that perhaps the armadillo is the strongest of my totem animals. I mention that animal has to do with setting boundaries. He adds that it is also about trust, protection and recognition of some of my reclusive behaviors. It's true that I usually prefer privacy and enjoy being alone.

According to Osiris, I awakened the lizard when I spoke with it in the garden. I say that the information that I've read about lizard says it helps you to look into the future so you can decide what you want to manifest.

Osiris adds that lizards are quite flexible, they adapt very well to circumstances and they can make themselves invisible using camouflage. "They are considered to be by themselves. They do much to keep themselves from harm for there are many who fly above that would make their dinner from them. The lizard is becoming important to you."

I've never heard of a lizard as big as an alligator (Liponie told me that.) so I ask Osiris what kind of lizard Pootie is. He says Pootie is very ancient and that he is an unnamed dinosaur type lizard that was much bigger three million years ago.

"True Heart, can you put the totem information in a form I can comprehend?"

He suggests we call upon the hedgehog. The idea of such a tiny, prickly-seeming creature assisting me is fascinating and I ask how it would help me. True Heart says it would spur my intelligence, my resourcefulness and my intuition. I agree I'd like that kind of assistance and ask him what I need to do.

He offers to work with me on the totems when I'm not addressing the council. I immediately and happily accept and ask if there is anything else I should do. His advice is that I continue to read what the white tribe considers to be the meanings, and then develop beyond that with my own insights.

In order to transmit the totem information to me, True Heart says he will first make it in English. It is an expanded version of fifty thousand years of the greater understanding of totem. "We of the Ohkuhnasha tribes have different beliefs than the modern. You are receiving the full library…and you now have the full measure of this."

He speaks to me in his tribe's language and I answer in what sounds like the same tongue. He tells me that I am now an official Ohkuhnasha.

"Good! I love being one of the people. Thank you, True Heart. I look forward to you tutoring me about the totems."

Yesterday, I heard that there are some codes that are back. Now I ask Charlie if there is anything he can do with that. He says I can bring some of the codes to the council. It takes me a bit of thinking before I remember that the Atlanteans had codes they worked with to ascend and that Aconna Shareeah is an Atlantean on the Joy Council. She is willing to give Charlie all the information about the evolutionary path of the Atlanteans from the 3rd dimension to the 10th dimension. That should be incredibly helpful.

With the addition of the Atlantean codes, it's time to do the transmission. Charlie says that the orbs we got from the galactic councils last night are very important, especially the one about death. He explains that the knowledge I placed in the past when I worked with the boomerang stone was transmitted forward through generations. That raised the vibrations of the different areas I visited and carried forward to the progeny of those whose footprints I stepped in.

Charlie continues by saying that True Heart is helping them with an understanding of the Earth's evolution. He also tells me that Aconna Shareeah lived on Earth as an individual of Atlantis during the time True Heart lived on Earth. "He was a member of the tribes and did not make the transition the Atlanteans did."

There is so much information to compile that Charlie thinks they can use it in two or three different directions. He agrees to be ready with all of that when I'm back in three days.

"We have one piece of many pieces completed. What you brought to us with the three orbs we have already prepared and this can be transmitted. We have also put pieces together from that which you streamed to support the attraction of those energies of knowledge in the past. We have one orb to transmit which will assist these areas."

I move quickly through the very familiar steps of sending out a transmission; however, I have a challenge speaking a language that several times my body insists I vocalize. I mention my difficulty to Tonas and he agrees that there are different configurations of the throat and the voice box that are required to speak as I wished to speak.

"I wanted to speak in much deeper tones."

He says he can speak it for me, but, after making the attempt, he admits he can't do it either.

"What language was I speaking?"

"It was so beautiful. You were speaking the language of Lisseecora."

"When I do something like this would you tell me afterward what I said?"

Tonas agrees to whisper in my ear and then says that Nosahdean was very proud that the transmission also went out to her world in her language. "That was a stroke of genius. You are a great negotiator."

That must have been Osiris at work but I accept Tonas's compliment and add that one day I'll even know what I say. Ever encouraging, he says that of course I will.

As I'm saying farewell to the council, here comes another surprise. Out of my mouth comes a very high-pitched, choppy-sounding language that is very different from the other new one I just spoke. I hope my face doesn't look as astonished as I feel.

Tonas says that Zahseet is smiling because I am speaking her language. Another surprise is that even though I didn't really know what I said, somehow I knew it was in her language.

"She wishes to give you a crown. You must accept it, of course."

"All right, thank you."

She and I now have a conversation in her language. It seems that I am able to be diplomatic in a completely unknown language because she says I am very kind.

CHAPTER SEVENTEEN
November 7, 2014

"Two nights ago I heard, 'I will consider more parts of the Earth, and so you will have no more scratching.'"

Esthra says that this was about my greater vision for Earth and I was tapping into something I was doing as Great Father. "Have you noticed that more things are flowing in and out as you are tapping into these alternate realities that are occurring simultaneously?"

I reply that bits of information like this frequently just confuse me and it would be better if I knew the full context of what I was hearing or doing. Then it occurs to me that knowing everything I am doing would probably be way "over the whelming." Maybe I'm only hearing pieces of information because that's all that I can emotionally handle right now.

"That same night I heard something about, 'So that I can respond to your heart.'"

"This was part of a conversation you were having with Tonas. He does not want to rush you or do anything to push you beyond your timing. He wants to be careful with you because you're not at the place where you could make the choice for yourself that would be the kind of commitment that would mean a lot to both of you. The full meaning of the sentence was that Tonas wants to respond to your heart but he also wants to be cautious because of that same heart. You're not ready and he knows it."

It's a good thing Tonas is patient because I'm not; however, I do appreciate that he's being careful with me. I want to be sure about us and I'm not, yet.

I've been wondering how to help people feel how sweet the release of disempowering beliefs and fears they've been holding onto is and see/feel that there is something so much better to reach for. I know there are now energetic ladders bridging each dimension into the next but there has to be more to do.

Moving into the Fifth Realm with Sananda, I call everyone forward who is safe for me to work with and ask them to give us multiple gifts for themselves: if they've ever prayed for assistance or for answers;

if they ever wished for something different or didn't like some aspect of their lives but didn't know what to ask for or what to do. I suggest that they could give themselves a vision of what the ideal answer or solution would be in each instance. They could ask their angels for extra support, to attach angelic energy to the answers and to light up the paths that would most assist them.

I also suggest they might give us gifts to help them see, feel and know the sweetest paths for them to move gracefully and easily into a higher dimension.

At the Joy Councils, Tonas says, "Greetings to you from my heart."

I return his greeting and ask him if I'm wearing something nice. I've not been feeling well and I am still wearing my pajamas and bath robe.

"You are, and I have a crown of flowers for you."

After thanking him, I ask him if I've ever visited wearing my pajamas.

"There was a time when you wore interesting clothing with holes in it. We see holes in the knees of pants in the media and assumed that you were wearing that fashion."

I don't say that my clothes have holes in them because I've worn them out but I still like them. I do say that sometimes when I come to the council at night I'm wearing my pajamas with little red hearts on them. He assures me that he has not seen me wearing those and that today I look Grecian.

I'm glad Liponie's magic wardrobe presto change-o is working. I don't imagine Tonas would ever complain about anything I wore, but I'm definitely glad I'm showing up appropriately dressed.

With Aton before we join the council:

After he greets me, I say, "Last night I was asking you about the two final spheres I haven't received yet and I believe you said, 'They are like systems that will erase outdated technology.' Is that correct?"

"This is one function. They become so bright that the old technology will not be able to be seen."

"What is it that the twenty-seven spheres in my aura are doing?"

"These are moving and exciting the orbs of creation energy that are within everything around you. They are supporting your physical body and they are preparing you for a time when you will not require them. As for all of the other non-dual masters, they will be part of instantaneous creation. They are sharpening your senses."

I agree that will definitely be helpful and thank him.

With the full Joy Councils:

After everyone is seated, (Yes, Tonas is still directing the up and down.) I say good afternoon and add that, as usual, I have a few questions.

"Who told me, 'Life has been a balance of joy and sorrow, but it won't always be.'?"

I hear Marilyn's voice acknowledge those were her words. As soon as she says that, I begin crying; my father is now in the hospital.

"You have had an experience of your life that was very trying, and as someone who has had similar experiences it is the joy that awaits you that you must focus upon and not all of the old stories that are holding you back from a brighter vision, my dear."

I tell her I really don't want to talk about any old stories because I'm struggling to deal with my father's ill health.

She says the council is aware of my father and is holding the candle high for him. "He is nearing the time when he will be joining us. We will ask him to be on the council, of course."

I really can't picture working with my dad on the council. I think I only managed to persuade him two or three times during his life that he was wrong about something. My comment to Marilyn is that would be an interesting experience for me because he is very strong-willed. She replies that the human is.

It takes me some moments to collect myself, but eventually I begin questioning Osiris in the hopes of finding out if there are more suns with Earth-like planets on different dimensions.

"As I'm looking out at the stars at night, am I seeing just dimensions four through seven?"

(The people of Earth are divided among these dimensions. Some are in only one of those dimensions while others might be in a blend of more than one dimension.)

Osiris says that I am seeing the stars through veils and reminds me that since I am embracing only the 6th and the 7th dimensions, I only see the stars in those dimensions. Then he says that they are the same stars seen by those in the lower and higher dimensions. Finally, he tells me that a good exercise for me to do would be to ground myself in the 6th through the 25th dimensions in order to witness the stars with the flavors of those dimensions.

"What if I put myself in the 8th dimension?"

"This is what I am speaking of. If you put your feet in the 6th, 7th, 8th and all the way to the 25th, you will witness the same stars and yet the flavors and colors would be different in each dimension."

"I thought you said that different dimensions had different stars."

"The stars do not change in the higher dimensions; it is you who changes. Let me give you the example of Giza; it was a three sphinx complex. The Atlanteans moved two of them to the 5th dimension and then onward; they now reside on the 10th dimension. Had they been left in place, those that transitioned to the 5th dimension would have found the exact same three sphinx complex there."

"I was just trying to get around the fact that our astronomers are not finding the suns or planets that they believe will support life. Of course, you said that there are planets where beings do not have physical bodies but are just energy."

"There are many layers of dimensions. I can tell you that if someone from the 21st dimension, from somewhere else, were looking at Earth, they would see no people on Earth. Because you have anchored your energy to the higher dimensions, you would be able to see the trees and waters all the way to the 25th dimension but you will see no buildings. It will look as if no one is alive on those dimensions until you arrive at the 10th dimension. Once you are within that dimension, then all the implements from the academy tutorials and two of the sphinx plus much that was associated with Earth's advancement that the Atlanteans took with them can be witnessed in that 10th dimensional frame where they currently exist. When you look upon a dimension, and you are not of that dimension, you cannot see into it."

"Is there something outside of the cluster of universes?"

Osiris answers that the one place that exists outside of the universes is called the Origin. I had a feeling he would say that. I ask him if there were universes that existed before the current group of universes and he says there was nothing.

"All there was in existence was the collective oneness of the essence of Creator. Imagine that there are no masculine or feminine genders. All there is, you call this God, is the God and the great experiences of the God. Then within the great expanse of that experience there was a spark that put its little feeler out and said, 'I have an idea for an experience that will advance your grand experience. I shall become in great oneness of self with a balance of a different flavor.'

God said, 'Ah, this would be a wonderful experience that I could have. Please do so my son, my daughter; go out and have your experience, take this dollar and a fishing pole...' Here Osiris laughs. '...and make your way.' From that point was the beginning of the Origin. We all came from that one spark and the flavor of it grew to become that essence of balance between the masculine and feminine. It had never been done before; it was an original thought. This story was played for a very long time. There are not enough numbers to encompass how long it would take to create the vision of how long the Origin was and all that played out within it before our journey began."

"Would you speak a little more about the nature of the beings that created the universes? Did they come through Lyra?"

"There were forty-seven that moved through that pinhole of light. One came through who spawned the seed of my beloved and I. Forty-four of those who moved through the pinhole became universe builders. They scattered throughout the universes creating worlds that have evolved to a non-dual state and some have not. Those forty-four bore the seeds of duality; my beloved and I do not. (The unaccounted for individual represents the neutral lineage, while Osiris and Isis represent the masculine and feminine lineages.) We were very much involved in creating and supporting this universe. We had much assistance; it was not only our 'wand' that was being moved around to create. It is truly the evolution of remembering the self that draws that spark of neutrality that is embraced fully. My beloved and I never lost sight of the sweetness of that neutrality."

"Did they have names?"

"They do have names; they are considered to be forever living, as myself. We are eternals, as you call us, because we are embracing the full neutrality of the non-dual. We have not written degradation and death into our existence so there shall be none."

"Are eternals the same as immortals?"

"Yes, it is impossible for us to die."

I don't think he wants to tell me their names and I'm not going to ask again. I've had about all the esoteric knowledge I can handle for today anyway, and I finish our conversation by thanking him for the information.

"True Heart, this morning I heard you talking with me about an animal which you said could guide me to the fullest measure of my strength. What animal were you referring to?"

He says he was speaking about the badger because it is strong-willed and determined. I feel like I already possess much determination, but I guess more can't hurt.

I ask True Heart if he knows what Pootie and I are talking about. He says we are communicating telepathically in the language of the lizard. I've been enjoying this lizard's energy so much I find myself wanting to pet him.

"Gaia, how did Pootie come to be in the fairy garden? Was he killed and the fairies brought him into it?"

She says that there are layers upon layers that have been created within the dimensional fields for specific species that are choosing to remain as part of Earth history. "These have special tasks to support the evolving Earth. Pootie is a species of the dinosaur. There was a time when the job of Pootie and others would have been erased from Earth. He is low to the ground and all that he is anchoring is very important, and so there is a garden for these."

Gaia reminds me I can meet Pootie in person when I'm on the 8th dimension.

I explain to Charlie, and the core group, the work we did in the Fifth Realm before I came to the council and ask them if they noticed anything. He says that all in the council felt it and some of the tribesmen were part of receiving the work.

"I felt like it would really help so I'm glad you did notice a change."

"We love your flowers."

"Oh! Tonas put them on my head but I don't know who made them."

Tonas says he went with Gaia to our garden to make the ring of flowers. Charlie says the Swizzlers would also like to have some of these and asks Liponie if they can have a project. I tell him they are welcome to the flowers in the garden.

I ask Gaia if we can do anything with the honey bee. She says they are no longer welcome on Earth and they are moving into the fairy gardens to be released back into the Earth at the right time.

I am really glad to learn that. I have wanted to do something to prevent their deaths but haven't been able to figure out what to do. I explain that what I meant to ask was if there is a way to use the honey of the bee to enhance the sweet paths people are being shown.

"The reality is that I and all parts of me are of the purest of sweetness. When one allows themselves to recognize the sweetness of this world, then you recognize the greatest sweetness of self, for truly you cannot separate the one from the other. There is the feeling that Earth is in trouble, that Earth is angry and striking back when there is a quake or fires or a volcano. These are simply part of the experiences of the body of us, just as a pimple on the face of a teenager is not a representation that they are bad or angry at their face or body. It is simply a part of the function of the hormones."

"There are all kinds of concerns about global warming and pollution. People are frightened about a lot of different possibilities."

"That is their story. It is the flavoring between the chapters. Soon there will be no fears such as these, my dear."

Her assurance is wonderful to hear. That reality can't come too soon for me.

Charlie informs me that the things we talked about last time are perfected; there are more than a million pieces in the configuration including an expansion on the concept of death. He adds there is no reason for death but there are those who still desire this to be their reality. I know he's right. Some people look at me very strangely when I mention that death will become strictly optional.

"Let's put it in place then. Is there a sphere or an orb?"

"I put it in my tooth."

I'm laughing and completely befuddled as I ask him if he is giving up his tooth.

"I like the look of the jack-o'-lantern, and I am not using the tooth so I thought I could use it as something to instill. It is like a little pocket. When you have something you are not using, it is possible to find other uses for it. It is called recycling."

I agree that recycling is a good thing but the only way I know to do that for teeth is when children put them under their pillow for the tooth fairy. As this explanation is coming out of my mouth I can't believe I'm telling Charlie this story. I feel like putting my hands over my mouth to keep from saying the words, but I've already said them. I lamely finish by agreeing to use his tooth if he wants to contribute it.

"It is a good vessel and we can use it over and over again. I have all the teeth I pulled out of my mouth in my pocket except for this one. I may put them back later but for now I like the jack-o'-lantern's look. This tooth is hollowed and the package to be released to the Earth and beyond is within it."

I ask him to place it on the table. Tonas whispers to me that he thinks Charlie is a little confused about recycling and offers to do research about it that perhaps will help Charlie. I whisper a request to do that right away.

In my regular voice, I ask the council to focus their attention on Charlie's tooth with the transmission in it. The languages I use to begin this transmission and several places during it sound like the ones I used last session when I was speaking to Nosahdean and Zahseet. As I feel the transmission move out through the Joy Arrows to Earth I say, "I hope that all of you enjoy the sweetness of your lives because if they are not sweet they can be, if you choose, very sweet and very lovely."

Tonas informs me that Liponie has completed the council buildings for Nosahdean, Zahseet, Fractinuta and Choshe Ahsahneeuh and asks me if I'd like to do the inaugurations today. I agree to do that many if I can do expedited versions and he prompts me as I go. He says he will be happy to do that and adds that Zahseet's council is beneath big waters. (I learn later that she is able to walk gracefully around on a fish tail instead of legs. And I thought it was hard to maneuver in high heels.)

He also reassures me that I won't have to worry about breathing underwater because I'm going to be within something. I know Zahseet doesn't need to be in the water all the time because I've talked with her at the council. I saw her face there the other day. She was very interesting looking and had a little crown on her head.

Before we begin this round of inaugurations, I remind Tonas to cue me at each place. I'm already feeling a little fuzzy from the work we've done, and I don't want to get names wrong like last time.

To begin, I take his hand and gate with him to each of the universes starting with Nosahdean's universe of Lisseecora, followed by Zahseet's Zhorin Universe, Fractinuta's Ackvidohnon Universe and Choshe Ahsahneeuh's Eyeintoreenah Universe. At each place I greet the council, activate the sword and crystal on their table and the transmitting device on top of their building, transmit all of the work we have done for Earth to their universe (It's calibrated to be appropriate for each universe.) and thank them for joining our fellowship of the one tribe.

In each universe I find myself speaking what sounds like several different languages. The toast we drink in Zahseet's universe is, according to Tonas, a sacred elixir from the fountains of Loree which are located in their high mountains.

Tonas says that the Eyeintoreenah Universe will be celebrating for days after the inauguration and that the Folgor dancers are present. Before we begin the inauguration, I ask Choshe Ahsahneeuh (Choshe) if Doshie is present. He replies that Liponie made sure he would be present.

I wave to him and Choshe tells me Doshie is waving his hands back to me. After the inauguration, Choshe says I am welcome in all parts of their universe. He asks me to be present regularly at their council and says they are grateful for the opportunity to serve.

Tonas reminds me that we must stay to see the Folgor dancers, and so, for the second time, I am grateful to experience the feel of their performance. When they are done, I promise myself that one day I will experience their dancing with *all* of my senses.

Back at the Joy Councils, Tonas says that everyone was able to witness the inaugurations. I want to know if I said the appropriate words at each place. He sounds puzzled when he assures me I was perfection in itself.

"Can you tell me a couple of things I said that you thought were nice?"

"You were very complimentary to Nosahdean's world and to all of the people in the council. You welcomed them from your heart and said you wished them to know that this is a collaboration, not a dictatorship with you directing. The message you gave to each of these councils is that the true measure of our connection is one of heart."

I'm always surprised after I finish chattering away in a new language that presents itself. It's good to know that *some* part of me knows what it is saying.

"Charlie, two days ago I had the sensation of amplifying all the work we've done. What did I actually do?"

"In viewing, I can see that that which has been in place for quite some time, and even the new works, were transmitted from your deepest heart. There is a very bright light that is a part of your consciousness that was amplifying these timeless potentials and possibilities."

"What is the bright light?"

"There is within your consciousness a very bright light of awareness that sparks for reasons that you define. If you have a very important decision about something, you open up this consciousness and that which is within that consciousness that supports this transmission of amplification is lit like a sun. It is very much part of that which has been activated by your certain works that have been put in place. You have a very busy ethereal body."

"I wonder if I need more of it here because this physical body is feeling very tired."

"Your ethereal is in constant motion now supporting the physical, mental, emotional and all parts of yourself."

"Thank you, Charlie."

"Jesus, do you have anything I can tell my dad?"

"My dear, most individuals believe that they must meet some dedication in order to be accepted into the heavens. Please tell your dear, sweet father that I am beside him and will lead him into the land of promise. I will do this for him and I will stay beside your mother until her time. This will mean something to them; I am of great stature for them."

"Yes, you've always been the man for them. Thank you for your help. I'm saying goodbye to the council."

In privacy with Tonas, I admit that I'm having a great deal of difficulty dealing with my parents' ill health. He says he wishes to minister to me, to hold and soothe me and asks me to return. Hoping this will help, I agree to do so.

CHAPTER EIGHTEEN

November 11, 2014

Tonas greets me then says it has been somewhat wild and crazy. Feeling slightly alarmed, I ask if there's something I need to know about.

"There are many preparations for a big feast and already the decorations are being strewn about for a Christmas celebration. This is a holiday that is quite well-known on Earth."

Since the stores here seem to advertise Christmas and Thanksgiving almost simultaneously, I make a stand and say that we must celebrate Thanksgiving first. He says that is the feast we are preparing for and the Indians are very much involved in it.

"You must be riding your bicycle because I heard your bike ringer in my left ear yesterday."

Very proudly he says of course he is and he has *no* extra wheels.

"Oh, that's exciting! I was going to tell you that it's better to go faster sometimes because if you go too slow you get wobbly."

"We are involved in, not races, but it is quite spirited riding. Liponie has made us a track. There is also a different kind of bicycle I have not tried yet that does stunts. The Swizzlers are very much involved."

I agree there are bikes you can do all kinds of twists and turns with and add that some bicyclists can ride down the street without holding the handlebars. Then I realize I should not have mentioned this and immediately ask him not to try it. He makes the point that if we say anything to the Swizzlers about it they are sure to try it. I promise to keep quiet about riding with no hands.

Tonas wants to know if the little tassels on the handles have a purpose. I say that they are just for decoration and that usually only kids have those on their bicycles.

"We have little baskets."

"Those are handy to put things in if you go shopping."

"Shopping? You are confusing me, my dear."

"If you take your bicycle to the store and buy a few things, you put the items in your basket so you don't have to hold them in your hands."

This statement is met with a few moments of silence during which I can feel the light bulb go on for Tonas.

"Ah, so this is… Ah! This makes so much sense to me now. I have been keeping my bell in this."

"No, no! It goes on the handlebar so you can ring it when you want people to get out of your way."

More silence…followed by, "I see. I have also been keeping the helmet in the basket. I think this helmet is not necessary; I am sticking very close to the path."

I tell him that is his decision, but where I live it's a rule that you have to wear a helmet when riding a bike.

"Osiris, two days ago I heard you say, 'You are straining, my dear. Let us move beyond that.' Then you gave me a whole download of information but the only word I could discern was 'Galilee.' What was that about?"

"It is almost as if you are forcing your abilities to be achieved more swiftly than the natural course of this. With all that Aton has activated within you this shall be a graceful transition, and so, I gave you a sedative."

I burst into laughter and he laughs with me. Then I ask if he downloaded me with some boring information about Galilee.

"This is a story about trust. Jesus had walked upon the waters and others wished to also step on the waters. He was instructing them how to do so. Of course, he learned how to do this somewhere else than in his mother's arms. These individuals were stepping on the energy he laid for them and their lack of trust made it so there was more flailing and fighting of the energies. It is easy for you, my dear, to simply trust what is."

I vehemently disagree with this advice. "Trust and faith don't interest me. I really just want to know. I have worked on this issue, but, obviously, it's still an issue."

Osiris chuckles and says there is no manner of energies that can keep me from what is to be. He adds that I might as well trust it. I suppose this is good advice, but it doesn't appeal to me at all.

"Does each universe have forty-seven lineages?"

"Everything that exists is part of that pool of lineages. They are spread evenly throughout all universes. The beginning was an explosion of creating, and there was no concern of what lineage of the soul an individual created for their experience. It is not the body of the individual that makes the choice; the soul chooses the lineage for the body. It is not differentiated that a universe must only have souls from a certain lineage. It is simply one great big journey; all is part of the great circle."

"From what you are telling me it seems that all the universes came through Lyra."

Instead of answering yes or no, Osiris says that everything began in the same moment.

"The other issue that is of concern to me is the languages that I am speaking. Tonas has assured me I'm doing just fine and that I haven't said anything I shouldn't. But words are just pouring out of me and I have no idea what I'm saying. That feels very awkward for me."

"Nearly every human being who is speaking the Language of Light, or love or an angelic language, is speaking it without a dictionary. Some have an understanding of what they are speaking. I think the great wonder will be when an individual creates the dictionary."

I'm impressed with my 10th dimensional self when Osiris comments that that part of me can speak directly to an individual in their own language.

Speaking privately with Aton, I ask if he was the one who told me that my fluid connection with the orbs will help me to understand nearly everything he talks about. He says he was and that this is already working.

"The transmissions will continue to flow and you will feel a tremendous recognition that begins to build upon itself. I believe that there will be less of the questioning and more of the knowing in the days ahead. All that which is within your ethereal is now connecting with the orbs which are cycling through the fluid space of your aura. Each of the conduits is in fluid energy streams. I believe that you enjoy these."

"I must, but I still have plenty of questions. I really would like to feel smarter, Aton."

"Oh, we see you as such a genius."

I comment that I don't feel any smarter than I've ever been but he says that is a fallacy.

"I should *feel* like I'm smarter, shouldn't I, like I know more?" Now I feel like crying and realize I'd better change the subject before I do.

"I feel that you are dissatisfied with something. How can we assist you?"

"I don't know that there's anything else any of you can do at this time. Maybe this is just something I need to wade through."

It's too bad he agrees that is the answer; I had hoped he would mention another option.

My greeting to the council is, "Hello and ho, ho, ho. Please, can we have Thanksgiving and the winter solstice before we have Christmas?"

Liponie assures me that we have all of these things in place. "It was little Charlie's idea as well as the other parts of their collective. They are quite unified when they make their foot down that they wish for something. They say in the supers market as well as in the stores there is already Christmas and so it must take place here!"

I still maintain my belief that you shouldn't have your Christmas tree out before Thanksgiving dinner. Liponie reminds me how beautiful Christmas is and I give in.

"OK, you can have anything you want in the way of decorations for however long you want, but Thanksgiving is important. I hope you've done the research on the first Thanksgiving so that maybe we can do a re-enactment of that. Then we can eat all day long with more traditional foods."

Tonas says the native individuals are working on this with Liponie.

"Liponie, do you come to Earth to get ingredients and then bring them back here to fix things?"

"Sometimes I do! And many times it is easy to use my wily ways, of course. I am a genie."

Now I am inspired to request one of my favorite dishes that can be found in Indiana in the fall, persimmon pudding. I offer Liponie my Grandmother Crystal's recipe for it, but he says he will do research.

"Charlie, will you tell me more about the 'bright light of awareness' that is within me?"

"The bright light of awareness within you is the spark of your genius that is aside of your spark of the essence of self. This spark is part of the physical body that exists as particles and light; it is an emanation that can be felt and even seen by those with the gift of the sight."

"It's the spark of my genius you said?"

"It is the spark of your genome, the history passed from your ancestors, and your genius. It is associated with an amplified version that occurs when the essence of the Great Spirit enters your body. This amplification becomes ever brighter; it is your true spirit. This is the part of you that never leaves. If your body was to die, this spark of your individuality would, in its connection with your soul, transition into the next frame of your existence.

When the body dies or ascends, the individual part of self that blends with the soul essence brings the individual into the next stage of evolution. It is not that you ascend and your soul moves through its perfection, it is you, your mind, your individuality, your spark that is so bright, and you are blinding... You do not believe me."

"It's not so much that I don't believe you; it's that I don't understand what you're saying. I was just saying to Aton that I wanted to be smarter."

"Ah, we consider you to be one of the great minds."

"I just feel like I'm really struggling to understand things that I want to understand. It's not easy."

"This will come very soon. Eat more apples."

I appreciate this humorous advice and thank him for it.

(I believe two things are contributing to my frustration and lack of understanding: I have always had difficulty with understanding auditory instructions, and nobody here speaks English. By that I mean, what I can say in ten words, everyone here needs a minimum of twenty words and forty words seems to be the average. Except in Osiris's case it's more like eighty words.)

During a discussion with the council about releasing the 4th dimension, I mention that although we have attempted to address religious issues we haven't done much about nationalistic principles such as: this is our territory and don't come here; you're not the right kind of people to be here; or there are too many people coming here; each country has its boundaries and stay out!

Mr. Kennedy answers, "And they are being called to battle with one another throughout the world. They are fighting instead of being. The fighting of tyranny, the fighting of poverty, the fighting of disease, all of this is truly a war within itself. When individuals stop fighting, that is when there will be truly the freedom of heart."

I answer that I don't want to denigrate individuals who have joined a branch of the service, but I don't want my sons to go to war.

"I was not in favor of anyone ever going to war, and yet, we were called to arms. My belief is the same. That we should not ask what all of us can do for them, it is they who must raise their standards so that they can do for themselves and the world. That is what we are supporting with our works here, the one tribe. We are holding that light high so that the energy and the faith and the devotion that can be brought into the hearts of individuals can be lit again as a flame within them. The people of the world have forgotten themselves."

"Thank you Mr. Kennedy. Charlie, can you do anything with what we've been talking about?"

"I have been listening very carefully. I believe that there is a belief that God will fix things and that if you pray all will be made right. Perhaps it is time for people to know that the God of that miracle is within themselves."

"Is there a representative of another universe who wished to speak with me today?"

Tonas answers that there is a very interesting individual named Ihroenees who is an emissary from the Sehhoetica Universe. I welcome him to our council meetings and ask him to forgive me for not repeating his name, explaining that I will need to practice pronouncing it.

"How may we assist you?"

"My greetings to you, I am the Emissary Ihroenees. There is a full council of us here requesting to your pleasure adding us to your council."

I reply that I would love to have them join our council and if their building is done on Friday I can do their inauguration then.

"We are most grateful. All of our stars and worlds are of duality and so we do have a ways to go. This will be of great assistance to us to be part of your affiliation."

I'm ready to leave, but Tonas asks to speak with me in privacy first.

I first ask Tonas if Liponie has done anything with the food rooms. (Some time ago Hathor requested that we always have cake available. An idea I completely supported, of course, and I asked Liponie to make desserts always available.) Tonas says much pie is being eaten and there are new treats every day. He also says there is a room full of marshmallows, things to dip them into and even ways to melt them.

I wish I could have seen the look on Osiris's face when he walked into that room. I bet his grin went from ear to ear.

Tonas now describes Ihroenees as being incredibly tall, a very beautiful green color and instead of hair he has a feathered bird head. I don't believe I have ever been more surprised. All I can think to say is, "My goodness."

"He is quite beautiful although he is wearing clothing and I cannot see what is under it."

Tonas doesn't know if Ihroenees has wings because he is completely covered with clothes; he even has gloves on his hands. Both of us think he is trying to appear human. I suggest we invite him to meet with us privately and Tonas does so telepathically.

After Ihroenees joins us, I explain to him that I don't usually see what is in front of me because, although my energy body is here, my physical body is on Earth's 6th and 7th dimensions. He says that he understands, but my lack of vision is not really relevant.

"It is! Tonas just told me these wonderful things about your appearance. You are green and your head is that of a bird."

"Yes, does this offend you?"

"No! I'm very excited. Even though we are one tribe, I really want to celebrate the diversity of all the beings that come to our council. Please feel free to dress or not dress as you do in your universe. I've already told people that it's not necessary for them to learn English which is the language I speak."

"Oh, but you are speaking my language."

"But to me I'm speaking the English language. Osiris is translating for us."

"I see."

"I hope I'm not being rude, but may I ask if you wear the clothes that you currently have on in your universe?"

"No, we do not."

"May I ask if you have wings?"

"Indeed."

"Oh, how beautiful you must be." I feel my eyes fill with tears at the thought that Ihroenees felt he must hide his appearance from us.

"You accept me?"

"Oh, I want to see you! You must be gorgeous. You see, humans dream of flying. I would love to see your whole group of people discard the clothes, unless you want to wear them."

"They are quite constrictive."

"I have to wear clothes because of social rules, plus it gets very cold on Earth, but you could just say goodbye to clothes."

"Will the others accept me?"

Tonas asks to speak and I welcome his input.

"Dear emissary, you come from a dual world and my beloved very much knows what that is, for Earth has been a dual world from its inception. Please know that everyone of this council is either an ascended being or they are of non-dual. It is impossible for them to be of anything except the greatest delight at your presence however you wish to appear.

You noticed the dear, thin, little people with the colored hair? These individuals have become from a collective, individual within themselves. You can see that they are quite unique in their dress and in their actions and we love them for that uniqueness. They are the first of their kind and they are lovely. How, too, can there be anything less for you? We accept you and all of the beings of your world as part of our tribe."

"I am of speechless. I will report this to all within what you call my universe. This is what we aspire to achieve within our very selves; that advancement which allows us the pleasure of the purity of self. The awareness of that is our greatest privilege to learn from all of you. We are ever grateful to be a part of this council and also to become acceptable as we are."

"I can't wait to see your beautiful feathers. Tonas, thank you so much for your eloquence in explaining that we really enjoy the uniqueness of everyone here."

CHAPTER NINETEEN

November 14, 2014

My curiosity bump has been itching to know more about Ihroenees and I've decided to scratch it by inviting him to speak with me in private. Through a series of tactful, I hope, questions, here's what I learn. There are many different species, including humanoid and aquatic ones in his universe. The name for his species is Homa and although there are many species of Homa, they are all two-legged and with wings. They come in many different colors, are considered to be quite educated and they only fly during ceremonial occasions. (I was a little disappointed to learn that.)

Their young hatch from an egg which the parents watch over and care for. I find it humorous when Ihroenees says we are kinsmen in this since, he reminds me, I also came from an egg.

The Homa do not live in trees, but their homes are made out of tree branches. Ihroenees resides in a very large home with his mate, Shashirah and their sixty-one children. I'm surprised by that large number. I'm also surprised that they are adults when they are twelve years old and they only live fifty or sixty years.

"Is there anything else you'd like to tell me about the Homa?"

"We are very pleased to have this opportunity. There is even more of a passion for this fellowship for it is in our belief that he who shall become a part of this affiliation shall become forever living."

"Yes, that's right."

"You seem to be ageless yourself."

"I'm considered to be past middle age for a human being and this part of me that's talking to you from this 6th and 7th dimension does not look anything like the me that you are seeing. My body is not the way I want it to be yet, but I am told that it will be and that is exciting news for me."

"So you have the same vision for yourself as I do since I am of forty-five cycles. Our cycles (years) are a little longer than yours, and yet at forty-five cycles I have only a short time left. I am choosing to erase that reality using SVH."

(Sananda has been teaching SVH to anyone who wishes to learn it.)

"I am a practitioner of that modality and I congratulate you."

I have been waiting to share with Ihroenees my love of birds and their feathers, and now seems like a good time to mention that I have some feathers on display in my office. Ihroenees wants to know how I removed them from the birds. I explain that birds here periodically lose their feathers and grow new ones; when I see them on the ground I pick them up.

"I was only interested in the ritual if it was of deflocking. We are considered to be quite magical and there are beings that come to our place of living and capture some of our Homa."

"Would you like those returned?"

"Explain please."

"Earth had lots of creatures that were taken to other worlds. We had a way where instead of actually taking our creatures the people took holograms of them instead of the real creature."

"What magic is this?"

"It's something we can do using SVH."

"We would be forever grateful. There are other stars and planets that have this same issue. The individuals of the human species wish to have our coats, for they are considered to be magic."

Ihroenees explains that they are killed for their feathers since they only release when a Homa is dead. He asks me if he is supposed to do something to assist us with returning the missing Homa. I say that will not be necessary and release him back to the council.

Private meeting with Liponie about Christmas presents:

I have a Honeycrisp apple for Osiris since he has been such an important teacher for me. Liponie assures me that he can make it so that it won't spoil. I can even eat it and still be able to give it to Osiris since people at the council are only consuming the energy of food. I don't understand how that works yet, but it's a bonus to be able to give a gift and still eat it. Sort of like giving your cake and eating it too... .

My idea for a present for Charlie is a train. I offer Liponie the option of making a miniature one or one that Charlie could actually ride in. Liponie says he's most excited to create it, he has the size in mind and he's going to make it so that it won't need to stay on a track. It's so wonderful to have a genie in house; shopping is effortless, or rather, unnecessary.

With the full council, Tonas informs me that a woman named Plany Ohsheer, an emissary from the Nordahnee Universe, wishes to speak with me. I address her and ask if she's interested in joining our council.

"If you will accept us, all of our inhabited worlds and stars are of dual. It will be a great task to bring them all into the vision of what you have even at present."

"I am not daunted by what you tell me. Be assured that all of us welcome you with no judgment about any of the challenges that you face, because on Earth we face them also."

She shares that they are busy selecting people to be on their council and they intend to have an emissary from each of their inhabited systems. I thank her for stepping forward and explain that as soon as Liponie has constructed their building we will do their inauguration.

I ask Osiris if we can restore the Homa taken from Ihroenees's world back to their homes. He replies it will be a pleasure to do this but adds that many worlds in the Sehhoetica Universe have had their winged ones stolen. We can restore them during the inauguration but first we will need to connect with the essences of all who were taken in order to get their permission to replace them with holograms for the thieves to take.

It takes Charlie about fifteen seconds to connect with the essence of every stolen Homa. Our plan is, as we enter their universe, to send out a transmission requesting approval to use the holograms.

I thank Charlie and get ready to inaugurate Ihroenees's council. Before I can gate anywhere, Tonas says there is something wrong with Ihroenees and suggests we meet with him in private. I mention that maybe he's just happy, but Tonas says he doesn't appear to be so.

Privately with Ihroenees, Tonas, Osiris and myself:

Tonas asks if we have done something to offend Ihroenees and asks him to give us counsel.

"I… I am overcome for two of my own were once taken. To imagine this I cannot even allow myself to have the faith in it for I am in fear of being disappointed. I believe that my heart and the heart of my dear one will break if it is not so. I cannot tell her."

"I used a similar process to restore many creatures stolen from Earth so I think it will work for you. Osiris, will you speak with him?"

Osiris asks Ihroenees to have his mate and all of his children with him for the inauguration of their council. He requests that Ihroenees keep our plan secret and asks him to have faith in our project.

He also suggests that Ihroenees invites parents from all of the realms within his constituency who have lost children and not tell them why they have been invited. He asks Liponie to make an area for these guests and their children.

"It will be a grand reunion for your realm when the missing ones who are alive today are restored in your council chambers. This will inspire every corner of your universe."

"I am without words. But you may believe me that my words will be spoken at the culmination of this event, and I am grateful."

I learn from Ihroenees that their Joy Council chambers are on the highest peak of his world. Osiris explains that when we enter their universe Liponie has the ability to offer individuals a stopped moment of time in order to make their decision and he will also transport them all to the council.

In the Sehhoetica Universe, Ihroenees introduces me to his beloved mate, Sahshirah. She greets me and thanks me for including their children on this momentous occasion.

I can't resist asking her what color her feathers are and she asks me if I'm blind. I explain that she's seeing my ethereal presence.

"Oh, you are a transmission. You feel so very real!"

"I guess I am, but I'm not. It's confusing for me."

"Ah, you are quite beautiful. I am… What is my color, dear?"

Ihroenees says she is more than just blue. Tonas says that in Earth vernacular she is a beautiful azure color.

"I know I'm going to see you one day so I'm just trying to imagine right now how beautiful you are… Anyway, we are here to do your inauguration! I'm saying hello to all your council members. Tonas, are they all different colors?"

"Indeed, it is a very colorful group. I have in my hand the special sphere from our dear Charlie that you can apply after."

I describe what I'm doing as I move through the steps of energizing their sword and cone. I explain that the work we've done for Earth has been calibrated for their worlds and universe and ask them to assist me with their hearts and their love to send the transmission to every corner of their universe.

Tonas now asks Ihroenees how many stars and planets are in this universe. Ihroenees answers that there are forty-seven million inhabited stars and planets and nearly half of them are home of the Homa.

Tonas directs the Homa who have a special invitation to step into the main council chamber along with their children. He whispers to me that Liponie is stretching the room. Then he says, "Through the heart and the spirit of this council there is a gift for each of you. Each of you has lost something and it is within the power of this council to restore it."

I activate the special sphere and transmit it out to this universe.

Tonas whispers, "Oh, my dear," and I hear someone give a very long excited-sounding speech in what must be the Homa language. Tonas says in a shaken voice that he is overcome. He reports that Liponie seems to be unaffected and is serving champagne. "Ah, he is seeing the joy in this, of course. I think you may give a magnificent toast, my dear."

"This is to the one tribe and to your reunion with your loved ones. I drink to you, to your universe and to your participation in our evolution together. Joy forever."

Ihroenees asks to speak, and, of course, I give him permission.

"As you will hear me in this language, the others hear me in their own languages. It was the inspiration for us to step into a role that would join the councils affiliated throughout many universes. It was our desire to help others, but our full mind was to help ourselves. These beings of this council are of great power; you have witnessed it today. They have shown us that to be a part of a tribe, a one tribe, is not to be self-serving; it is to be individuals within a group of one.

I pledge today and I pledge with all my heart for all of you that each of you will come to this same feeling of unity that I have burst within the very heart in my chest in this moment. This is a commitment to assist our worlds, and through that also, all that exists within all of the dimensions, whether they are a part of our council or they are not. Today we commit to the vision of the one tribe as our tribes are now restored to our families. We are ever so grateful and we bow to your power."

Too overcome to continue, he stops for a moment then finishes by saying, "We shall live up to this commitment and we give you our hearts as well as that commitment. May I raise my glass in toast and thank Liponie, whose great power has made possible each of you to be here so that we could all witness. Take this vision back with you to all corners of our universe, whether you are of Homa or you are not. We are of one tribe. I raise my glass now to that tribe."

After we drink the toast, Ihroenees tells me I am welcome there always. I promise that I will return one day when I can see really see them.

In privacy back at the council, Tonas repeats that he was quite overcome and that this was great work. "I do not think there was anyone there who was not tearful with joy and also in celebration. The only ones who were not tearful were Liponie and Osiris. How can either of you be unaffected?"

Liponie answers that he was as overcome as the rest; he simply hid it well.

With the full Joy Council:

"Two days ago I heard someone say they might try to tell me something. Will that person speak to me, please, and tell me what they wanted say?"

"Yes, thank you. I am Emissary Plany Ohsheer and I wish to tell you that our worlds are at war. It is not the beautiful ceremony I have just witnessed that perhaps you will experience at our inauguration. There might even be those who would wish to thwart that collaboration."

"I don't have any concerns about that. We have some technologies that will keep us safe."

She asks how their council chambers can be kept safe. I ask Osiris to explain, but he turns that task over to Liponie who announces he is now a Level Two SVH Practitioner.

I'm completely surprised and excited that Liponie now has the tools of SVH at his disposal. After congratulating him and blowing him a kiss, I ask him to explain for Emissary Ohsheer what he plans to do.

"We will have a hologram in place that looks as if your Joy Council has been bombed to oblivion. It will look as if there is nothing but dirt and ashes. There will even be a crater beneath. But there will be no harm come to you or to anyone affiliated.

Perhaps we can create a special transport for those from different stars and planets who are making their way into this council. I will work with Sananda on this. There was something from your ancient academies where you could step on a plate and be immediately where you wished to go."

"Please know that if anyone requires protection, simply bring this to the council's attention and we will make preparation."

I didn't recognize the voice of that speaker so I ask who it was. I'm surprised and impressed when Tonas says it was him. He sounded much more authoritative than he usually does. Later he explains that was his commander voice.

"I got something about a vision for an alliance of the 4th dimension with the 3rd dimension. Is there a council that would help us with that?"

Osiris answers that this is a tricky business and that there seems to be tremendous resistance to releasing the 4th dimension. He feels that damage might be done by pressing the issue. "There is so much resistance now that it is almost creating waves of very disturbing rippling energies. This is of concern."

I ask Choshe Ahsahneeuh if he has any ideas to share with us.

"I am in favor of the graceful approach. It is somewhat disconcerting to see the action of the Earth as if it is rippling. I have seen this before and it can be quite dangerous. Most of the non-dual worlds within my universe elevated collectively, and so there was an energy wave that carried and uplifted them. If some of the non-dual worlds would join with those who are choosing to elevate we could make a 'bridge of hands' to assist in elevating."

Osiris suggests that those who are of the non-dual and those of duality that have ideas to offer could make one transmission for all to receive. He asks if they may have permission to begin. As soon as I say yes, Osiris says they are ready.

"You're ready for it already?"

He says of course, laughs and asks what I was thinking.

"Things don't move that quickly here. We have to have committees, sub-committees, votes and approvals. Is it a sphere?"

Charlie says he has a transmission for Earth that shall come from all of the non-dual beings that Osiris quickly allied with telepathically. "These collaborators will be streaming through this energy that I hand you now. Those who are willing to put out their hand and raise their energies to meet those of the non-dual shall find their pleasure in this. Those that are resistant will feel acceptance and patience."

This seems like a good solution to diffuse the tug of war that Earth must have been experiencing. After we send the transmission out, Charlie says they can feel the effects already.

I've brought boxes of my Christmas ornaments to the Joy Council for Liponie to duplicate and use on our tree; now's my chance to show a couple of my favorite ones.

"Here's an angel my son Mike made for me when he was little and it's one of my favorite ornaments. This little ornament is one my son John put together for me. These kinds of decorations are the most special. You can look through the boxes I brought; I made a lot of the ornaments or bought them at craft shows. If you have a workshop to make ornaments I would like one from the Swizzlers, please."

Charlie adds there will be one from each of them.

I ask him if any of the others can speak yet. He says they have not made a single sound; they are choosing to have speech move through him. "They are choosing not to experience that part of being an Earth human, though they are leaning close to that time because of the apple pie."

I find this hilarious and amusedly comment that if you're going to have a weakness, apple pie is a good one to have.

"I think it is the apple pie that is guiding them to want to be closer in alliance with experiencing physicality. They are enjoying the games and all that is a part of our affiliation here. They are all proficient now in many of the instruments. We are planning a special orchestra for Christmas songs. It is possible that I can coax these ones into making the voice work so that they can sing the songs."

"Charlie, your voice is so pretty when you speak individually. I imagine they would have lovely voices too."

"Do you not like my voice when I am of the collective?"

"Your voice sounds gravelly when you speak as a collective. It is more pleasing individually."

"Oh…"

Here I realize I've made another mistake because he sounds very downcast. He says he will adjust his voice.

"Wait, wait, Charlie, please. I'm used to hearing your group voice and I'm OK with it. I don't want to do or say anything that's going to stifle you or your collective in any way. The other day, when you were dressed as Santa, and I noted that you were skinny, I regretted saying that Santa Claus should be fat. I want you to be happy, Charlie, and I don't want to say anything that will inhibit your happiness."

Charlie says, in his singular voice, that he is happy to comply.

"I don't need you to comply! I want you to do what feels joyful for you. Please, Charlie?"

"It might be possible for us to adjust the voice. This is the sound of all of our voices together."

"I'm OK with it. It is gravelly but I get a chance to hear all of you speak. I do like your individual voice so you can do both. OK? And if you want to be a skinny Santa, you definitely stay skinny."

"I must understand skinny."

"That's very thin; like a swizzle stick."

"Ah, Swizzler, swizzle stick!" Here I'm treated to prolonged laughter. "We are skinny. We are the Swizzlers!"

Charlie is still laughing when he says he will remember this forevers.

"You didn't know what I meant by skinny?"

"I did not understand fully the skinny."

"In our reality we've gotten used to seeing Santa fat, and it just popped out that you should be fat. I need to let go of the 'should,' because there's nothing you should do, Charlie."

"It is our great pleasure to should. There are many great works to do. There are many shoulds."

"Should implies a burden or an obligation."

"That is not our interpretation. Our interpretation is that there are many opportunities to be of service."

I acquiesce to Charlie's interpretation and ask him if he's taking time to do fun things. He answers that they are painting and playing tennis on tables. I remark that Tonas has told me Charlie is good at everything.

"We become quite proficient. When we are less proficient is when we are disconnected from our collective mind. Then one can be of less proficiency than another. You are right, I am good at everything."

"I heard that you are playing the drums."

"I am very good at the drumming. I like the cymbal."

Tonas whispers that the playing is incessant and asks me to get Charlie a flute.

In my sweetest and most neutral sounding voice, I suggest to Charlie that it might be nice if he had a room by himself where he could practice drumming. He answers, of course, that then no one would be able to hear him. I explain that after listening to drumming for a long time, especially if it was loud, I would want some quiet time.

He catches on right away and says he will request a special place for practice. He also asks for a place where people can gather and listen when they have orchestra concerts. I approve both ideas.

"Tonas, are the people who haven't joined our council able to participate in all the activities that are going on?"

"Most certainly. Each of these individuals has someone who is a personal guide to them to take them to any function. They are all made aware of everything that is open to experience, including food."

"Good, next time I'm here I want to hear about the preparations for Thanksgiving because basically here you just eat all day long. And you give thanks that you *can* eat all day long."

CHAPTER TWENTY
November 18, 2014

Tonas greets me and says they have been sending little "bubbles" to me; there are two new council members who wish to speak to me.

Before we do any work, I ask Liponie to join us. I've been bringing articles to the council for him to store or fix up: more Christmas ornaments, my thirty-year-old, dilapidated bicycle and a jar of cranberry spread that I make every fall. He assures me that the ornaments are stored, my bicycle is restored (with the addition of tassels and a basket which I find rather amusing) and he's stretching the cranberry spread so that everyone can have some.

My next suggestion is that we should have a big room for cooking. There is quite a pause before Liponie asks me if the room we have is not big enough. I explain that I didn't know we had anything like that. He says that we have a very large oven and work station that has been here since the experience where everyone had a chance to cook something.

"OK, I'm going to telepathically give you some recipes for: Six Layer Cookies, Russian Tea Cakes, Christmas Wreaths and Honey-Baked Apples."

Liponie says he has them. I hope I actually managed to send him the complete details. Then I console myself by thinking that if I didn't I won't be personally tasting anything anyway.

I ask Aton to join us in hopes of finding out about the interesting things that are happening in my head. After he greets me, I relate that yesterday I saw a couple of pages of words go into my third eye; the words were blue in the last part of this.

"These were formulas that have to do with some of the works you are doing on this council."

"All right. Yesterday I saw wings pop out on either side of a little round thing in my head." (I later figured out it was a symbolic representation of my third eye chakra.) Aton doesn't know what that was but he suggests I prepare for many unexplained things. That's not something I'm looking forward to since the perfectionist in me longs to have an explanation for *everything*.

"There's been lots of organizing going on, especially in the front part of my brain. I saw a whole bunch of clutter and disorganized wires there, so I asked to clear that. I heard you say I was just processing, so I said to my brain, 'Simply process.' My brain said back to me, 'I am your computer so I know.' Then I hear in my brain, 'Tis the season to be jolly.' (I realize how odd it sounds that my brain and I were having a little chat, but it didn't feel out of the ordinary as I was experiencing it.) Then I felt a beam of light shoot down through my brain. Was that you shooting light at me?"

"It is actually the filaments as well as elements that are within your many consciousness levels. All of the orbs are dancing in your aura and interfacing with the physical aspects of your body as well as the energy of your body. This is focusing on what is within the levels of consciousness and how it can interface with what is being directed through your conscious mind, your heart mind and all of those other brains that exist within your being. These are all applying themselves and building their strength. They are also interfacing in the smallest ways possible, for it is not meant for you to bring forth great expansions of use of the knowledge you have yet. (I like his implication that at some future point I *will* be able to bring forth great expansions.) Now, only baby steps are being used to develop these areas of your new consciousness expansion."

"This morning there were also some kind of blue cords for my heart."

"Ah, this is delightful news. This would be your Sirius and Andromedan genetics that are showing themselves."

"I like that! Thank you, Aton."

With the full Joy Council:

"Happy day to all of you. We have snow here and are approaching our winter season. May I speak with the first emissary who is interested in joining our council?"

"I am grateful. I am Emissary Nicetorrine or Nicktorrine from the Annahkolee Universe. You may call me Nicky if you wish, since others have had difficulty with my name. (I'm glad that I'm not the only one who experiences pronunciation difficulties.) I have seen great wonders at your council. It is a unique association, is it not? Playful, yet serious at the same time and most magical."

I agree that his description fits our council perfectly. Nicky continues by saying that they look forward to the new way that they will be able to experience as a result of the work we do. "Our goal is to be able to say that our universe is non-dual, and we see membership in this council to be a catalyst for this. So we are very grateful. Thank you."

Through a series of questions I learn there are many inhabited planets in his universe, but some are only periodically inhabited since there is another species, the Fanacordee, that moves from planet to planet. He says the Fanacordee are intelligent and well-educated with a strong desire to keep to themselves. Although they stand on two legs, they also have a tail and they are cold natured. His race has had an agreement with the Fanacordee for more than two hundred thousand years that they will not step upon the planets that species uses. Nicky's humanoid species inhabits more than nine hundred planets and stars.

"Nicky, I'm most delighted to have met you. Are you human color or Osiris's color?"

"I am near the color of yourself."

"Are there other colors for your race of beings?"

"We have the browns and different colors of browns. Is this a factor in our becoming part of this council?"

It seems that potential council members have not taken to heart my message that we won't turn anybody down if they ask to join us. Instead of repeating that, I explain that I was simply curious and add that I hope to learn as much as I can about all the beings that come to the council.

"I wish for you to know that both species of our universe will be a part of the council."

"Good. That's important. Thank you very much."

Next, Tonas introduces Council Principal Lowcahn from the Zhansarrah Universe. I welcome him and ask if he is also interested in joining our affiliation.

He says that he is, and adds that his universe is a mixture of dual and non-dual worlds. He also says the world he lives on is nearing a leap into non-dual, much as Earth. I reply that we keep thinking we're going to leap, but we've had a little bit of a challenge with releasing the 4th dimension. He still thinks the work our council has done is very impressive.

Curiosity impels me to ask him if he knows how many inhabited planets and stars there are in his universe. He comments that our numbers are interesting; it's logical that we would have a different system of counting. He figures it out though and tells me they have a little more than one thousand inhabited planets as well as forty stars.

"Liponie, if you make the persimmon pudding it will taste good, but it will not look good. It will be brown and lumpy but that's how it's supposed to be."

I hear him give a big sigh and admit that he is very relieved. He has attempted every means possible to make it look good. I apologize for not mentioning that sooner.

I suggest to Gaia that maybe we should consider having a meeting for all the fairies. She wants to know why. I explain that if any of them have seen a woman having a baby and put two and two together we don't want them to try having babies that way.

Gaia says that their bodies would not allow it, although a fairy queen could create the physiology that would make birth possible. She suggests shielding all fairies from witnessing past, present or future human births.

I agree that's one way to handle it; the other way would be to explain that the birthing process for humans is going to change. "I'm going to have children sometime in the future, I think, and I'm certainly not going to have them the way I did for my first two. (At this statement I hear someone—I bet it's Tonas—draw in a deep breath.) Another

208

approach might be for you to explain that the way they are having babies is the most divine way for them."

Gaia agrees that we should have a meeting soon and says it can be transmitted to all the fairy gardens from our council. She also likes the idea of sharing with the fairies that the Earth is evolving away from the old ways and that our new path will perhaps lead to the same painless birthing rite that is experienced on a non-dual world.

I suggest a strategy meeting the next time I come to the council and ask Gaia if she has decided whether or not to give the other fairy gardens the new body parts that she gave to the fairies in Sheliah's garden. She says she hasn't decided yet, but she would hate to see any species not have the wonderful experiences she's been exploring with Aton.

"How did this happen for the fairies? As soon as they opened the sex book you gave each of them did they then get their new parts?"

"It was my gift."

"Wow, that would be quite a surprise. I can almost hear them saying, 'Whoops! Where did that come from?'"

"Yes, for them to discover this was most enjoyable for them. I would like to tell you something that was so tender. Sheliah's honeymoon experience was quite delightful for her; however, little Rosebud's appendage was most visual whereas her area was hidden. She wished to see it and she could not make herself bend. It was quite hilarious for she kept trying to see it. Finally, she went to a smooth stream, stood over it and squatted deeply down so that she could witness what was below. She told me she was quite excited by the discovery of her pleasure palace."

My other idea for Christmas is for everyone to have a secret Santa. I explain the concept of this to the council, but I'm really not sure they all understand how to be secretive. I can just see someone walking up to their secret Santa, introducing themselves and asking the person what they want for Christmas. Mr. Kennedy says he will explain more details.

It then occurs to me that drawing names out of a hat won't work. Almost nobody reads English and it won't work to ask Mr. Kennedy to read the names out loud. I mention maybe we could use pictures and, thankfully, Liponie says he will rain pictures from the sky.

"One last thing before I go. Charlie, have you learned to dance?"

He says that Liponie has a school for them so that they can learn all dances and he can do the cha-cha.

"I wanted to make sure because once I get to the 8th dimension and dance with Tonas, then I want to dance with you."

He's excited that I want to dance with him. He's also excited that Liponie gave them playing cards to attach to the spokes of their bicycles with clothing clips because they make sound. As he's sharing his excitement about his new experiences, it occurs to me that Charlie will never be bored. He's going to be absolutely thrilled with everything he experiences because *everything* will be completely new.

CHAPTER TWENTY-ONE
November 21, 2014

"Two days ago I heard myself say, 'We're also indebted to you for you are the very first.' Who was I speaking with?"

Sananda says I was talking with Nicky about how they are making an interconnection between species to support the advancement of the worlds in their universe. He says that has never before happened in any universe; however, in Nicky's universe every inhabited world is aware that our council exists. The worlds also know they are being contacted from outside their universe to become part of something that is a collaboration of all the universes.

I ask Sananda if the other universes we've worked with are aware of us. He says there are certain places that know, but not all do.

Speaking with Esthra, I explain that this morning I had a dream about Charlie. "I was telling everyone with me in the dream about him and how I miss him so much, and in the dream I was sobbing. What was that about?"

Esthra explains that Charlie is a symbol of innocence lost. "He is the most innocent being ever and at the same time he's incredibly wise and able to do wonders."

As soon as Esthra said the words, "innocence lost," I knew his assessment was correct and now I'm crying.

"Think about the little barefoot girl you were and some of the experiences you had in the old paradigm that helped to rob her of her innocence. You had to become strong and tough to keep your sanity. All those experiences made you who you are today, but I think you would like to have that little girl back within yourself."

"I would. I think this is what I've had touches of on those days that I've felt good, although good is not an adequate description. It's a feeling of clarity and peace, like my head has popped up above the clouds and I can see, feel, hear and be clear. My life experiences feel like a smear over the top of who I really am."

Esthra suggests I might address this issue with SVH. I've done a lot of work clearing childhood issues, of course, but I don't remember ever addressing the issue of lost innocence. After I do a clearing, it feels really good to scrape off another layer of old stuff.

At the Joy Councils:

Tonas always greets me so pleasantly, but I'm also always in a hurry; today is no exception. I do manage to say hello, then I ask him what we are going to do about Santa Claus.

He answers that Liponie is scavenging Saint Nicholas from somewhere in the Fifth Realm to be brought here. "He will be wearing his typical costume which was quite furry. Liponie has instructed each of the Swizzlers that humans have expanded on Santa but they are going to witness the *real* Santa. It was the only way to do this appropriately."

I feel a sense of relief at this ideal solution and gratitude that Liponie and Tonas thought of it.

"Thanksgiving has been the date selected for Saint Nicholas to be present so that the Swizzlers can each sit upon his lap. Someone gave each of them a catalogue of gift ideas for children and they each have wishes. There will be Lincoln's logs which made Abraham quite excitable."

Tonas says one of the gifts they are getting (I asked.) is indeed Legos. This is exciting for me to hear because I spent hours upon hours building Lego buildings with both my sons, and now I get to do that again! Maybe I'll even know when/what I'm building. I can hope, anyway.

I'm told that Liponie has created a play room with tables for the Swizzlers to put out their puzzles and any other things they choose. He's also creating the council chambers for our three new universes.

Now here's a question that comes from the part of me that lives in a world of duality and has the ability to be suspicious. I ask Tonas if he is aware of any council members who have not yet spoken up who are perhaps here with subversive intent.

Sure enough, Tonas admits that has not occurred to any of them. Osiris and Sananda join us and I repeat my question. Osiris assures me there are none who are subversive that are actively in our council although there are others who have been in presence and observing, in order to see what is in it for them. He says that one safety measure we have in place is that no communications with subversive energy can leave our council. Since it is important not to allow any introduction of outside forces into the universes that have their new councils, we have also put extra security in those universes.

"Because of the duality factor in all the universes we are working with, I don't want anything tracked back to me or to the Earth that would cause any harm to us."

Osiris assures me that protection has been in place since the beginning of our work and that the emissaries were hand selected. I acknowledge the emissaries are probably OK, but we're dealing with duality and sneaky people.

"Perhaps we can put some education together for all of the twelve universes that are to be active after today. We can show them an endless supply of positives including infinite awareness and perpetual regeneration. I agree with you, my dear."

"If someone figures out that all this good work is coming from Earth, and they want to stop it, that would not be good. This is my home after all."

Osiris agrees that it is time to move into a new level of vigilance and to have it be part of everything we have done. He suggests that Commander Ashtar could redirect some of his ships, if that is acceptable to me. I immediately accept this offer. After Ashtar joins us and asks how he may be of assistance, I apologize for not including him from the beginning and explain my concerns.

After Osiris updates him telepathically on what we've been discussing, Ashtar says he will devote a legion of High Commanders to all the universes that have joined our affiliation. "As the universes come aboard it will be one of the perks for them to receive a portion of our support. We can be under the direction of each of these councils."

I ask if it's possible to do anything concerning the universes that haven't joined us yet since their representatives have been watching us. Ashtar says the command cannot enter a universe without the acceptance of one of the emissaries. He suggests there could be a bit of a buffer in place while individuals are in presence here and that the borders of these universes could be put into our loop of shield protection for the other universes.

He also reminds me that I have a very incredible resource in the Swizzlers and advises including them in our planning because their strategies are flawless. I thank him for his excellent suggestions and ask him to please implement them.

I ask the small group I'm consulting with, Tonas, Osiris, Ashtar and Sananda, if it is impolite for me to ask each emissary, when they step forward, how many inhabited planets there are in their universe. I'm told that everyone knows that information.

"How many inhabited planets and stars are in our universe, Sananda?"

"In our universe there are more than sixty inhabited planets and there are thousands and thousands of stars that are inhabited."

That's exciting information for me; I've never thought of stars as being inhabited.

With the full Joy Council:

"Good morning, good afternoon or whatever time it is here. I have a little bit of a speech to give you today. Do you remember when I was chatting with Nicky the last time I was here and he had some concern that the color of his skin would be a factor in determining if he could be a council member? Let me reassure all of you who have not yet joined us that your appearance, or the appearance of any of the beings in your universe, does not matter. Neither does it matter what is going on in your universe.

The only factor that determines whether or not you will be accepted into this council is what is in your heart. If you honestly desire to join and you are hoping for improvement for your universe or for yourself, you are welcome. You can be ten feet tall with a ten-foot tail, purple with green spots and fangs down to your knees and you will be acceptable to the council if you truly want to join. Have I made myself very, very clear to all of you with that statement? Would you please nod your head if you understand?"

Tonas says they are all laughing at the picture I created for them.

"There's another thing I want to share with you because perhaps you haven't yet figured this out from the work we've been doing. *Nothing* is impossible; I'll say that again. Nothing is impossible with the Creator's assistance, with the brilliant minds around this table and with the Serenity Vibration Healing work that I and others of our council can implement. You might be thinking that there's something special in your universe that will be very difficult to handle and you are hesitant to join us because you don't think we can manage it. We can and we will.

I have a gift for those universes that have joined our affiliation if you all approve. I'm going to offer Five Star Serenity Send-off to all of the sentient beings in your universes who have died or been killed. Sananda, please telepathically transmit what that means to all those present."

He says they all know now. I ask if there is anyone who does not wish for me to offer this to the people of their universe and he tells me that all have accepted.

I ask Creator to offer the Five Star Serenity Send-off to all the sentient beings that have died in the universes that have joined our Joy Council. I also ask Creator to put this in place for those who accepted it. "I don't know the capabilities of those of you from the different universes that have joined us. But if you can, ask about a person you loved or someone you knew who has died and find out where they are."

Tonas says we can recognize Chief Council Choshe Ahsahneeuh.

"I will share that the answer to that question is that they are in a state of higher awareness within a place in your universe. They are experiencing a very important next stage in their journey of the life. This is a little shocking and yet acceptable to us."

I inform the council that they are in a place we call the Fifth Realm, and it is where beings with a soul from every universe will end up. Choshe asks why this particular place was selected and I ask Sananda to transmit that information to the council telepathically.

"Ah, it is a bigger picture, is it not? For myself, I am ever more gladdened that we have joined this council to assist in the fulfillment of that great design."

"Thank you. It's where everyone gets to have the wonderful experience of rewriting their life."

"I believe it is even more than that, my dear. I have just found the piece that I have been looking for forever."

"If you still have concerns about joining us and you feel you have something you need to share in private with one of the council members, I encourage you to do that. Discuss with them any specific issues that you have or any hesitations, concerns or doubts so that they can help you decide to join or not to join. Is that agreeable to those of you who have not made up your minds yet?"

Tonas answers that is agreeable to them and then continues by saying there is no time pressure for any of them. "We are simply making this council positon open for you to participate and enjoy all that we have here for you to experience. Naturally, if you are choosing to be in affiliation with this council, this same set of parameters will be offered to you and your universe.

If you feel it is not to your liking to join this council now, but perhaps in the future of time you might wish to join, please know that you are welcome. I believe that it might be a good thing for us to mark March 15th of 2015, as the final date for those who are in observation of our council. So they have this full measure of time to experience the council and at that time will be able to, if not interested, return when they are in agreement with joining us."

I was so impressed with the authority and power in this voice that I forgot it was Tonas speaking and ask who the speaker was. Tonas answers it was him and explains that he feels that this date will be a turning point for Earth. I clap my hands and thank him. He acknowledges my enthusiastic endorsement with a whispered thank you.

I've been curious if I've been doing any bike riding at the council. Charlie says I have won three races. I find that incredible but he assures me that I have great power in my legs and competition in my blood. I suggest he tell the part of me there to quit being a show off.

"I think that it was your bell that was the show off. It was a delight for us. Do not consider that I am being of pussy footing."

I must be a much better bike rider there than I am here because it was pretty scary for me to even get on my bike the one time I rode it here last year.

Inaugurations follow the same procedure I have used for the previous universes:

In the Nordahnee Universe, Plany Ohsheer is waiting for us. Tonas tells me that she has a throne directly opposite mine and that this is a very large council; there are more than sixty thousand members present.

After welcoming everyone, I say that I'm glad to be here with Tonas, my partner and my… I want to say more about my relationship with Tonas, but all I can come up with is, "…and maybe more than that. With your assistance, I'm going to inaugurate and energize your sword, crystal and transmitting device and also gift you with the work that we've done in our universe."

Tonas reminds me that we installed special shields for this council since all the worlds in this universe are dual and many of them are at war. After the work has been transmitted, I say it was sent with our blessings and our hopes that they can come to peaceful solutions for their wars.

Tonas offers Ohsheer the opportunity to make the toast with Earth's champagne.

She says, "It is my pleasure and it is our great honor as a universe of many species, many worlds and stars that are learning the way to peace…. We are very grateful to be a part of this council and for the opportunity for each of us to have the heritage of Ihconnakashetah. This is what you would call ascension. The right of Ihconnakashetah is for all of our ancestors and that is a priceless gift that is offered to us as well as affiliation. We would ask that Joy now transmits this to all of our peoples."

"With the Creator's assistance, all of the sentient beings of your universe who have died are being offered the gift of Five Star Serenity Send-off. If they are in acceptance of this they may have it."

Plany says, "Each of you here who represent all of the worlds and stars of our universe, know that it is not only our world that we are holding the light for the future. It is for all worlds, all stars and all universes. We take on the greater mantle now for the one tribe. May Ihconnakashetah be the truth for all of these beings."

We gate to meet Council Principal Lowcahn from the Zahnsarrah Universe. He informs me that there are more than forty thousand in his council.

After the work is transmitted, he says, "Just as you speak of your gratitude, you must measure what ours truly is in comparison. You bring to us a vision of hope and of that picture which is much grander than we would ever have imagined. The empty seats that you witness are open for people from different stars and worlds to be able to sit at council during different times."

Tonas says that we are in celebration about the leap that this world is about to make into the non-dual and asks that it be graceful and memorable for them.

At the Annahkolee Universe Council, Tonas says we are happy to see large contingents from both the Annahkolee and the Fanacordee present. He also mentions that some of the ships in the Ashtar Command are moving into position to be of assistance. He explains that council members shall define the measure of service the command offers; then clarifies that the command will not be their servants but they will be of service.

The language that I speak for this inauguration, perhaps Fanacordee, sounds very forceful. I thank the council members for their willingness to cooperate and for the model this provides for the rest of the universes.

When we return to the council, Tonas tells me they wish to give me an ovation. I agree this was a wonderful day and thank them for their recognition of that.

"Who was the person I saw this morning holding out a very pretty colored blanket?"

"It is I, Nokeenosah Shertee. I am ambassador of the Kallahshar Universe."

"I caught just a glimpse of the blanket, but it was very lovely." I can't resist asking him if it is a gift, because as soon as I saw it I wanted one just like it. Alas, he says it is part of his garbing and it is also the garment worn by a council head from their world, Gasnar.

⊘ "We are an enlightened world, we have been in witness of the great wonders here and we wish to become part of this affiliation."

I reply that we would love to have them join our council, and, unable to stop myself, I ask him if it is possible for me to have one of the blankets. I don't normally care that much about clothing, but that blanket really was exceptionally beautiful. I'm delighted to learn that the day I become one of their council heads I will receive one!

I offer to do their inauguration when I come back to our council on Thanksgiving if their building is done. He says they will plan a great celebration on that date and asks if he can return for our feasting.

I welcome all present to partake of our feast even if they haven't joined our affiliation. "I don't know if our foods will appeal to you, but I'm sure Liponie can make something that will. I think of you all as my family."

⊚ Tonas remarks that we are a family of essence. Then he asks me to show everyone the particles of being that they are made of so that they may see that we are all made of the same spark. After I admit I don't know how to do that, Osiris offers to demonstrate and I accept his help.

⊚ "I wish now for you to look upon Gaia. Please, Gaia, show all these in presence the particles of light, geometries and golden streams that you are made of. Now relate that to the full measure of her presence as a planet. Witness through your consciousness the transmission of that bigger picture of her as a planet, as well as all that exists within her, including this Joy element who is the leader, the loophole that makes all of our work possible, and our dear heart, our friend. Now, may I show them yourself, Joy?"

"Yes."

"Now you may witness the particles that make up Joy and you can see the collaboration between Gaia and herself. Do you see that she is a part of Gaia and Gaia is a part of her?"

Osiris continues his demonstration using my sword, then Shertee and his twelve council members. Finally, he asks Charlie if he may have his little Matchbox car. I find it surprising and interesting that Charlie is playing with a toy like that. He does such incredible work at the council it's easy sometimes to forget that he is a little kid.

"I wish for you all to see, first, the joy that this little car brings this fellow who is part of our council. Now expand to see the sparks of light that emit from the fabric of the creation energies that are its makeup. Joy is, let us call it, the soul of that spark of essence and it is also a reflection of love. Now that you have seen this there is no denying the fact that we are all the same. We simply have our own personalities and stories of our experience, and we have our hearts, our minds and the spirit of who we are. These are the defining elements of everything, and so, we are all truly of one tribe."

Private meeting with Tonas and Liponie:

Liponie says the tree is nearly decked with the balls (not boughs) of holly, fa, la, la, la, la.

I've brought him a lot of apple recipes with the hope that maybe they will tempt the Swizzlers to speak. Knowing what a marshmallow fiend Osiris is, I brought recipes for S'more Pie and Rice Krispie Treats. I also brought more of my favorite Christmas cookie recipes and suggest to Liponie that maybe he might want to wait to fix them.

"Why wait for anything? We are having the Saint Nicholas for Thanksgiving so we must have the Christmas things. You are the lighter of the tree."

The little remaining resistance I had to a pre-Thanksgiving Christmas crumbles. Fa, la, la, la, la.

CHAPTER TWENTY-TWO
November 24, 2014

The last time I visited the council I was inspired to give them all a tour of my home. I pretended my eyes were a video camera and walked around looking at and describing some of my favorite furnishings and pictures. Now I ask Tonas if he was really able to see anything. He says they could see the energy of my house and that it has a very happy, artistic feeling. I don't understand what "seeing the energy" means and ask him to explain.

◎   "We can read energy. Let me give you the example of a banana. If the banana is old and has the brown spots on it, we see the perfection of it. It is still brightly orange. Ah, the word is not orange; I apologize. The color is brightly yellow. As we moved through your abode it was quite exciting for us to see your home and the perfection of it. Did you wish for us to see if there was dust under your refrigerator?"

I'm a bit too embarrassed to reveal that I actually did dust before giving them the tour. Plus, I still don't understand what he sees; from his description it seems like he doesn't see anything as it actually is. I suppose, though, that he would say the same thing to me—I don't see things as they actually are.

"I saw myself leap into your arms yesterday morning."

He says I've been doing that more and more often and it is a real gift for him. I run, he catches me and spins me around. I ask him if I get dizzy. (I'd be extremely nauseated by spinning like that here.) He says I don't and adds that sometimes I make the squealing laughter.

"Have we watched any of the tango DVD's?"

I have about fifteen of those that I brought to the council for Tonas and Liponie to watch. I'm determined to *someday* be a top-notch tango dancer.

"Yes, of course, and actually Liponie found many different resources for us to learn from. There are many dances we will be dancing in celebration."

Then he asks me not to hold him to this, but he believes that those remaining will step forward on Thanksgiving. I've been wondering how they could wait so long. I hope he's right.

I ask Liponie to join us so I can tell him I saw him this morning. I say I was surprised by how handsome he is and that he was playing the violin.

"You did not know that I was handsome? I have told you so."

"I know, but it was nice to see for myself."

"Ah, look at Tonas; he is a bit jealous that you have seen me first."

"I've seen you twice! I wonder why I haven't seen Tonas. Maybe I'm afraid to see him because he's too handsome."

Tonas says he is very pretty and that he believes I will like his looks very much.

I mention to Liponie that I brought more recipes and he asks me to give them to him in his head. I do that, then, in order to see if he received them correctly, I ask him if he can tell me the first ingredient in the divinity recipe I just gave him.

He says he can't! Naturally, I ask him how, then, will he create the candy? He says he will make the transmission of what is to be created and it will appear. The recipe is only of benefit if I wish to have *exactly* that which I desire.

This explanation takes the concept of cooking by adding a pinch of this and a lump of that to a whole new level for me. When I cook I still dutifully measure ¼ teaspoon amounts for recipes.

"I was reading them so that you would get them exact, but if you think there's something you can do differently to make them taste better, you have my permission."

Then he assures me that he can make the exact recipe I transmitted. "This is what is waiting for you in your future. You have the desire for what you desire to fall exactly into what you desire. See, the desire, the desire, the desire I brought into the conversation? I said it many times because the desire is what is cooking the brownies."

This is another thing I don't yet understand. Not understanding something has been popping up often enough lately that I'm getting pretty good at just letting further explanations go, at least for the time being.

Ready for an Abbott and Costello routine? (If you don't know who they are, watch, "Who's on First?")

Speaking to Liponie, I advise him that it's not balls of holly, it's boughs of holly.

Silence… Followed by, "I know the word of bowel."

"I thought you said balls of holly."

More silence followed by, "Is not the bowel part of the human anatomy?"

"I mean ball instead of bowel, but that's OK."

"I think it is disgusting, my dear."

I try again and say, "I don't want balls of holly, I want *boughs* of holly!"

"Oh, my goodness, and whose bowels shall we pull this from, a chicken?"

"No, no, I mean a branch of holly. Branches of holly are what I mean."

"Well, you see, to me a bowel…"

"No, I wasn't saying 'bowel,' I was saying 'bough.' These are different words."

I give up and tell him to just forget it. I wonder if he was just teasing me, but his last words are that he will research this and make sure it is not a ball. Agh!

Now I learn that they have been only relying on my recipes for Thanksgiving. Although it might be interesting to have a Thanksgiving dinner composed completely of desserts, I suppose we should have a few other dishes on the side. I suggest that Liponie asks some of the Americans for dinner suggestions. He tells me not to worry. He's researching Thanksgiving and dinner will be a triumph.

"Do the Swizzlers have Christmas stockings to hang up?"

Liponie actually sounds a tiny bit panicked when he admits he let this slip through his fingers. I know he can create stockings faster than I can say the word, so I move on to ecstatically making suggestions for gifts for the Swizzlers. I'm feeling like a kid again as I list toys I used to love to play with. Yo-yo's, (I wasn't any good but I liked trying.) pick-up sticks, blocks, kaleidoscopes and snow globes are on my list. Liponie's going to create an arena with a high ceiling so they can shoot off rockets and fly remote control airplanes. We are both determined to make their first Christmas extra special.

Still consulting with Liponie, I ask him if he can make a special pipe for the Native Americans for smoking tobacco. He says he would like to create a special place for the tribes to meet with homes of their standard abodes; they would have the night sky and the pipes could be brought to them there. I enthusiastically approve this plan.

Then he says we are going to have a grand celebration because people are getting really excited about their secret Santa. That reminds me to ask how I'm going to find out about my secret Santa. Liponie admits there has been some cheating and asks Tonas if he's going to confess or will he have to tell me. I'm laughing as I tell both scoundrels that cheating is not allowed.

Tonas now confesses he wished to be my secret Santa so he made a personal request. It was granted but he did have to promise he would speak to Jill Marie on Liponie's behalf.

Liponie asks me if I would like to know who I will be Santa to, but before I can guess he says it is Princess Zahseet. He cheated again to match her to me because he thought she would be fun and Charlie had already been picked. Seems like not much was left to chance, but I'm fine with the results of Liponie's manipulations.

"Commander Ashtar, can you give me a short description of the fleet's function? Do you prevent outside interference for Earth?"

He asks what I mean by outside interference and I say being attacked by beings not from Earth.

"The councils are the ones who give us direction on this. Since our tenure here as guardians, we have on occasion received acceptance to block outside interference. There have been times where individuals have come in to make a specific action toward other individuals. We have not been allowed to stop them because their own species is a part of the species of Earth. It has been a bit difficult for us to sit and watch on occasion, for it is our excitement to jump in and help as best we can. There are things we are capable of doing to limit the damage. They have no desire to destroy Earth. It is the human species that is of less interest to them."

"We were talking the other day about the fact that the transmissions in these other universes had gone out to assist their people but most of them didn't know about it. Wouldn't it be nice if they felt hopeful that things were going to get better?"

Osiris points out that the emissaries are involved in determining when individuals in their universe will be ready to know they are being assisted by extra-terrestrials. He asks me to imagine what it would be like for the human beings of Earth to know that someone from another universe was interfacing with them. It brings me up short to realize that others would consider *me* an alien.

"Does anyone wish to say anything before we join the full council?"

Aton says that he believes we are headed into some interesting times and that, to him, the 4th dimension feels as if it is warring with itself. He explains there is an element within the 4th dimension that would like to keep all of its toys as they are; it does not wish to see what the toys look like in the 5th dimension since that dimension does not promote tight control. (I learn much later that he is referring to the same species Ashtar said was not interested in human beings.)

I ask Charlie if he has any ideas. He first asks me if I like the way his voice is today. He's been trying new ones every day and this one seems pleasant. I remark that he sounds quite a bit like Marilyn. He tells me he thinks her voice is beautiful and thanks me for the compliment. I don't have the heart to tell him that it is strange to hear him speaking with a woman's voice. I'll just wait and see if he decides to keep it.

Now he says that he feels every human being wishes to have fun. "They have forgotten the child within themselves. I am experiencing my childhood." With a touch of pleading, "I never wish to have it go away, Joy. It is far too much fun. Perhaps we can help those who are resistant to wake up that little child within themselves."

"I would like that. Some of the qualities that I treasure about you are your innocence, your enthusiasm about everything you try and *your* child-like quality. These, and you, are precious to me."

"Thank you. We will work on this immediately as our collective."

In the full council, I ask Gaia if she's made any decisions about the fairies. She says she's been relying on me. I mention that it might be a good idea for all of the fairy gardens to know how Sheliah and Rosebud's garden is. She offers to make a projection explaining their garden, have a meeting for all the fairy queens (There is one queen per garden plus many guiding councils.) and show it to them. "The queen would then have the choice to provide the projection to their guiding councils and from there to their garden."

"I think knowledge is power and it is a good thing to have. I like your idea."

"I feel that they will all be very excited and open to make the move. My idea is to integrate slowly into each garden; when several understand something that makes it easier for all."

"True Heart, I felt snake energy really strongly two days ago and I got quite a bit of interesting information about the snake totem. Snake senses the Earth currents, is able to undulate gracefully, knows which way the wind is blowing and sheds its old skin, of course. What I thought most interesting is that it is able to keep a low profile like an ordinary snake or a high profile like a cobra. In the Fifth Realm, I asked for gifts to help rewrite the history of snake for our world because it has been portrayed as a tempter that should be killed. People will embrace whatever reality they choose but I'd like for them to realize that snake also is part of the one tribe."

True Heart agrees that snake is good medicine. He says it is about enlightenment, the shedding of the past and the old ways and embracing the new skin. I ask him if snake medicine would help us release the 4th dimension.

"You must realize, as librarian, I like this title, that the world has been somewhat happy with its old story. It is comfortable like an old blanket. The snake can give, I think, an important message to the evolving world which is perhaps frightening to some because it is a new skin. They are afraid to let go completely of the old skin. Once they let go of it, it will be gone and they do not understand what the new will be. Snake is about rebirth and the transformation that is ahead. It is perhaps considered impulsive to move beyond something that is tried and true, and yet I see this as wisdom; the wisdom that opens the way for the new light to shine.

You are becoming the young girl that you desire. Your old skin is the one that you are wishing to shed only it is comfortable to be in that skin that has been a part of your whole life journey. It is the same skin that was birthed with you through your mother, so it is also a part of her old skin. It is a new world when the 4th dimension is fully gone from Earth."

I ask him if there are other totem animals that could assist the release of the 4th dimension. He suggests maybe the toad because the toad helps one to look upon oneself. "Toad is also a reminder of the strength within that will help them carry into that new tomorrow."

"Thank you, True Heart."

"I did some work about assisting people who are physically and/or mentally lost, and who are put in places where other people are trying to care for them. My dad is in a rehabilitation facility. As I was helping him eat dinner the other day, I experienced much unease with the people around me because of their disabilities. Many of them didn't know where they were, couldn't feed themselves or weren't interested in doing so. The lady next to my dad at the table kept tugging on my clothes and asking me if I was protected. Nothing I said reassured her.

I put together work to help people like that who don't know what the possibilities are for them if they choose to release their current reality. I know you can add to what I did and create something for the other universes that have joined us."

Charlie asks me to transmit it to them. After I do, he says they will have it ready in four minutes.

While they are doing that, I decide to show the council something fun. I ask Tonas to guide me to a place about ten feet from the Christmas tree and turn me around so that my back is towards it. Once I'm in position, I say here's something we used to do at my house. Then I toss a small, spiky, metallic ornament that looks like a star over my head and hope it lands on the tree. Tonas tells me it did land on the tree, but then it slid down several branches.

"My two sons would take turns doing variations on this Christmas toss. If anyone wants to throw an ornament on the tree, they may try it."

Tonas asks if he may toss it and tells me his heart skipped a beat when he threw it. It always felt daring to me, too, when I threw it. Sometimes, when my boys weren't at home, I'd take it off our tree and give it a toss just for the fun of it.

I ask if anybody strung popcorn to put on the tree. Tonas says that is being done by the elves in the striped socks. Liponie volunteers that we have the true North Pole complete with Santa's workshop.

"How could you not tell me that?"

"There is so much. The workshop is in a bubble so that anyone walking by can witness all of the little elves making things. After our meeting today there is another meeting where we are making gingerbread boys and girls to trim the tree. We also have decorations of holly berries and popcorn on strings. We are keeping busy."

Although Charlie has the work done, I decide to do the inauguration for Nokeenosah Shertee's universe first, that way they will be able to receive it.

"Before we leave I need to speak with a little girl named Kindeera. I believe she has a kiss for me."

Tonas asks her if she would like to come and sit on my lap. He says she has the prettiest feathers he has ever seen, deep, golden yellow with a little pink mixed within. He lifts her onto my lap and suggests I hold her.

"Hello, Kindeera. Is it all right if I stroke your feathers?"

She giggles in a little girl voice and then says, "Yes."

"I love feathers. Yours must be beautiful."

"I want to thank you. My Sahshirah tells me that you saved me. I am six of our years and my heart is very glad I get the right to be bigger. I am to tell you from my Sahshirah that I am alive for you, and that I will give this wisdom to others. None of us that were made dead are dead now, and so we are grateful."

She speaks their language which is, unsurprisingly, birdlike, with very short sounds some of which are high-pitched. She explains that is easier for her to speak and thanks me again.

"You did well. Give me my kiss, please."

"My Sahshirah tells me to remember this kiss forever because it is the kiss of my life."

"You are so pretty and I love you!"

"We are all bound for good things now."

"Yes, we are, and you get to see them all!"

"My Sahshirah tells me that it is my freedom."

Now that she and I have finished conversing, Tonas thanks her and asks if there is a kiss for him.

"I will kiss you too, but you are not Joy."

"Yes, but I am in joy. Come little one, you may go back to your Sahshirah."

Inauguration for the Kallahshar Universe:

Nokeenosah suggests I call him Nokeen. In answer to my question, he tells me there are less than twenty thousand council members at present but their building is developed so that there may be many more.

I move through the inauguration process and transmit the work we have done, calibrated for their universe. I suggest we do a toast but Tonas tells me that Nokeen has asked for a moment of my attention.

"I understand the toasting and the drinking of the elixir. I wish to bestow upon you one of our council mantles. You enjoyed mine and its beautiful colors. It is woven from something like your opossum's hair and it is our ceremonial garb. We wish to offer you this mantle, making you our honorary council member from the universe of Chailee."

"I'd love to have one."

"May I place it upon your shoulders?"

"Yes, please."

"As I place this upon you, I ask that all of you raise your glasses in celebration of this connection of heart to become one tribe. I wish also to thank your Liponie who has made a smaller version of our mantle for every member of the Joy Council who is in presence now and also for anyone else who joins in the future. The one you have is made by our tribesmen specifically for you. If you wish to do the toast now I will step back to be a part of the drinking of the elixir."

I thank Nokeen and ask Tonas to give the toast. He speaks very eloquently, as usual. Then I remind Nokeen to come to our Thanksgiving celebration and extend my invitation to anyone he wishes to bring.

"I would not dream of missing it. All of us here would be most grateful for the opportunity to experience the flavors of your world."

I wasn't expecting him to ask to bring twenty thousand people along and I hesitantly answer that we can probably make room. Liponie laughs and tells me to fear not.

Back at our Joy Council, I ask Plany Ohsheer if she's had a chance to explain to any of our council members what the war that's going on in her universe is about.

She says that many have forgotten what the wars are about, but the primary wars are about ownership and the power of resources. "Some of the worlds are very highly prized for their metals; some are prized for their consumable foods and others for their crystals. There are attempts to control or even own planets and to enslave those who exist on that world. It is unfortunate that there is not plenty of everything on each of these worlds, although I think there might even be wars so that they could have more of it. I believe the only recess for war will truly be the enlightenment."

"I wonder if there is a way to allow those who enslave others to feel what it is to be enslaved."

"Perhaps there is, for I believe that every world that has been a conqueror has also been conquered. Perhaps this is what gave them the flavor of taking back. Once the conquered have been liberated, then the hunger is to take revenge upon those who enslaved them."

I ask Sananda if he has any thoughts to share.

"It seems there are some enlightened beings on each of the worlds in this universe because each of them has a member on the Joy Council. If you were to create a vigilance council of your own, these individuals could also develop and focus transmissions to assist your elevation. If you look at the history of Earth over the last thirty years you will see that the exponential advancement has been due to the collective focus of awakened beings. It has not been from outside sources as much as from within. I believe a primer on this will assist you."

Finally, we make the transmission to assist all who are mentally and/or physically challenged who could benefit from it. Tonas tells me that it could be felt. I hope this begins to make a difference because what many people in the nursing homes I've been in recently are experiencing seems tragic to me.

CHAPTER TWENTY-THREE

November 27, 2014

Private meeting with Liponie at the Joy Councils:

Since I'm starting to feel a little of the Christmas spirit, I've brought some presents for Liponie to wrap and hide. The first thing I hand him is a very dark blue-black stone filled with tiny sparkles that look, to me, like stars. It's called a blue sunstone but it reminds me of the night sky. I ask Liponie to use the stone to make matching rings in plain silver settings for Tonas and myself for Tonas's Christmas present.

Then I display what I think is the perfect gift for Osiris, the marshmallow lover. It's a very large marshmallow resting on top of a cookie with a small candy cane on the side that represents a cup handle; there's melted chocolate on the top of the marshmallow and a little bit is running down the side. This all represents a cup of hot chocolate. It probably doesn't taste very good but I found it irresistibly cute.

I do a completely unnecessary demonstration of equipment and toppings used in making Christmas cookies because Liponie's been doing research with Martha Stewart!

That brings to mind a question about how he does research. He says he connects to our media; I ask if that means he watches TV. His answer that it is somewhat like that and it is very entertaining doesn't enlighten me at all. I've got presents and Thanksgiving on my mind, though, so I don't ask anything more right now.

"The last gift idea I have is another one for Osiris. I want to give him a big wheel of cheese along with the apple I gave you the other day because when someone is very important we call them a big wheel or say they are the big cheese."

"You must tell him that he is the big cheese and explain to him that he is the Stilton."

I'm not sure what kind of cheese Stilton is, (Google says it's the "aristocrat of cheeses.") but I suggest Cheddar cheese would be the tastiest.

Now I ask him if he thinks Zahseet would like a surfboard. There is silence for a moment and then he says the word "surfboard" very slowly. I picture one for him and describe how you lay down on it and paddle out into the ocean. I hear him start to sing *Wipe Out* and then he says, "Surf City here we come!"

"Good job, Liponie! How did you know that?"

"I have made it my passion to know everything of the modern world."

"Do you know if they have surfs or surfboards on her world, and do you think that's something she could do?"

He says they have surf but no surfboards. I'm really excited that this could be something everyone on her world might enjoy. Liponie suggests that we set something up here so she can be trained. I immediately show him a vision of a water park with a wave pool and both of us realize that the Swizzlers would love something like that. We're going to have a special unveiling at Christmas and Liponie assures me that our park will be even more exquisite than the most magnificent water park on Earth. I love plotting with him!

Tonas joins us and addresses me as, "beautiful treasure." I savor that yummy compliment as he tells me that Liponie has a table that seems to go on forever with screens all around so that everyone can be seen.

Before we enter the council, I ask him to clarify something he told me quite some time ago. I know he said he was an initiate of some of the ancient academies of Earth, but I ask him if it's more accurate to say that he wasn't actually an initiate. He says that is more accurate. It could be that he was just at the academies to catch a glimpse of me as I did my tutorials, but I don't feel like asking him about that now. Instead, I suggest that if he had been an initiate he would have experienced some of the tribulations of living on a non-dual planet—Earth.

He agrees that would help him to have a greater understanding. (In particular, I hope, a greater understanding of me.) Since, "the past is not stolen" from him, he's going to petition to become an AMS initiate in the past.

Talking about academies reminds me to ask him how the initiates of the Academy of Enrichment are doing. He says it is more than either of us ever dreamed. There are no new innovations, but all that has been put in place will take the students many years to fully engage.

Tonas now says he needs to warn me about something. Wondering what it could be as I imagine some kind of crisis, he informs me that Charlie is dressed as a turkey. After I quit laughing, Liponie tells me it is simply a costume because Charlie wishes to honor me.

"He wanted to be the center piece of the table. I told him that it was impossible because the table is too long and he must be in presence. I coaxed him off of the table by telling him that he can sit next to you. You must come back later for our dinner, my dear."

I agree to do that after my dinner with my brother's family.

As we enter the Joy Councils I give my best turkey imitation of, "Gobble, gobble, gobble."

Charlie answers me and he sounds like a real turkey! Then he says, "Leave my drumstick on me! I will play with it later with my drums."

"Charlie, you and the Swizzlers are such a delight for me. Thank you for honoring the tradition of Thanksgiving and let's bless all those poor turkeys that won't see another day. I won't take much time because I know you have a big celebration planned but, as usual, I have a question. Yesterday morning I heard, 'See all Nagahnsay papers and toss them in your heart like a bunch of fresh leaves.' Is Nagahnsay a new world?"

Tonas says they have a little gift for me and asks me to please sit down. He then asks the delegates who wish to join the Joy Council to step forward. They are:

Kamala Shrow, Universal Presence from the Joeshrahnah Universe. Her world is Ahrowsh and it is primarily dual.

Rahnosah Prahnic (Rahsawsee for short), from the primarily dual universe of Lindar. His world is Candarfor.

Joyyahl Kindar, newly elected Council Presence from the Corena Universe. Her world is Darroan and it is primarily non-dual.

Harahnsha (Har), from the primarily non-dual universe of Fonar. His world is Coriah. He says they want to put their crowns in the ring, a turn of phrase which I find delightful.

Silgah Holinrah, Governing Presence from the completely dual universe of Lowmeereeuh. Her world is Nahshegrah.

Yarah Homma, Emissary from the Inseanahrah Universe. Her world is Nahgahnahsayyear. She says, "It is our heart, not papers, that we offer you and the journey of what have been the pieces brought into place to support our newly and fully non-dual universe."

Monahquah Senet, from the primarily non-dual Gaygoreeah Universe. His world is Kaireesha.

Haireetah Voreeneeuh, from the primarily non-dual Ahkahnay Universe. Her beautiful world is named Zihcorahn.

Toemarrah Metahn, Emissary from the Neftoo Universe. His world, Eesha, is primarily non-dual.

Bohnar Comeen, Council Presence from the primarily dual Comahleeah Universe. Their main world is Zeefmah.

Neftee Voenesh, Councilman from the primarily non-dual Deeohnah Universe. His world is Ahsha.

Ohniuh Comb, Council Presence from the nearly even dual/non-dual universe of Porneeseesee. Her world is Eeshenarrah.

Kallahm Amar, Emissary from the mostly dual Booseeuh Universe. His world is Santee.

I'm glad I'm sitting down because my head is swimming from hearing so many interesting names. As they were introducing themselves I soon gave up trying to remember anything anyone said. Tonas is going to have to repeat these names for me many, many times.

"I'm just as excited to have those of you from primarily dual universes join us as I am for those of you from the non-dual universes who joined us. Earth is a dual world. What is the balance in our universe?"

Kennedy reports that our universe, Chailee, is even-steven.

"I welcome you all. It is lovely to hear your names, and, at some level, to be able to witness you. Thank you so much for stepping forward on this day of gratitude that we celebrate in America as Thanksgiving. I'm glad you all jumped in the pool with us. Let's see if we can swim our way to the unity that we've been hoping to manifest. Can some of you tell me how you travelled here?"

"Yes, I am Emissary Toemarrah Metahn. I am assisted by many different principles; we are primarily non-dual and evolved and so it is easy for me to transmit my consciousness and then to affirm my presence here as a physical form."

This is my chance to tell the new delegates that I'm looking forward to being more physically there because it's just my energy body that is speaking with them now.

"If I may speak, I am Bohnar Comeen and my world is primarily dual. Though we are an enlightened society, we have been assisted greatly by those of your council to make our transmittance here."

I should have figured there would be a variety of ways for people to arrive.

"True Heart, there's something about the animal bear in May. Can you tell us what that is about?"

He says the bear is connection. "It hibernates and then awakens to the new beginning. Because of the Earth energies and the celestial forces, there is an energy that helps the bear to know its awakened time as well as the full measure of what lays before it. It is the same now for this evolving Earth and that which is the nurturing sense of Gaia as she assists all who are awakening just as the bear in May. It is perhaps another window for quiet and sweet awakenings."

That sounds good to me and I'm also grateful when True Heart tells me he is still tutoring me about the animals.

"I'm assuming that the representatives from universes that are primarily non-dual can put their heads together and come up with some things that would be possible for you to reveal to Charlie and the gang about ways to stair-step us up to that kind of a reality. If you could drop some hints that would be great. I do hear some of the goings on here when my full consciousness is not here and then I bring them back here for you all to elaborate on. It's a rather circular way of moving forward but it has been useful."

Osiris agrees that in conversation almost anything could be said. I ask them to help me tune my ears.

"Jesus, I have been considering asking you to talk about the details of your birth, but I don't know how much awareness you had when you were just a baby."

"It is easy for me to look back to the moment. May I say that I have gratitude on this day of Thanksgiving for the day that you held me in your arms and whispered to me? I remember this; do you remember it?"

"I remember that a group of us in SVH assisted your mother, but I'm fuzzy about what we did for you. Tell me about it."

"You made healing for my dear mother and when my birth was made, you were offered the little one, myself, to hold in your arms. You did look into my eyes and you spoke to me that there were to be people who would hate me and there would be people who would remember to love me. You were working to do just that. This shared with me the complexity of humanity, that which was to be my great experience of being loved and hated. It was such in my life. I was loved and I was hated. And now here we are together, and, of course, you love me most deeply."

I have been crying as he speaks to me and am unable to answer him.

"It was a great message for me, for many gave me the same kindness of healing for my mother, but they spoke only of the syrup and sweetness of what life would be for me. Your truth helped me to build strength; it was your words that prepared me."

"Thank you for sharing this with me. I'm grateful that I was able to be of assistance to you, but I'm *most* grateful that I can finally love you."

"There is one more item on my agenda. I'm wondering if I should rename my sword. Arthur, how did Excalibur receive its name?"

He explains it was dreamed into reality and named in the dream by a great sorcerer. He also says that the Lady of the Lake did indeed give him the sword, and someone, he doesn't say who, threw it back into the lake when he died. He suggests I name my sword the Joyous Spear and adds that Liponie could take the spear to baby dragon Joyous and have her breathe a little fire on it.

I really like that idea! I thank Arthur for his suggestion and agree that's what we will do.

"Now, tell me if we are having the traditional Thanksgiving foods and then the foods that the Native Americans gave the first settlers? Who can share that with me?"

"It is I, my dear, Marilyn. It is quite traditional; there are even pretend turkey slices. Your Liponie has been very busy. There is the cranberry and your grandma's persimmon pie."

I tell her it is pudding, but she says it looks more like a pie to her. Pumpkin pie, many root vegetables and corn are other foods. The decorations are as if for the first Thanksgiving. People will be wearing pilgrim costumes at dinner, while members of the different tribes will be wearing their traditional garb.

"What group of the Native Americans were the ones who assisted the first pilgrims?"

"There were several, actually. This particular celebration opens into the theme of the one tribe that is celebrating the unity of one another. This shall be transmitted at your discretion. There is a feeling among us of the spirit of gratitude. If this is transmitted by all of us it will be as if an immersion onto the hearts of all human beings, whether they are of the Americas or of the other countries of the world."

Mr. Kennedy says, "Our good old USA could use some help. Perhaps in this focus we can make it so that the tradition of America is held as a mark of the spirit of its original focus and thought. That was to celebrate, not only the harvest, but to celebrate the new world that was open to all of these new settlers. They were on these new soils for a reason; they wished to have the freedom to worship as they desired.

Perhaps this is a message that can be blended with our message together, that each individual has the spirit of their own means to worship the essence of themselves, and the essence of their beliefs, whether this is of Mohammed, Jesus Christ, the Great God, Jehovah, Abraham, Great Spirit, Buddha or Shiva. This includes the ancient teachers of Isis, Osiris or any of the others present here. We have a long history of beliefs; may they all be held in the same attitude of acceptance."

Whenever Mr. Kennedy (I'll never be able to call him John.) speaks, I treasure every word. He was such an important figure when I was a teenager, and it is still hard to believe I'm able to talk with him and work with him. After I thank him for his suggestion, I ask Charlie to put the transmission into a sphere. His gobble, gobble, gobble is followed by real turkey sounds and then laughter. I comment that he sounds real and he says he's been practicing.

"Have I managed to tempt any of the other Swizzlers to speak yet? I've been bringing lots of apple recipes."

"They are fully reticent."

"I don't know how I can tempt them anymore. If they could speak I'd have a chance to know them better."

"Ah, I will be the intermediary for all in saying that we know your heart and you know our hearts. How can we be any closer than we are now? We are in your tribe, and, of course, we live with you. We see you naked."

Startled laughter erupts from me and I declare that they don't see me naked! I don't think they do; maybe they do.

"Were you teasing me, Charlie? Is that true?"

"It is a joke."

"OK, I'm going to have to be careful now."

"We close our eyes."

I'm left not really knowing if they can see me in the altogether or not. Hmm.

"All right, let's do this transmission. I'm looking forward to learning about all of you, and certainly learning how to pronounce your names. I'm sending special blessings out to all those people who could use more food than they currently have. I'd like to send them a feeling that no matter what they have to eat today there is abundance for all and it is their birthright."

I ask the council to assist me to send out the energy of joy, appreciation, gratitude, love and an acknowledgement of the oneness that we all are to the Earth, our universe and all the universes who have joined our council.

Tonas wants to know if I will return for their festivities.

"I will. I'm going to celebrate Thanksgiving with my brother and his family." I start crying again because my mom is in the hospital and my dad is in a nursing home. I don't believe he will ever leave it. "I would appreciate it if you all hold the lamp high for my mother and my father."

"It is our honor, my dear."

With Tonas in privacy, he asks if I would like for him to come with me for the day, energetically, of course. I can use some support and tell him so.

"I will be most pleasured to be at your side. It is the time for me to be more in presence and more assisting of you. Lean on me and remember, I am like Woonfred, anything you ask is always, 'Yes!'"

CHAPTER TWENTY-FOUR
December 1, 2014

The other day I heard Tonas ask me to marry him. I've been in quite a dither since then. I'm too nervous to approach the subject directly, but maybe I can sneak up on it. He and I exchange greetings and I tell him we have to talk. My voice must reflect how nervous I feel because he asks if he has displeased me.

"No, I heard something the other day and I think you were talking about marriage."

"We talk about this quite a bit, my dear."

"Oh, this is the first I've become aware of that. What have we been saying?"

"We talk about the days when you can see me before you and what it will be like, perhaps, for us to have children together and our great travels. It is always in our hearts and minds that you will have that period to allow me to take you to court. This will assist very much because we will date."

"Take me to court?"

"Yes, you have requested that I take you to court."

"What does that mean?"

"You said, 'You must court me.' So I assumed that we must go to the court and that there would be something there that we must achieve. I am very fit; I can meet any challenge."

Even though we are still generally talking about the subject of marriage I'm able to relax quite a bit because of his humorous misunderstanding of what courting entails. I explain that it simply means we will date, but he is still confused and plans to speak to someone about it so I elaborate.

"Courting means you bring me flowers or take me out to a nice restaurant and we have dinner. Maybe we see a movie together and we walk and talk and just spend time together."

I hear him take in a breath and then say, "Oh, this is much easier than I thought. I thought I had to win your hand through combat or through some human ritual. I have done some research and some of this was quite bloody, but it was, of course, something I assumed we would evolve beyond in any event."

I assure him that no blood needs to be shed and I am now able to open up a bit about my feelings concerning marriage. "I was married once and it was supposed to be 'till death do us part.' I know I'm not going to experience death, but I don't want to be with someone and then feel like I can't stay with that person any longer. That was how I felt when I was married." I hear him say "Ah!" at this point but I continue with, "I wouldn't want to ever feel that way if I was married again. I would want to know, just like Gaia and Aton know, that it is forever. This part of me is not at the point yet where I can feel that way."

"We have discussed that we will begin at the very starting point. That I will court you and then you will make up your mind. We have several hundred years to play with this."

"My other concern is what happens when two people who have children decide to part? If you would have had children with Sironea, what would have happened with the children?"

Tonas answers that they would remain incarnated and not evaporate. Obviously, I need to rephrase my question.

"Let me explain what I'm asking. It was my choice to divorce the man I was married to. After our divorce, the children spent some time with me, and some time with him. This was very difficult for both of them, but especially for my younger son. It was very challenging for them for all of us not to be together in one household. Do children experience that feeling of loss if parents split in your reality?"

He assures me that although children on a non-dual world grow up very quickly, they enjoy their childhood and never experience a feeling of separation from their parents. "If I was to be in relationship, let us say with you, and for some reason you would design that you are no longer interested in being in relationship with me, it would be, of course, sadness for both of us. But immediately good things would come into play to honor both of us and we would move aside from one another. The children would never feel separate from us."

This information does calm some of my concerns but still I feel it's necessary to tell him that I will have to be at a lot different place emotionally and physically than I currently am before I would even consider marriage. He says we have also discussed this and that I'm overly concerned for nothing.

"If you believe it will assist you, speak with Sironea and she will give you many scoops. I have nothing to hide; I am not an ax murderer."

I say I might speak with her, but I probably won't. I don't think I will pursue this subject again for quite some time, and maybe never. I am somewhat reassured, but I'm still very uncertain about what the part of me that is spending almost all of the time at the Joy Council is saying to him. I didn't even know we'd been discussing these issues!

Liponie joins us and I ask if Cory is still sitting at the table looking like an iceberg.

"Oh, yes, never melting."

I mention that I've been thinking about Ashtar as a potential partner for her. Liponie agrees that could be exciting and suggests I speak with her. Once she is present, I say that I consider her to be a universal woman since she is connected to everything in all the universes. I then point out that there's a man on our council who is about as close to being a universal man as you can get. "He's a very dashing figure and very instrumental in assisting our evolution. His name starts with the letter 'A' and he's a commander."

She tells me she's interested in what I'm suggesting! This could be a great match!

"I'm assuming that it's OK to tell you that he was in love with someone who left him a long time ago. Tonas tells me he's been so involved with his work with the fleet that he has not even given a glance to anyone else. You've been watching our work on the council and observing Charlie, his collectiveness and his oneness. I just want to encourage you to broaden your horizons a little bit or a lot and consider having a body and Ashtar as a potential partner."

Cory says she is fascinated by the relationship of Gaia and Aton, and Isis and Osiris. "There is so much love. It is the storybook."

I advise her she could make her own storybook. She says she would need some legs. I reply that Liponie could assist her with that detail and Hathor would be a good resource person to talk with. Cory remarks that Hathor is quite spirited and I agree that she is very womanly and sensual. Finally, I hear the admission I've been waiting for Cory to make.

"I do not feel this ice body is me."

I agree that I don't feel it fits her and tell her she is a warm woman. She says the word "woman" as if testing the flavor of that idea then adds that there are interesting things ahead. I point out they will be a lot more interesting for a woman than for an iceberg. Cory admits she has been interested in consuming some of the food. Liponie tells her there is plenty of good food here and offers to practice with her to help turn Ashtar's attention towards her. He suggests they have a meeting with Ashtar since he will be guarding many of the universes that Cory is part of; perhaps she could be Ashtar's advisor.

I assure her that Liponie will not push her but will provide guidance for her. She giggles and thanks me. I am so delighted at the possibility of her falling for Ashtar that I can hardly wait to see what develops.

Private meeting with Liponie:

I request an outfit that honors the Homa: a blouse the beautiful blue color of Sahshirah, with pink buttons that are the color of her daughter's feathers; a pair of brilliant green trousers that are the color of Ihroenees; a coat that has all the colors of his children and a little sporty hat with a simulated feather that looks like one of Kindeera's gold and pink feathers.

Liponie says that is all possible so I go on to request a surprise for Tonas. "I don't know if he wears underwear, but I would like a pair of boxer shorts for him that are the colors of the bird people."

"Boxers, like the fighting men?"

"Boxers are underwear that men here wear under their trousers."

I know I'll never see the underwear unless Tonas and I actually do get married, but I like the idea of knowing he might have them on under his trousers. Liponie doesn't sound familiar with underwear; I bet nobody on this dimension wears anything like that. I suggest research.

Continuing to discuss Christmas gifts with Liponie, I ask him if Charlie is set on the drums or is he still trying other things.

"My dear, he is everywhere doing everything. He wants to bring in millions of years of experience all in this little window of time. We are keeping up as best we can."

I brought a DVD with me that chronicles the history of surfing and suggest that Zahseet could watch it after she gets her surfboard. I ask Liponie to talk with her to see if she enjoys physical activities. He agrees to do so and tells me he is ready with a long, flowing gown of feathers as well as a beautiful cape.

I'm surprised my outfit is already done, but Liponie tells me that once he has the inspiration it only takes him seconds to create an object. Also, I didn't ask for a gown but it looks like a gown is what I'm getting. I'm sure it's beautiful; it's just not trousers.

Osiris and Tonas join us before we move into the full council and I ask them if there is something we need to sort out before everyone will feel comfortable with joining.

Osiris replies that it is a matter of time. I'm surprised to learn that individuals who have not stepped forward here are not the only ones who can vote. They are here to gather information which they constantly bring back to their universe. Then there is voting that takes place in their universe. Upon hearing that information, I realize it is a miracle that *any* universe has joined our council. Imagine trying to get the majority of inhabitants in a universe to agree upon something!

Osiris comments that I am a vision and asks if it would be possible for Isis, Gaia and Hathor to enter wearing the same kind of costume. They join us, think my outfit is exquisite and Liponie creates similar clothing for them.

After we enter, Tonas says that everyone jumped to their feet. I explain to the council that our clothes are in honor of the Homa, especially Ihroenees, Sahshirah and his family, but also all the bird people. I also say that I hope they don't mind if I call them birds, because anything that has feathers is a bird to me.

Ihroenees tells me they are honored and he transmits a copy of our dresses through his consciousness so that all his people might see them. He tells me it's all right to call them birds; they are winged ones.

"I also want to tell the Annahkolee people that I love them. I love all of you actually. They were talking to me three days ago and when I asked them what they wanted to say, I heard, 'Simply that there is time, there is love and that we love you. You are the joy for us.' It's interesting that I'm hearing universes speak now."

Someone asked me three days ago if I wished to meet a young man. Today I ask the council if there is a young Annahkolee man here. I hear him chuckle and then he announces that he is here. When I ask his name he tells me he is called Tutti.

"Oh, good, an easy name! In one of the languages of Earth your name means all. You have a wonderful name."

"I am very shy."

"Did you wish to say something to me, Tutti?"

"Yes, I wish to say to you that you have made our existence even more exciting. We are working, of course, always together and we are always functioning as one mind toward the greater good of all. And yet, somehow this Council of Joy gives us… We have the feeling that we are meeting our destiny."

"I have that same feeling."

"I am of gratitude to you for this."

"You are most welcome. Thank you for your words today, and you can say to all of your people that I am delighted that they are tutti."

He says they will think that is funny.

"We have some work to do today that has to do with black people. I had a dream the other day in which a black man told me he was getting beat up. This brought home the point to me that blacks do not feel like they are part of a one tribe. They have their own rules, social codes and even language in some cases. They've experienced some terrible things from people of other races, and especially white people. What can we do?"

Charlie says that when he looks upon all of Earth there are very few places where the color of black is acceptable. "In the thoughts of many they are to be spurned and they are not human. I feel that they have been separated from the tribe. Mickey Mouse is black and everyone loves him, and so, this about the black tribe of Earth escaped me. They need to meet Mickey and then they will feel very much acceptable."

Remember that although Charlie's collective has existed since the very beginning, Charlie himself is just a little boy, and so, Mickey Mouse is one of his favorite "people."

I also explain that two days ago I received a packet of something for goodly men that might assist. Charlie says he is viewing the package now. He believes Council Principal Lowcahn can help us with this since his universe is very nearly completely non-dual and blacks are acceptable there. "This can be important to our focus of the one tribe. I believe all of you will agree that when this goal is met, it will be an inspiration to all other worlds and universes of that greater fellowship restored."

I agree that anything to help clear prejudice would be helpful and leave this issue with the council to address again when I come back.

When I mention that I know more emissaries have stepped forward, Tonas offers to announce them and I gratefully accept. He introduces Chief Kahsheenah Vohnsheer as the representative from the Nasconerah Universe. Vonsheer's world is Lahkashnah.

I heard someone speaking to me last night and I even heard complete sentences. I ask who told me, "Mansepwah is a volcanic cloud. You'll have to look through it to make out Jardaniveeah. We, the peoples of this world, are fascinated by your council and are interested in joining."

A woman who introduces herself as Lana Fahreetwoah tells me that Jardaniveeah is her world and their universe is Zahnahsh.

The final person Tonas introduces is Council Presence Jenairrah Magursha from the world of Paireeleeah in the Insear Universe. I tell Jenairrah that I spoke with him last night and saw him as a bearded man. He confirms that he does have a beard.

Tonas says that all three are interested in joining our affiliation. Liponie says he has all their buildings ready and I tell them we will do their inaugurations on Friday.

Then I ask Charlie a really important question. "Did you get to sit on Santa's knee?"

"I am speaking with my new voice. I sat on Santa's knee and I told him everything. I had a very long list, and I also wished for peace on Earth and goodwill to all of the men and women. Santa promised to give it to me."

I remind Charlie that part of our work is to help Santa and he agrees it is important for us to do that. I tell Charlie that I haven't met the Saint Nicholas he spoke to. According to Charlie, there are many who pretend but this one is the real Santa.

I move on to try to find out if Charlie is staying with the drums or if there is another instrument he prefers. He says he likes the flute and the piano, but people put their fingers in their ears. I suggest he could take some lessons. That is acceptable to him and I ask him to pick one instrument to start with. He chooses the accordion since it is like the piano. It's too bad I don't care to dance the polka, because that's about the only thing I can relate accordion playing to. Surely there is a good accordion player in the Fifth Realm, so I ask Sananda to find a teacher for Charlie.

I mention to Sananda some people my dad and mom have told me they'd like to see after they die. He tells me there would never be an empty welcoming space and *all* of the people I listed will be present.

"I don't know who is going to go first, but they are both in bad shape."

"They are not in bad shape, my dear. They are in preparation, but it is difficult for you."

He's right. I've been exhausted the last two days.

"Osiris, could we show someone who is looking at another person and considering them an enemy or that they're too different that the other person has the same make up that they have?"

"The geometries are all the same; all have the same spark of light, the same essence of presence."

Charlie says he thinks this is the answer for the black people of Earth. "It is for all species, everywhere, the same story. If everyone and everything sees itself as a part of the other, even if it is a rock, there will then be that stream of energy that is the tribe."

"There might be another piece to that. Three days ago as I was asking about releasing the 4th dimension I heard someone say, 'This is our view.' I would like for the person who told me that to repeat what they told me."

"Thank you for this opportunity to speak. I am your Joyyahl. We are the ones who gifted you the Joy Arrow. It was always in our mind that the transmission to All That Is brings to heart the vision of the oneness. It is our view and the spirit of our vision that all who reach the greatest flavors of oneness shall know that we are of that one tribe. There is no way to separate us. And so the Joy Arrow is the vehicle to transmit that vision of unity. Our world is primarily non-dual, and our universe is the same. The only true path to recognizing that which is that spark of oneness that unites us is to open the heart to see what one is so that they may recognize that same spark in others. Do you see? If you recognize this in yourself then you can recognize it in others."

"I heard one of the worlds or universes, perhaps ours, say that they want the illusion. After that I heard, 'Have faith in me,' and then I heard 'for the Earth itself.' Maybe it's Earth we're talking about."

Joyyahl says she thinks it is time for Chailee to speak with us. She adds that although I am representing Chailee, she is also energetically present at our council. Joyyahl suggests that perhaps Liponie could give her a body so that she could have lips to speak. I ask Liponie to please do that and here is what she tells us.

"I am your universe, Chailee. I greet all of you in presence in the name of Joy and in the name of myself. We are quite mixed in our feelings of where we wish to be. I say this because there is a war between those who wish the evolution and those who wish to have the conflict. They are part of Earth and so it is that Earth, of which so much energy is placed in presence, is very important to the full universe of us. We are watching Earth and accepting the steps being made to create that non-dual within the space of Earth. All of our other worlds are in watching and in waiting for Earth to make her mark for when she does there is no one in this universe who is unaware of what will come next. It is only a matter of time before *all* match that same pace of forming of unity. All are reaching to match Earth if they are in a dual. All those who are in a non-dual are watching so that they may be of assistance.

There are three worlds in our universe that are in conflict and wish not to see that of the illusion fall aside, for it is in their interest to keep the veils. It is their right and privilege to experience this for however long it will continue. The motion of that which is the continued evolution will take that one and then the other and the other forward to meet their unification. It will be a divine choice on their part. It will not be because we make it to be so. I am supporting and yet I am also observing. I can be in no other state and yet I hold that great wonder and vision that you hold, my dear, in my heart for I know the ultimate is to reach that goal that you are wishing and shall achieve in the most opportune time. I can tell you from my observation that the journey is close at hand to reaching that goal."

That is encouraging information for me, but then I remind myself that this was a universe speaking. What would close at hand mean to a being like that? I decide to look at that information positively and just keep working.

"Sananda, the other day I heard you speaking about, 'celebrating the eternity.' Can you tell me the full version of what you said?"

"There is a beginning thread that lights the way to a destination that has no end, for those streams of infinite light are exciting everything and pushing the way forward. As this applies it shall be in its spur and fueling in a wave of forever."

"Mmm, that sounds delightful. Thank you."

Speaking with Aton, I say that I think I unplugged something in my head this morning. He tells me to put it back quickly and I feel momentarily panicked that maybe I did something I shouldn't have. He says he was only jesting and that instead of unplugging I was adjusting; something I am doing almost constantly.

"Do you get a chance to spend any time with Gaia in your abode?"

"Precious little. We are very focused. I am most dedicated to my beloved and this is what you would consider a pinnacle moment in time for Earth. Soon, a part of her will release, like the skin of the snake, and a new birth shall occur which is free of that old skin. It is part of her evolution and I am ecstatic to be in the position that I am and able to assist."

"I am also grateful. You know, of all the people I've met, and I've met some wonderful people, the work that you've done has been the most significant for me."

"I am grateful for this compliment. I am most dedicated, as you know."

"I know you are and I love you for it."

"I've never lost sight of Earth and I never shall."

December 1st seems like a perfect day to take a Christmas tree to Sheliah. If Liponie can put it in a snow globe that will be a way for her to have snow in her garden, something I think the fairies will really enjoy. Liponie says that it will always be snowing inside the globe and there are Christmas lights and ornaments all over the tree. He makes it as tall as ten fairies standing on each other's shoulders. (That would be twenty inches tall.)

"Hello to you my Joy!"

Just hearing Sheliah's voice makes me smile. I return her hello and tell her I have a present for her garden. For some reason, Liponie doesn't instantly manifest the tree. Sheliah asks if she can bring her children and says they now have nine little Joys and they are all perfect.

"As you know, I am very important to this garden. Rosebud is helping me by being the papa. He is very good. I knocked him on the head with my star and gave him gratitude."

Well, that's one way to keep your marriage happy. (I asked Gaia about this later and she said it was not manipulation. He would have experienced it as a gift.)

"We are teaching some to walk so we will have them here now."

Rosebud says, "Hello, my Joy. I am a big daddy."

I say that with nine babies he must be very busy. He agrees he is and says they are very blessed.

"I know you are and I just want those blessings to keep flowing. I have a present for you. Liponie, are you there?"

Liponie says he has been waiting for the moment and then he asks Queen Sheliah to gather her subjects and all of their children for a very important ceremony. Once everyone is present, Liponie clears his throat and says that there is a present for their garden for perpetuity from dear Joy. I hear Sheliah draw in a big breath and then say it is very beautiful. She asks if she should conk it to make it light and I tell her to give it a conk.

She sounds very excited as she tells me the tree turns around and around and there is now snow in the garden. Laughing, "We never have snow in our garden. This is a beautiful tree. You know what it reminds me of? Looking out at your world, and instead I am looking at it in our world! It is all sparkly! Thank you, Liponie, and thank you Joy and thank you kind man."

"That's my partner, Tonas."

With a certain tone in her voice she tells me that now that I have a Rosebud I should talk to Gaia because she will get me a book. In a very confiding voice she adds that the book will show me how to do many things. I admit that I am interested in seeing the book and Sheliah says it is the best gift they ever got. After I remind her that body parts came with the book, she laughs and says she and Rosebud play with those toys all the time.

Although it is never cold in the fairy gardens, Sheliah is aware of what is happening in my dimension because before I leave, she reminds me to stay very warm.

CHAPTER TWENTY-FIVE
December 5, 2104

At the Joy Councils with Liponie, he says he has been quite busy and all the council chambers are ready.

"Oh, Liponie, I bow to you. Now, did you get a chance to see what boxer shorts look like, because I like the idea of wondering if Tonas is wearing them underneath his trousers?"

Liponie says he is sure this will add to the flavor of our relationship. I specify multi-colored, comfortable and silky boxers and request that Tonas join us. Since I am still giggling as he enters, he comments that we are up to our designing.

I check with both of them to make sure they heard the Swizzlers' Christmas lists because I bet they are all intent on toys. Tonas says they are aware of the lists which are very creative. That prompts me to ask what some of the items on their lists are.

Tonas says he thinks they did research in the toy department of the internet. "Charlie is very excited about a basketball hoop and yet he wants it to have wheels underneath so it can be moved around. One of the little cuties desires to become an Olympic champion, and so there are all of these different mechanisms. Bars that you spin around and something that is called a horse although it does not look like one." (Must be a pommel horse)

I thought the Olympic equipment might be just for Champ, but Tonas says it is for all of them. He adds that for individuals who did not even want lips, they are certainly now embracing the human aspect. All of them wish to have shoes with roller skates underneath and ice skates. I'm told that Liponie is already creating a pond for ice skating and everything is completed for the water park. Tonas explains that he has been doing research and helping Liponie since he has been so busy creating the council chambers.

They have also decided to make a very large amusement park with the little rides as well as the very tall and scary ones. Tonas says he is not interested in the scary ones. That's fine by me; I used to do those rides when I was young and foolish but the time I went on the Tilt-A-Whirl as an adult I was nauseous for the rest of the day. Now I stick to the Ferris wheel. I ask if he's talking about a carnival. He says I am correct and then tells me that there is no mountain that is magic. He and Liponie looked everywhere to find out why they named it Magic Mountain and settled for copying much of what is in the Magic Mountain.

I'm thinking this is a Disney ride since Disneyworld is the Magic Kingdom and I try to tell Tonas that the Magic Mountain is in the Magic Kingdom. He tells me it is not and it has Six Flags. I realize that he's talking about a different park and quit trying to convince him otherwise.

I want to know if they have an accordion for Charlie. He says they now have one. There was every possible instrument in our storehouse except the accordion. (I want to say, "naturally," but refrain.) Tonas says they bought, as in purchased, an even hundred; Liponie manifested them, of course.

"You mean one hundred accordions?" OMG, I hope they don't all decide they want to play one. Listening to one person play an accordion might be only purgatory but one hundred people learning to play an accordion is my idea of musical hell.

Tonas confirms that we do, indeed, have one hundred accordions. I am unable to fathom why they felt it was important to have extras. I feel like saying one is plenty, but again I refrain. Instead, I ask if Sananda was able to find a teacher for Charlie. Liponie says he has already done research on this and he will ask Sananda to bring Myron Floren from the Fifth Realm to teach Charlie. It seems that Charlie has been watching *The Lawrence Welk Show* and is enraptured by the music and the dancing. Mr. Floren was the accordion player on that show so Liponie's choice is perfect.

Next, I ask Liponie if he has had a chance to find out if Zahseet is athletic. He says she is and will love our water park; it even has surf.

Liponie's mention of doing research prompts me to again ask him what resources he actually uses.

"We use the net. Even the television is available on the internet. It's a flawless way, my dear."

I was afraid he would say that. Now I remind him that when I read to King Arthur the astounding fact that he did not exist, I had found that information on the internet.

"But Arthur is in the other room."

"But according to one source on the internet he never existed. You have to be discerning about what is true and what is not true on the internet."

"O-h-h-h, it's a riddle."

"Yes, so you might want to check several sources to see if the information is accurate. Remember what you got with the 'Cone of Silence?' We knew it was a joke but you thought it was the real thing. Things like the 'Cone of Silence' can be sprinkled all through the internet."

I'm laughing but Liponie is saying, "Oh" and "Ah" about this information. He tells me he is most concerned. I tell him he has lots of resources on the council. Osiris and Isis have been around almost forever and they would have seen lots of things. He agrees to double check his facts and I reassure him that it's fairly safe to assume that entertainment is legitimate.

I ask Liponie if Cory has decided whether or not she wants a body. He tells me that she is testing out bodies of Disney characters and that today she is Snow White. Charlie loves Disney movies so I bet he put her up to that; Liponie says I'm correct. I'm sure this is not a good idea, but I don't address it now because Liponie is already talking about a quandary he is facing with a hurdy-gurdy. I've heard of it but I have no idea what it looks like or how to play it. Liponie says it is a stringed instrument that Charlie wants, but he hasn't been able to find any recordings of study.

Liponie admits he is concerned that Charlie may be over whelming himself. We decide that I'll have a talk with Charlie about quality versus quantity.

"Are you making any cookies?"

"We have a cycle that moves through with different kinds of cookie dough. We have an automated process where all of the dollops of dough drop onto a cooking platter which moves on a production line through an oven which heats and cooks with light. When the cookies come out there are long lines of individuals waiting for them. They like to pick them up fresh and hot."

It makes sense to have something like this in place since there are so many thousands of people here; otherwise, Liponie would never get out of the kitchen. I learn they have made all different kinds of fudge and a favorite is peppermint fudge with marshmallow; I bet Osiris loves that one. These sweets sound so good I may have to make some cookies or fudge in this reality.

"Surely there is someone among all of the millions of people here who knows how to work a yo-yo."

"Kennedy gave it a try but he was not good at it."

"I know it's hard but people who get good at it can do marvelous tricks."

"I think it is important for everyone to watch the study we have and then attempt it for themselves. Before we go, let me tell you that the most fun for all is *not* to make it easy. They seem to enjoy the challenge. If they could use their super powers it would not be nearly as fun."

With the full councils:

"Recently, I heard a woman ask me if I am a side of Joyce. Her question startled me but I realized that I am a part of Joy and Joy is part of me. As I'm sitting here on Earth talking to you, I can see my hands and the sofa I'm sitting on, I can enjoy our conversation today, and then when my consciousness leaves you I go about my way in this world. My father is currently in hospice and I believe he will be gone in just a few days. My participation in my Earth reality is a side of me you perhaps aren't aware of. What I want to tell this woman, and all of you, is that all of us have many sides. All of us are in our evolution, and I've really been working on myself to disregard and not complain about things concerning myself that I want to change. I've done quite a bit of that in the past and I'm determined to not do much of that, if any, in the future.

For those of you existing on worlds of duality that are in a process of evolution, like I am, there is an Earth expression of: 'Give yourself some breaks.' That simply means give yourself permission to acknowledge and honor where you currently are and know that you, and all of us, are moving towards manifesting our perfection. I'm not there yet, but some part of me is; for example, I recently talked to a part of me that exists a couple of hundred years in the future who has a lot of answers that I don't currently have."

Osiris asks to speak and says this is a very important message to all in presence. "It is not necessary for you to join our affiliation. We are most pleased to have you witness. Joy, I believe that you are speaking of the council woman Candahriah, who asked this question of you. I wish for you to know, Candahriah, that this description given by Joy is true through all dualities. In the nature of duality it is true that there are many sides to every individual. The only true side though, that is the reality that all of us of non-dual worlds see, is that she is of the purest of perfection of light. That is also how we see you. We are never in judgment; we are in celebration of every stage of evolution. We are celebrating you, Candahriah, for asking this question. May your universe and your world be most blessed by that perfection within yourself that you are in the process of restoring."

"Thank you, Osiris. Was this of assistance to you, Candahriah?"

"It is very much so and it is with my pleasure that we of the Kallamiah Universe pledge ourselves to this council."

"I welcome you."

"We are in gratitude for your explanation, and all of those who have been waiting for this answer have agreed that this is the time for us to make our commitment."

"It is thrilling for me to hear you say that."

I now explain what goose bumps are and that I am experiencing them. She surprises me by saying they also experience these but they have a different kind of skin. She adds that she is from the world Lowdeenar and that it is a water world. When I ask what her skin is like, she is at a loss to describe it. Osiris volunteers that her skin is much like that of a dolphin and that her face is very human-looking. He adds that she has arms, legs, a finned tail and is nearly the same color as he (dark green-blue). He says that she is more green than green-blue and tells her that she is a beautiful color.

I hear her giggle and she informs us that she is overcome. When I ask her if there is any land on her world, she says that the planet has a center of stone but all above that is water. I love learning things like this. I wonder if they would like to learn to water ski.

I mention to the council that it's winter here so if they want to do any winter games they could try sledding and building snowmen. "There's a game to play in the snow where you tramp down a big wheel with a center hub and spokes. I don't remember all the rules of it but it's a form of tag. Did you ever play that game, Mr. Kennedy?"

"I have never even heard of it, and yet it does sound like great fun."

Charlie immediately adds that they will try it today. They have already made "snowmans."

"And you can build snow forts. One year my son Mike took a machine called a snow blower (I briefly describe one.) and used it pile all the snow in our front yard into a heap so that he could make a big snow igloo. You could have snow ball fights, too."

Tonas whispers, "You should see the look on our little Charlie's face. Oh, his mind is working."

"Charlie, I want to give you just a tiny bit of advice. There are worlds and worlds of things to do and explore, and I know you want to try them all. Maybe this is not possible for you, but we have an expression called spreading yourself too thin, which means you're trying to do everything at once. Most humans who get involved in too many activities don't do very well. I know you are very qualified and you can do lots of things well, but maybe if you just focused on one musical instrument for awhile you would get a better idea of which ones you enjoy the most. This is only a suggestion."

He reminds me that there is only three hundred years, or a little more, to do everything. I agree that I'm also starting to feel we don't have much time left before the culmative. I explain that the point I was trying to make is that sometimes focusing on one thing gives you a deeper enjoyment of it. He answers that he is having the deep enjoyment and I say that's all that really matters.

I share with the council that a few days ago I heard the words golden platform and I'm sure that is about something important. Liponie says this is something the Earth Vigilance Council came up with. At this revelation, I ask everyone to stand and acknowledge both Liponie and the CEV for their diligence, their work and their assistance with everything we've been doing. "Their work is magical and I would like for everyone to give them a big round of applause, please." After I clap for them I add, "Thank you. You are an integral part of our team, just like every person here."

Liponie now tells us that he has perfected the vision and schematics for three different golden platforms for each council. One is for the full council presence of the Joy Councils of the other universes so that they might be in complete connection with our council. The other platform is for a smaller number of individuals from a council and the last platform is for one individual council member. Our council table has been enlarged to include forty-seven seats (one for each universe) and Liponie is ready to move into production of the platforms.

Charlie adds that there is no hurry for those who haven't joined to do so. We just want them to know they are welcome to join our council.

I ask if they are able to do two of the golden platform options simultaneously and Charlie says yes. The golden platform will automatically transmit the chief council person, for example, into their seat. For most individuals it is the difference between being present and having their consciousness transmitted. This sounds like a great idea and I give Charlie and Liponie the go ahead to create the platforms.

"I heard myself say something yesterday that I want to share. I believe I was talking to all of the universes. It is interesting to be able to do something like that (putting it mildly). Here's what I said, 'To those of you of the different colors and different worlds, please note that this is only temporary and will resolve.' I also heard myself say, 'Every heart is opening to the oneness of love that they are.' I assume that I was talking about our situation with the black people of Earth."

Charlie says I was and that we have the vision ready to transmit. It has been expanded for all of the universes so that each color, shape, size and configuration of every species on each world is brought into that frame of honoring of their position.

My idea is that we do some inaugurations so that the new universes can experience the benefits of our work. Tonas agrees to assist. I ask Jesus and Charlie to combine, while we are doing the inaugurations, some of the energies of the new teachings that Jesus wants to bring forth. I add that this is a great time to begin that because people are thinking of Christmas.

I gate Tonas and myself to the Joeshrahnah Universe to meet Kamala Shrow. When I ask her if she would like to say anything before we begin, she asks me to simultaneously inaugurate Rahnosah Prahnic's council since they are of the same soul lineage. Before Tonas and I energetically split to go to that council, he informs me that their council building is on a sun named Ihlowsha. Taking that information in stride, I gate with Tonas to this other universe. I ask Rahnosah if it is acceptable that I inaugurate his council at the same time that I do Kamala's. He agrees that is a wonderful idea and tells me he wishes he had thought of it himself.

I follow the procedure we have used in the previous universes to inaugurate the swords, crystals, and Joy Arrows for both councils and then send the transmissions out to their universes. We finish with our traditional toast using champagne. Tonas tells me they already have their golden platforms and that a golden light will indicate for them when I am in presence at the Joy Council.

I gate us to the Corena Universe to meet Joyyahl Kindar. Before I begin her inauguration, she tells me she was aware that a council from her universe offered us the Joy Arrow and that they collaborated with Liponie to create all the Joy Arrows for the other universes. She asks if Liponie may join us and Tonas transmits a request for him to do so.

Joyyahl thanks Liponie for coming and formally thanks him for making it possible for each of the beautiful councils to have the benefit of their arrow. "This is a joy for us to make this commitment to be the centerpiece transmission for all universes, for through this arrow we truly are one of the tribe. We welcome you and are ready to receive all you have to offer."

I thank her for her gift of Joy Arrows to all the universes, telling her I was not aware her universe had done this. I proceed with the inauguration and transmission then offer the Five Star Serenity Send-off to all sentient beings of their universe who had died. I explain that this offers them the option of either entering the Fifth Realm or an ascended master temple. When we have finished the toast, Joyyahl tells me she does not understand what an ascended master temple is and asks me to explain.

Oops is my immediate thought. I explain that on Earth there are forty-seven of these temples, and then ask Tonas if this universe has temples of their own they could go into. He tells me that all universes that have always been non-dual will not have had any deaths, but he doesn't know about universes experiencing duality. I send out a call to Osiris to come and help me. When he arrives, I ask him if it was incorrect to offer ascended master temples as an option for those who have died in this universe.

"Ah, this is an Earth experience, my dear. They were designed for the initiates of the ancient academies so that individuals might prematurely ascend and yet remain on Earth. I am not aware of an ascended master temple on any other world."

That remark catches me by surprise, but before I can admit that I've really goofed, Osiris tells Joyyahl, "Once we have a council meeting we can make an offer for such temples to you and create them from the beginning of your universe. This would be a wonderful offer for individuals who would wish to remain in your universe to be of service to those who are still evolving."

Osiris suggests we give this work to the Swizzlers and I thank Joyyahl for asking her question, adding that I think these temples will be a wonderful gift for the other universes. She confirms that they are excited to be able to experience them. Tonas tells the council they have their golden platform and that Liponie will explain how it is to be used.

The next Joy Council to inaugurate is on the planet Coriah which is in the Fonar Universe. Harahnsha greets us with excitement in his voice and explains that he feels our transmission will be the turning point for his universe since it is already primarily non-dual. After the inauguration and transmission I reveal that in addition to offering the Fifth Realm through the Five Star Serenity Send-off there will be an additional offering of the option to enter an ascended master temple once those are created. After I offer the Send-off, I can sense that some who have died are on "hold" waiting for the temples to be created. Osiris explains that the pause will only be for this moment because when the temples are created they will have been in the universes from the beginning. We drink a toast with Cristal champagne and then depart for the world of Nahshegrah in the Lowmeereeuh Universe.

I greet Silgah Holinrah and ask her if she would like to speak before we begin the inauguration. She says that this is the finalization of a dream for them, for they have been watching Earth and the pace that it has taken in the last few years. They have the same wish for their many worlds and they are grateful for the opportunity to use the same magic as we do.

I facilitate the inauguration, the transmission of our work and once I've explained the new option added to the Five Star Send-off, I offer that to all who have died in this universe. After a toast and a few parting remarks, Tonas and I make our way to the world of Nahgahnahsayyear in the Inseanahrah Universe.

After greeting Yarah Homma, I request that she keep me informed about how the transmissions affect her non-dual universe in the days ahead.

She tells me that they are here in service to us. Then she asks if the transmissions may be made in the past before their universe became fully non-dual. That sounds like a great idea, so I ask Sananda to join us and repeat this request to him. He says it will be easy to calibrate all transmissions to be sent into this universe in their ideal timing when the worlds in it were dual in nature. I suggest that we need to do this for all the universes. Osiris says that we can, with Charlie's assistance, recalibrate our Joy Arrows so that all the transmissions we have done will have been sent out in the ideal timing for each universe.

I thank Yarah Homma for her request which will allow us to enhance the transmissions we offer and then I move through the inauguration, transmission, Five Star Send-off and the final toast. I'm getting really good at these, which is a good thing, because we still have a lot of universes to do. Maybe I'm just getting used to universe hopping because my head doesn't feel quite as fuzzy as it has in the past from doing this much work all at once.

Tonas and I rejoin our Joy Council where he informs me that everyone is clapping for us. He tells me there are many geese here. I want to know what he is talking about. He asks if that is not the plural for goose. I agree that is correct, but want to know where the geese are.

He replies, "The geese bumps, my dear."

Through my laughter I manage to inform him we still call them goose bumps even if everyone has them. Then I tell the council that although I reached my limit of universe inaugurations today I do feel able to do the work that will assist people of different colors.

Charlie says that the transmission to recalibrate our Joy Arrows is in a sphere and ready to be activated. I ask for the council's assistance and then transmit the recalibration into the sword, the crystal and the Joy Arrows. When I ask about the ascended master temples, I am told that Sananda will be working with the different universes to create them.

Jesus informs me that the transmission for beings of all color, size and species includes the inner teachings of the present day and that, "There is a journey that begins in the heart and from the heart is a path leading to the ultimate destination that the heart knows. This destination is designed by the spirit. In that, there is no color, no shape or size or species. It is the spark of that which is the essence of the true being that is the guide to that destination. We truly are, within the origin of our being, and throughout the journey of our life, one tribe. That is what I added, my dear. Charlie tells me that they are ready for you to take the orb now."

"I think this is the best Christmas present that we could ever give to the world."

Jesus reminds me that this present now goes beyond our world and even our universe.

"Yes, and I am so grateful to be able to offer it. This is joy to the worlds indeed!" And with that, we send this transmission out.

Tonas tells me it was beautiful. "It was, and shall always be our Christmas, our holiday and our celebration of Earth Day, and now also to all the worlds."

"Jesus, I would like to see the three wise men. Mary, I would like to hear about your journey and if Jesus was indeed born in a stable I would like to say hello to the inn keeper. I want to hear the full details of all that transpired before and after Jesus's birth sometime before this Christmas."

After I bid Tonas and Charlie goodbye, I hear an unknown voice say, "Goodbye, Joy, do you like my voice now?"

I say that it sounds a little like Sheliah's voice and Charlie tells me he is basing it on a character named "Boy" from a movie he's seen. Tonas tells me no one knows what movie Charlie is talking about and that he, Charlie, has a part of himself in the cinema. When I ask Liponie to find out the movie's name he tells me he will but by tomorrow Charlie will have another voice.

Before I leave, I thank everyone for being part of my life and ask them to continue to hold their vigil for my father who is in the process of transitioning.

CHAPTER TWENTY-SIX
December 8, 2014

Two days ago, my father died in the house he was born in ninety-seven years ago. I'm glad he was able to be there when he transitioned because he deeply loved the farm. My brother and I brought Mother home from the hospital to be with him, but she won't be here much longer. She has some kind of infection that the doctors have not been able to halt.

I set it up with Jesus that he would wait on the ascension bridge with whichever of my parents died first until the other one died. They were married for seventy-two years and have been miserable since they were frequently without each other these last two months as they took turns being either in the hospital or a nursing home.

I ask Sananda to go with me to talk with Dad since I need an interpreter; my telepathy is great at transmitting but not yet good at receiving. Sananda says he checked on my father this morning and he was in deep conversation with Jesus. He was doing most of the talking. (This is no surprise to me.)

"Thank him again for all the support he gave me through my whole life."

These are Dad's words via Sananda: "He's really glad he was able to financially support you more in the latter part of his life. It was always, to him, an honor but he didn't understand why. He thought the only way to assure he was doing a good job was to line you up with Jesus. He's been talking with Jesus about who you are and what you're about."

I'm very glad to hear that because I could never explain SVH to either of my parents. Their spirituality was exclusively trying to live a Christian life, attending church and reading the Bible. This was a great program for them, but not enough for me.

Sananda also tells me that my father has decided to remain looking old until he sees how my mother looks. If she shows up looking young, he's going to quickly switch; if she shows up looking old, he does not want her to see him looking youthful.

I ask Dad if he likes his body. I'm told he says he loves his body and he always did but he's going to change to a youthful version.

"Dad, can you jump and click your heels together in the air now?"

"He said, 'This one's for you,' and he did just what you asked. He'd like you to know that he knows everything about your purpose and what you're doing now. He's very proud that he got to be your father. When he moves into the Fifth Realm he's going to be able to assist you because Jesus has explained what's possible."

What Sananda is referring to is that Dad can go back and rewrite everything he ever did that could have pushed me in a wrong direction or limited me, then hand me a file that will also assist me. Sananda says that my father plans to get my mother involved and that both of them will be able to assist me.

"What he would like you also to know is that the version of love that he had for your mother and the one that he knows that she had for him is different than the vision that you have of what a love would be but it is exactly what he wanted because that was all he knew. He says that she was the best wife that he could have ever asked for. When he looked at her he saw her as she was but also as his young bride. He always felt young and like he was that young man who fell in love. Times were really, really hard sometimes but the one thing that he knew was that she was right there. He is so proud to have been your dad and your brother's dad. He said the thing that he loved the most about you was that you looked like your mom when they were young together. He says that your brother loves you very much and that he's always going to want to take care of you, so let him."

"Thanks Dad, I love you. We're going to have your funeral tomorrow."

Sananda says Dad replies, "I'll be there."

Talking with Aton at the Joy Council about my progress, he says my consciousness levels are being affected by the orbs. I want to know exactly what that means. He says the orbs are awakening the latent knowledge of the masters instilled in my consciousness levels. They are also stimulating knowledge which can assist me right now. He asks me if

I've noticed how quickly I am able to complete tasks now and I agree that I seem to be able to edit material for my books faster than before.

"May I take one little quick bow for this, hmm? Things are moving quicker in your mind. There is no rhetoric to slow you down or create sluggishness."

"I'm puzzled, though, why I don't remember conversations people have with me. My mother said, just a couple of days ago, something about how she would be with me always, but I can't remember her exact words. Conversations just seem to flow right over my head and not stick."

Aton points out that I have been under considerable stress, and I agree that is probably a major factor in my inability to remember.

"May I give my congratulations to you and to your patriarch that he has made his elevation?

"Thank you, it was a relief for me."

"It is his ascension and that is quite magnificent. Before you began your grand scale of things, imagine what it was like for people to simply die."

"Oh, terrible."

"It was quite lovely on the other end where they all gathered and waited for everyone to come into readiness. At the same time, it is a very wonderful thing to now have had the culmination complete with that exquisite entry into the Fifth Realm. I intend to ascend with my beloved. Did you know?"

"I know, and I'm so glad you two are together."

"Ah, we can attribute this to you, my dear."

"Osiris was at the bottom of it. He's the one who gave me a little nudge and, of course, I leaped at it."

"It is in your nature, my dear."

"That has been a surprise for me to find out. I just want everyone who wants a partner to have one."

"This is the sweet part of yourself."

Aton says that with Marilyn's help, Cory picked Sophia Loren's body as a model for her own. He adds that Cory's research was carefully done to assure that Ashtar's former partner did not look like Sophia. Cory wanted to make sure that it was herself who was attractive to him.

I ask Tonas, Liponie, Hathor and Cory to join us. When they are present, I tell Cory I'm really happy with her choice because Sophia is such a classic woman. She says she likes her body and that Marilyn has been teaching her how to walk in high heels, very, very deliberately.

I hear Liponie's raucous laughter and he adds, "I have been in charge as well, my dear, though when I sashay around it is not the same."

My advice to Cory is that no matter what happens with Ashtar, I hope that she thoroughly explores every avenue of enjoyment that her body can give her.

"Thank you, I am sure that I will guard my heart until there is a question in his eye. There is someone else that I have interest."

I ask her if she can tell me who it is and she asks for privacy. When we are alone she whispers to me that it is Liponie and adds that he is so beautiful. There go my plans, but I don't care one bit. I agree with her that Liponie is a jewel.

Cory makes a little growling sound and says that she feels like a woman next to him. Wow, she has leaped into her womanhood with her heart and both feet! I have to tell her that Liponie has had a crush on Jill Marie; she likes him, but she really cares for someone else. I've been trying to help him with her, but my heart has not been in it because I know she will never fall for him.

Cory says that Liponie is *everything* and follows her declaration with another growl. I ask her if she wants me to give Liponie a few hints, but she prefers I help her by putting them both in charge of a project. We discuss some options and then Cory says she feels it would be best if they could both have their hands in something.

She suggests I could have them make plates and bowls for the kitchens. "You could explain to him that it would help me to feel more human if I have my hands in the clay. If we had to make many of these crockeries it would give us a chance to develop our friendship. Now he is committed to teaching me how to be a woman and he is so hilarious. He creates everything with a thought so there must be a reason why he would need to be with me for a long time, perhaps to teach me how to be in presence with a man. He could teach me how to be sensual. I have had quite a few lessons but nothing about engaging with a man."

I ask Liponie to join us and I make the pottery suggestion that Cory mentioned. He's amenable to making models that he can use to then mass produce using his presto change-o method. Now Cory takes the initiative to ask if she may make a request. I'm really delighted, of course, and give her the go ahead.

"Liponie, you have been so helpful. Do you think there is anything that I could do to make my body better?"

He pauses for a moment and then says that he cannot see any place for improvement. She is perfect.

"Ah, thank you. I wonder if you could teach me how to dance. I know that you are already doing so much for everyone. I just do not trust anyone else to teach me certain things like, if I'm going to be in a relationship as an embodied being, I do not know what it would be like to have the smalls talk. Perhaps you could show me what it would be like in a relationship if I was walking in Joy's garden with a man. What would he do? Would he walk for a little while and hold my hand; would he perhaps find a little place and kiss? Will you teach me how to hug and kiss and dance and things like that because I will need to know how to do those things? I would like for you to teach me how to swim and I would love for you to design all of my clothes and my swimming costume."

I'm wondering why she asked me to help her, because she has this situation well in hand. I do ask Liponie, though, if he would be willing to take some time to fulfill some of Cory's requests because he has been working so hard.

"Indeed, that will be quit lovely. I will show you everything. Of course, you must know that Ashtar has interesting tastes. He likes to embody himself in the normal Earth atmosphere and have little coffees and be among the people. I can show you what he likes."

Cory thanks him and says she just knew he would be the perfect teacher.

Speaking privately with Liponie, I ask him the name of the universe of the man who created him. He says it is Neftoo. When I ask him if the man is on their council, Liponie, in a clipped and emphasized tone, says the man is dead. He adds that his owner was from a dual world and that he had the most interesting hungers for things. I explain that the reason I was wondering about his creator's location is that I wished him to know what a treasure he dismissed.

"Hmm, he used me quite much, my dear. I let him destroy himself."

"What do you mean by that?"

"I gave him everything that he wanted. It was my only escape."

"Then I'm glad you did it and I'm glad you're with me."

With the full Joy Councils, I ask Charlie to clarify the work we did when we calibrated the Joy Arrow.

"The calibration of the Joy Arrow was initiated so that it would be supporting all of the energies in all of the different realms that we are connecting. There will be many worlds that are of dual and many that are non-dual. In each of these it is important to have the energies be calibrated specifically for them for the works that are to be brought into their world. This was already in place, and yet it was also important that the arrow itself be raised to be in a position that can graduate for each individual that is receiving based upon their acceptance levels."

"So we calibrated the different ideal timings for the transmissions, and we did it for each individual person in each universe?"

Charlie confirms that is correct. I tell him I'm really impressed and thank the Swizzlers.

"Sananda, did we put any of the ascended master temples in place?"

"We are prepared for all placements in the eventuality of each universe's desire to enter this affiliation. Each universe that joins will have forty-seven ascended master temples. Forty-seven is a number of great importance because that is the number of the soul lineages. We have made it possible for individuals with an individuated soul of every world and star and every universe who has accepted the Five Star Serenity Send-off to choose either an ascended master temple or the Fifth Realm."

"Charlie, have you started any accordion lessons?"

He says he is waiting for his instructor and he was told that he won't get his accordion until Saint Nicholas comes.

"You will like my new voice. It's a very nice voice that I heard on a movie."

I don't like it at all. It's very choppy and nasal-sounding, but I agree that it's different. Then I tell him that I liked the first voice he used. He changes immediately to that one and asks if I like it. I say that I do and he says he will use it because he wishes to have the voice I like. I encourage him to keep experimenting and ask if we are singing any Christmas carols.

He says there is a great deal of singing, mostly by the angels that Liponie brought here. I ask Liponie and Cory to get together some caroling groups and to just pick anyone who wants to sing whether they have a good voice or not.

"Candahriah, do you do anything on the surface of the waters on your planet or do you do only underwater activities?"

"It depends on what you wish."

"Do you have boats?"

She asks what a boat is. My next question is if she spends her time underwater. She says she does and then I ask her how long she can be out of water. There is a long period of silence. Finally, I remark that she is not underwater here. Liponie explains that there is a transparent bubble of energies around her that I am not aware of.

"Oh! That's cool. Does Zahseet have one of those also?"

He explains that Zahseet doesn't need one because she can be aquatic or on land. Then he asks to speak with me privately.

"I did not wish to say this in front of the others. Those from Zahseet's world seem to age and then they reverse. They keep their wisdom."

I ask him if he thinks it's because of the fountain they drink from and he agrees that is possible. He says he hasn't felt comfortable asking her about it. I thank him for this information and say I'll ask Osiris about it some other time.

Tonas and I move to the Gaygoreeah Universe to the Joy Council on the world of Kaireesha. Monahquah Senet greets us; we inaugurate his council and then transmit our works to his universe.

Next, we gate to the world of Zihcorahn which is in the Ahkahnay Universe. Haireetah Voreeneeuh greets us and we follow the same procedure here. Before we leave, Tonas states that the Ashtar Command will not support wars but they will support the council.

In the Neftoo Universe, Tonas asks to speak with me privately before we enter the council. He explains that he spoke to the previous council about not supporting wars because he was concerned some in that universe might want to involve the Ashtar Command in their conflicts.

Toemarrah Metahn greets us and we quickly move into inaugurating their council and sending out our transmission.

We move to the world of Zeefmah in the Comahleeah Universe. Before we enter the council, Tonas says the required drink is fermented discharge from an animal called a moosheah (not as tall as a camel and without a hump). Although it resembles camel spit, it is their special drink and he wanted me to know about it in advance. He suggests perhaps we should not mention the word discharge and I agree. I thank him for warning me and add that I'm glad I don't actually taste any of these drinks; unfortunately, he says that one day I *will* remember the taste and that he and Liponie fixed the drink. I hope they made it taste not too bad, but I wonder how good they can make discharge taste.

In the council, I greet Bohnar Comeen and ask him if he would like to say anything before we begin. He replies, "We are feeling the energy of this union even now and we are feeling the hope of all of Comahleeah is at hand. All of your works seem to be so very much open and from heart. We are learning this from you."

"Thank you. I'm learning it too. Remember I'm still in a world that is also experiencing duality. It can be quite challenging, can it not?"

"Indeed, only we did not realize that we were dual. We did not realize that there was anything different. We have learned much from you."

"I didn't know that either, so we are learning together."

274

The inauguration and transmission go smoothly. Tonas then announces, "We have one of the traditional drinks, and yet I think our dear Liponie has found the premiere fermented moosheah elixir. Each of you has a beautiful moosheah horn, created by Liponie, to drink from." Tonas's voice sounds a little fake to me as he announces, "This is such a delightful tradition and we are very excited to be a part of it. Let us all raise our horns, and in the raising of it we hold the vision for the hope of all tribes knowing that Zeefmah and all of the Comahleeah Universe are experiencing their destiny."

I take a little sip and proclaim the drink interesting. Tonas says it is quite a delicacy and tells me I must drink the full horn.

"Thank you, Tonas."

"Yes, of course."

We make a few parting remarks and then escape. After we gate to the Deeohnah Universe, but before we enter the council, I emphatically label Tonas a stinker.

"Everyone was watching! You took the tiniest sip. It would have been an insult."

"I hope I didn't make a face."

"Perhaps you can use your SVH to rewrite this. Go ahead my dear, Neftee is ready."

I learn Neftee Voenesh is two words instead of one. He explains that there are many names in the middle of his two names because they keep all of their mother's family names. I ask him how many names there are. Tonas answers that in Earth terms there are sixty-one names. I thank Neftee for not telling me all of them and ask him if he wishes to say anything before we do his inauguration.

"We are primarily non-dual and it has been a great journey for us to reach the status we are in. We are very much excited about the days to come and living in the moments for our final steps. We can see ourselves taking them with Earth."

"I like that idea. We've got to do some catching up with you because we've got some challenges."

After we complete the inauguration and transmission, Tonas gives the toast to "unity and the final steps leading us into the fellowship of one tribe."

Back at our council, Liponie is laughing as he tells me everyone was in tears and in laughter when they saw my face as I drank the spit. He tells Tonas he shouldn't have said anything. Tonas answers that he had to say something to me. I immediately use SVH to rewrite that I had a pleasant expression on my face as I gulped the discharge. There's no need to cause offense.

Earlier, Liponie reminded me that today is dedicated to the elevation of the consciousness spirit on Earth. Now, he suggests that perhaps we could send a focus together for the vision of enlightenment and that perhaps Buddha could give us something special to add to this. I notice on my calendar that it says "Bodhi Day" which is a Buddhist celebration. We invite Buddha to come and I'm told that now he is in presence.

He tells me he's worked with the council and that they have all put their hearts into a transmission that will be universal. "That transmission is the full vision of everyone's true journey. It is not necessary for us to walk in each other's shoes to understand one another. It is to understand ourselves. In understanding the spirit of our own selves, we are able then to witness the purity of spirit that is the truth of all beings."

"Thank you for your assistance."

"Thank you for this opportunity to take an important day that has been dedicated to enlightenment and making it a multi-universal day."

Charlie tells me I have a sphere and it is multi-colored.

"Focus with me, please, your enlightened minds, and your light hearts as we bless the sphere." I then guide them in assisting me to send the transmission out to all the universes in our council.

As I'm wrapping up the meeting, Tonas asks me if I would like for them to hold a special intention for my mother and I say yes, their support is appreciated. I tell them my father's funeral is tomorrow and that I'm OK with that. I know he's waiting for my mom. Tonas lets me know Cory wants to speak privately with me again.

Cory sounds very distressed as she tells me she cannot go on with the charade about Ashtar; when she is with Liponie she feels like she's going to explode with love for him. I offer to tell Liponie she's not interested in Ashtar, but I suggest not saying anything to Liponie about her interest in him. She agrees with me and I ask Liponie to join us.

"Liponie, Cory has informed me that she is still interested in learning how to relate to a man, but it's not going to be Ashtar."

"I'm still very committed."

"I know you must be a wonderful teacher. Enjoy your work with her, please."

"It is always very enjoyable."

"Bye, Liponie. Bye, Tonas!"

"I thought perhaps you were going to leave without bidding me farewell."

"No, and here's a kiss, too. We need to have some mistletoe hanging around."

"That doesn't sound very good."

"You get to kiss people when they are standing under mistletoe."

"Ah, but the toes are not good."

"Mistletoe has little berries."

"I will do research. At first thought it was not very appealing to kiss you under a little gaggle of toes."

CHAPTER TWENTY-SEVEN
December 12, 2014

December 9th was the evening of my dad's funeral. As I was trying to go to sleep, I saw the faces of many people as they filed past me. I later learned that they were council members who came to his funeral to honor me. That same evening, I heard Sananda say that there are many ways to meet death and each is divine. I knew he must be right, but that really didn't help me much. I was grateful, though, that Dad slipped away peacefully.

Since Cory is so interested in Liponie, I ask Jill Marie to share her true feelings with Liponie. She steps back two weeks in time to speak with him. The result of their conversation is that Liponie now knows she has feelings for someone else and they agree to be just friends. I decide I will say nothing to him and just carry on.

At the Joy Councils, Aton pulls me aside to ask me to do an exercise that he explained via a phone conference to some of the AMS initiates. I explain that I didn't listen to it because I was with my mom who is in the process of making her transition.

"We are taking turns being with your mother."

"Thank you. She's been seeing people and we keep telling her they are not there."

"Do not tell her that. Even I have stood in her presence."

"She was describing things that seemed rather strange. I knew there were probably people there but I believe she was hallucinating too."

He agrees that is possible. I tell him I will listen to the recording of the phone conference and ask if there is anything additional I can do that will assist me with regeneration.

"There is a very important piece that you will be able to manage, I am sure. It is called patience."

I'm better at being patient, but I still have a long way to go. I share with Aton how, as I was getting my teeth cleaned at my dentist's office the other day, I started thinking about what my hygienist will say when she begins to notice that my teeth are getting better. They've been holding steady for a year or so with no new little cavities, but there are some spots she's watching.

Figuring it can't hurt, I ask Aton to pray for my teeth. He asks me if praying is like beseeching for a miracle. I agree that miracles are one benefit of prayer and it will take one for my teeth to improve.

During a conversation with Osiris, I learn that the elixir Zahseet's people drink is similar to a milky fluid that can be found in Vilcabamba, Ecuador. People there call it the milk of the mountain and those who drink it have great longevity.

I've never heard of this place or this drink. Since I don't have the time or the inclination to visit Ecuador, I ask if drinking the elixir from the fountains of Loree would help me rejuvenate. Funny, as I think about how it is so much easier to energetically visit another universe than physically travel to Ecuador.

Osiris tells me it is possible. He says that Zahseet's race grows to be a certain age and then their age reverses. "Zahseet looks like a sweet little princess yet she is quite elderly. If you were to drink this elixir it might benefit you. Perhaps talk to her privately and suggest that you would like to experiment with their elixir. I must tell you that drinking it is part of a ritual. Elderly individuals make a pilgrimage to the great fountains, drink from the fountains then make their way back down the mountain. When they enter the waters again they would be at the beginning stage of the reversal of aging. Zahseet is becoming as if a child."

"That must stop at a certain point?"

"I believe she has had this same appearance for more than one hundred years. She is quite sprightly."

I tell him I will talk with her because I don't want to intrude into one of their rituals. Osiris says I can do no wrong in the eyes of any of the council.

Tonas greets me and asks to kiss my hands. I return his greeting and ask him to tell me what's going on with him since I never seem to take the time to find out. He says he is in bliss every moment and adds that what is happening with the council as well as being in my presence is a great deal of excitement for him. "It is as if we have ninety-four little children between us and they are such a delight to all of us. It is amazing for us to witness their development. They are so wise and yet also so innocent."

Speaking with Sananda and Jesus, I ask if there is a chance Mom and Dad would want to attend our Christmas party. My reasons are that I'd really love for them to meet Tonas and I would love for them to have some fun.

"Maybe Mom had some fun when she was little because she spent a lot of time reminiscing about those years, but from my perception, fun was not part of her reality. Do you have any thoughts about that?"

Sananda answers that I am selling my mother short and that she enjoyed her life. He reminds me that her perspective was different than mine.

I answer that she felt her lack of a high school education prevented her from doing as much with her life as she could have. Also, through the adult part of her life, she seemed to worry almost constantly.

"Have no concerns of this, part of her enjoyment was the worry. Have you ever heard someone say they're not happy unless they are worrying? The pay-off for her worry was that she felt she had control of something if she was concerned about it."

I suppose he's right, but since this is not an issue anymore I reiterate my hope that they could come to one of our parties and dance. "Mother never danced with Dad; she said if they did it was a shuffle."

Jesus says he believes my father has made his choice to transition into the Fifth Realm. He asks me if this influences my desire for them. I'm feeling so emotional it is very hard for me to talk, but I am able to say that I would have loved for them to see the people I'm working with. Jesus says we can show them and that my father is already aware of what I have accomplished.

"I know, but it's not the same as saying, 'Dad, here are Emmon and Firona, and Mom, here's a wonderful man who may be my forever partner.'"

Tonas says I am giving him hope. "She is going to introduce me to the parents. This is a big step for us."

I'm sure he is trying to cheer me up and I do manage to laugh at his remark. Jesus tells me that Mom is very close. Through my tears, I reply that I know she is, but at least my brother and I have had some nice talks with her.

With the full council:

"We did some work with enlightenment and I want to get some feedback from Buddha about what enlightenment is. I was thinking about this the other day and defining what it means to me. One thing is that I'd still have questions but in most cases I would be able to get the answers myself. Secondly, I would feel good every moment of every day. Who would be the best person to define enlightenment for me?"

"It would be my pleasure to answer you. I am Buddha. As a human being likened to yourself, a journey of enlightenment is a never-ending journey. There is always that little fruit ahead with the nectar so sweet to reach and take to your lips understanding and recognition. The sweetness of that fruit when taken into self is the greatest of pleasure.

The harmony that you speak of is a field of resonance that exists. In that field if there was blood flowing from any part of your body you would simply look upon it with great wonder and stop it with your mind. Enlightenment is within and yet it radiates outward to create not only the field for yourself, but you also know that all who come upon your field are in that same space of grace and sweetness that is your truth. That is enlightenment. Nothing is out of reach; it is simply a step away."

"I have heard of this field you are talking about. It sounds like something wonderful to have."

"It is something that is developed and you have it. You are simply creating within it the components that you would wish to be ever present."

"I don't feel like I know what I'm doing."

"That also is part of the journey. If it is just out of reach, how can you know the taste of it? You can imagine, you can project forward and take that essence into yourself and live it in advance of developing it. And

282

yet, nothing is sweeter than the nectar which is achieved. You are designing yourself in this moment. You have many very important and heart-felt companions. I call them important because when I was in my evolution days and evolving piece after piece, it was as if I was taking a puzzle and putting the picture together for myself. As I did, I had assistance from some of the same individuals who are assisting you. And yet, I had to reach a certain plateau where I was in readiness for the receiving of what they had to offer and when I reached that point what they had to offer became ever possible and ever present. You are in a place now where you can have many fruits offered to you and they are for your picking."

"Speaking of fruits I heard something about 'carrots' and I believe there is some kind of gateway."

Buddha answers that individuals throughout the Earth are holding a vision of a world that is free of conflict. "Each of these individuals have their own idea of what the vision might look like, and yet it is the exact same vision with different flavors. You are of the academy and so you have your feet within several positions leading to the 25th dimension. Even if you are not fully aware of what it feels like in each position, you are experiencing it. Those of the world who do not have that privilege have only the vision they can imagine. Many of those visions were spawned within the 3rd dimension and so the pictures of what enlightenment and an enlightened world will appear to be are somewhat similar and hold some of the same components. Many people are wishing to skip several steps ahead, but the Earth itself must make its progress.

The individuals of your AMS affiliation are holding open bridges for those who are ready. Each of these bridges has a gate and the gate leading onto each of those bridges is held in a resonance that many are ready to embrace. Your affiliation will have an easy time holding together the vision of what is to be.

We also have the CEV which we all honor most greatly. They have been working on several projects to assist in immersing the Earth through these individuals of your AMS who are spread far and wide throughout the Earth holding their vision. Many of them are already moving into the next day and they have held the vision of the gateway all through their day."

"Do we do anything today with what Charlie has put together?"

"It is important for your day for this to be applied by our council and then members of your AMS can distribute this vision throughout the Earth."

I propose to do some inaugurations, then the work Charlie has and then say I hope to be able to speak with Jesus since there is a focus on his story this month.

Buddha agrees there is energy to be traded on the myth of his birth in this month. "As an instructor of dear Jesus, he was an apt pupil. Many of us at this table instructed him in his academies, and, of course, there is much to be traded on the energy of his birth at this time. There are eyes and hearts and minds focusing on his birth as well as the gifting of one another."

For each inauguration, I activate their sword using my sword, that energy moves through the crystal and arrow to activate them, we transmit the work through those implements, I offer the Five Star Serenity Send-off, drink a toast, usually champagne, and Tonas offers the support and protection of the Ashtar Command. Different languages of what I assume are specific to each universe are always a part of the work I do during these inaugurations. Here are the inaugurations in the order that we do them:

Ohniuh Comb's council on a moon, Hahkah, of the world Eeshenarrah in the Porneeseesee Universe.

Kallahm Amar's council in the Booseeuh Universe.

Kahsheenah Vohnsheer's council in the Nasconerah Universe.

After that third inauguration, I have a couple of small pieces of chocolate since I'm feeling very dizzy; hopefully, that will help to ground my energy but if not, it's a good excuse anyway.

Lana Fahreetwoah's council in the Zahnahsh Universe is the largest yet at over ninety million.

For Jenairrah Magursha's council inauguration (Insear Universe), Tonas asks them all to stand and whispers to me that this is their custom.

When I ask, Tonas tells me that for Candahriah's inauguration (Kallamiah Universe) Liponie created a "bubble" for me since their council is underwater. I also have a costume in honor of their culture. Tonas says it is a green gown that is clinging to my body quite beautifully. My face and hands are my regular skin color but every other part of me is covered by the gown. Tonas uses the word "clinging" three times during his description, so my gown must be very fitted.

Back at our council, Tonas tells me all here witnessed the work through a projection. I ask Charlie if we have something to offer the universes in our affiliation.

"We have a package deal. Take it or leave it. I am only joking. It is like a little ice cube which will melt and allow people to receive the transmission when they are ready. Sometimes an individual has a resistance to the whole ice cube and yet if they were to have the little pieces as the cube melts they are then able to accept more. Individuals will have an option to see the world as it can be and feel that which is clinging to them from the 4th dimension as well as the old ways of the 3rd dimension melting away." Charlie delivers those last two words very dramatically and asks me if I like it. I reply that I do like it and that I love him and all of them.

"Before we activate that, I wonder if Jesus has anything to include."

"I believe that what I would offer to our world of Earth, more than anything, is a vision of hope. For in the hearts of many there are still the beliefs that there is no escape from the bondage that is linked to the old stories. May the vision of the future also reflect within this ice cube."

Charlie says that it does and yet he believes that we can add that heart-felt energy, for certainly there is no being on Earth who has not felt the pure energy of Jesus's source of being.

I ask to share something that my brother told me yesterday and Tonas says I must.

"Much of his life he has been very concerned about the affairs of our world, politics, our money situation and those kinds of things. He's very successful and a wonderful, generous and kind man. He shared with me that he was feeling downhearted as he was driving to visit with my mother and me. He was at a stop light and he looked up and saw an older lady in the car behind him, and she just smiled at him. He had a moment of awakening where he realized that it was his… I don't remember the exact words he used when he was describing this to me but I believe he said it was his responsibility to be happy and that he was going to do so. I was so glad that he shared that with me. There's so much I want to tell him that I really can't at this time; I know that's divine also.

Years ago I was driving along in my car and I suddenly knew that nothing outside of me determines my happiness. I could feel happiness inside me. I'd love to help people release blocks to allowing themselves to be happy with even the simplest things in life: a woman's smile, a great piece of chocolate, a gentle rain, the sound a breeze makes blowing in pine trees, a bird singing outside their window, a baby's laughter and all the myriad other small events that people encounter during a day. For those who are ready, let us help them become aware of those small delights in life because they are huge."

Charlie answers that, "We are many times come and other times overcome by that which is your generosity. It is your spirit of that desire to assist that gives us our passion as well. We are complete and ready for you to take this jewel, a gift for Earth that will also be calibrated for all of the universes that are in readiness. It is a gift for you, Joy, for you are the bringer of Joy to all of us. Look upon our faces when you enter the room and feel our admiration."

I'm feeling a bit overcome by Charlie's words. In order to keep from crying, I ask Liponie if we may have some champagne for a toast. Laughing, as usual, he says he is ever ready and asks all within the council to please hold their hand outward. "Into your hand will come a cinnamon roll and in the other hand a crystalline glass. Cory and I have been working on cinnamon rolls all day."

"Do we have the aroma of cinnamon rolls?"

"Bring it to your nose. It is most delightful. We have been in laughter all this day so there is much laughter and joy in the cinnamon."

I decide to do the transmission first and ask everyone to focus their joyful and happy hearts on it as I send it out. Then I make a toast to hot cinnamon rolls, love, joy, companionship and all of the councils.

"Mary, tell me a little bit about the story you'd like to share with me about Jesus's beginnings."

"You must know that I was quite young when I realized that I was to become the mother of this dear one. It was in special ceremony that he was conceived. Yes, indeed, and there were many in presence. The conception of him was most divine; it was a part of a very specific ceremony that was designed to bring about the energy being that we all see in presence here. It was as if the conception of a non-dual being and yet it had to be of an Earth-sparked essence. Naturally, as he grew, and I neared his birthing, there was a need for us to travel. It was also important for him to be born in a place of neutrality. And so it was that he was born within a cave. You have been in this cave, Joy. Yes?"

"Yes."

"Ah, this gives me great gratitude beyond that of your support and healing of myself and the greeting of our dear one. You also stood in presence there in your physical body."

"Yes. There is a star placed on the floor there. I waited in line with many other people as one by one they knelt and kissed the place where he was born. It was very special for me."

"The birth of my dear one was the beginning of a very important journey for me. Naturally, it was important to save his life for there was a death sentence upon him. All of the boy children born during that time were to be murdered. And so it was that we left that area and did not return for years. It was a joy to me to raise this little puppy. He was so very sweet."

"Were other people at his birth? The story we tell is that there was no room in the inn and that you birthed him in a stable."

Mary confirms it was a stable in a cave. I ask if she knows the innkeeper's name. (It would be fun to invite him to our Christmas party and tease him about not having enough room for the Messiah.) She answers that she did not meet him. Joseph entered, found there was no vacancy and they moved on.

"It was not considered to be our first choice for someone of noble blood to give birth to their first born within that place of the animals. And yet, for us, it was a sacred place, for we knew that it was a place of history, you see. It was already known to us that there would be a legacy left behind."

The other details she furnishes are: the animals in the stable consisted of their donkeys along with one horse and a camel; over a course of days a star did indeed appear over the stable which led the kings Gaspar, Melchior and Balthazar to their presence.

"Do you think they could join us for our Christmas celebration?"

Mary laughs and says, "How delightful! Naturally they were very helpful to us. They gave us priceless treasures that would help us make our way to Egypt."

"Were there shepherds that came to see you also?"

"Of course, there were many who came. And the story of the little drummer…"

Wondering if there was such a little boy, I prompt her with the word yes. She says it was her heart that was beating fast like a drum. "The face of this one radiated the greatest gold; I knew of the aura. I birthed my child, thanks to you and all who assisted me (other SVH practitioners), free of pain."

I am so glad that we were able to assist her and I tell her so. She says her heart was filled with such joy to have the little one placed in her arms and to know in the forever of forever his heart would be joined to hers. "He is made of the body of myself and he is made of the light of that which is sparked from the heavens."

I'm crying at her beautiful description of Jesus's birth and say that children are very precious. She answers that none are more precious than me. I have difficulty embracing her kind words and now I'm crying even harder.

"You have had a long road to this place you exist within now, and yet, if you look upon it, what a beautiful journey. Some of it was fraught, it is true, but it led you to this place you exist within now. Truly, if we look upon it, every step of that journey was sacred, was it not?"

Her words help me to regain a bit of composure and I agree I am grateful for my journey. Through more questions I learn that they stayed several days in the cave and then made their way very quickly by night to Egypt where Jesus would be safe. (There was no edict in Egypt about killing first born sons.)

"We were in a church where our guide told us you had sheltered. Is that possible?"

"Saints Sergius and Bacchus Church is the church that was built over that place which was, in truth, a crypt. We took shelter and lived there for some time."

"In that church we saw a picture of you and all of us saw you blink your eyes at us. It was amazing."

"It was a special message to each of you. There were many of your SVH fellowship in presence."

"What were you transmitting with your blinks?"

"I was transmitting an awakening pattern to assist those of your fellowship to awaken. I was transmitting to all of you evenly the same rain of beautiful, great wishes for your journey so that you could find the path that is of the greatest comfort leading to that which your heart and conscious mind bring to your presence. It is not for any of us to lead you by a leash around your neck. It is for you to be in your freedom step and find your way. For us it was, and is always easy, to guide and to lead, and yet we are never pushy. We are always uplifting."

"I have finally found my path, so I'm grateful."

"It was quite unceremonious for me to have my picture leaning up against the wall there. And yet, it was in perfect position for people to see me. I believe you have named this church. Say the name for all of us please."

At first I'm drawing a blank for the name and then suddenly I remember we called it the church of the blinking Mary.

"Yes, indeed. Do you all hear it?"

She tells me she has developed even more transmissions and that sometimes they (Jesus is pictured with her.) make their mouths move.

"Sometimes Jesus's little feet move. It is quite comical to see the faces of individuals who can see this because most do not believe their eyes."

I know she is right. Even with all of us standing there, staring at her for several minutes and affirming to each other that she was blinking, it was *still* hard to believe. Seeing his little feet wiggle might have put me over the top.

I ask Mary if Jesus was a large baby and she confirms that he was. She adds that this was a blessing for as they crossed the Jordan and on into Egypt it was important for him to look older, to appear as though he was born perhaps even as much as a month before. This was because there were people that could tell the tale of an entourage of individuals that were in guardianship.

"When I come back I want to hear more details from you and also Jesus. Let's have some of the shepherds or people you would like to invite to our Christmas party, if that's possible. It could be a reunion for you and I could talk with them and see what they thought about the baby born in a cave."

Mary explains that the cave was most important for the animals for the Sun could be quite hot.

"I'll be back on Monday and I want to hear more about the Christmas preparations. Have we sorted out the confusion about mistletoe?"

Tonas sounds sheepish as he says that all have been educated now. I thank everyone for the wonderful work we did today, tell them goodbye and ask to speak with Cory in privacy.

Cory sounds ecstatic as she tells me that she and Liponie have had the most wonderful adventures. He shared with her that a man should have his arm around the woman when walking, and he also showed her how to walk with their hands clasping one another. They went to a movie, sat very close and shared a soda pop.

"At any time if you want me to give him a little nudge let me know. I don't have to say your name but I could tell him that he has a secret admirer."

"Oh, let us explore this a little longer. I wish for him to come to this on his own. Tonight, he is going to show me the kissing. It is impossible on the Moon to have moonlight and so we have starlight in your garden. I'm nervous but the girls are helping me."

"I know you'll have a great time. Good luck, he's a wonderful man."

CHAPTER TWENTY-EIGHT
December 15, 2014

I have been trying to get to the root of why, even as a little child I felt like I was a sinner and also why I never felt I was good enough. Why, as an adult, did I spend so many years feeling depressed?

My future self tells me, "When you were little, nothing that you experienced could measure up to the purity of the reality that you knew you were. All the experiences you had, made you feel you were getting dirtier and dirtier. You weren't able to discern that you really weren't getting dirtier. The experiences of sexual abuse were a constant reminder and then later on the dogma you heard in church reinforced those beliefs about yourself."

I'm still dealing with judgments about things that happened to me but this information gives me another angle to do some clearing and rewriting using SVH.

I've decided to speak with Sananda about things I recorded in my journals several years ago. "In February 1999, I heard, 'With that knowledge the spark of the divine within can be manifested.' Then I remember seeing white symbols flowing in lines in front of me."

"A link was being restored to you so that you could sing or speak the knowledge. Do you know what you're saying when you speak Language of Light?"

"Only once did I hear myself speak a few words of it and know what I was saying. It was something like 'Ya ka osh mah aloy' which meant 'self returning to Self'; otherwise, I have not a clue as to what I'm saying."

Sananda explains that I am speaking the languages of the different universes, but also sometimes I'm speaking a universal language they can understand.

"In November 2001, I heard myself say, 'Children of all ages are going to be coming to me, little ones and big ones.' Then I heard a little boy say, 'Even a little boy like me.' I heard myself answer, 'I'll love it.' Who was/is the little boy?"

He says it is someone from the future who is not born yet.

At the Joy Councils, Tonas greets me and I can hear the smile in his voice as he does so. I reply with a cheery, "Hello," because I'm happy to be speaking with him again. "I have to ask you a quick question. What did you have to do in order to begin the ancient tutorials?"

He says he went to the ancient council that one would enter and petition millions of years ago as any other initiate would have done, and that now he was an initiate of the AMS.

"I petitioned to be in the same academies that you visited at different times. It was an excitement for me to be able to see you strolling through the courtyard to attend a new tutorial. To be able to experience some of the same tutorials was delightful."

I ask if we spoke with each other. He says he looked upon me and I made eye contact with him. I wonder what I thought of him.

"For your next tutorial, if you wish, you and I could make an agreement that when you step into the ancient academy I will be there and make some kind of overture to you."

His request takes me totally by surprise and I am immediately unsure about how to respond. Finally, I reply that I'm feeling really good with how we are now and if we did something like that I might be dancing in front of him naked right now. He says he would have no problem with that.

"I still want to see you. I know you think I've seen you, but I have not. I've not seen you, I've not seen you and *I have not seen you.*"

"Yes, this is true."

"I'd like to manage to do that before we do anything else."

"And we have the rest of time."

Content that he will not push this proposal, I let it go.

Liponie joins us and I explain that Jill Marie told me about their conversation. He asks if he can be very open about his situation. Of course, I say yes.

"Liponie is my name; Liponie is my life. Liponie, Liponie! The name Liponie means open heart, openness and acceptance. Yes, I desire for there to have been another story, and yet, I must tell you a bit of a secret. Tonas, I must beg you to be quiet of this. I have another interest and it is most exciting for me."

I say that is wonderful news and add that I guess I can wait to find out who the person is.

"Ah, if you had known you would have been trying to fix me with her. She is the beautiful one. I will have you guess."

I pretend to ponder but he can't wait for me to guess. He says that I positioned him to be her teacher and I'm finally able to exclaim Cory's name.

"Indeed, I feel a great draw to my heart. She is so sweet and innocent and so open to learn. Of course, she is a very good student. She leans into me and we walk and we talk about everything! She is so interested in being embodied now."

Then he seems to rein himself in as he explains that since she had her eyes on someone else he is biding his time. I hasten to explain that pairing was my idea and I don't believe it was ever hers.

"Ashtar was the only one I could think of who was free. Maybe she feels the same for you if she's so warm and cuddly." I am biting my tongue because I really want to say more than this, but I manage to restrain myself.

"Oh, it is our study, I am sure. I am teaching her how to be the optimal partner. I have something that pushes the envelope a little. We will have a special showing on Christmas Eve of the movie *White Christmas*." Liponie explains that he will be Bob Hope, Cory will be Vera, I will be Rosemary Clooney and Tonas will be Bing Crosby. Liponie is even going to give Tonas singing lessons.

I can't resist telling Tonas that I really love it when a man sings to me. He doesn't respond for a moment and when he does he doesn't sound thrilled as he asks, "Really, my dear?" I'm a little disappointed that maybe he can't sing; nevertheless, I assert that a man singing to me is very appealing.

Liponie resumes his explanation and says that at the end of the movie both couples go behind the tree and kiss. That will be his overture. He asks us to keep it a secret because he doesn't want to overwhelm her.

"If she does not respond as I hope, I can always say that this is just part of the movie…and, of course, my heart will be broken again."

Those words compel me to give him a bit of encouragement. I tell him my insight is that I think his heart will open even wider after he kisses her. There is a long period of silence followed by a very soft, "Oh…" Then he adds, "I am of great interest in her. My heart goes pitty-patty, pitty-patty."

With the full council, I relate that two days ago I saw something that looked like a DNA helix. It had a lock on the bottom of it but it seemed to be moving as if to unwind. "When I spoke about it with Sananda this morning, he said that issues holding the 4th dimension can be tracked to people's DNA helix. He explained that everything happens in a person's energy body and then it transmits into the physical body and into the DNA. Is it possible for you to view the issues that would be in DNA and then we could do some work to release them?"

Osiris agrees with Sananda's statement and adds that that transference stimulates many deep primordial responses which are linked to the 3rd dimension. "The important piece that I will throw on the table is that there are no 3rd dimension qualifying energies within thought patterns that come from the heart."

I want to know what Charlie can do with this information. He says they must make sure this is applied to the very deepest measure because it could be the turning tide for everything. The winter solstice "can be a bigger day than we ever dreamed if we are capable of bringing this idea into its higher focus."

I knew there would be something to do on the solstice! My plan is to give Aton a big hug when I come to the council on that day. I always feel almost like I've been holding my breath through the winter until that day, and once the solstice occurs I can start to breathe again. It's wonderful to have more and more daylight returning!

"I think some people who are very dear to me have become more cuddly."

Charlie explains that eight of the Swizzlers are trying out new bodies and have become almost human looking. He adds that Liponie helped them and they enjoy wearing their clothes more. "There is a report from this one over here that when he fell off his bike, he bounced. It is better to be more cuddly."

"I'm glad to hear that you are still experimenting with things. It's wonderful to be able to play like that."

Charlie replies that it is not play for them; they are very serious. I answer that if I could do something like that it would be play for me.

"There is someone here I would love to speak with. Recently I heard Rostropovich say, 'Hi there, Joy.'"

Osiris says this was a special gift for me, but Slava is no longer here.

"Oh, darn! I really wanted to speak with him."

I can't believe I've missed the opportunity to speak with someone whose skill as a cellist I greatly admired. I'm hoping I didn't miss a performance, too, but Liponie says that after Rostropovich and I talked for awhile he played a song for me.

"It had something to do with Romeo and Juliet and you very much liked it."

I am not aware of any cello piece with that title. Liponie tells me Rostropovich called it Suite No. 1. It was made for a large orchestra, but he wished for me to hear it (Liponie's words) plain-sounding.

Here comes another of our language merry-go-rounds. I say it must have been Bach; Liponie says it was Rostropovich. I say I meant the composer of the music. Liponie says he is disappointed because he thought Rostropovich would play one of his own compositions. I say that Rostropovich didn't compose much. Liponie tells me that I seemed to enjoy it and there was a full orchestra accompanying him.

"Then it wasn't a Bach piece because those are unaccompanied. It wasn't the Dvorak?" (This is a famous cello concerto and one of my favorites.)

Liponie says no, it was Rostropovich.

"I understand that Rostropovich was the player. What I'm trying to find out is the name of the composer of the piece he played."

"I wonder why he did not give us any reports on this. It was a special gift from me to you."

"Thank you, Liponie."

I swallow my disappointment along with words of complaint. I don't want to hurt Liponie's feelings but the part of me *there* got to chat with and hear Rostropovich play his cello while the part of me *here* didn't hear a single word or musical note. Bah!

"Sananda, can we offer all the members of the councils who might want them all the SVH processes? I would also like to offer those to all the people in the universes who have joined us as well as their friends. I assume the processes would need to be calibrated for each species."

He agrees they will be unique and asks if I wish for him to make some directives with regard to this. I confirm this plan and leave the project with him.

I report to the council that my mother has not yet passed. My brother and I have spent hours with her watching as the time between her breaths continues to lengthen. It has been very difficult to witness the process she is going through and although we have both have attempted to ease her transition, we don't know if she is aware of anything we do.

Aton says her body is taking it's time to release. "I wish for you to know that her body seemed always to be so very tender and weak and yet it is a very strong body. You spawned from that body so you must know how strong and vital it is. It is important for you to be in patience."

In a brief conversation with Tonas about my sword, here is what I learn. If I'm standing and the point of it is touching the floor it would reach to my waist (forty inches); the handle is not a swirl but where I put my hand moves as if it is fluid; the jewels on the handle are ruby, emerald and sapphire; the handle also has a golden stone from Lyra that was a gift from Tonas's parents and there are smaller, multi-colored stones that look like they have rainbows in them.

I wonder aloud about my sword-wielding capabilities since I've never held anything larger than a butcher knife in this lifetime. Tonas says it looks impressive when I draw the sword up and touch the crystal with it.

"I've been reading through my journals. I was in so much despair for much of my life I'm surprised that I'm still alive."

Sananda comments that they are also surprised and that it was not without their efforts. He adds that there was also a great deal of anger and I remind him that I've been working on clearing it.

"My dear, there is very little that would be considered anger within you and it is instantly expunged. Have you not noticed?"

"Last night I was doing clearing on releasing any last bit of anger towards Jesus. I hope that I have."

Jesus answers that he is always pleased if I hate him or love him, "For even the thought that you are bringing your kind attention to me is a gift in itself."

"You've gotten a lot of attention from me then, but it wasn't a good experience to have felt that much anger for so long."

"There were reasons behind it, my dear."

"I think I've discovered a lot of the reasons, but if you have anything to add, that would be great."

"The only thing that I have to add is that your heart is bigger than any other part of you. It is so grand and so giving and so filled with heart spirit. It is attractive to anyone. Have you not heard your own laughter? It is like a bubbling brook. It carries to the world and there is a healing quality within it. You are not the same person you once were."

"I know that."

"You were so desperate, so very sad and so very condemning of yourself. Now feel the new acceptance you have for yourself in this very moment. Each time that you were angry at me, all I could see was the bleeding heart of one who is so precious to us all. You are aware that I am of the Council of Origin, as are you. Those in that council know that anger and hate come from pain. It has been our collective focus to lead you to your greater understanding and you have achieved this; the past is the past. Listen to the fairies; they are great teachers, are they not?"

"They are, and I agree with you that much of the time I am accepting myself. I am feeling so grateful to be able to talk with all of you, to do the work we are doing, to meet new people and to discover new abilities within me. The list of things I am grateful for keeps getting longer and longer. I'm especially glad that I am finally able to be your friend and to love you.... Give me a moment here before I continue."

I turn my attention to Gaia in order to ask her how many babies Sheliah has now. She says Sheliah is working on her twelfth baby.

"I know you said no worries about too many babies, but are there concerns about that at all?"

"How could there be?"

"She mentioned one time having thousands of babies and that is a *lot* of babies. When she told me that she conked Rosebud with her star to give him gratitude, I wondered if he wasn't happy."

"How can you think this? He is so accepting and loving."

"I just thought it odd that she gave him gratitude. I don't want things to go awry in their fairy garden."

"Ah, he is learning how to be."

"So the gratitude bestowal was a good thing then?"

"Of course."

"Is there someone here named Khoronosar?"

Gaia answers that he is not present. "His name is Kronosahn and he is from the Kahshar Universe. You had a conversation with him. All of the names of this individual, the universe and the worlds all start with a 'Kah' sound. Their language has very few sounds."

Tonas informs me that Kronosahn has returned. After I ask to speak with him, I hear the interesting attempts of someone trying to speak English and not having any luck at all. I advise that they take a deep breath and relax and then I hear a series of very short words most of which do indeed start with a "Kah" sound. Then I surprise myself as similar words come out of my mouth. He replies to me and I say to him, in English, that I accept. Tonas whispers that was wonderful and asks where Osiris is when you need him.

"I agreed to something, but I don't know what it was. Can someone help us?"

Isis offers to assist as translator and I now hear Kronosahn awkwardly speaking English.

"I am Kahkahnohsar Kronosahn and I am wishing to be of pledge in this grand and very important council. I am of the universe of Kahshar and we are already in preparing for that number of council. Our position is being made ready for your blue man to prepare for us if you accept. I must say that you speak Kahkahsha Uhkah very well."

"Thank you. It was a surprise to me. (I tried to speak some of this language after I left the council and was unable to make it sound anything like I did here.) I definitely would love to accept your universe. Thank you for speaking with me and stepping forward."

He again speaks briefly in his language. I answer with a few words of it and then he thanks Isis for assisting.

Privately with Tonas, he asks if he may kiss my fingers. I answer yes and add that I'd actually like for him to kiss me.

"Mmm, did it curl your toes?"

"It was dreamy." It is difficult to describe what happened when he kissed me. I didn't actually feel the kiss, but I somehow did feel it. I told you it was difficult to describe.

"I can do better."

"Oh, no, I might faint. I'll be seeing you in just a few days. I do love you, Tonas."

"Ah, I adore you my dear one."

CHAPTER TWENTY-NINE

December 19, 2014

My mother died at home on December 17th, eleven days after Dad died. They have left this dimension, but this morning I was delighted to learn that they are not through with me! I got that they were preparing genes for me, but I'm not exactly sure what that means. Sananda is the master to talk with about genetics and after I explain to him what I heard, he answers that, "All the things that you will get from your parents in the Fifth Realm will begin when you were seven and eight. This will assist you in the past to step more into your role. Your parents are now prepared and capable of assisting you by giving you files that are going to enhance things quite a bit for you in the past."

"Three times this morning I heard Dad say the words, 'Your mother.' He paused after each time he said that and I had a sense he was trying to give me a bunch of information. Will you go with me to talk with him and tell me what he wants to say?"

In the Fifth Realm, Sananda relays that Dad was trying to tell me, "You always wanted certain things for your mother. She didn't really need anything, but you always wanted her to have more. She now has everything and more; she's in heaven."

I ask how long they each were in Master Academy. Sananda says that Mother spent the equivalent of seventeen years in it and my father spent seven years there. I ask Mom to tell me about what her transition was like. Sananda says she was really grateful my father was waiting for her on the ascension bridge. "He looked old, but he quickly switched to looking young when she showed up looking youthful. Everybody was there, including many ancestors she didn't know. She didn't want to distress my brother and me, but her body just took that long to die."

"The hardest thing for us was that she kept calling for her mother."

"She says that she knew she was dying, but she wasn't trying to find her mother. She had reverted back to being a child wanting her mommy because she didn't feel comfortable. Your father wants you to know that he really enjoyed his time on the bridge with Jesus; it was a wonderful gift.

He also wants you to know that he and your mother are soul mates. Neither of them had the skills to know something like that when they were alive but he knows that means something to you. They are together and mated forever. He says they've been planning and putting together a place for themselves. They've already done some work for you because Jesus explained the possibilities to him on the bridge."

Dad asks Sananda and me to move to the house that they have created. Sananda describes it as being a white, one story house with green shutters and a roof of rust-red colored shingles. The front steps are rounded tiers that get bigger towards the bottom. There is a picket fence around it and there is a little pond near the house. In the back yard there is a garden with a scarecrow and rows of cabbages, carrots and beets. There are perfect little cages around the tomato plants and tomatoes are sticking out through the cages.

We always had a huge garden when I was little and even in his last years Dad always attempted to grow tomatoes. I don't think anybody needs to eat in the Fifth Realm, but Dad was a farmer. It looks like once a farmer, always a farmer.

"He says this is the place he always wanted to give her and so he created it. They have chickens and even though they don't do clothes he put up a clothesline."

I ask Mom if she likes the house. Sananda reports that Mom takes Dad's arm, leans into him, looks up at him and says she loves it. "They are very sweet. They will be able to experience a thousand years of life like this."

"What kind of chickens do they have?"

Sananda says they are Rhode Island Reds. These were the kind of chickens we had when I was a little girl and this reminder of the farm life I shared with my parents brings tears to my eyes. I've always loved chickens and it's good to know that these won't be killed. They don't even have to lay eggs; they can just be chickens.

I suggest that their farm ought to have a horse and a couple of cows. I'm told that Dad says he's just getting started and he hasn't had a chance to make them yet. There will even be a little barn for the animals off to the side.

I ask Dad if he has had any of his relatives visit.

"Your father says he hasn't because this is their place, and people here are not invested in what others are doing."

I'm really surprised by that because Dad was an avid researcher of his family tree. I was sure he would enjoy being able to discover the origins and names of all his ancestors. Mother has seen one of her sisters and her mother, but Dad hasn't even bothered to see his two brothers or his parents.

Mother loved roses and I whisper to Dad to suggest that he could create a rosebush for her that would always put out perfect, long-stemmed, red roses. We move to the front of the house to see the rosebush. I'm told that it is already there and that Mother appears to love it.

Sananda says Jesus gave them many ideas about how they could help me. They have altered their genetics so that the work I've done on mine will fit better. They have a file containing that assistance and it also contains their changed story so that I was raised like, for example, Mother Mary.

"Your mother is saying that you are the treasure of their life and that now the memories that will be able to be recreated in your life story will reflect that. Before, they were just living their lives."

"What do they say about Ron?"

"That he was their baby boy and they'll always see him as their little boy. They are very proud of him. They said they're so proud of both of you. They're over the Moon that they got to be your parents. When the time comes they will help him, too. They don't regret anything but they are in a position to help now. Do you want to imagine the hug because they would like to give you one?"

"OK." I'm crying again as I hug them, thank them, take the file they hand me and move to the SBT to put it in place.

At the Joy Council, Tonas asks me how I'm feeling. I answer that I'm feeling weepy and that I'd like to speak with Liponie. Immediately, I hear him say that Cory told him of my match-making role in their relationship.

"We are in the love; we are in the passionate love like I have never felt in my life! She is beside herself with love for me. I took her into your garden, my dear. It was for kissing class and I could not stop my kissing; I continued to kiss her face and her hands and her lips. Her lips are so soft."

"Oh, dear."

"She did not want to quit either, and after the kissing I had other things to teach her."

"Liponie! Whoa, advanced class right away."

"I am romantic. Gaia tried to give us a book. I told her, 'No, I will teach.' I am in the roll of teacher, yes?" Liponie gives two big sighs and says, "My dear, thank you from the bottom and the top of my heart. You have made it happen, again. If it was not for your thought to put me in this position, I would still have been pining for Jill Marie. Who is, of course, a lovely dear, and yet it is not the same as my dear Cory who wants me. Oh, she wants me with all of her being. I am not second rate with her or even third. There is no way to describe it. I have never been in love like this in my life. I have never felt this passion. I wish this for you!"

"Well, maybe one of these days, Liponie."

"Your fellow is winking at me."

"Do you know how to give the gifts to the Swizzlers, because here the kids have to go to sleep and then Santa sneaks in to bring the presents?"

Liponie reminds me that kind of pretense is not necessary here. We can just have Saint Nicholas and the elves come in and give the children their gifts.

I warn the full council that I just finished conversing with my parents and I'm feeling really emotional today. "Charlie, I heard something yesterday about being free of imprints. Is there something that you can help us with about that?"

He says they have an idea that there are collective imprints that keep individuals stuck and that there must be a singular point or resonance that imprints on that stuckedness. "If it is universal, if it is something that would be the same resonance frequency, it is something that could be assisted to elevate by finding the opposite resonance and transmitting that through the arrows. We would start with small bursts at first and continue to build while watching very carefully to make sure there are no upheavals. You and I have completed it and it is ready."

"Well, I guess I'm good for something there instead of just being a party person."

"I am confused. We have worked very diligently on this for many days."

I now admit to everyone that I'm having some difficulty with the part of me that exists there because I don't feel that person is me. I'm angry and jealous of the part of me that gets to experience all the things that I've not been able to experience. I'm also frustrated and sad and I want to know about all the things I've been doing there that *I* am not aware of doing.

Charlie remarks, "It will be like having amnesia and then waking up to know who you are, I think."

"I guess. I feel like you don't really know me at all and I don't know that part of me that's there."

"I live with you. Believe me that I know you. You are emotional because of this transition of…"

Charlie's reassurance brings more tears to my eyes. I agree with him that the deaths of my parents are a factor in my emotional upheaval but there's more to it than that.

"Liponie, I know you were just trying to do something nice for me, but when Rostropovich did all that wonderful playing for the part of me that's there, I didn't experience any of it. I didn't see him; I didn't hear his beautiful music. All I heard was, 'Hi there, Joy.'"

Charlie says he understands and encourages me to do some SVH clearing so that my anger goes away. He began speaking with his collective voice, but finished speaking with his singular voice. He explains that this shall be his new voice.

"Until you decide to have another voice."

He agrees, "Until the very moment that I decide to have another voice. I love you, Joy, and I live with you. I know you in every way possible. You are lovable; you are perfect in our eyes."

I'm crying even harder now.

"This anger will make its way from you." He declares in his plural voice, "We all love you. We would marry you if it were not for Tonas."

Although I am still sobbing, I am finally able to laugh.

"It is true. We may be in a stone but we have a heart."

"I know you do. You have great big hearts. I'm so glad I know you. I've got so much going on right now and it's an extra emotional time for me with my mother and my dad."

Tonas tells me I don't need to explain, and adds "We love you unconditionally; you are everything. You may think that you do not do enough or see enough or believe in yourself enough, but without you there would be no council. Without you there would not be all of these universes stepping into line. Believe me that you are enough."

"OK, I think maybe I just need to let the things Mom and Dad gave me settle in, because they did a lot of rewriting about how they were with me during my childhood. Maybe I'll feel better."

"Yes, and I think sleep."

"Yes, the funeral is Sunday and we're going to bury Mom tomorrow at 1:00 in the graveyard of a church I used to go to when I was little."

Tonas asks if it is possible for them to be in presence to support me and I invite everyone to attend.

"I'm going to read the things I want to say about her on Sunday and you are all invited to both ceremonies."

Tonas says they all will be there and the only work I need to do today is the work that the Swizzlers and I have put together. I agree that I want to put that in place, but first I've got to blow my nose.

"Ah, Kennedy explained to me what blowing your nose is. I was confused."

His lack of knowledge about this common human body function prompts me to ask him if he ever got constipated or had a cold when he was in the ancient academies. He says he doesn't know what a cold or a constipated is so he can't confirm if he had them or not.

"Maybe Kennedy can explain that also."

"Ah, he has just done so…vividly. I must tell you that I had all of those experiences."

I'm finally able to laugh and say, "Oh, that's great!"

"And the one with the water coming out of the wrong place."

"What do you mean?"

"Just one moment. It is called the diarrhea. Thank you, Kennedy."

I stop and ask myself if I should feel guilty for hoping he would experience these things. I decide not guilty, because it gave him a taste of what it feels like to be human.

Tonas says it's not possible for him to truly know what it is like for me during this time I live within. "In the ancient academies there was a different kind of energy that was free of adversity, and yet, it was fairly dramatic for the first two or three hundred years."

"Thank you for doing that, Tonas."

"It was what you call a labor of love, and it was something that fueled my passion. I have been cold, I have been hot, I have had the diarrhea and the constipate. I have had the stomach ache, I have had the head hurt and I had skin taken off my body from falling. It was very dramatic to be of Earth. I have you to thank for these experiences."

"You're welcome."

"I am grateful. It gives me the opportunity to understand humanity and Earth and help from a different perspective. As a commander I am quite expert, and yet as a being on Earth I was anything but expert."

As we begin the work for today, Tonas remarks that Charlie has put the transmission inside a Santa's stocking. The vision of that helps to cheer me a bit as we move the transmission out the Joy Arrows to the universes.

CHAPTER THIRTY

December 21, 2014

Conversing with Sananda, I say that I heard Mom and Dad communicate something to me this morning that didn't make sense. "One of them said, 'We are there, and then that energy moves into the heart.'"

He explains that there is a life force that can be passed on to another when there is a death. "It wasn't necessary for your father to pass it on to your mother because she chose to die quickly. The life force that was governing their energy bodies is just sitting there waiting. It didn't go with them into the Fifth Realm and it would help you."

Sananda suggests that all I need to do is intend to get the pieces of this force, move into the ideal positions in the SBT for each installation of it and put their gift in place using SVH.

After doing that, I mention that yesterday I heard Mom tell me she and Dad are working tirelessly on my behalf. "This morning I heard her say, 'I'm going to say, I love you.'"

"That's not typically what people in the Fifth Realm do, but you are different and they are going to be making a very special effort to assist you. Your mother is not the old woman you remember; she is an ascended master."

Sananda says that Mom wants me to know that in her new story she told me she loved me all the time. "Both of them are dedicated that they always super saturated you with love."

At the Joy Councils, Tonas greets me and then says it is good that I am there for them at this time. He explains that there are issues of great importance that must be brought to my attention and that they did not wish to begin without me.

The tone of his voice and the statement he just made put me on high alert. I ask him what is wrong.

"It is a very serious issue. We are devoid of several key players in our council. Isis, Osiris, Sananda and others handed their voting privileges over to others and moved to the Nordahnee Universe. The whole universe is at war, and it is nothing that the council has been influencing.

It would have happened in any event and yet I must say that it perhaps could be considered as a direct result of Plany Ohsheer making a full commitment to be a part of our council. Nordahnee is at war and this is affecting the other universes."

I ask if Charlie is still here and I'm greatly relieved when he says he is. He adds that these individuals are not aware of Christmas. I assure him that we'll be able to celebrate—at least I hope we will—and not to worry. I have a couple of things that might help.

"Yesterday, I heard Sananda say something about 're-awakening the imprint of fetal knowledge.' That would help people have more of an awareness of who they really are."

"This might be very important. I believe it must be instilled to everyone within all of the councils; otherwise, it could be considered an act of war. These individuals are not pleased with our universe and it is important for them not to make aggression to our universe. Osiris and others are in position making negotiations. The Ashtar Command is in full presence to guardian Earth, yet there are many outposts within our universe that could be affected by this."

I've been trying to stay calm. So far I've managed not to scream, but I'd really just like to go hide somewhere. Dealing with a war in another universe is not something I ever imagined I would be involved with and dealing with a war that might affect our universe is definitely not something I feel qualified to handle, especially since Osiris, Isis and the others are gone. I'm scared.

"Both my parents have now died. When they ascended they did not take their life force with them and Sananda helped me to get it. I don't know if that would help but at least it would be a gift for everyone in the universes."

Charlie agrees that could be important because of all who have ascended during our inaugurations. He says the fetal memory is also very important. His next bit of advice (I'm *so* glad he is here!) is that everything we do must be evenly distributed. "If there is anything directed to these individuals, it is possible that could be viewed as an act of aggression. They are at high focus to vanquish those who are choosing to blend with the greater collective of this council."

"Are you saying that they don't want parts of their universe to have the things we've been offering?"

"I believe it is much bigger than that. I believe this is the piece that none have been able to witness with their thoughts. It is a given that these individuals are the 'burrs under the saddle' that could hold the collective evolution in its standstill. Have you an understanding of having one faction of individuals holding up the full progress of a situation?"

"Yes. We know what they are against; what are they for?"

"This is an important question. Let us commune. They wish to dominate their universe and spread their domination into other universes and encompass the full measure of all that exists. They are choosing as their designation to impede the collective evolution."

"They want to be the top dog."

"There are no dogs involved."

"They want to be the rulers of everything."

"They have an agenda for this."

"I think we should put these ideas I brought in place and see if that shifts anything."

"I am now making a direct communication with everyone on the full council in all of the spaces of this council presence within Earth and on the Moon. I prefer the Moon; it gives me a beautiful view of the Earth.

There are several who are making offerings now. We are adding these concepts to the full measure. Our council is working with all of these additions. The most important feature is to protect Earth, to protect this universe. This universe is seen as the cause of their upheaval. They do not have Christmas spirit."

Even though this is a really scary situation and I am still trying to remain calm, I can't help but laugh at this statement. I am sure Charlie did not intend to be funny, but in spite of this looming potential for disaster his observation feels very humorous to me. It feels good to laugh, even if for only a moment, and I agree with him.

"I believe if we showed them that there is giving of the heart. Oh, I am in awe of my own genius. Let me give you a vision. What if we were to show these individuals what they will receive if they are successful in overtaking all universes and the feeling of this within themselves so that they see what victory brings to them? And then I realize this is a bold move and might give them even more energies to move forward. I am being countered. It is suggested that part of the reason why these individuals are in great upset is that the full communion of all universes elevating together to one pinnacle moment narrows the field of experience to less than three hundred and fifty years. They wish to live forever creating havoc."

It never occurred to me that other worlds would be experiencing war, let alone that an entire *universe* would be at war. I ask Charlie if any of them understand the benefits of what we've been doing.

"What they see is that their story is becoming shorter and they have a long range plan to swallow all of the universes. This might take as many as a million years, and so, they see three hundred and fifty years as a thwart to their plan."

The words "live forever creating havoc" lodged in my mind. How do you deal with people who have a plan like that? My thoughts are running around in circles; luckily, Charlie has another idea.

"If they were to play out their roles in the SBT, they could have their experience. I must communicate with Sananda; he shared something with me about line clearing. (This is an old SVH tool that supported the evolution of beings in all timelines of Earth. It was so successful that we in SVH don't need to use it anymore.) This must be discussed as a gift to them; I am communicating with Plany Ohsheer. She is transmitting to all their council members to move to our council. They are all now in presence and voting. It is suggested that while they are in discussion we put together the package of what you have brought to the table and what we added."

When I ask about transmitting the life force gift, Charlie suggests that Jill Marie add it to the Five Star Serenity Send-off Process in the past. That way, everyone will have received it. I remove my awareness from the council, contact Jill Marie and tell her about Charlie's suggestion. She upgrades the process and I step back into the Joy Councils.

"I believe that the line clearing experience along with the wisdom of the fetus will turn the tide of the war. That is important because these individuals, who are causing imbalance for themselves which ripples out

314

to others, have the opportunity to learn what they knew at their fetal stage. We are ready for the transmission of the fetal knowledge. I have just received a transmission that individuals have accepted the addition of the line clearing experience. Naturally, there was extra information added to this to match their universe and the species that exist there, but the most important aspect of the line clearing tool is that the Creator and the higher consciousness and soul of the recipients will work in harmony to implement the parameters of the expansion. We will not be transmitting this; it will be taken care of in their universe."

I send out the fetal knowledge transmission to the universes that have joined our council and as I do so I ask the Joy Council to add additional blessings.

Charlie says that he can feel the importance of this and that it is a Christmas miracle. I also feel a difference and Tonas agrees that there is much to be benefitted from what has just gone out. He explains that they have been greatly concerned but they didn't wish to bother me. "You have your important experiences. As many as possible will be present for the 'send-off.'"

He is talking about coming to my mom's visitation. As soon as this session is over I have to deliver her eulogy.

"Can anyone give me any feedback about what is happening in that universe now?"

Charlie says he can feel that there are minimal ripples but there is a wave that is building. "These of our affiliation that have put their full presence in that position believe we will still have Christmas."

I explain that I'm laughing at his words because I'm nervous.

"We are nervous as well. We are embodied now and in this universe."

"I'm sitting with you on my lap right now."

"It is a nice place to be. We are feeling now that there is more hopefulness. I believe that we could offer their council something else. They have been excited about their affiliation with our council and perhaps they have made some enemies by creating rules that others are not willing to follow. I am communicating now with Plany Ohsheer. You can assist them to reverse what they spoke by offering them time capsules in which those words are muted. This will take care of some of the energies but those who were dramatically affected will still remember.

I am communicating with Ashtar now who says he has a large enough fleet to create a wall of support that blocks transmissions from these individuals that would reach outside their universe. The Nordahnee Universe is bordered by other universes and I believe that those universes need to choose that they will not allow these warring factions to cross. This may also create discontent so it must be done with strategy.

Ah, I am speaking now with Shannara. She offers her affiliation to block. There is one universe that borders that is not yet activated as part of our affiliation. It is the Lowmeesha Universe. This is the link that is the weakness. We are communicating with Chief Council Bowginuhsar. He wishes to put, let me say this in American, their hat in the ring."

Charlie explains that Bowginuhsar doesn't wish to provide an avenue for the Nordahnee Universe into his universe which has some dual worlds that don't want to be involved in the wars.

They don't have a council building, but Liponie moves into the past and creates one for them. Ashtar agrees to patrol the borders of their universe until I can get there and inaugurate it.

Tonas and I move to the Lowmeesha Universe. He says that there are only six people present at this time for their council. I'd be glad even if there was only one person there since that's enough for an inauguration. After conducting the fastest inauguration I've ever done, we move back to the Joy Council.

There is just enough time for me to get to my mom's visitation. I've done all I can do right now and I resolutely put this situation out of my mind.

CHAPTER THIRTY-ONE
December 25, 2014

This morning I realized I am involved in a hopeless dilemma; I'm jealous of myself! The 10th dimensional Joy gets to wear beautiful gowns, jewels and even a crown. The most difficult thing for me to swallow, though, is that she is with Tonas all the time, and she even *sees* him. I struggle with that fact for awhile and then realize that holding onto jealousy will be a deterrent to me moving into the higher dimensions. I have to let it go. Later, I hear myself ask for a totally new movie; hopefully, it's one in which *I* also get to see Tonas.

At the Joy Council, Liponie greets me by saying, "You are waiting for me."

"That was my line. Don't tell me anything. I just want to get a couple of things straight for Christmas presents and then I'll find out everything that's happening."

I know this is a delaying tactic but maybe it will also help to calm me. Liponie says our skit was cancelled. I ask him to fix on old watch that belonged to my dad so that I can give it to Tonas. He gives me the ring I plan to give Tonas for Christmas, and, after I put it in my pocket, he says that I might wish to step into the council now.

"I'm going to. I'm a little nervous, Liponie."

"You have reason."

"Oh, don't say that! I may just not even go!"

"A lot has happened. You will wish to have the report and there are decisions to be made."

Instead of stepping into the council, I ask for Tonas to join us in hopes that he will give me some information that will prepare me to address what's going on. He agrees to give me a report and then asks me if I'm ready. I want to say no, but obviously that's not an option. I equivocate and say, "Yes…maybe."

The news he gives me is that Plany Ohsheer was murdered and has been held in stasis for three days.

The words, "Oh, no, we need to fix that," pop out of my mouth. I have no idea how to go about fixing this situation but Tonas does. He says it will be important for people to witness a miracle. Before he offers any additional information, I know who's going to have to perform it… me.

He says it's simple for a non-dual being to re-awaken an individual who has closed their eyes in this manner—something I didn't know—and, since I'm the figurehead of our council, the miracle needs to come from *me*. Obviously, something like this has never been on my resume and I'm starting to feel light-headed at the thought of even attempting such a task.

The fact that Solomon has given me a diopside necklace to use as an implement to facilitate a transmission doesn't reassure me all that much. Tonas also explains that I received a large preparation for this work which freed me from any impediment to performing the miracle. He explains that I will transmit a message from my heart; the essence of it will come through the diopside and awaken Plany. (I hope.)

"It is in our favor that she has been dead for three days. If her restoration was immediate, I think it would not have held the great shock that will wave through this whole universe. This must be done in the Nordahnee Universe, for she is held within a light configuration upon a platform there. Individuals from many universes have been moving past and paying homage. She has been watched over 24/7 and this has been 'televised,' let us say, throughout all universes. When you step forward, transmit onto her and awaken her, we believe this will turn the tide for those who are on the edge of choosing to step into the favor of what they desire to see for this new era for their universe. Many have been shifted by the works we applied in our last connection."

Instead of worrying any more about *how* I'm going to do what is required—I'll just do it, as they say—I ask if we know how she was murdered or who murdered her. Tonas says she was poisoned. The additional reasons he gives me about why I have to perform the miracle and why it will have such a huge impact on those who see it are, first, I come from a dual world and I'm not as well-known as Isis and Osiris, and second, I'm not forbidden from awakening Plany, but Isis and Osiris are.

I knew there would be good reasons, but I'd already decided to do what he asked. I tell him I'm ready and then he says I *also* need to give a speech to all of the worlds and stars of this universe which will then be transmitted to the councils of the other universes.

"Oh, jeez."

"There is no pressure. Your heart will know exactly what to say and it will be translated by Osiris. There are those of Earth, Mary, Jesus, Buddha and Saint Germain, who wish to remain in presence as counselors to assist these individuals for a short period of time. These emissaries from your world who lived in the 3rd dimension must be mentioned. You can mention that even now there are wars on Earth and that these conflicts do not have to be part of the duality. Do you understand?"

"Well, I'll just do the best I can, Tonas."

"This will be enough."

I hope he's right and that the diopside necklace will be the element that assists me to do this seemingly impossible deed.

At the Joy Council in the Nordahnee Universe, Tonas begins to whisper and instructs me to step into the viewing arena where Plany's body is placed.

"We are all with you and are walking up. Now we are in front of the body. She is laid out beautifully."

In place of the fear that I was feeling, strong feelings of dismay, anger and sadness are coursing through my body. I am relieved and grateful to find that the words I need to say flow easily.

"I'd like to speak with all of you, please, for a moment. I've attended two funerals lately and I really don't want to have another one. I lost people who were very dear to me, but death was part of the natural course of their lives. It was their time to go and they are now together and happy in the Fifth Realm. But this young woman still has a lot to offer to the people of this universe, and I don't want to see her not be able to experience the life she was planning on living."

I speak Language of Light and then say, "Plany, I call you back to us. Creator, quicken her again, please." After a moment, I hear Tonas say there is a heartbeat.

Encouraged, I address her again to say that we still need her and we love her. "Please come back so that you can help us with your universe. You have many magnificent works still to do."

Tonas reminds me that Plany has the vision for her universe.

"What I have to tell you of this universe, and all universes of duality, is that there is nothing that can compare with the mastery of self. There is no conquest or victory that is more supreme than that mastery and the awareness of your inner power, your inner God/Goddess.

There is a beautiful plant called a poinsettia that we have on Earth at Christmastime. There are many legends about it but the only fact I know for sure is that it only blooms after a long period of darkness. I think that, if you choose, it's time for you and your universe to bloom. I hope you've had enough darkness. I know I've had enough. We have darkness in our world; we still have wars, terrorists and people who are killing others, but we are moving away from that. I want that for your universe also. Plany, come back to us."

Tonas says that her eyes are opening. I speak more Language of Light and then tell her, "You are precious to us and precious to your universe. I'm waiting for you to embrace me. Rise, Plany."

Tonas asks Plany if she can speak. In a strong voice, she replies that she can.

"I thought I was bound for the Ihconnakashetah, and yet, here I am in my body."

I'm delighted that she is back and I ask her if we may embrace. Instead, she suggests we stand together in strength and peace and, "Look upon our worlds as a unit of fellowship moving together toward a goal that is greater than we have ever known. The vision of where we are is nowhere near the vision of where we are destined to become. Why should we struggle together or with one another, when the vision of what is to be is so grand and so glorious?

I could feel myself coming into life as your words spurred the beating of my heart. I heard your words that there is no war or conquest that is more divine and more powerful, no treasury that is of greater richness than that of the awakened spirit.

Look upon these that are with this Great One who is of the duality world. There is Isis, there is Sananda and beyond there are millions that are part of the council of all the different universes that have stepped forward. Imagine the power, the drive and the force of light to bring that which is our destiny into the forefront and into our lives. Why should we see conflict as more fulfilling than this? How can it be so? It is not, it is the illusion.

I would tell you that the force of light that drives this Council of Joy, this tribe of one, is the destiny of your makeup. There are teachers here that can help you, if you only wish to hear their words. There are teachers here from the worlds of duality, the world of Earth. They can share with you if you are willing to learn, if you have the heart to learn. If your heart is open and if you are not afraid to learn something new."

I delighted with her masterful challenge; I'm sure that none of the warlike people here would want others to perceive them as being afraid.

Plany continues by saying it is understandable if they are afraid, "And yet to open your heart and your mind to receive truth, is in itself an awakening that scares away the fear and brings to you an awareness of truth that gives you comfort."

She asks me if I wish to speak of the emissaries from our council.

"I do. They all have lived on Earth and I believe they could offer important assistance by sharing information, new ideas and new concepts. In my reverie last night, I saw children who are anxious to learn new ways. They are your future and I invite you to discuss with our emissaries schools for your children and adults. I know that they would be willing to share ideas with you about how to bring these things about. They and I know what it is to live on a planet of duality. I've witnessed death and wars and these are things I no longer choose for my world. I hope that your universe will share with me the vision of releasing conquest because that is not the way."

Tonas speaks to say that it is now time for us to step aside and allow them the privilege of making their own choices. "The Ashtar Command is in presence on all borders and is here to assist."

"Plany, I loved hearing what you had to say. Thank you for coming back!"

"I am grateful to you." She laughs and says, "I am most grateful because I have a vision for our universe and the unification of all universes, all beings and all parts of ourselves. I would like to offer all those of our universe a vision into the future. This is offered through our dear Jesus and Saint Germain. They have a desire to show us what is to be. If you are not afraid to see this, please join us. We will have this exercise later today."

Tonas cues me that it is time to leave.

At the Joy Council, Tonas says that except for the emissaries our consortium has returned. He adds that was quite an amazing experience to witness. I reflect that sometimes being unable to see what's happening is not so bad; seeing her rise from the dead might have unnerved me.

"For the universes that have joined us, can we offer some instruction for their children? We have schools here but they don't teach the important things."

"The important things?"

"The things about who you really are, your true nature. We're taught how to read and add, all the mundane things to be able to live in the world, but not the important things. Those things are supposed to be taught by parents, who never, at least in individuals of my generation, received any teachings like that themselves. Those values could also be taught in church; however, I'm of the opinion that what is taught there has not been very helpful. I imagine other worlds of duality are in the same boat. Charlie, what are the rules about something like this?"

"For those individuals who are willing to create an academy for their children so that they may learn the attributes of the future for all beings, this must be brought through each individual council. We believe we can put a program together for each universe, based on all of their species and their abilities to learn at the level of their understanding, one that can grow with their greater awareness. We have this program created in orbs for each of the councils. They may collect them and apply them as they wish. We will also create an intermediary program for each of these individuals so that we can explain and help them to further develop this worthy project."

"The teachers are crucial. It's very important that they be the perfect people for helping the children. Young children are so impressionable; we want to make sure they are just encouraged to blossom."

Tonas agrees this is an excellent idea. I suggest that there could be schools for adults, but almost as soon as the words have left my mouth Charlie says the CEV has already created a project for all adults of all species; they even completed a fetal program.

"What we have to transmit is in an orb that must be delivered directly to each council to distribute as they wish."

"Is that something you can do without me?"

"You have made me the intermediary. It is done."

There's a slight pause and then Charlie asks, "Now can we have Christmas?"

My announcement that it's definitely time for Christmas is followed by a very loud, "Yippee!" from Charlie.

Addressing Osiris, I explain that an apple is a traditional gift that a student gives one of their favorite teachers. As I hand him the apple that Liponie has given me, I explain that it is a very tasty, sweet Honeycrisp apple, and it comes with my thanks for being my teacher.

"Your other gift is a wheel of cheese. There are two expressions we use on Earth to denote someone very important. The first is that they are a big wheel and the second is that they are a big cheese. And so, here is a delicious edible representation of your stature."

Osiris says he understands the tradition of an apple for a teacher and he likes it very much. Next, I present Isis with silver earrings shaped as wings. I hear her gasp, exclaim that they are beautiful and that she is grateful.

It is finally the moment Charlie has been waiting for and I tell him to have at it. He doesn't understand that expression and asks me if he may open his gift. The excitement in his voice as he does so catapults me fully into the Christmas spirit.

"It is a train! It is a train! It is a train! It is our own train? May I be the captain?"

"You may be the captain."

"Oh, there is a whole car load of candy! And Liponie has me in the dress of the engineer. Toot toot! Everyone, you must all... OK, just the council then. There are little seats that are made for our little bottoms. I will pass the candies to each. Ah, and the train has tracks that go a long way. May I please leave you? I wish to drive the train!"

"Yes, you may."

Tonas says he will, "Oh, my gosh," me because they are so adorable. "They have all jumped in the train. Charlie has given them all the canes of candy and he is pulling on a string and making a very loud sound. He has said, 'All must be aboard,' and he is making a 'chooka, chooka, chooka, chooka,' sound. As you know, they have bridges to go over water ways. We will not see them for awhile. We have the instructor, Mr. Floren, to teach him the accordion when he is ready."

"They have stockings, right?"

"Yes, the Santa Claus filled them and then he 'turned with a jerk' for each. There was a recitation of *The Night Before Christmas*, earlier."

"Yes, not even a mouse."

"We did our research about the mice. We are glad for the opportunity to know about all these things that are part of Earth's history. Mice seem to be something that have been a bit of a scourge, and yet they are beloved creatures on Disney."

"Yes, the Mickey Mouse. Is Charlie driving the train around the whole place?"

"It is quite a track. They are so quick with their work and so diligent it is important for them to have this play."

"I'm not quibbling about that."

"What is a quibbling?"

"Disagreeing with you."

Before I leave, I ask Aton about a special passageway that I felt open in my brain several days ago.

"You have so many brains, but if you are speaking of your cranium brain, you might be experiencing the full measure of that expansion which is always evolving. The seed that was planted is growing. Soon it will be bearing fruit."

I like to hear Aton's reports on what is happening in my brain. Even though I hardly ever understand the meaning of his explanations it's reassuring to hear the words. I also appreciate that, so far at least, he never sounds worried or in doubt about my progress.

"Thank you, Aton. I think that's it for the day then. All of you enjoy your apples and cheese and I'll talk with you tomorrow. Merry Christmas."

In privacy with Tonas, I tell him I have something for him. He says he has something for me and asks who is to be the first. Since I have two presents for him, I suggest that I give him one, then he can give me his and I can finish by giving him his second present. He says it's unfair that I have two presents for him. We both find ourselves laughing at his complaint.

"It is unfair for I only have this. Let me explain to you what it is. It is a most beautiful ring with a diopside stone that matches the necklace you are wearing. The stone is from the mines in South Africa and I worked very closely with Solomon so that the quality would match that of your necklace. This ring is a promise ring. I promise you that I will forever be your support no matter what you choose for us. I will *always* be there for you. This is my promise."

I am touched by his promise, for I know it is authentic. The eloquence that came so easily to me when I addressed Plany has deserted me and none of the replies that come to my mind seem adequate. Finally, I simply thank him and ask which of my fingers he would like to slide the ring on.

"I wish for you to make your choice. There are ceremonies that you are attuned to."

"Please put it on the third finger of my right hand."

"Now I must, of course, kiss your fingers. The romance of Liponie and Cory has taken the hearts of all of us. She is so happy to be in a physical form."

I comment that her current incarnation is a big improvement over being an iceberg and add that I hope their relationship continues to be a happy one. (I still have those nagging doubts about *any* relationship being permanent, let alone permanently happy.)

I pull the ring I have for him out of my pocket, hold it in my outstretched hand and say it is for him.

"The stone is quite exquisite. It looks like it has stars in it."

"Yes, it's the night sky, Tonas."

"Oh, my beloved, indeed it is and on which finger do you wish I should wear it?"

"You choose."

"I will place exactly as you, on the third finger. What is this other?"

"In the little box is a pocket watch that belonged to my dad. I loved it for a long time and so he gave it to me. He didn't remember where he got it but it is very old. It's so pretty with the little bluebirds and things on it."

"It is very tender and special that you would give me your father's watch."

"I know that you can have it there and I can have it here."

He chuckles and agrees that is the loophole.

"I'd like to have another kiss before I go, please."

"I would like to… Oh, let me think of the words… I wish to lay one on you."

Laughing, I encourage him to give me a big smooch. He wants to know if his kiss curled my toes. I can't tell him it didn't. I say the kiss felt nice—on some level it really did—and we exchange wishes for the merriest Christmas ever. It's certainly one I will never forget.

CHAPTER THIRTY-TWO

December 26, 2014

In the Fifth Realm with Sananda, I call into presence every being there and say, "I would like for all of you, if you choose, to have the experience of being tutored in the things that really matter. In my opinion, that would involve personal growth and mastery as well as an expansion of the vision that we currently have about the oneness of all of us and the gifts that come with the knowledge that we are all love.

Please give us a vision from your current perspective of the most amazing and divine life experiences you would wish to experience which are free of limitations imposed by the experiences of your genetic lineage. You are the only ones who understand these impediments because of the cultural realities in your worlds. We are looking for incredible gifts to give to all of you that will assist you to be able to embrace master awareness and the ability to make the leaps which lead to our unification in this Fifth Realm."

At the Joy Councils: I've brought along a plate of Christmas cookies and as soon as Tonas and I finish exchanging greetings, I ask him to take one.

"I will have two cookies and I will also tell you that the children are having the time of their lives."

"What have they been doing?"

"We cannot get them off the train. There is no way for us to sit in the train, and so we stand with our feet where their bottoms would be."

I mention that Liponie could make some seats for the regular size people here, but Tonas feels the train should be reserved just for the children. He explains that everyone has had the study about surfing and the adults standing on the train have been pretending they are riding the waves.

With the full council, I explain the work we just did in the Fifth Realm. Charlie agrees to apprise all of the universes in our council of this offering (It will be archived for universes not yet part of the council.) and suggests that it be part of each council's initial meeting. If the first individuals to receive it are part of the councils, that will allow them to demonstrate that the work is not above them.

I agree with that plan. Charlie answers that he is in joy of this and asks if I have other works.

"I want to do something with a new American Dream. It's a new vision that is not about a chicken in every pot and a car in every garage; that was part of an old dream. This new dream is about abundance and mastery for all."

Charlie adds it is also about initiation of the self, as well as remembering the true purpose of existence, which is to remember. His idea is that capturing the American Dream from each individual that had achieved it from the future of time would amplify the possibilities.

I agree that is a great idea and prepare to step into the Fifth Realm with Sananda.

"I will wait." Charlie adds, "I will ride my train."

Before we move into that realm, I realize that getting just an American Dream isn't nearly enough. What I'm really looking for are the soul essence dreams of individuals in *all* countries, worlds and universes. Moving into the Fifth Realm, I call everyone forward safe to work with and ask them for gifts containing information about their soul essence dreams that can be made into a transmission.

Back with the council, I announce that the package I have contains the Ideal Dream from individuals of all worlds. Charlie says he likes it very much and then tells me he is moving into his individual presence.

"I must always remember that I am still part of this collective, as long as I am. I, I, I… This is my call to freedom. I wish to be an individual, and yet it is important for us to remain in this collective for a period of time to do the work. We are happy to do this. I have the piece; it can be transmitted out to the everything.

The idea that the New Year marks a new beginning is held within many individuals of Earth. Let us also instill within this gift a vision of the

contract with the Self that is free of any entanglements from beliefs that
are linked to old stories. This is a vision that will be shining to all beings
of every universe and fits within the parameter of this offering. We simply
move it through the councils because they are now part of our affiliation,
and we hold it for later for those that are not part of our affiliation.

This Ideal Dream piece of the work is a gift from your heart. We
have added our own flavor of whipping cream and nuts to make this a
treat. Individuals will not turn this down. It will be too sweet."

I love all the opportunities for laughter that Charlie furnishes and
I'm giggling as we send out this transmission. Charlie's sweet tooth must
be as big as mine.

"We all accepted, of course. I included candy canes. Those who
accept will receive a sweet taste in the mouth."

"Can someone update me on what has been happening with the
Nordahnee Universe?"

Tonas says there is a great wave of support that is rising
throughout different areas of that universe. "Individuals who were simply
sitting on their fences are now ready to step forward and make claims for
a forward thrust of peace. This is all being orchestrated and applied
through what you would consider the sweetest of energies. They are not
wishing to change anyone, only to be an instrument for peace. Plany is
very much becoming a great spokeswoman for her individual groups, as
well as for the full council. She is a very fine leader."

"Yes, I was impressed with what she said yesterday."

"It is a time for change, and those who are stepping in for this
change are very much in passion to step forward. There is quiet on the
warring fronts. It is as if they are in a pause, and there are some who have
accepted the challenge. She had much wisdom in her wording of, 'if you
are not afraid.'"

After agreeing that was an excellent strategy, I ask for information
about the warring factions. Tonas says there are many different species;
some are united and some are even at war with each other. The species
that is most involved in the war is similar to one we have in our universe.

At this time, I choose not to ask any questions about this race of beings. I remind myself that there's no need to go looking for trouble; enough of it has found us lately. Anyway, I'm sure I'll find out about them later.

Next, I ask Charlie if the Swizzlers have had any more thoughts about things we can do to assist the 4th dimension to release. He says they have been considering the importance of the elevation of the species that is in conflict with the harmonization.

"They are forgetting that they are one of you, as you are one of them. It is our opinion that there is a very good chance that if an individual saw the molecular make up of themselves and the molecular make up of someone like ourselves, or Isis, or yourself they would find corresponding elements. It is too easy to be in conflict when you have a feeling of being different. It is our opinion that individuality with sameness is the most important message."

I remind him that Osiris told me to leave that species alone until I'm completely in the 7th dimension. Charlie agrees that is good advice and continues by saying that the Swizzlers are always creating a vision of the unity of the one tribe.

"We have an impossible description for what we have as a gift to our new world. Once it is offered it can be expanded to other universes. The concept is, my heart is good; your heart is good. There is no reason for there to be conflict." He pauses for a moment and then says that transmission is ready.

"There's one more topic. What about religion?"

"It is a social club."

I can't help but laugh at this assessment while secretly agreeing that it is at least partially true.

"Tonas was talking about how in his dimension he can experience a winter setting and the person living right next to him can have a tropical environment. I didn't quite understand how that could be, but those of us on a spiritual path have heard over and over that you create your own reality. How can we have the fun of doing that but also have the picture of the bigger reality we are all part of?"

"There is a fear of separation which makes it so that people feel the need to control one another. If you are afraid to be alone or you are afraid that someone else will want something from you, then the survival of the fittest comes into play in the old paradigm. This belief of a central figure requiring one to apply specific rituals in order to be acceptable is an illusion. There is no fact to base this upon for I have a great vision of that one. That one that is within all of us is the same."

He summarizes by saying that the common theme is based on fear and is always about the need to control others. You can feel safe if you can control others; you can also feel safe by allowing yourself to be controlled by others who appear to be stronger.

"What can we do about this?"

"This is a story that has no basis of truth. I know this because I have reversed the vision to the very moment of the beginning, that beginning where we all came from the same place. It is the same essence within all of us. There is no differentiation between me and you beyond our individuality and the essence that our form is encapsulated within. There is only one consciousness that you call God. There are different names for these."

The transmission Charlie puts together is the vibration of oneness with individuality. He announces that they are almost complete, and then they will have pie—a plan I totally agree with. One of these days I know I'm going to have a sensation of tasting food here. Today might be the day!

"Have you had a chance to open any of your other presents?"

"We are waiting for you. We made love notes for everyone and we delivered them with the train."

He hands me the transmission and says this is the Swizzlers' Christmas present for me. As we send it out, I call upon the council members to open their hearts wide with the joy of this season, the joy of self-mastery and the joy of knowing their oneness while still retaining the flavor of their individuality within that oneness. As a finishing touch I add the energy of, "Nothing is lost, everything is gained."

In privacy with Liponie, he says he's been waiting to unveil the water park, everyone has had the study of surfboarding and Zahseet is at the council today. Sounds like today is the perfect day to open the water park. We move back into the council, I announce to Charlie that we have a surprise and we move to the park entrance. I know there's a big bow on the door so I direct Charlie to pull one end of it while I pull the other end.

"Ah, a big drape is falling." After a moment's pause I hear him yell, "It is a park!"

The next two times he says that are even louder and he wants to know if it's for him. I say it's for everyone, suggest we enter and ask Zahseet to accompany me.

Tonas says that she wishes to take my hand. I ask her to guess who her secret Santa was and she tentatively asks if it is me. I finally get to shout, "It's me! I have something exciting for you. I hope you think it's exciting, anyway, because I thought it was. There is a wave pool here, and there is also something here especially for you."

Tonas asks everyone to follow us then suggests they enter the little bungalows if they wish to put on their swimwear. He tells me Zahseet already has a swimsuit on, courtesy of Liponie, and then directs her through a special gate to a pool where she will see waves that have been manufactured by Liponie.

"Zahseet, this is your very own surfboard and it is your secret Santa present from Joy. There are greeneries painted on top of it and there is actually a handlebar, a stick from the center for you to hold onto. It is a training bar that you may take off at any time."

I hear her say very softly that she thinks she understands. And then she gives a piercing shriek that lasts for a long time, followed by laughter. "We must have one of these at our council. Ah!"

When I ask her, she admits that her people have never done anything on top of the water. I wonder if this gift will revolutionize her world. Even if it doesn't, she seems really excited to try it. She says Charlie is already surfing and he is very good. (That figures.)

"His board does not have the handle. I think mine has a handle because of my tail. It gives me more stability."

"I hope you enjoy the board because I thought it would be a lot of fun to do something in the water you've never done. Are many of the worlds in your universe water worlds?"

"No, and yet there are some. "

Since she's excited about the surfboard, I can't resist mentioning water skis. She wants to know if Liponie knows about such things and I say he probably does. She asks to borrow him and I say that's OK with me. Liponie joins us and apologizes for being late. When I mention that Zahseet is eager to learn about other water activities, he says there is another section of the park with jet skis. There is also underwater gear for Charlie and the others but that will not be released until they have had scuba diving lessons. I didn't know about any of those other things but they certainly will be fun for the kids.

Liponie asks for a private conversation. When we are alone he wants to know if I was pleased with the rings. Scrambling for a reply since I didn't actually see them, I tell him that Tonas said his stone looked like it had stars in it, so I was pleased. I also congratulate him for the great job he did with the water park and mention that Zahseet was excited about the surfboard. He says he did simulations that showed it would be impossible for her to ride without the handle.

"I think I'll give Tonas his underwear on Monday, and maybe even a swimsuit."

"Perhaps a Speedo."

"Ooh! Even not seeing him I don't think I can handle that yet, Liponie."

"Would you wish to know something?"

"What is it?"

"I wish to ask our little darling if she will be my bride."

"I'm sure she won't turn you down."

"We are so in love. It is like nothing I've ever experienced. There is a piece of Cory everywhere, but for me, everywhere she is that's where my heart is. Lips closed please. I have not decided where or when. I am thinking it must be special."

"When is your birthday? I want to know because you are an important person to me."

"I am corresponding with the dates of Earth and I think it is January twelfth. I had to do a great deal of factoring for you are aware of my age. It is a secret from Cory. She must not know I am…"

"Wait, I bet she's older than you are."

"I do not wish her to think me a baby."

"Oh, gosh, Liponie, things like that are not important when you're in love with someone."

"I know. It was a joke."

"I was worried you were serious."

"I wish to surprise even myself. Will you honor us?"

"Oh, I'd love to do that. I'm getting really good at these unique marriages. Quite a resume I'm going to have. I married the Sun and the Earth, all the fairies in a garden and now a marvelous genie and a former iceberg."

"I was thought into being for Lowmoeshee and I'm going to ask him to be my best man."

"How does it work, Liponie? Someone created a body and then your soul said that's the body for me and popped in. Is that what happened?"

"Gogohsha thought the body of his son, Lowmoeshee, and he also thought my body. I am not a Pinocchio. There was no fairy that tapped me on the head and made me a real boy. When the body is ready, then the soul makes its entrance."

"That was your soul's choice, right?"

"It was. Who wouldn't wish to be me?"

"I'm pretty happy with myself, but I bet a lot of other people would enjoy being you. Give me a kiss and I've got to go."

"Ah, remember, my dear, you made another love match."

"I just gave a little bit of a nudge and your love match happened on its own. I'm happy for you, Liponie. Bye, bye."

CHAPTER THIRTY-THREE
December 29, 2014

On December 26th I heard myself say, "Something happens just before I was born." Our current timeline began on January 17, 1948, in the northern hemisphere and January 18, 1948, in the southern hemisphere. In SVH, we don't normally work with anyone who died before those dates; I've always wanted to be able to assist people who lived before 1948 and since I was born in February of 1946, meaning I was alive at the end of the previous timeline, I might be able to do it.

I have put things in place using SVH so that when I was born I entered a little bubble of 8th dimensional energy. I know it's a kooky idea, but if I stretch my aura out to encompass the whole Earth, everybody who was alive on my birthday, February 9, 1946, could feel the 8D bubble I was born into. They could choose on that date to be part of an energy field that would help them glide into our current timeline.

This seems like a plausible plan, but I decide to speak with Sananda first. If I present it to him in the form of a request rather than a query, I think he might agree to assist me.

"Sananda, will you and the other masters of light I work with add things to my aura so that when I'm born and I stretch my aura out to encompass the Earth, people alive on Earth then will be able to ride with me in my bubble of higher dimensional energy into this current timeline?"

He agrees that they can do this and when I ask him if it is possible to do something like this for the other universes, he says yes! All I need to do is give this information to Charlie so that he can work with a council member from each universe that lived in the previous timeline.

At the Joy Council with Liponie, laughter precedes his speech, as usual. He informs me that he is more joyful than ever and I echo his sentiments. He's agreeable to me just diving into discussing the clothes and memorabilia that belonged to my parents that I've brought with me. My brother and I donated most of their outdated clothes, but they each wore a few things so often that I just can't bear to part with them.

I ask Liponie to make Mom's clothes like new and enlarge them so they will fit me. They are: a little blue sweater with tiny white flowers that I always loved how she looked when she wore it, a white sweater and an old (maybe forty years) black and white checkered coat that she wore doing things outside on the farm in the winter.

"This old denim work coat belonged to my dad, Liponie." I start crying here because I can still see him wearing it outside in these last years when he was doing things like burning the trash. "I don't want you to change anything about it. Leave even the spots and dirt on it. Can you just create it here so that I can look at it every once in a while?"

"I will put it on a manikin and you may have it forever."

When you are an old-time farmer you must have a straw hat and Dad had several which were in various stages of falling apart. I brought two with me, one for myself, which I ask Liponie to repair only enough so that it doesn't fall completely apart, and another for Tonas. Liponie is to just repair the holes in it and leave it looking old. I'd love to be able to see the look in Tonas's eyes when I hand him this hat.

The dress hat Dad wore in his later years was a black fedora with a small, jaunty feather in the band on it. I might wear it myself sometime when I'm feeling especially masculine and so I ask Liponie to spiff it up for me.

"Thank you for this, Liponie."

"It is so easy for me. What is life without a genie?"

"It would be so less magical. The next things I have are clothes my mom saved that I wore when I was a little girl. The only one I remember is this little, red velvet dress, because I never had anything this smooth and luxurious feeling before. If I get around to having a little girl, I might like to have some of these clothes for her. They need to be perked up because they've been stored for over sixty-years and they are a bit musty smelling."

Liponie says they are now like new. I show him just two more items: a blue, crystal vase that Mother usually always used for bouquets she would select from the many flowers she grew outside around their home and a beat-up-looking tin cup I used to drink from when I was little.

"You do not wish for me to make it as new?"

"No, I want it to look just like this."

I'm crying, again, as I realize how much I already miss Mom and Dad. They are never going to call me on the phone again, something Dad did almost daily the last few years. I console myself with the knowledge that although they are dead, they are OK.

"Liponie, I know that I will get better at connecting with them as I keep visiting the Fifth Realm. It's just that they aren't like they were when I knew them—not that I want them to be that way again!"

"They are better!"

"I know, but they're different now. It's hard to explain, Liponie."

I share with Liponie my plan to give Tonas his underwear today. Liponie tells me he made some silk ones and some flannel ones. Those are, he explains, to keep Tonas's buns warm. He also made him beautiful silk pajamas with a matching robe and slippers.

"Before you give these to him you might like to take him into your abode because I have created a special man's chamber, a special wing for him which will be a surprise. It has all of the books that he loves and his own, you call this, television. There is also the tired man."

"The what?"

"The chair that lays."

I burst into laughter when I realize he's referring to a La-Z-Boy Chair. Tired man, indeed.

Liponie suggests I make my way there, there's a bow on the door, and he will send Tonas. I intend to move to the location and a few moments later Tonas greets me there. I ask him to please take the bow off the door and explain it's a little chamber next to my room, courtesy of Liponie.

I hear him say, "Oh," with a definite tone of interest in his voice. He continues, "It is very beautiful. It is like I would imagine a special man chamber in a palace and there are the volumes; they are uploads of stories. There are many presents here. Ah, it is unfair! I wish to have presents for you."

"It's really fun to give things to you. Let's open some of them."

"I will. Ah...I don't understand."

"You'll have to describe to me what you are seeing."

"It is like pants and a shirt that are very soft."

"They're pajamas."

"Pajamas?"

"Yes, you wear them when you're lounging around or watching TV or lying in your recliner. Liponie calls it the tired man chair."

"Tell me about this tired man chair. Is it this one here that is very puffy?"

"It must be. You can lay back in it."

"It does not lay back."

"It should. There should be a handle on it somewhere so that you can recline."

"Let me sit here. I see there is a lever on the side."

Before I can explain, he obviously pulls it because I hear a startled, "Oh!"

We both laugh then Tonas asks how to make it reverse. I suggest pulling it back with his feet which seems to work. Since it is big enough for two he says we could have long talks and maybe a little kissing while being lazy in it. I answer that I am agreeable to those ideas.

He opens another present and asks if they are swimming costumes. I tell him it is underwear.

"Oh, underwear... I have heard of this. This one is soft like the pajamas and there is another that is more rough textured."

"Right, that's flannel to keep your bottom warm."

"The bottom of what?"

"Your bottom."

"Are we moving into an ice age?"

"No, men and women here wear them under their outer clothing. I've never asked you about anything like this because underwear is considered a private thing and not something to show to other people. You don't need to wear it every day, but if you wore one once in a while, I could be imagining that maybe you have underwear on today or maybe you don't. It's kind of a sexy thing, Tonas."

"Liponie made a joke to me that he was going to warm my buns. It all comes to light now. I thought he meant a food, of course. He is a comic."

"You always just wear black so I like to imagine you wearing some really colorful underwear."

"I look very handsome in black, but to have these colors against my skin. There is nothing we have that is of this softness. You call it silky. You told me this word once when I held you in that beautiful gown. Do you wear these underwears?"

"Yes, but not like yours. Mine are abbreviated."

"They are what?"

"They are much smaller."

"It is because you are much smaller."

"Yes, but mine are made more like the bottom part of a bikini swimsuit."

"Ah! And you do not wear this in public?"

"I wear them underneath my outer clothes. Mine aren't as sexy as yours, but I could buy some sexy ones I guess. Mine are just kind of plain cotton ones."

I can't believe I'm saying these things about my underwear and even thinking about buying some prettier undies. Hmm… Well, maybe before I get to the 8th dimension that would be a good idea. Then I remember that creation occurs instantly in that dimension. I'll wait.

"I don't imagine underwear has been part of your reality, but it is for us here on Earth."

"There is no reason that anyone would wear such a thing, and yet, it is quite exciting and sensual as well. This sensuality is a new side in you."

"I've been working on it. I do have a lot to do today, though. Can we meet somewhere in private with Charlie and Osiris?"

"Can I show you that I am wearing all of my—you only wear the one?"

"Right."

"I will take off all but the one then."

Oh, oh! I start laughing and ask him if he was actually putting his underwear on in front of me. He agrees he did so, but he did it very quickly. Even though I didn't see him, for some reason I'm embarrassed. He wants to know if he offended me. I tell him he didn't but I can feel myself blushing. My face must be red there, too, because he notices it and thanks me! Emboldened suddenly, I tell him that maybe one if these days I'll really see him in his underwear.

"I am living for the day of this."

Before I get myself in any deeper I suggest it is time to get back to work.

In private with Osiris, Charlie and Tonas, I tell them that we have a real dilemma. What kind of party can we create without the assistance of our ultimate party planner and what kind of gifts can we give someone who can create anything he wants?

Osiris agrees this is a dilemma and says he only knows of one person, a jinn known as The Great Comahlee, who might be able to trump Liponie. It seems highly unlikely to me that any being in any universe could trump Liponie, but I don't know of any other options.

I explain that there is nothing I could think of in the way of physical things to give Liponie that he couldn't whip up for himself, but I did ask him if he would have liked to have had a mother and father. "He said he'd never really thought about it so I didn't pursue the subject."

I hear Charlie's singular little voice say, "I would like a mother and father."

His request stops me in my tracks. I never stopped to examine the fact that Charlie and the rest of the Swizzlers don't have a mother or father. They could be considered orphans. Orphans! It seems like the most perfect and natural thing in the world to tell him that I am his mom and, without even asking him, I volunteer Tonas to be his dad.

"Ah, oh, oh, you are the best mother, and he will be the best father."

"And Liponie can be your special uncle who gives you presents all the time."

"Uncle…yes, I will research this uncle."

I am now, officially, the mother of ninety-four Swizzler children and Charlie is number one of the bunch. That feels just right. Now that that's settled I move back to the topic of potential gifts for Liponie and ask if anyone knows if he has friends he hasn't seen for a long time.

Osiris says he is sure Comahlee, who is on Andromeda, (Liponie's previous home.) knows about Liponie's existence. He summons Comahlee and almost immediately I hear laughter that is somewhat, but not exactly, like Liponie's laugh.

Comahlee acknowledges the great Osiris and comments that this is an interesting place. After I thank him for coming, he says that he knows I am Liponie's queen. I don't think of myself that way, of course, but mention of Liponie gives me a chance to say that we have been trying to make plans for his upcoming birthday.

"Wait, wait, what is a birthday?"

"We call the day you are born your birthday and on Earth you celebrate that day. He wasn't born, he was thought, but he figured out that day was January twelfth, which is only a few days from now. We want to help him celebrate and are trying to figure out what to give him."

"It is a surprise?"

"Yes, definitely. Do you know of friends in his past that he hasn't seen in a long time?"

"I will need a disguise. Hmm, I shall become a woman for this (more genie giggles). I know of many people in his past. I just now created a name so that I can become the great Kee Kee. I am beautiful, can you not see me?"

"I'm a little challenged with that Comahlee. It's just my energy presence there and the part of me that's talking to you is on Earth in the 6th dimension right now."

"Oh! I'm sorry of course. I must make my voice…" Now I hear his version of a sexy woman's voice saying, "I am quite beautiful. Can you not imagine? Yes, I am the party planner."

I do not have a good feeling about this genie. His focus seems to be centered on himself rather than on any discussion about Liponie, but at the moment I don't know anyone else to turn to. I ask him to find out things so that we can have a good party for Liponie and he agrees to be very vigilant.

His first request, which is a good one, is for Osiris to find a way to integrate him into the group as Kee Kee. He explains that he won't interfere with our work but he needs to listen. Osiris agrees that if Liponie knew Comahlee was here, he would definitely know we were up to something. He's going to keep Kee Kee at his side as an advisor.

So far, the only thing I've been able to think of that is essential to the party is trumpets. Liponie thinks that when anyone of importance enters a room, trumpets must be involved. As I think about a party room, it occurs to me to ask the group where we are going to have the party.

Comahlee says he can make the party place. I'm feeling more optimistic about his abilities, but then he wants to know if I like his voice. He also proclaims, "Yes, it is true. I am a great advisor. There is no mistruth in this; I am an advisor. The space I create can be integrated here at the last moment. We will cover his eyes, bring him into the room and have the surprise party."

This genie has an ego bigger than the Grand Canyon. I hope I can keep him focused on the party and the person we are planning it for. I agree to his plan but then I have an inspiration. Jill Marie had so many great ideas for the solstice party that I'm going to ask her to be my back-up assistant just in case Comahlee's plan turns out to be a dud. Now I'm feeling much better; when she and I put our heads together we can come up with awesome ideas.

"Osiris, two days ago I heard myself say, 'I'd like for Liponie to have something from the mother.' I'm not sure who I meant by the mother."

"Ah, Cory comes from a bigger crystal that expanded to become fully present in many arenas. I am thinking that he is becoming quite serious with Cory. I believe that what he would desire would be to meet her mother or to ask her for the hand of her daughter."

I wonder if Liponie is really that serious about Cory. Osiris says that anyone with eyes can see that he is. He then asks Kee Kee to arrange for Cory's mother to be embodied. As soon as he makes that request, I know that's exactly what I was hoping for.

With the full council, I explain the "slippery slide" I recently made for people on Earth who were alive on my birthday and ask how we can do something similar for all the worlds.

Charlie is experimenting with a new voice and I have to ask his identity before I telepathically show him everything I did. He says they are calculating the steps and asks me to do my part in the Fifth Realm. Since I don't know what my part is, I ask him to explain it.

"I have contacted individuals from every world in all of the councils, and we have brought together individuals who are willing to be the source of being for this energy transference. It depends on the higher dimension that is achievable in the future for each of these worlds. The current line of time that exists for some is several thousand years. There are individuals willing to be in presence."

"For thousands of years?"

"They are willing to be the instrument on their world, as you were for Earth. It is for you now to move into the Fifth Realm at the moment of the collective ascension and communicate with all those there who are from the other worlds. This time is prophesied to be three hundred and fifty years from now. They will know what you are there for; bring what they give you to me."

I do that and when I bring it back to Charlie he says it is correct. He says, "Each individual is ready. This offering will be transmitted to each of the councils for them to disseminate amongst their different worlds."

It seems best to inaugurate KK's universe before doing this work, so I gate with Tonas to the Joy Council in the Kahshar Universe. We spend some time trying to figure out how to pronounce his name and then Tonas says we have KK's permission to just call him KK. I move through their inauguration and the transmissions, and, although it is very difficult, I am able to utter a short speech in their language.

Back at the council, but before we step into the main room, Tonas says in a rather sultry voice that he wants me to know he is wearing his underwear. Feeling considerably flustered by this piece of information, I ask him how am I supposed to be able to concentrate on work now. Without any hint of remorse he adds that it is very silky against his skin. This is a side of him I've not experienced before; he is actually teasing me!

He relents slightly and explains that he also pulled me to the side to tell me that Liponie has created all of the council buildings so when someone becomes ready to join there is no waiting, ever. I agree that was a good idea and now that I've regained my composure, we rejoin the full council.

Charlie says the transmission we're going to send out will only be received by each council emissary, and then disseminated. After we finish the transmission, Tonas says it went to every universe except our own. At first, I wonder how I could have goofed like that. Then Tonas asks if it would be all right for Osiris to offer this instead of me; he can connect with each of the individuals directly. I approve and then finally realize this was a strategy so that I did not have to meet face to face with emissaries in our universe who are in conflict with Earth. Osiris tells me that the council is watching my back.

It's time to find out if Charlie sinks or floats. I don't need to ask him if he enjoys the water park; I know he does. He confirms that he floats. When I ask Liponie if he can help Charlie swim underwater, I'm told that he will learn that when he has his scuba lessons. Liponie adds that Charlie can surf sans surfboard. It figures that he would think of trying something unique like that. Zahseet has been practicing and having the time of her life. The Swizzlers also enjoy surfing. I decide not to ask Liponie if I've tried this sport. I'm 99% sure this is something I'm content to just watch.

"Charlie, did you open your stocking?"

"We opened our stocking and we have eaten all of the candy."

"There were other things in there too, weren't there?"

Bluntly honest, he says there were other things, but the main thing was the candy. I decide that next year he will get a stocking with nothing in it to take up candy space.

I only know the one present Liponie and I planned to give him, so I ask Liponie to pick out another present for Charlie to open.

"Ah, it is the hurdy-gurdy! I am so excited! I must have my classes immediately."

I can't even picture what a hurdy-gurdy looks like. For some reason I'm seeing a man who is turning a little music box with a monkey sitting on his shoulder, but surely that can't be right.

"I thought you just turned a handle for the hurdy-gurdy. Do you have to do other things?"

"Yes, there are lots of things on it to make music."

"I don't know anything about it so you'll have to get someone else to help you."

Liponie believes Charlie will be able to master this instrument by himself and that's the way we decide to leave it until I find out more about it.

I check with Tonas about some of the council member's names because I realized many of them are probably two words and I have them as one word. After trudging through that, he asks me, "You did not wish to meet in our chamber?"

"For…"

"I think it is important for you to make sure I am wearing these properly."

"Oh, stop!"

Tonas tells *everyone* he is wearing a special uniform.

"Stop it, Tonas. Oh, dear, I've created a monster. I'm thinking of you in your special uniform as I say goodbye for today."

Before I can leave, he asks me for thirty seconds of privacy. Once we are alone he says, "I only wish for you to know that you have given me such a wonderful gift. The gift is that I am feeling so very open and carefree with you. Have you noticed?"

"Yeah!"

"You have given me such a hope, but it is beyond the hope of an opportunity for us to be together. Even if that was to never happen, the feeling of inner-connectedness and freeness is such a sweet energy."

Tonas reminds me that I am leaving without speaking to Solomon. I have time, so, addressing thin air, I ask Solomon if I could speak with him for a moment, please, and hope that he hears me. I'm gratified when I hear a new voice say, "Yes, my dear."

345

Immediately, I make what I consider a daring request and ask him if I can give him a hug. He says he would feel lost without one! I get to hug Solomon! I'm feeling really honored and, I admit it, smug about that hug. Then he tells me we took a risk.

"A risk?"

"It was a risk to give you such a powerful tool and not tell you what it was for."

"I actually saw you wearing a beautiful crown and I saw the green necklace you gave me. What did that necklace do, because I couldn't have done something like that on my own without help?"

"It was something that was already prepared to act with your intellect. It is one very important stone that can bring back life. I think you call it chrome diopside. To us it is the life stone and it looks exactly like an emerald."

"It exists in our time but people don't know about it?"

"Many humans know of the mythology of the stone. They actually put these on dead people but they do not understand the abilities. Nor did you understand the abilities that you activated in yourself. What you must know is that you have abilities that are a part of your heritage that are within your consciousness levels. This is what was summoned to apply the utilization of this tool."

"Thank you for your assistance and for the necklace."

"Would you like the earrings for your upcoming birthday?"

"Oh, I would. Will you come to the party?"

"Certainly, my dear."

I blow both of them a kiss and say goodbye. I got to hug Solomon… Wow.

CHAPTER THIRTY-FOUR

December 31, 2014

I lined up some potential hurdy-gurdy teachers for Charlie, because when I watched someone playing it on the internet the other day, I realized it's a more complicated instrument than I originally thought. It seems most of the candidates are from France. Sananda agrees to offer some of them a chance to go into an ascended master temple and from there they could come to our council. It will be interesting to see who is selected.

"Yesterday, I received knowledge that someone named Kahleah has a position of great importance in my soul lineage and that she has information for me. What does she want to tell me?"

Sananda says she is an Atlantean and suggests I speak with her directly.

"I am Kahleah. I wish for you to know that through all the works you have been endeavoring over the years you are in possession of something quite valuable. You have within you a conformity of genetics that is, shall we say, quite unique. Are you considering that you could add the genetics of, perhaps, myself to your formula?"

Of course, I am immediately interested in having her advanced genetics. The Atlanteans are on the 10th dimension!

She goes on to add that she has suggested this only because part of her genetic makeup is human. "The other part is Lemurian which, for many, would be a bit too much, but not for someone as yourself with all of your consciousness levels and all that has been laid before you as a beautiful rose path. These attributes could guide you to assimilate my unique blend of human and Lemurian.

I have not brought this suggestion to you without contacting all those who would be in a position to allow this. You may move through the same channels and check the facts. It is within my pleasure to offer you my genetics which would be woven into your genome within the ovum and the semen. You are nearing a time when, I believe, my genetics will elevate you to that space that you are quite anxious to reach."

That seals the deal for me. I chat with her for a bit more in order to be polite. She says that although we both live on Earth, the country of France in the 10th dimension, where she exists, is as if on another world.

With her permission, I move to the Joy Council to speak with Osiris. After I explain Kahleah's offer, he agrees we must speak with her. We move to a private room, I ask Aton, Sananda and Khnum to join us and as soon as they are present I hear Kahleah announce that she is in presence.

"Thank you for coming. Is Sananda here, Osiris?"

"Yes, he is embracing Kahleah. I did not know of your close friendship, Nanda, with the great queen. Kahleah, we would be honored to have you join our council."

It occurs to me that maybe she would enjoy dancing at our party tonight and I invite her to come. She thanks me and sounds slightly interested. Then I remember that Ashtar is still an available man and ask her if she knows the commander. Her voice dripping with sensuality, she answers, "Oh, we are familiar with Ashtar."

I'm somewhat taken aback by the instant switch in the tone of her voice, but I've started something and I'm not backing out now. I comment that I've been told he's a very handsome man. She says I was told correctly and adds that she would be very pleased to join our party.

"Do you have a king to go with your queenship?"

"Periodically…it depends on my nature of the moment."

"So there's no steady partner for you?"

"Hmm, steady is an interesting word. You are of interest in this? Everyone is making faces and rolling their eyes."

They are onto my plan. I can't conceal my laughter and tell her that I'm known as a matchmaker. She asks if that means I make alliances for individuals. I say that it does and that I united Gaia and Aton in marriage awhile back.

"Ah, we were aware of this phenomenon, and it leads to you. You have given me even greater notoriety for myself. I will, of course, call all to notice of the great wonder of that one of my lineage who brought the Earth and the Sun together in love."

"They really loved each other already and I just gave them a little nudge."

Moving back into business mode, I inform Sananda that Kahleah has offered her genetics to me. This causes her to explain that she is also offering her abilities and instruction on how to use them. When I am fully in the 7th dimension, if I wish it, she will be my personal coach. I agree that I like that plan.

Now she addresses Khnum, says he is looking fanciful as always and asks him if he would consider doing the weave on this work. He says it will be fascinating work for him and very beneficial for me. Thoth joins us and he gets her sexy voice greeting. I'm now sure this is standard procedure for her when introduced to any male.

Aton offers his opinion that this could assist me perhaps more than anything he has done to lead me into the higher dimensions more swiftly. Sananda says all are in agreement that Kahleah's genetics will be beneficial for me and then he asks to speak with me in private.

When we are alone, Sananda repeats that this is an amazing offer for me and that Queen Kahleah is quite evolved. He also says that her offer to council me personally contains infinite possibilities. Now that he's pointed out the benefits, he mentions that Kahleah is quite sensual and although there is nothing wrong with that, it might be best to filter her genetics since she is one with "appetites."

By the time Sananda asked for this meeting I was wondering what I had gotten myself into. Although I wouldn't mind a return of some of the sexuality I used to feel, I bet her unfiltered genetics would have set me on fire. I admit to Sananda that I'm relieved and grateful for his advice and assistance.

"Whether you wish to explore many relationships or not, it would be best not to be driven by these genetics to do so."

I instantly agree. I don't tell him, of course, but I'm just hoping to eventually feel sexual towards *one* person, Tonas.

"It is good that Tonas was not included in this gathering for I know that his mind would immediately run to concern for this. Not because he would wish to hold you from having the exploration and the experiences, it is simply that he would have the same concerns as I. We can filter this. She is quite free and beautiful and everyone wishes to please her. That pleasure brings her to even a higher degree of desires. It is not a negative thing, my dear."

"No, but that is not me."

"That is why I have brought this to your attention. You are more interested in authentic long term connections that are meaningful."

"Yes, that is true. I had some short term connections in my younger years and none of them were pleasurable. Of course, I'm a different person now, but exploring multiple intimate relationships is not of interest to me. Her genetics will need to be skillfully filtered because I would not want to have to deal with those kinds of appetites. I'm glad I've talked with you."

"She has many abilities that are attractive to what you would wish. It would not be possible for us to do this if she were not of your soul lineage. If you will allow me, Thoth and Khnum to be of the greatest delicacy in this, we would be carefully sifting through. Since I know already what genetics you have in place this also gives me an opportunity to very easily enhance that which would assist you and your abilities. You also have my genetics as well as those of us who are of the Origin Council so this would be a very good blend."

"Go for it."

"We shall then. Before we go back, let me discreetly bring the others here and add Melchizedek if you accept this."

Osiris and the others of our group join us, but they also leave themselves in position to interact with Kahleah. Sananda tells me that they all knew why he wanted to talk with me.

Osiris says, "Joy you are a treasure to all of us. There is no judgment of wrongness for finding pleasures in the body. Several of us have had the joy of Queen Kahleah, and yet I must say, it is not you, Joy.

She is enjoying speaking with one of us and we are celebrating because it takes her attention away from the rest of us. We will collaborate and filter through the genetics. There will be fail-safes in place so that they only activate in a framework in time that is less than one year ago. This activation will also very quietly stimulate some of your other genetics. We assure you that all that is applied will be enhancing constantly. When it comes time for Queen Kahleah to tutor you, you can make the choice to maintain with our council or with her. She is a worthy instructor; I suggest we all become part of your classes."

"Yes, now that I have more background on her, I would be glad to have your support."

"She will know that her genetic has been filtered and we will make known to her that this was at our discretion. You have given us permission."

"We don't need to tell her that right away do we? I don't want to offend her."

Osiris agrees they will not have any cats leave the bag yet. Sananda suggests I could tell Kahleah that I've been working with Aton, Melchizedek, Khnum, Thoth and him and that I wish for each of them to be a part of a special council in charge of weaving this genetic I am so very honored to receive. That would allow them to blend with Aton's project.

After I agree to this plan, Sananda says it won't be necessary for me to let on that they left the room, because they didn't. He advises me to just bring my consciousness back to our gathering.

I address Queen Kahleah to explain that Aton and Melchizedek have been assisting me with brain expansions, and Sananda has worked for seven or eight years with my genetics. "I really would appreciate them being part of a team for me working with you when we get ready for the genetics and also for the tutoring you have offered. I am so honored to receive these gifts and I want to take full advantage of blending your genetics with what I already have and the counseling of these people I've been working with for so long. This is with your approval, please."

"I believe that it would be enhanced evermore by these beautiful men. This will be our crowning glory, my dear, working together as such. When will be begin, dear council?"

Sananda says it is important for me to have an opportunity to get to know her and asks her to periodically take time to visit our council. "It is not necessary for you to make this a permanent space, and yet we would be happy to put a chair for you at the council table anywhere you wish."

"Hmm, yes, of course, perhaps the chair can move a bit. (I bet she eventually ends up sitting next to every man at the table.) This is a feast for me, dear. Thank you for inviting me to such a pleasurous buffet of wondrous beings of light. I agree very much so and I believe we can collaborate and put something together. I am willing to hand over to you now the special strands, as you would call them."

Sananda says that is exactly what they needed, and that we are grateful to her. "Shall we let you know as soon as we are ready?"

"Yes, I will take my leave now."

Sananda tells me Tonas just entered and has been updated about what we've been doing. (I feel like I've been handling fire and am maybe just a little bit scorched around the edges. Having her as a tutor is certainly going to be interesting.)

"She is welcome at our council table. It is no more a distraction to have her there than the children. She will eat Kennedy with a spoon."

Something like that is exactly what I pictured her doing when she thanked me for inviting her to a buffet of beings of light.

"Sananda, this morning I saw my dad sitting on a motorcycle. He was dressed completely in a black leather outfit that even included a black leather cap with a little brim. Then I saw a picture of Mom and Dad. I felt the energy of that picture go into my heart and I heard myself say, 'Thanks, Mom.'"

"They are having a grand time."

"They did have a motorcycle for a brief period of time before I was born."

"They are rewriting their lives and doing many things they never got to do. You were thanking them also for taking care of themselves and doing what's right for them. They are having experiences in their minds which seem to be happening in real life. In the Fifth Realm, they are capable of doing millions of these scenarios at once."

"Next, I saw pictures of my two boys go into a pile and then I heard, 'We're done.'" (Mom and Dad had a lot of pictures of my boys and I've brought them back to my house to sort through.)

Sananda suggests we go into the Fifth Realm. "Your mother and father are going to hand you a file for you and one for each of your sons. They have been rewriting their lives to expand on what they gave you before."

While we're there, I tell Dad he looked great on his motorcycle and I ask Mother if she ever finished high school. (The fact that she didn't was a great regret for her when she was alive.) Sananda tells me she says, "Many times over." (That means she has experienced completing high school in many different realities.)

With the Joy Councils:

Tonas says he didn't know of Queen Kahleah but he is very grateful to our friends here; otherwise, I would have "stepped into a puddle of great loss of innocence."

"Yes, I was glad Sananda spoke with me."

"Did I embarrass you with my nakedditity, my dear?"

"I want to ask you about that. When you saw the underwear, you just vanished your clothes and you immediately had the underwear on. Is that what you did?"

"Yes, the part of you that could see me liked what you saw."

I'm feeling so put out with myself there that rather than give him any encouragement, I only murmur a neutral, "Hmm…" I wanted *this* part of me to enjoy seeing him wearing clothes. I'm just going to pretend this didn't happen, after all *I* didn't see him.

I've brought some more items for Liponie to restore (quilts and more dresses I wore when I was little). Even though I know I'll be able to do this myself when I'm in the 8th dimension, it's comforting to have him do it now. I've also brought Christmas cookies and fudge I made to share with everyone here. The problem with this is that I'm also going to have to give some of it away to my friends on Earth; otherwise, I'll be left staring at a full pan of my favorite kind of fudge.

Liponie joins us and I explain what to do with the things I've brought. Then I announce that we're going to have a dance tonight and I plan to kiss Tonas at midnight.

Liponie says, "Ooh, there will be more kissing."

"How is your relationship coming along?"

"Ah, she loves me. She adores me. She truly does. We laugh and we talk and there is so much for us to learn about each other and about everything. She has experienced everything. Because she is everywhere she witnesses everything. I listen to her for hours."

"Oh, my gosh, Liponie, you two could talk until the end of time. I'm so happy for you."

"We are taking it slow."

"Well, you've only got three hundred and fifty years. That's not much time, but maybe it will be enough."

"What color would you like your dress to be?"

"Midnight blue with stars all over the dress."

"This is exciting, indeed. You will have it."

With the full council:

After I say hello to everybody, I move into queen mode and declare we are going to have a dance tonight. It's a great feeling to know that when this part of me finally gets around to actually experiencing what happens at the council I will never be left sitting beside a dance floor and hoping somebody will ask me to dance. Never, never, never.

"Charlie, I transmitted something to you last night."

"Indeed, it was a very intricate grid connection pattern that will assist to bring that universal alliance between all of the different councils into a very unique harmonic."

I heard what he said, but I can hardly believe I was capable of doing something like that. Charlie explains that there is much in my levels of consciousness that I am not aware of consciously. I decide not to comment on that conundrum because he continues by saying that I have millions upon millions of thought patterns that are coming together.

"All you must do is have a thought about something and when you fall into sleep it begins to formulate and the answers come together through your brain processing and all the knowledge that you have. This is a loophole for you."

"Good, I'll take all the loopholes I can get."

"The other thing I want to discuss is something that Tria, the Atlantean, said after the solstice party. Her words were, 'Earth itself is encoded with all that is necessary to create the balance that you can vision and even beyond that to what you have no concept is possible.' Is there something we can do with that now or do we have to wait until we get to a certain dimension before we can access any of those codes?"

Charlie says they have put something together that contains very powerful encodements. He thinks that if we add the flavor of higher vibrational energies and then transmit those energies to individuals who are ready to embrace them, this will enhance the collective. He explains that immersing the collective consciousness of those with a higher vibration will assist those with a lower vibration more than sending the energies directly to them.

Next, he says it might be relevant to immerse this work into the previous timeline. (That timeline began on January 7th and 8th, 1781, and lasted one hundred and sixty-six years. The timelines always have two dates; if it begins on the 8th in Australia, it is the previous day for America.)

"Can we send everything we've done to the previous timeline?"

"There is no valid reason why not and some things will be supported. This is ready."

Charlie claims they are geniuses and laughs the Swizzlers' collective laugh. As soon as we finish sending out the transmission, he says there is already a ripple forward from the distant past. He states, and I agree, that this will be a very good new year.

"Charlie, I feel like I'm your mom and Tonas feels like your dad, but, stop and think about this. Everyone here is my family, right? That means all these people are related to you. I am hereby proclaiming that everyone here, unless they choose not to be, are your honorary uncles, aunts, nieces, cousins, grandparents, great, great, great and so on grandparents."

Charlie's singular voice says, "Oh, all can be my family." His collective voice says, "For all of us." His singular voice asks, "For all of us, really?"

"Yes, if any of you in the council don't want to accept, you'd better speak up right now!"

Tonas says everyone is clapping their hands in cheer. "We all love each of you; you are our genius babies, the stars of the show."

"You see how special you are, Charlie?"

"You made me an individual."

"You chose that."

"You gave me the way to be an individual. I am having so much fun."

Charlie's mention of fun reminds me about the hurdy-gurdy. The pictures I saw of it looked like the inventor had a slow day at the shop and decided to have some fun by combining a violin, a guitar, a miniature piano his kids got tired of playing and then added the crank of a Model-T Ford to really get it wound up. I mention to Charlie that the hurdy-gurdy looks complicated and he says that's why he selected it. I should have known he would pick the most difficult thing he could find. No autoharps for this kid.

Sananda says they will have a teacher for Charlie tomorrow. They are working with Kahleah's genetics right now.

Charlie says that after he has a teacher, he plans to give a concert the very next day. I'm a little concerned about that plan and suggest that I hope he will be patient with himself if he is not a masterful hurdy-gurdy player after one day of instruction.

"OK...like the drums. People held their ears."

"Yes, I think it's important to have people who spent their lives mastering their instruments show you some easy things to start with and do right."

"Yes, and it's wonderful that people feel that it's safe to cover their ears."

"Even though playing loudly would be a lot of fun, it is also possible to play softly on the drums."

It seems that possibility had not occurred to him because he says, "Oh…"

"Is there another present for you to open today?"

"Yes, they're going to give me a man."

I have no idea what Charlie is talking about so I call for Liponie. He explains that we have an expert hurdy-gurdy player named Giuseppe who will be Charlie's teacher.

"True Heart, a few days ago I got the energy of ostrich. Then this morning in my reverie I saw myself wearing some kind of vest and all of a sudden a green frog popped out of it and looked up at me. What do I do with the energies of ostrich and frog?"

"Both of these are new energies that are birthing into your life experience. We will first look at the ostrich. What has changed in your life, my dear?"

"My parents have gone and I'm cleaning out their house."

"Those are big changes. The frog energy is important because of the change. It is a rebirth of self and of the world; a rebirth of good things and opportunities opening for you. There is also an opportunity for you to have someone else step in and assist."

I wonder out loud who that would be. True Heart suggests it could be someone in the future and notes that, many times I bring them information from the future. I remark that I'm noticing that more and more but I have no idea how I do it.

"From your abilities. How can you not know how you bring these forward?"

"I just don't."

"The ostrich and the frog together are important to your physical and emotional support. You are releasing things that are less important to you and opening up to things that are more reasonable to what you are choosing. You are choosing the spiritual, the journey into awareness, and that which held you in a secret of this is now in collaboration with you. Your energies are opening; you are ready to become who you are. That is the ostrich, you see. You know the story about how an ostrich thinks it is hiding."

If that story really were true, my ostrich persona would have had its beak full of sand for much of my life.

"Are you saying that even though I thought I was in hiding, I haven't been?"

"You are not in hiding; your people that were closest to you are now supporting you. They are guarding you, protecting you, giving you support."

He's right about the dramatic change in the kind of support my parents are now able to provide for me. They assisted me financially when they were alive, but they weren't able to comprehend the healing work I do. I'm glad they understand it now and are even able to help me with it, but, as I tell True Heart, I still miss them.

"And you will."

"I'm really happy that they're having a wonderful time. It's just that the sixty-eight years they were with me are finished. I might feel better if I remembered more about my childhood. There's so much blank space."

"You were a free spirit. Simply remember that when the ostrich feels safe, it holds its head high. You are safe. It is time to bring your head high."

"You are still tutoring me about the animals, right?"

"Of course."

"That's really important to me, thank you."

Before I tell Aton about all the weird things that are going on in my head, I take a moment to be grateful that no matter what I say he won't think I'm crazy and have me carted off to the "funny farm." Here's what I report: "Something clicked into place in my brain this morning. Later I saw the cut open half of a lemon in my head. I saw a square clear crystal, shaped like an ashtray go into my head. Something fell over in my head and made a popping sound. Then I got turquoise. What does any of that mean?"

Sure enough, he says this is all part of the process. He calls these events, "little automatic expansions" and tells me to expect more of them.

"There's nothing special that I need to know about any of that then?"

"The only thing special that you need to know about is that you are special. And thank you for the dance tonight. I have already spoken to Tonas and he is arranging for costumes for all of us."

"A masked ball would be fun."

"I do not understand."

"You wear a mask so, just like the ostrich, you can hide. Most people will know who you are, but it's kind of freeing because you can pretend they don't. Maybe you can kiss someone that you wouldn't have the nerve to kiss without your mask.

That's it for today but I'll be back tonight. I'd like to have big smooches from lots of people, but especially one from Tonas at midnight. Liponie, please have champagne and other beverages. I'd like to see if I can handle margaritas in the 10th dimension. Remember to caution people about getting tipsy, especially me! I love you all. Goodbye, Tonas."

"I adore you, my dear."

"I'll see you tonight and tomorrow."

CHAPTER THIRTY-FIVE

January 1, 2015

Today feels like the perfect day to go to the galactic councils of light and get things for the New Year to give to Charlie. I intend to split my energy bodies to do this and it feels like I enter thousands of councils. I bow, move forward and ask for support and catalysts for graceful and glorious shifts and transformations for this year and beyond for Earth. Using SVH, I put this in order and take the sphere to the Joy Councils.

After Tonas greets me, he says that Ashtar has been diligently waiting for me. "There is something he wishes you to witness."

I'm still feeling skittish from dealing with war and assassination so I comment that I hope we are not going to have to deal with something awful again. Tonas says he is unaware of what it is. I'm able to relax a little bit now because surely he would know about any disaster looming on the horizon. Still, I mentally collect myself and take a deep breath before we enter the council.

I hear Ashtar summon Tonas to the front of the council and ask him to kneel. Oh boy! Something good is going to happen.

Ashtar says, "All may witness that I now elevate you to Supreme Commander. You may rise, Supreme Commander Tonas. Of course, we could not do this without you, dear Joy."

"You had me so scared! I was afraid there was another catastrophe to deal with. I don't know anything about your ranks of command but this sounds impressive."

Ashtar says that Supreme Commander is the highest ranking. I think Tonas deserves it, of course, but I'm curious if there was something specific he did to bring about his elevation. In answer to my question about that, Ashtar explains that, "Everything that exists as the possibility for what we as the collective of this command have worked for many thousands of years has come into a quickening due to the great works of you, dear Joy, and the collaboration of this Supreme Commander. Should he not skip through nine ranks?"

Now I'm squealing with glee for Tonas while Tonas says he is overcome.

"What a New Year's present! You have really big boots now."

"There are boots? I am most grateful. This is a great honor for me and for all of us here. We are a team with one mind and focus for this evolution. We recognize there has been a complete turnaround since the beginning of this council, and even before the council began with our work on Inishimora. Again, I am quite grateful and I am sure there will be a great pay rise. That was a joke for you, Joy."

Ashtar adds that imagining the culmination could be in a handful of years is a great celebration for all of them. "We salute you both, of course. We would raise your rank, Joy, but how do you rise more than queen?"

I agree that I'm quite content where I am. I also mention that since I'm getting things from the future I know that there will be at least two or three more universes that will be joining us soon.

Ashtar agrees that all universes will eventually join us and says the Ashtar Commanders believe by the end of January there will be a complete turnaround for all of the warring factions in the Nordahnee Universe. "All the works that you have done within the council here and the works that have been done in the Nordahnee provinces are recalibrating the views of these different species as well as different individuals from the warring planets. We shall no longer call them warring planets; we shall call them worlds that are finding peace. I must take my leave. I give you my greetings, all, and congratulations, Supreme Commander Tonas. Naturally, you may elevate to a larger ship if you wish."

"Never, I shall always wish to have Inishimora, please."

Ashtar grants him that privilege and I am secretly glad Tonas chose to keep our ship.

Osiris says he is observing Tonas's very big pants. "I have watched you grow these months and you have become someone with a glorious personality. I find that to be very valuable. Do you not agree, Joy?"

"I think he's actually able to have more fun now than he did before."

Tonas says we are speaking of him as if he is not here.

"Yes, I'm commenting about your personality because I've noticed some light-heartedness about you recently, especially with your new 'uniform.' I'll ask you about your new rank in private."

"Before we do any work, I want to find out about the party. Jill Marie told me my dress was magnificent. She said it was like looking into the night sky to see the stars and that was just what I wanted."

Tonas assures me that the dress is now hanging in my closet. This is one I really, really want to see.

Since I've been a little bit concerned about my behavior last night, I ask if I took off any clothes and danced on top of any furniture. (I remember when I was in college dancing on top of a radiator in a friend's apartment after having too much alcohol.)

Tonas says, "Sadly not."

Then he tells me that not only did I have a margarita, I was the bar mistress with four blenders working at the same time. I find this hard to believe because I don't know anything about mixing drinks. Tonas explains that Liponie was making eggs constantly. The picture I have of Liponie wearing an apron and scrambling eggs does not fit with what we've been discussing. I ask for additional explanation and Tonas says Liponie was encouraging me. Oh, egging me on. I tuck that little gem away and move into work mode.

With the full council:

I explain the work I did before coming to the council today and hand Charlie the sphere. Then I ask what the medallions of Earth are because I heard something this morning about a special project to assist them.

Charlie says they are awakened individuals like me. The CEV have a transmission which he adds to the one he has prepared from the sphere I gave him. I ask him how many medallions of Earth there are. He answers that there are currently 943,000 medallions that will receive. Then he adds something to the transmission for those who will be medallions later.

Before we send the transmission out, I ask if it will assist the other universes. Charlie says no, but suggests I could get things from councils in the other universes that would make the transmission more valuable. I split, gate to those councils, take what they give me and move back in a flash with another orb. I love travelling this way and can't wait until I can take my physical body with me.

Once the transmission is sent out with my added wishes for a Happy New Year, I hear Charlie's singular little voice say, "Mama, Mama, I can play the hurdy-gurdy. Giuseppe is teaching me and he says that I am a natural. He talks funny."

Charlie tells me he is not yet ready to give a performance but he will be. I learn that the others are playing instruments of an orchestra. After imagining the Swizzlers banging, honking and screeching on drums, trumpets and violins, I immediately suggest they might enjoy some lessons. (I'm certain the council members would appreciate that also.) Liponie says he is already on this assignment and laughingly suggests getting an angel to teach the harp.

"I have a story to share with the Swizzlers. It is one my dad would frequently relate. Of course, he had lots of stories, but this is one I especially enjoyed. It's about a person in our family nicknamed P.G. who lived during the depression. This was a time when many men didn't have any work so they would roam around the countryside looking for work or whatever they could do to sustain themselves.

P.G. and another companion were, the expression is, 'bumming.' They were walking and looking for food. P.G. went up to a house and someone there gave him a loaf of bread. He rejoined his companion and they continued walking while P.G. was eating the bread. As they came to a bridge, he'd had enough of the bread and he threw the rest of the loaf right into the water. His companion protested that he was hungry too and asked P.G., 'What did you do that for?' P.G. said, 'You've got to learn to beg for yourself.'

Now, if you substitute the word, 'speak' for the word 'beg,' that is my advice for the rest of the Swizzlers. One of these days Charlie is going to be traipsing around the universes with me and exploring where Buzz Lightyear has not gone, and you have to be able to speak for yourself. That's my lecture for the day."

Charlie's collective voice tells me this was heard by all. He adds that they said to tell me, "We love you, Mama."

"OK, kids, I love you, too. I do want you to be able to move into your own individual mastery, though, and speech is a part of that. I love you all and Merry Christmas."

I'm curious about which of his presents Charlie enjoyed the most. He says he liked everything but he very much liked the train, the candy canes and the caramel apples. My son is obviously a foodie with a sweet tooth.

Next, I learn that Pinky got a special closet from me. I wasn't aware I gave her anything like that so I ask Liponie to tell me what's in it. It contains cheerleader outfits and other clothes for a little girl including two things that, he says, I might enjoy: a poodle skirt and saddle shoes.

"Oh, Pinky, I can't wait to see you in that outfit! Thank you, Liponie."

I move into a discussion with Gaia about what we are going to do with the fairies. There is an important meeting of the Grand Council which will be held in a chamber next to our Joy Council inside the Earth. Liponie made the chamber, as well as a large orb—floating in the middle of a Christmas tree—that is going to act like a television so that all the gardens will be able to see the meeting. He also made a special pedestal for the fairy queens to stand upon and when they do, their energy will be transmitted into the council chamber.

I tell him he's a genius. Laughing, he says he can never tire of hearing that. I reply that I could tell him that every time I talk to him. Now that I have a picture of the mechanics of the meeting, I ask Gaia what's on the agenda for discussion.

"It is important to offer these queens a chance to understand the full measure of what is possible and then to make their determinations for their gardens. It will only take a moment for them to decide. They are very excitable. We have decided to give them an opportunity to experience the new parts for three days. They can cast them aside if they are not of interest. You and I know that they will require a book."

"Shouldn't Sheliah be the one to talk to them about her experience?"

"It is important for you to be recognized and then Sheliah may give her interpretation. I will introduce you."

Gaia asks me to take her hand and we move to the chamber for the meeting.

After greeting her children, she tells the fairies that they are here today for a very special reason. "It is important for you to know that the world is nearing a time of change. This is the first council meeting we have had in a very long time. You are each a part of me and we are, in these next days, weeks, months and a few years, to become a very important support to Earth as a whole.

You have a chance also, to apply your bodies in a different way, and we have here with us today the queen of the Earth council of human beings. She is an advocate for yourselves as well as for you each having the opportunity to create babies and also male species of fairies. She is what you consider to be a maker of love matches and she is the one who brought my dear Aton and me together. We are grateful to her. I wish to invite each of you of our world to know the heart of Joy. Joy, do you have words to speak to these dear ones?"

I keep my speech short because I'm really interested in what Sheliah is going to do. I mention that I'm looking forward to getting to know more of them and I thank them for the care and the love that they have given the Earth for all the eons of time they have existed. I introduce Sheliah as the new queen of her garden and the fairy that I played with when I was a little girl. I then ask her to tell the queens about the new body parts that she and Rosebud are enjoying.

"Yes, hello, and greetings from my heart to all of you, and to you, Joy! I am a new queen as you know, and I am very excited to tell you about the many possibilities that are available to each of you. I am in a marriage and many in our garden are married. We have babies and I have forty-three. Rosebud has a penis; I have a vagina and we put them together. We are made to fit and it is very pleasurable. Gaia has a book for all of us and it is possible for all of us to have these body parts of the penis and the vagina."

She has absolutely no inhibitions about her new body part because she now invites them all to see her vagina. I'm not sure how she is able to demonstrate this body part, but I bet it would be fascinating to see her attempt. She explains that her vagina is like a pleasure palace and Rosebud, her husband puts his penis into it.

I'm stunned when she announces that Rosebud gave her his penis to demonstrate how it works. As I'm contemplating a detachable penis, she shows the assembled fairies how it fits and explains that he "makes it go really fast in and out. There are many positions that are shown in the book. There is nothing else that is more fun to do, ever. Although, I must say to you all, I like to conk people with my star, too, but I think the penis and the vagina are very good.

Gaia tells me that each of you will get to experience this. All you need to do is have your vote now. In my garden we enjoy the vagina and the penis already, but all the rest of you might like to have this to play with. I will be quiet now while you all vote." Immediately she laughs and says that everyone wants the vagina, the penis and the book. She adds that she doesn't think they will ever cast them away. I hasten to explain that is an option; they don't have to keep the new body parts.

Moving to a topic that is a little more comfortable for me, I ask the fairies to share with Gaia or myself any ideas they might have that would help us to move easily and gracefully into the higher dimensions, specifically the 8th dimension.

Gaia says she wishes to continue the meetings because now there is so much change happening. She offers to convey to them telepathically through a universal matrix. "There are many other species that you will be coming into contact with and we wish to keep you informed and prepared. Please enjoy your new body parts. Each of you has a wonderful book in your little home. The transmission begins to you now…and we are complete. My blessings to all of you, and our gratitude."

"And mine also. Happy New Year."

Gaia suggests we make our leave and then she asks me how I think the meeting went.

"I'm glad you suggested additional meetings. I think that's going to be important. Rosebud gave her a replica of his penis?"

"No, he gave her his penis. She can conk him to reattach it."

"I didn't realize she could do something like that."

"A fairy queen has a great deal of power, my dear."

"So she said to him, 'Give me your penis so I can show everybody.' Is that what happened?"

"He was very happy to do so."

"Keep me posted on what happens."

Back with the full council, I give Tonas a brief description (which doesn't include the words penis or vagina) of the fairy meeting. The update Tonas gives me is that Jesus is still at the Nordahnee Universe and, according to Ashtar, it might be two or more weeks before he returns. Looks like I'll have to wait until next Christmas to find out more about his beginnings.

The next area I'm going to investigate has to do with the tarot. It is a system of divination I've studied a bit, although not for some time. Recently, I consulted one of my books in order to discern which tarot card represents this year for me. It is the Wheel of Fortune card which is supposedly allied with the planet Jupiter.

I think it would be fun to chat with another of our planets and Osiris says Jupiter can attend a meeting if I would like to speak with her. I ask what her name is and he says it is Sheearah.

More questions reveal that all planets are female since they birth life; suns are all masculine and stars can be either masculine or feminine. If life exists upon them, then they are female.

Now I explain why I'm interested in speaking with Jupiter and ask if anyone here is familiar with tarot.

Osiris chuckles then tells me that everyone is smiling. He adds that tarot can be "real" if I choose for it to be. When I explain that a Wheel of Fortune year is about major change and maybe fame and fortune as well as luck and fate, he says that nothing could be closer to the truth for me.

Even if she doesn't have any information about fame or fortune, I think it would be interesting to find out about Jupiter. Osiris announces that she is now embodied here and Liponie has outfitted her with a beautiful gown.

I thank Sheearah for coming to speak with me and compliment her for her gorgeous bands of swirling energy. She agrees they are quite beautiful. As we converse, she reveals that she has many dimensions with embodiments of individuals in different forms living upon them.

"What is the giant red spot that you have on the surface of your world?"

"You speak of my vortex?"

"Yes, does it do anything special?"

"It is decorative."

(I wonder how many scientists will be satisfied with that explanation. I think it's delightful.)

"OK, yes, it's lovely. What else can you tell me about your planet?"

"All areas of our mass are held in special gasses that feed the species. We are of love; we are awake and aware. All parts of us breathe love and the sounds, the energy, the sweetness of the resonances of the sound of each of the gasses. We consume the love of all that is a part of us and we adore the vision of all that is around us. We are pure consciousness. We are many species and yet each of them is energy. Each of them is held in the vision of the light of our truth. It is where you are in your direction of achieving. One day, we will be a part of you, and you will feel our great love, our communion of heart. Each of the dimensions is as if a different colony of energies. We can move between the different dimensions and experience them. There is no way to describe how unique and yet the same we all are. Each of the different energies on the dimensions feeds the whole with a glorious harmony that does make the song that we all feel in our very presence."

"Your words are very pleasing."

"I am very pleasing; all parts of me are pleasure."

"One of the reasons I wanted to speak with you today, besides wanting to learn about you, is that we have a system called tarot." After repeating the explanation I gave Osiris, I ask her if there is any truth to it.

"Energy is truth and energy feeds all that comes within our range. We are a giant; as a great giant we influence many worlds, many stars and your Moon and Sun. The consciousness of Jupiter is joy and it is also fulfillment of all that is desired. Does this fit with your wheel of the fortune?"

"Yes, it does."

"Then so too shall I magnify this to you."

I am thrilled with this gift. What could be better than having a planet as large and beautiful as Jupiter beaming joy and fulfillment of desires to me? After thanking her, I invite her to visit our council in her embodiment any time she chooses. She says it is very freeing to have limbs and lips.

I suggest that before she leaves she might wish to speak with Cory, a former crystal who is really enjoying embodiment. As I'm making that offer, a vision of all the planets, stars and suns embodying and having a wonderful time flashes into my mind. Never one to hesitate where there is a potential for divine partnering (at least for others) I suggest to Charlie that if there is a love match that would potentially enhance a planet, a sun or a star's experience, I'd like for them to know about that possibility. Charlie says that is a tall order but I remind him that other universes have councils similar to our vigilance council. He agrees to make it a focus.

It is possible to do my genetic work today and all who are part of this project move with me into a private room. I explain to them that since I possess the genetics of Isis and Hathor, I'm choosing to have none of Kahleah's genetics that have to do with sexuality and sensuality. Khnum tells me they sifted her genetics with, as we call it, a fine-toothed comb and removed those flavors. They left all that would support the natural abilities of moving energy and solid objects, telepathy and trans-locating; all the things that are important to me.

After Thoth adds his assurance that they have taken every precaution in the filtering they did, I give my permission to proceed.

Sananda says he put together the foundation for these genetics to be activated in my pre-conception state (Mom's egg and Dad's semen). I put the genetics in place using SVH.

Sananda says that now that I have this genetic, it might be one of the great secrets of my success. "None will truly know what is possible through the advancements of your personage. Once you are in the 7th dimension, what is brought forth will be very fortuitous."

Aton says, "When I look upon that which I was able to offer you, and what will now be changed in the past, you have an even greater advancement."

"All right, thank you gentlemen for your work today."

Private conversation with Tonas:

I ask him the significance of his new rank. He says there is only one other Supreme Commander and it is Ashtar himself!

"Oh, Tonas, that's marvelous! How do you feel?"

"It is the greatest honor I can imagine. I have skipped past Insigne, Insigne Commander, Triton, Regleah Triton…" The rest of the names are a blur because he's almost yelling and spouting them too fast for me to catch.

"I didn't catch those ranks but they sound impressive. Here's a big kiss to go with my congratulations and wishes for a Happy New Year. Did we dance last night?"

"You said you were going to dance my feet off, but they did not come off."

"What kind of dances did we do?"

"We were very much into our tango, of course. We did the waltz. You did something funny that was so beautiful. You required me to wear these almost painted on pants, and you wore tiny outerwear that had little fluffs on it and you danced on the very tips of your toes. You threw yourself into the air and I caught you. Of course, I would not have dropped you ever. You were telepathically directing me with every step. Naturally, everyone was in awe of you."

Never having danced ballet or even desired to learn, I have a sneaking suspicion that the only reason I attempted something that ambitious was so that I could see Tonas in painted on pants. I'd like to dwell on that picture for a moment but he is too excited about his promotion to talk about ballet.

He says he was unaware of what was going to happen since it had been cloaked from him. He adds that Ashtar is the only person who has moved through all the Ashtar Command ranks, and to have been elevated to Supreme Commander is beyond his understanding. He claims he owes his elevation to me and I immediately correct that statement by saying his promotion is because of the work we have done together.

"I am in gratitude to you forever, my dear."

"I love you, Tonas."

"I adore you. My love for you is unmeasured, because it cannot *be* measured. One day I will show you this love. You will see through my eyes all that I have seen, and you will see the true spirit of yourself that is still hidden from you because of the dimension that you exist within."

CHAPTER THIRTY-SIX

January 2, 2015

Yesterday, I saw Kahleah shoot some kind of beam of electricity out of her third eye. I didn't understand the purpose of this demonstration and I don't really want to ask her what she was doing. I ask Sananda to join me in the SBT and explain what Kahleah was demonstrating.

He says she was showing me a means to transmit and shift the energy of the field she was in; if she was in, for example, the Arctic, she could activate that and make herself warm. "The reason she chose to show you this was to open that possibility in your mind. It's easier to do something once you've seen it done and you have the capability for this based on your genetics."

I'd really enjoy having that ability. My body temperature is a degree cooler than normal. You'd think that would be an advantage in summer but I don't notice any benefit. What I do notice is that most of the year I'm cold. I've never bothered to buy any kind of lightweight, evening wear because no one would see it beneath my coat.

At the Joy Councils with my genetics team:

Tonas says that Kee Kee has been preparing for Liponie's party on our ship because it is the only place secure from discovery by Liponie. I'm not so sure there is any place like that, but so far we've kept the secret.

It's my turn to mention that I was able to speak with Thoth last night while sitting on my sofa. In other words, not during my morning reverie when it's usually easiest for me to connect with the masters. Thoth agrees that I definitely did speak with him and says that he hopes I will continue to choose to communicate with him.

"I felt a definite 'zing' with you, so I'll keep working with you."

Tonas asks what kind of a zing I experienced. I explain it was just a zing of connection with telepathy. He surprises me then by asking me not to give Thoth underpants. I've experienced enough jealousy from male partners that I'm immediately relieved when he says he was jesting and that he does not have "jealous bones."

Aton says Kahleah's genetics are stirring much of what he has put in place and that it is quite impressive. I mention that I saw her last night. He says she is in presence and asks me to explain what I saw. I repeat what I saw her do and add that it was impressive.

She agrees, of course, that her demonstration was very impressive and says I will have the same abilities. "It was less a beam of light than a transference of energies. A stream of light was something you would notice. I wish to continue showing you these visuals of your abilities. Your many consciousness levels will give you further mental training. I was not of the AMS so it is not possible for me to instill my knowledge in your consciousness levels. It is much easier for me to simply show you."

I agree it was fun to see her demonstration and thank her for showing it to me. She asks if she may be released now because she was in the middle of something very stimulating. For an instant my mind wants to picture what she might have been doing, but I put up a mental stop sign and quickly agree she may leave.

Osiris says Aton has been very impressed to witness that my orbs are moving in a different pattern. "This pattern, as well as the resonance of the orbs and how they interface with your filaments of energy that are linked to your consciousness levels as well as your amazing brains and the consciousness levels that are interfacing with those brains, is very impressive. I had the thought that perhaps Isis or I could mirror to you the perfection of the movement of our orbs. This would assist your orbs to move in a more confluent way. It is prepared for you and would take no time at all to put in place."

Immediately, I agree to his proposal; he's the patriarch of our universe!

Osiris explains that he gave this to Sananda to implement for me and that Isis would do the same. I ask him if her orbs move in the same pattern. When he says they don't, I request having the mirroring of her orbs as well. Isis joins us and asks why she was summoned.

"Osiris is going to mirror for my orbs the way his orbs move, and I also wanted to have a taste of the way your orbs move."

"Ah, well, you know that my orbs will be moving in a very graceful manner that supports the feminine energies of yourself. Since you have a balanced masculine and feminine, it is possible to create a marriage of these for the two of them are in their unity and focus very often. When they are connected of heart, perhaps we can capture this unity, for in that unity the orbs are dancing most exquisitely and can be considered to be at their most powerful since they are both quite balanced in their own rights. Blended, they will be even more so. Do you agree, Aton?"

Aton says he has implemented a simulation of their individual orb patterns and also of their united focus. He feels that Isis is correct and this will be quite a feather in my hat. Sananda offers this work to me and I put it in place using SVH.

I can hardly wait to find out more about Tonas's new position and what his parents think about it. He says they are in the "seventh of heaven. Every thought is of what a wonderful honor this is for me and our family, as well as an honor to you. We believe it will be of great assistance to Ashtar to have someone to share the quest, especially now with all of the universes to oversee. It has been Earth alone that we have been focused upon."

I ask him if his new position will mean that he won't be able to work with me as much. He says he has been asked not to stray his thoughts beyond the works we are doing together.

"It was in the mind of Ashtar that this elevation for me to Supreme Commander, I still love to hear it, is important for the position that I have in working beside you. It elevates the stature of our Joy Council. Be not of concern that my time will be split between that of the fleet and the council. With all of the universes that are within our council I have a higher ability, as you would say, to make command decisions, and Ashtar and myself have an open conduit between us."

"Yesterday I heard, 'There is a universe that has reached critical mass to become non-dual.'"

"The Corena Universe is within moments of this."

"Have you had a chance to talk with representatives from the universes who haven't stepped forward?"

"It has been brought to our attention that it is best for us not to speak to them about this, simply because they must come to their decision without any pressure. Those individuals who are watching are from worlds that are of the strongest focus of dual. They are popping in and out of the council and observing. I believe that there will be some new interest, especially with what is happening with the Nordahnee Universe. None of these are as deep in war as the Nordahnee were."

"Thanks for that advice. Even though I'm here, *I'm* not really here. Let me salute you and congratulate you again before I leave."

"Liponie is having a little celebration party later if you would like to join."

"Of course I will…she will. Bye, Tonas."

"Farewell, my beloved."

CHAPTER THIRTY-SEVEN

January 7, 2015

January 4th, I heard Dad, as if from far away, shout, "Joyce!" This was so funny because when he was alive and outside doing some kind of work on the farm, he would almost invariably shout for someone in the house to come to the door so he could tell them something or ask for something he needed. He could be far away in the pasture and inside the house we could still hear him, but for me to hear him shout my name from the Fifth Realm really sets a record for long distance communication.

Sananda joins me for a visit to my parents in the Fifth Realm. He explains that they know about the genetic work I am experiencing now and they feel like they can support me by giving me a file. He says they also want me to see the new chicken coop my father built by hand.

Even though people are able to create with a thought in the Fifth Realm, making something by hand sounds like what Dad would choose to do. He loved to work on the farm but in his later years his hands were so gnarled with arthritis he couldn't really do much.

I'm missing my parents in ways I never thought I would: I keep looking at the phone to see if they've called and when I'm driving I see things that I plan to remember to tell them about.

"Let's see the chicken coop, Dad."

"He's really excited to show it to you. You know everything here is energy but he wants you to know that it has real hay in it."

"At least there's no chicken poop for the chicken coop."

I intend to give them both a kiss, thank them and tell them that I miss them. Using SVH, I put the genetic work they gave me in place.

At the Joy Council:

"Yesterday evening I was talking with Thoth as part of my channeling homework. He said to me, 'Purposefully draw to yourself the frequencies of 7th dimension. Tune into that frequency and release from your reality all that does not match it. See that path open before you and step into it with grace and ease.' After I heard that I wondered if it would be possible to create conduits of 7th dimensional energies for myself, like making a tunnel into that dimension."

Aton tells me that will be easy for me to do once he gives me the pieces. He explains that he is also tying the 7th dimension into the energy fabric that sustains me, but this will only be for the period I am in the 7th dimension. He comments that the upgrade I got today was quite efficient.

"My dad just built a chicken coop. This is a little place to keep chickens."

"He is ascended, is he not?"

"Yes, but he was a farmer and he liked to build things."

"Ah, I understand ever more why the individuals of this space are very much enamored by your parents. They are creating a unique atmosphere. Now everyone will want to have the coop."

"There were many things he wasn't able to do towards the end of his life but now he can."

"And he is."

"Once my dad gets going on something he is unstoppable. Kind of like me, I guess."

"There are apples falling close to the tree."

"Sananda, why Tonas?"

"You are questioning why you were drawn to the Ashtar ship of Tonas, and then rewriting your life story so that you had connection with him for the last fifty years?"

"Yes."

"There are 786 incarnations where you and Tonas, within the spectrum of those life experiences, were not Joy nor was he Tonas but they were very interconnected. This is very common in love matches that are spread throughout time and you have your fingerprints in several universes. I believe this is also why it is such a passion for you to bring the universes into the thread and the forming of the culmination.

When an individual has had many incarnations on non-dual worlds with someone who is a heart passion, these incarnations still exist. You also had some on worlds of duality, including Earth. To have such a deep connection and the heart alliance leaves an openness for this connection to occur in this incarnation. It is very simple, and the heart knows what the heart knows. Did you notice on meeting Tonas, even though you had less ability than you do now, that there was an immediate reaction for you as well as for him?"

"Yes, I was intrigued. Is this incarnation 786 or 787?"

"There are 786 incarnations other than this one you are experiencing now. You must know that you, being in the position that you are cosmically, are leading a charmed life. I know you do not believe that, and yet without the support that you have given yourself and we and others have also given you, life would have been a little different, including that you would be dead."

I know he's right, at least about the part that I would be dead. I used to wonder how I managed to get through some of the times I recorded in my journals.

Speaking privately with Tonas, I ask him if he knows about our 787 incarnations. He says he does and he wanted to tell me many times but he couldn't.

"Maybe this is the one."

"Of course, my dear, it is."

"Just for the record, can you name off all the ranks you skipped?"

"Captain is the first rank. Commander, then Insigne, Insigne Commander, Triton, then Regleah Triton."

"Where does High Commander fit in?"

"You can have several ranks within Commander. After Regleah Trition there is Seccleor, then Dawn, Supreme Dawn, Clarion and Supreme Commander. You know I moved from Captain to Commander, then to High Commander and then I moved beyond all of these as if I had wings of angels to Supreme Commander."

Through a series of questions I learn that Ashtar began the command when different galactic races began genetically assisting humans. This assistance was allowed only if the humans had some of the genetics of those who wished to assist them.

"The Arcturians elevated individuals by bringing them onto their ships and awakening their levels of consciousness as well as activating some of their genetics. The Andromedans assisted also but they came to Earth and worked directly with people. The short life span was their greatest dilemma."

"What about the Anunnaki?"

"They were involved with humans but they were not in favor of human sovereignty. They had their own agendas."

With the full council:

"Osiris, is it correct to say that the only nutrient you require to sustain your body is light?"

"We do not have pizza on the non-dual, except, of course, at our council. This is quite pleasing and when we consume it, it is the energy of the pizza. When we eat ice cream it is the energy of the ice cream; however, there are individuals on our council who are from dual worlds and when they consume the food it enters their body as a solid or as a liquid. It is not so much that we of the non-dual are eating light as it is that we consume the vibration and the spark of light that is within the food."

"Would you have to eat anything?"

"No, it is enough to consume the light. Let me say to you that the food is an illusion, even if you grow it yourself and prepare it. It is all made of the same creation energy and so it is formed into a configuration that meets the eye of what is expected, like a tomato."

I ask Mr. Kennedy how eating food at the council compares with eating food on Earth; for example, is it necessary to chew anything.

He answers that chewing is part of the excitement of the ritual. "In *this* place, as you consume a strawberry it is as if you are eating a strawberry because it is made from the same energy of a strawberry on Earth. The difference is that there is no mass. When you eat it you have the same sensory of it, and yet when you swallow it you are swallowing light, the vibration of it. It is quite interesting; the vibration of a strawberry and the taste of it are enhanced when you are energy."

"Osiris's reply confused me because he seemed to say yes and no."

"The difference is, that everything is light, so the answer is no and yes."

In spite of Mr. Kennedy's explanation, it still seems to me that eating an energy strawberry would be like chewing on air. Rather than ask any more questions about eating, I tackle the subject of food from a different angle.

"Liponie, if people from dual worlds are eating here, do we have bathroom facilities for them?"

"Indeed. When they consume foods within this council, even those of the non-dual make the poops."

I didn't imagine anything like that would happen here and I ask Liponie if we have magic toilets. He says they are like beautiful fountains of glory.

"What happens with the excretions?"

"Oh, we take care of it, my dear. We cycle it back into the food."

Both of us fall into fits of laughter. I know he's joking but I can almost sense the interesting expressions on the faces of people from dual worlds. He assures everyone he was jesting.

"Charlie, do you have anything for me?"

I hear his singular voice say that he loves me and I remark that I like his new voice.

"Thank you. I like this one, too. Why should the vision of love immersing the Earth be only for Earth? We have, from all the worlds that are participating, a vision of the highest expectation. We have brought this to everyone here at this council and each has offered their heart piece. We believe that when this is instilled into Earth and into all of the different worlds and stars in all of the different universes, this will light up the Earth so that it becomes as if a new sun. So, too, shall all the worlds. This is our idea as a collective and what we have put together."

Tonas asks Charlie to wait so that we can recognize Joseah and Festona Beshar. Festona admits they have been lagging behind and it is their desire that their universe, Slanar, be part of our work.

"And please do not leave us out of this opportunity. I am Emissary Sohmeeneeuh Toelinah of the Annapeenorah Universe. We have been waiting and waiting. We wanted to step forward earlier but all of the worlds in our universe are dual.

I spend some time asking her to pronounce these names again. When I check with the Beshars, Joseah tells me she is the mate of the Council Presence and so she is not important.

I say she is very important, but she insists that she is not. When I tell her that statement is incorrect, she says she will bow to me on this. Again, I state that she and everyone here, whether they are a Council Presence or not, is important. I'm glad when Festona agrees she's important; he says she is his inspiration.

Tonas and I gate to the Slanar Universe and Festona reveals that there are no members in their Joy Council at this time. He adds that they have witnessed our great wonders and asks if it is possible for us to bring their future council members into the present. Tonas suggests sending Liponie into the future.

Liponie announces that we may now witness a magical event. "The chairs are empty, and now they are full! Please explain to these individuals how they magically appeared, Mr. Beshar."

"Each of you here has been summoned through magic that comes from the Chailee Universe. We have been witnessing the great wonders in this universe and in others that are coming together in fellowship; they are all working together to create what can be considered to be miracles. Believe me, that all of this will be brought to your awareness. Please trust in me that what is to be is what you will choose."

I speak to him in his language. He answers, then says, "You are indeed eloquent. We are grateful that you have spoken our dialect."

After this, things go smoothly with the activation and transmission of the work. When we finish, Tonas informs them that with the assistance of Sananda and Osiris, they will have the opportunity to know all that has transpired up to this point. With their acceptance, that information is transmitted to them.

Before we move to the Annapeenorah Universe to inaugurate their council, Tonas suggests we send Liponie ahead to bring council members in because he believes they have the same situation we just encountered in Slanar. When we arrive, Sohmeeneeuh thanks us and lets us know everyone understands what we will be doing. As soon as we finish the work, I hear Osiris announce himself and ask me if I would be willing to inaugurate another council in the Moedayahduh Universe headed by Council Presence Historia Terreeah.

Before we head for that universe, Tonas informs me that Historia is very quiet and shy. When we get there, I ask to speak with her privately to try to encourage her. I suggest that even though she may think of herself as shy, she is a trailblazer for her universe.

Tonas says that she is someone who has looked forward and is brave enough to step forward to accept the wonders that we have for her universe. Her quiet reply is that they are grateful.

Before I begin, Liponie tells me everyone is "on the pages" in their understanding of what we are doing. The inauguration, transmission and toast go smoothly after this. Before we go back to the full council, I decide we should drink a toast to the Lowmeesha Universe since we didn't have time to do that when we inaugurated their building. I mention that even though they stepped forward under duress because of the Nordahnee war, they did step forward. Once that detail is taken care of, we move back to our council.

Charlie says the transmission is ready and hands me a sphere. I thank him, give him a kiss and ask the Creator to put a little extra zing into this gift of awakening of new love, new knowledge and new excitement and joy for this year and the years to come. Then we send out the transmission.

It's time to check with Gaia about how the fairies are doing. She says they are enjoying their new body parts and their books and none of them wish to go back to the way they were. She also dealt with the issue of birth by telling them it was not necessary for them to have the birthing experience that humans have.

"How did Sheliah demonstrate her vagina?"

"She bent herself backwards, put her hands on the ground and had her legs wide open; she was very acrobatic."

"And Rosebud has been fully restored?"

"Yes, and he is quite active with his new penis."

I ask Gaia if he needs any help with the babies. She assures me he doesn't because each baby is most aware. I'm still a bit nervous about the changes we've instituted for the fairies. She says this is an adventure for them and reminds me that until recently they have been the same since the beginning of thought.

Private meeting with Tonas, Charlie, Osiris, Sananda, Mel, Khnum, Aton and Thoth:

"Osiris is the patriarch of the masculine line; Isis is the matriarch of the feminine line. I don't know who the eldest in the neutral line is, but would there be any value in having the movement of their spheres mirrored to mine?"

Melchizedek answers that he is the longest-lived person of the neutral line at our council and asks me if I would like to witness his spheres. Suppressing a giggle, I say I can tell that they move differently than mine.

He says they are in creative motion and his voice becomes sensual as he describes their movement. "It is like swirling your energies in some whipping cream. If you took paint on your fingers and you were rubbing it very smoothly onto a canvas. My orbs move very artistically, very magically, very musically."

"OK! I would like some of that."

Aton says he is excited about how much I have evolved. "The conjunction with Kahleah's genetics is becoming quite interesting. I am adding the flavors of Melchizedek; it is done."

Charlie tells me he is now proficient in both the hurdy-gurdy, and the accordion. The Swizzlers found that when they link as a collective they all learn very swiftly. With that bit of news, I suggest that they could play their instruments for Liponie's birthday. Charlie agrees that now people don't cover their ears.

Now he sounds excited as he tells me that he has an idea. "Imagine the chairs of music; each time the music stops one of our council must move to the next chair and play that instrument. We will have the piano, the harp and every instrument, and we will have them mastered by the day of the party. I am, perhaps, the most fabulous designer of music and I will work with Handel on this."

I cringed when Charlie mentioned musical chairs. That was another of those childhood games I hated to play so I'm relieved his version is not a fight for survival.

"Handel is there?"

"I have asked for him. I am choosing to make a beautiful song for Liponie and Handel is the perfect person to help me make Liponie smile more than he always does. I will be making you very proud, Mommy."

"Charlie, you don't have to do anything at all to make me proud of you and love you."

"But you will extra love me when I have made the beautiful song for Liponie."

"I will love the song, but I'll always love you the most. Bye sweetie, bye Tonas, I'll see you in a couple of days."

"Farewell, my dear."

CHAPTER THIRTY-EIGHT

January 9, 2015

I ask Sananda to visit the Fifth Realm with me to see what Mom and Dad are up to now. When we step into where their house is, they aren't there! Sananda discerns they are involved in a think tank focusing on Earth and the other universes and structuring a vision that helps them to see the way the world can or could be. This is so unlike anything they would ever have been involved in when they were alive; I have to remind myself that they are masters now. I telepathically send a message (Sending is not a problem for me, just receiving.) to Mom and Dad to return to their place and they do.

Through Sananda, I learn that Mom has been making all kinds of cookies and she looks like she's about nineteen.

"She and your father are doing things there that nobody has ever done. She could think the cookies into existence, but your father just told me that going through the action of making them gives her much pleasure. She takes them to different gatherings, like the place where they just were, and she also offers them to individuals as they first enter the Fifth Realm. Your father says that people consume them and this is shifting the way people are thinking."

"I've been thinking of this place as a big cave where everyone is just sitting around reviewing their lives. Mom and Dad don't seem to be doing anything like that."

"The place where that is done is a space that is pure light into which people project themselves. They look like they're standing and doing nothing, but actually they are looking at and experiencing movies of themselves on millions of screens. I know that your parents have done that because they gave us a file for you."

"Are they through doing that?"

"Your father says they had a very unique life. The choices they made were, in many cases, one or the other or there were no other choices. They had to go forward and do this or do that so they don't really have a lot to redo. They have nearly mastered re-experiencing the options for their lives in the last two weeks, whereas, you have millions of life transforming choices to make. They have already experienced the choices they could have made in childhood and youth and the expansion of those."

I'm glad Mom and Dad are happy, healthy and together, but it seems like most of the time they're doing the same kinds of things they were doing when they were alive. It's time to suggest some livelier activities; otherwise, Mom might spend the next three hundred years making cookies.

I tell Mom that I know she likes to cook but how about riding motorcycles with Dad. Sananda reports that Mother's face lit up when I suggested that. Since it seems like I'm on the right track, my next suggestion is that Mom could learn to be a swimming star like Esther Williams. (Mom took swimming lessons when my brother and I were young, but she never really was comfortable in the water.) According to Sananda, Mom has met Esther in the Fifth Realm.

I'm getting really excited thinking about all the activities they could do and I begin suggesting the first things that pop into my mind: Mom could have her own motorcycle to ride; they could ride horses together; they could learn to dance. Mother loved to dance when she was in school but she and Dad never did things like that together. Sananda says Dad is up for dancing and Mother loves the idea.

I'm curious about what Mom is wearing now. After a slight pause, Sananda tells me she says she has on a house dress. This totally surprises me because even when she was alive, Mother never wore anything like that. Wardrobe help seems essential and I know just the person to consult.

I hear Liponie laugh and tell my parents they have a lovely little place. I suggest that Mother might be interested in expanding her vision concerning her wardrobe. Liponie asks me to leave him here in order to communicate. I hear him say, "Cookie? Mmm, I would love one."

Gosh, I love my mom. She's still as generous and gentle as ever.

I've been thinking that perhaps other individuals who end up here might need some suggestions, even though they are dead, about how to really live and have fun. As soon as Liponie remembers that the Fifth Realm is where we will all end up, he's on board for preparing the way.

He says Mom and Dad have offered to give him a tour so he will understand the full range of the Fifth Realm.

As I consider what Dad and Liponie might come up with, I don't think this place will ever be the same. I'm OK with that because if I'm going to be spending a thousand years or so in the equivalent of heaven, I want to have some fun.

Now it occurs to me that I could get assistance in the Fifth Realm from authors I've admired. Sananda agrees that is possible but suggests I only ask for help from authors whose genetics I have. After calling those individuals forward, I mention that I still love books from my childhood, for example, books by Kate Seredy and Eleanor Cameron. I also address Kage Baker and tell her I love her books. Then I ask for all of them to help me with my own quirky style of writing.

I'm thrilled when Sananda tells me I have some of Ms. Baker's genetics, but that makes sense because she is on my list of 30,000+ names. He asks me to telepathically transmit to everyone what I am writing. I share with everyone all that I have written up to this point and explain that the challenge for me has been adding my own thoughts and feelings about the things I hear and discover.

Sananda sums up my request nicely by saying, "You'd like to honor them by having your genetics stirred in ways that will assist you to add those flavors to your books and to have the energy of their wisdom. Now take the file they have handed to you."

Then, since I feel like I'm on a roll, I call all others on my list of 30,000+ names forward. I ask them for files to assist me with all the skills I have, or ones I will be developing, so that I can manifest them in my own way, my own timing and with divine grace and ease. Then I implement both files using SVH techniques.

At the Joy Councils with Tonas:

He warns me that we have a very big day today. I'm fine with that as long as dealing with war or assassination is not on the agenda. The good news is that a bunch of individuals wish to join our council; the only small challenge to overcome is that they all insist their inaugurations must be done in the past. They don't want to miss out on what was offered at our last meeting.

My plan from now on is to do as many inaugurations on one day as I can. Tonas offers to guide me step by step so that I don't forget anything when the energy gets intense.

"I have a thought that I have to put my foot down on one thing."

"Where is the foot going?"

I keep forgetting he is not going to understand those kinds of expressions and explain that my statement means I am making a firm decision about something regarding him.

"I proclaim that you may not wear a Speedo swimsuit until I can actually see you in it."

Imagining, even momentarily, how he will look in something that scanty makes my heart beat faster.

"I know of this Speedo."

"I don't want that part of me there to see you in it until this part of me here can see you in it too."

"I can tell you it is not impressive on Charlie."

It might not be impressive, but I bet it's cute. I'd love to see my son in his Band-Aid-sized swimsuit.

During a private strategy meeting for Liponie's birthday, I give Kee Kee one of my gold earrings to resize for Liponie. As soon as I mention the possibility of having Cory jump out of a cake, I hear her laugh and ask what she would wear. I didn't realize she was present and explain to her that I haven't been including her in our meetings because I was afraid she couldn't keep the party secret.

She says she can and that Kee Kee pulled her into our game. Kee Kee says Cory will enchant Liponie in the costume he has designed. I thank Cory for her cooperation and say that now she really must leave for the next part of our meeting. She assures me she will keep quiet.

It's time to find out if Cory's mom is willing to embody. Just as I feared, Osiris says they are still working on this and it is a difficult situation. He explains that she is as resistant as Cory was in the beginning and does not wish to be as if human. He told her that she would be playing a temporary role and that those who have embodied have had great pleasures. I know he's going to suggest that I speak with her, and, of course, he does.

I feel like crossing my fingers to help me be persuasive enough to budge a crystal. Osiris says he is expanding our space since she is quite large. He tells me her name is Zeezzz, summons her and then says she is here.

Speaking in my most pleasant and only slightly cajoling voice, I thank her for coming and say that I can feel she is really magnificent. I explain, as best I can, the situation and add my request that she temporarily assume a form that Liponie would be able to embrace since he is so in love with her daughter.

Osiris reports that she has asked via telepathy who has led her daughter astray and away from her form. She also wants to know if the one who loves her daughter so much would be willing to take the form of a crystal or is it required that Cory remain embodied.

These are tough questions to address, but luckily Osiris provides some great answers. He says he transmitted to her that Cory was resistant as well, and only after embodiment did she find this great love. He explains it is possible that they could join as crystals if they wished, but they do not wish to do so. He finishes by reminding Zeezzz that, "To have an offspring is not to define what the offspring must do."

I send her my telepathic agreement with Osiris's assessment. He says that Zeezzz has agreed to comply and I breathe a sigh of relief.

With the full council, I ask if there are more souls who want to embody in Earth. Gaia answers that there are many. I wonder out loud if there is a way to facilitate upgrades or expansions for the crystals in Gaia in order to allow more souls to embody in them. She says that all parts of her are evolving and suggests that Charlie might know of a means to expand on a more global scale.

He gives us, or at least me, some surprising information. There are many beings on Earth without bodies who are trying to find a way to embody. They are being snoopy and that creates problems for gifted individuals who sometimes become aware of them. The star they lived on was destroyed so they came to Earth because of what we are and what we will become. They are a collective, yet they are also individuals and they are doing things like simulating smoking and drinking alcohol. Charlie finishes by saying they are becoming little pranksters.

We have enough people occupying bodies that have issues with smoking, drinking and pulling pranks. We certainly don't need to add the entire population of a star to those ranks!

Gaia explains that she has been waiting to see what happens and adds that there are individuals from another species that could possibly create hosts for their bodies. She says she doesn't think that will fit with my plans because the individuals who would be offering the bodies would use them to create an army.

I have been becoming more and more alarmed as Gaia relates this current state of affairs. She reminds me the species who would offer the host bodies (if they were more aware of these disembodied individuals) are already creating, and have been for millennia, conflicts on Earth. I realize another potential catastrophe is not just looming on the horizon, it's settled comfortably right down on our ground. Ack!

I immediately ask Osiris or Charlie to give me some ideas for solutions. Charlie says there are billions of these displaced individuals and they have created ethereal embodiments in order to experience being human. They are just waiting for a chance to have bodies and then they intend to live on Earth. I experience a wow moment but it's not the kind I enjoy.

Charlie reminds me, unnecessarily, that an army like this could slow the progress we have worked so hard to set in motion. I say this is a real pickle. Charlie answers that it is a full relish plate. I appeal to Osiris for suggestions but he says it is their right to emigrate.

This situation takes the concept of immigration to new depths. I could probably make a joke about it if my brain wasn't so frantically scrambling for some kind of solution. Finally, I ask how we can make this a win-win situation.

I feel a ray of hope when Osiris says he knows the answer. He asks Charlie and the others if they have the same vision he does. My frustration that I don't know what he's talking about vanishes when I hear Charlie gasp and yell, "Mommy!"

"Give it to me, Charlie!"

"Osiris says this is not his idea. It is the idea that is floating around in the air."

"If it's just floating in the air, grab it, Charlie."

"The idea, Mommy, is to create a little pocket world within the Earth where they will have so much fun experiencing life in an embodiment that is of light. Everything that exists outside the true reality of the origin is an illusion; objects feel as if they are material, but truly they are only energy. We could bring an intermediary here to the council and offer them a grand spectacle of a place of residence that offers endless pleasures. They could have a water slide, Mommy! They could have trains; they are more sophisticated, though. I believe they will wish to have discos."

I am feeling hopeful enough that I can now enjoy my son's suggestions about entertainments they would like. I ask Charlie to tell me more of the plan.

"They would have the illusion of a physical form, just as yourself and myself. We could tell them that we are aware of their plight and we wish to offer each of them the most glorious experience of life on Earth and an opportunity to evolve and ascend with the beings of Earth. We explain that we created a beautiful space for them and they could even tour it. Then you would get the cheerleaders of the Cowboys to take them."

From what I've heard of the activities they are experimenting with, I'm fairly sure that would be an enticement for many of them; however, I want to make sure they actually will have the opportunity to evolve and ascend.

Osiris confirms that is possible and asks Gaia if she is capable of creating an area for them. She says she can and then she says, "If they are to have the cheerleaders from the Cowboys, they must also have the— what is the program that we saw of the dancing men? They were very saucy."

Now you may be thinking that I am making this up. Let me assure you that Gaia actually suggested this and Osiris answered in a rather grumpy-sounding voice that, "She is speaking of the men who take their clothes off and dance."

I'm feeling a little left out as I mention that the council is having a lot of fun I wasn't aware of. Osiris answers that they are watching the Americans more than anyone because they have the most fun. "The dancers are called the Chips and the Dales."

I mention that I've seen them and Osiris says Isis appreciates their bodies and their movements. He does, too, by the way.

It's time to involve Liponie in our project. As soon as he is present, I ask Charlie to transmit our problem and solution to him. Liponie mentions it is quite a challenge and might take him as long as six or seven minutes. Since he believes these beings will only be interested in playing, he asks Gaia if he can create their space within a non-dual arena so that they can create what they desire with a thought. Gaia suggests placing them on the 10th dimension with the Atlanteans but advises that we need to check with the Atlanteans to make sure the beings will not distract them.

Aconna Shareeah speaks up to agree that they will assist us as soon as Liponie is ready. Liponie says he is ready and the offer to live on Earth can be made to them as soon as we decide the exact location to place them.

Shareeah offers to give them the Americas. I'm not too thrilled with this idea but I mention that by the time we get to the 10th dimension it will be probably be OK for us to be there with them. Shareeah reassures me that the moment these beings enter the 10th dimension they will come into the harmony they are accustomed to.

She also tells me a contingent of Atlanteans just now visited the world they existed on when it still existed, and it was a non-dual world. She explains that they simply fell into some interesting habits while attempting to find out how to be human. (Humans do that too!) I find it very humorous that one of the interesting habits they fell into is visiting strip joints.

Shareeah's brilliant suggestion is to place them in a space linked with the 5th dimension that stretches to the 10th dimension and that the Nevada territory would be a location where they could more fully enjoy the gambling and the pleasure palaces they have been snooping around in. She explains that because of the activities they are currently involved in, we can't put them back to the harmonious place they were. The placement she suggested will give them a chance to evolve without creating havoc on Earth and the impenetrable stream of energy they will be placed within in the Nevada territories will not be able to be observed.

"They will be in their own world with their 501 genus."

"501 what?"

"They have an attraction to the 501 genus."

I'm still trying to puzzle out what kind of genus (genes?) she is talking about when Tonas whispers to me that she is talking about clothing.

I finally get that she is talking about 501 jeans. Alcohol drinking, cigarette smoking, aliens in 501 jeans, gambling, hanging out in Nevada and watching replicas of the Dallas Cowboy cheerleaders and the "Chips and Dales" dancers. Who would ever believe anything like that could be true. Even hearing it discussed, I have trouble imagining it.

Shareeah explains they created the jeans for themselves because they felt it helped them to blend in. She says that the Atlanteans will supply them with all the forming energies they require. She then asks Gaia to make it so that their evolution leading into the 10th dimension does not distract the Atlanteans existing there or the other Earth beings evolving into that dimension.

Liponie says he has created an area that is as if the full range of the Americas; it even includes skyscrapers and little cabins on ponds. He asks if I'd like to speak with an emissary. After I say yes, he tells me he has created an arena for all of them to be present so that their collective may be involved in the decision. Liponie says I may speak. I ask who I am speaking with and I'm told that I am speaking to Inoh.

"Welcome, Inoh, we have an offering for you so that you can be part of Earth. I know that you have been wishing to have that experience.

My genius friend, Liponie, has designed a place for you and your collective. Liponie, will you show them what we have?"

"You can witness here. Joy is the head of this great council of this universe and was well aware of your plight, my dears." Liponie adds a very sympathetic tone to his voice as he says that, "It was her decision to have this created so you can have the physical experience you desire. We have worked very diligently to offer this to you. There will be cigarettes and alcohol and all manner of opportunities to experience, as well as evolution to as high as the 10th dimension. In that dimension, you will wait until the others of Earth meet you there; then all of us may evolve together to the 25th dimension. I am offering each of you a two week stay embodied within this space. There are health spas, bowling and much food that you may fully taste and enjoy. There is an area which allows you to not struggle for money since you will be able to direct with your thoughts. The gates are open to this."

I'm not interested in gambling, drinking, bowling or Chip and Dales but the other features of this place sound appealing to me, especially no struggle for money. I remind myself that although that's not here yet, it's at least on the horizon.

Back to the moment at hand, I tell Inoh we're sorry that their world was destroyed, that we have room for them here and we welcome them with open arms.

"We are most gratified; this is truly a welcoming world. We accept your generous offer of this vacation, as you call it. And we will be embodied?"

"Yes."

"And we truly will have the tastes?"

"Yes, and you'll have the 501 jeans."

"We will have them for sure? Each and every one of us?"

"Every one."

"Oh, we most heartily accept. How do we enter?"

Liponie says the gates are open and all they have to do is step through them. "In two weeks, we will review to see if there is more that I can offer. If there is something that you would wish to experience, I am your genie. If you wish to return to your disembodied presence after this

396

two week trial of the territory, we will happily restore you. Of course, we would restore you back as if you had not had the experience. We do not wish to taint your experience of waiting endlessly for bodies by giving you this lovely experience. I think it will be easier to restore you back to before this offer was made."

They agree to these provisions and I suggest they step right in. Inoh says everyone is moving into a place called Equinox and asks what that means. Liponie explains he put a big banner over the top of the entrance and there is a turnstile to go through. He named it Equinox because that is a name he likes. He reminds Inoh that it is not a prison. He will be having a two week vacation in a place that can become their new world of Earth.

Inoh says they are grateful to us for this opportunity to experience and that he will speak with us in two weeks. Liponie closes the gate behind them.

I ask how long they have been disembodied and Liponie says their star, Airio, exploded in 2008. They knew that was going to happen and after they watched it happen they made their way to Earth.

I share with the council that I think this group will eventually be a great asset. Tonas agrees and adds that they might even assist us to move into the 7th dimension.

"Just when I think there won't be any more dilemmas, another one pops right up. Thank God for all of you! Wonderful work...high fives."

"There were many souls in our universe who wanted to embody. We made a layer of crystals in the Earth for them to do so. Are there souls in other universes who would like to embody and would be willing to embody in crystals in any of the planets?"

Charlie communicates with the different universes and says they wish for someone to communicate with these essences and from that position they will open up a space for them to exist, if they fit within certain parameters of the crystals. "They wish to always honor the crystal's evolution without causing distraction within the worlds of these universes and they are willing to create councils that souls can petition to embody."

Charlie says he likes what we did for the Airio essence of beings and suggests we could make a menu of possibilities so that beings could choose how they wished to embody. I agree that is a great idea and he says he would have accepted this himself.

"We didn't think of it then, but you still could."

"I would not leave you for anything, Mommy."

I'm really glad he said that. I couldn't bear the thought of losing him now.

Charlie says he is creating a link with the world of Equinox. "They are having fun. They have pinball. It was genius of you, Liponie, to suggest that they would have to give up even their memories of this. I do not think they will choose this. I think they will want exactly what they have forever. All is in place in all of the universes. There are councils and I will be in close connection with each of them."

It's finally time to do some inaugurations and I thank everyone for waiting patiently. I ask Mr. Gobi to speak with me since I heard his wife, Eesah, speak to me several days ago.

He says he is very pleased to be able to experience an inauguration. He's been told that it's possible for his council to be included in previous inaugurations but he can't understand how that is possible. I explain that the energy work I do allows me to move myself and other individuals backward and forward in time. Sananda confirms my ability to do that and that seems to satisfy Mr. Gobi.

He says we will go to Nahbinoshar but he has no council members ready. There are individuals who are interested but nothing is official at this time. I assure him that we have encountered this situation before and that Liponie can bring us their future council members who will even have an understanding of the work we will be doing.

He introduces himself as Demahtoo Gobi, Councilman from the Nahbinoshar Universe and his wife is Eesah Kohmahlee Gobi. She says she has been watching this great wonder and hoping for this day.

"We are glad to have you join. My partner, Tonas, is going to announce the other universes who wish to be inaugurated and then we can do them sequentially."

Tonas tells them we will move into the past in order to do their inaugurations and that Liponie already has their structures created. The council members that will be decided upon in the future will already be in attendance in the past. He finishes by saying that this is the great magic of energy.

I remind Tonas to help me keep on track with where we are going and we begin with the universe of Nahbinoshar. When we get there, Tonas calls me the queen of our universe. I'm going to talk with him about that after we finish the inaugurations because that is a title I'm not sure belongs to me. We inaugurate the Tollbeet Universe Council headed by Council Member Aheeshanarrah Kahteem, the Inzleeookeerah Universe (It's completely feminine.) headed by Matreeus Soonimarah Keylosh and the Antarrah Universe Council headed by Elite Presence Tassmarr Teetooareuh. With Tonas keeping me on track, I didn't make any stumbles.

"Liponie, what's going on in the Fifth Realm?"

"We have delightful projects in mind. No one will ever want to leave."

"Did my mom and dad share with you what they want to do?"

"I tried to talk to them about a glorious palace, but they refused me."

I'm not really surprised by that refusal. Dad and Mom were like little oysters snuggled in their shells. Dad was born in the house they lived in and he died in a remodeled version of it. They loved the farm and it would have been exceedingly difficult to pry them off of it. They might have been content with a newer, larger home but it would still have had to be on the farm.

"Are they going to be doing more things?"

"I have suggested that they become the premiere designers for all individuals to experience what they have thought. My understanding is that the individuals there look upon what they have chosen and what they have not chosen. They have a chance to experience what they have not chosen in its fullest measure. Yet what if they were never offered the vision of something? I am suggesting a special arena of offerings for individuals to experience. Those of Earth and other universes have had these experiences, so the menu can come from them."

"Mom and Dad, in my estimation, did not lead lives of wide experience, so it's interesting that you picked them. They will really have to broaden their horizons to be able to do that, Liponie."

"It is possible. They simply do not wish to experience these for themselves for some reason. Perhaps they will later when they see what others experience."

"Maybe. I just want them to have a good time. I think the Fifth Realm really needed something like this; if someone didn't know of a possibility, they wouldn't be able to choose it to experience."

"In the cumulative point, all will be experiencing each other's experiences, so why not do that first?"

"Good work, Liponie. I love you so much."

"There is such love that I have for you, my dear."

"It's marvelous to feel this way. Farewell everyone."

With Tonas, in privacy, he explains that the billions of people in Equinox are not part of Earth except for that stream of energy they moved into. A large bubble, nearly encompassing the whole of Nevada, was created for them and every place that the bubble is, there is no combining of space with abodes or individuals. They are not even close to a road.

I'm satisfied that their accommodations will cause us no problem and I move to a topic of great interest to me.

"Can you give me a little hint when I will be fully in the 7th dimension?

As I expected, he says he wishes he could. I propose that if we wrestle tonight and I win, he could answer *something* for me. He says he's seen mud wrestling but he thinks Jell-O would be better. I agree Jell-O would be way more fun.

"By the way, you called me the queen of this universe; you might not want to say that."

"Isis has agreed you *are* the queen of this universe. You have done more for this universe than any of us, ever."

"That seems like a pretty big crown, but I'll think about it. I love you."

"I love you."

CHAPTER THIRTY-NINE

January 11, 2015

At the Joy Council with Tonas:

"Oh, my dear, it is a joyous day."

"I have a question first, as usual. What is the significance of 568 in connection with us? I heard that number the other day."

"You are speaking of us as a couple?"

"Yes."

"Ah, I think I know. There are things I am not able to say."

"Maybe we were married 568 times. Is that possible?"

"There will be a time when you know the answer. You will say it to me and I will respond that you are a genius."

"Oh! I want to shake you! Can I shake you?"

"Oh, please do. I am wearing my under pants."

"Oh, NO!"

I'm laughing as I call him a rascal and admit I created a monster when I thought up that gift.

When the party planning gang is in presence, Tonas says that everything is ready. I share that my idea to get Liponie into the room is a simple one; I'm just going to tell him I have something to show him and gate him to the ship. I mention that I want the room to be dark when we enter. Charlie says the Swizzlers are all set with their instruments. I brought one of my favorite gold earrings to give to Liponie and I instruct Kee Kee to wrap it and the red Speedo swim suit.

Kee Kee now reveals that his birthday party idea is to have a circus with the Indians riding bareback and individuals playing with the tigers, as well as other attractions. This idea is not the quality of something Liponie would design and I am really disappointed. In fact, I'm so disappointed I can't think of anything to say. Normally, I would ask Liponie to fix it and I obviously can't do that either.

My last hope is that Kee Kee was able to invite people Liponie hadn't seen in a long time that he might like to see again. When I ask him if he was able to do that, his reply is an unenthusiastic "yes," and he adds that Liponie has not made lasting friendships like he has with all of us.

It looks like the only thing that's going to save this party is that Liponie will get to meet Zeezzz. She is practicing being humanoid. I use the term humanoid because she has insisted on having a long tail.

"Osiris, I was able to grab some information that was just floating around about the universes who haven't stepped forward yet. It seems they are involved in too many conflicts and wars to be able to reach any kind of agreement. I'd like to approach the remaining universe representatives about using a neutral space for discussion and perhaps have negotiators to convey options and possibilities to the warring parties."

Osiris agrees that is a good idea but he doesn't approve of my suggestion to bring their representatives from the future like we did for some of the previous inaugurations. He believes they might feel tricked if they saw themselves not involved in conflict anymore.

Next, I ask if there is a way to show representatives from the warring universes a vision of the possibilities. Charlie suggests that one member from each universe that has joined our council could talk to them and say, "'We are part of this, and we are learning how to be different.' And Mommy, we are going to play *Music from the Royal Fireworks* with fireworks about the top of the ship. Yes!"

I love listening to him when he's excited about something; luckily for me that is almost all the time. I am able to match his enthusiasm by saying that is a great piece and one that I've played myself. Charlie says the Swizzlers are going to have a chance to experience playing it with Handel as the conductor. Even though I probably won't see him, I'm going to enjoy just knowing he's there.

After discussing some more strategies, Osiris suggests that if the future council members from each of the warring universes are involved in our plans from the beginning they wouldn't feel like they had been tricked. We agree to implement this plan without me presenting the idea to the full council.

I can't quell my curiosity any longer and so I ask to speak privately with Matreeus Keylosh. When she is in presence, she asks how she may serve me. I'm not exactly sure how to proceed but it seems safe to ask her if she would be offended if I inquired how her entirely feminine universe works. Since she is willing to share information, I tell her we have not encountered a universe without any males and bluntly ask her how they manage reproduction.

She asks if those in our universe require males in order to reproduce. I confirm that we do and explain in a few sentences how we make babies. She replies that the females in her universe simply have the desire to create a baby and one will develop in the lower part of their body. There is a gestation period equivalent to four months of Earth time before the baby is released from a pocket on their physical body.

When she admits she is not familiar with the anatomy of an Earth woman, I send her a telepathic picture of a human woman's reproductive system and describe how the egg moves into the uterus. Although there are similarities for her species and the fluids of their bodies do feed their children, they do not experience the egg movement.

Then she explains that the pouch the little one is generated within is internal and yet also external so that the female can reach within it and lift the baby out. They experience birthing their young as a small disconnect that feels like a pinch. I experience only a moment of envy before a new question pops into my mind.

Still marveling that an entire universe could be feminine, I ask her if the animals are also feminine. She says that some plants have an interesting ability to procreate but before I can ask her about that she explains that their universe has an energy that, in a short period of time, changes anything masculine into feminine.

She must note the look of consternation on my face because she explains that they were aware Tonas would only be in their universe for a short period of time. She suggests we inform the Ashtar Command about this feature of their universe. Tonas agrees to do so immediately but first he wants to know the period of time before the change begins. Keylosh advises no longer than a cycle and informs us, "We have nine suns, and the cycle of what you call a day would encompass four Earth days. In that period of time, the nine suns and three moons make their transition. This is for our world of Renuhsha."

It seems to me that nine suns would make her world very toasty, but she says they are not so close that heat is an issue.

"Do you ever have night?"

"Oh, certainly, after the nine suns make their cycle we have what you would consider two days with our moons. We have two moons and yet we have one star that is like a moon, so you could say that we have three moons. You have these names for things that we are trying to match."

At this point, I ask what she looks like. She tells me that although her physiology is similar to mine, she is slender and much taller. She answers my question about how much taller than me she is by saying she would make three of my height. That means she's almost seventeen feet tall! More conversation reveals that members of her species live about nine hundred years and their coloring is similar to mine.

Now she admits they have watched some of our technologies and describes our birthing cycle as frightening while our mating rituals seem quite spirited. I agree that birthing is challenging and it's not much fun until it's over; then you're really happy to have your baby.

After thanking her for speaking with me so candidly, we rejoin the full council.

My first request is for a progress report on how the embodying is coming along. Charlie says we have started a small test program in the Ahkahnay Universe. Stars, moons and suns there were given the opportunity to step into a situation like our Equinox and all accepted a two week trial.

"What kind of dimension are they embodying into?"

"They are in a dimension of duality with the opportunity to move through the stages of evolution. These individuals are primarily of non-dual so they are excited to have the experience of duality with the option to evolve."

It's time for another update from Liponie about what is going on in the Fifth Realm. His laughter is followed by an announcement that my parents are having a barn dance and there is a large buffet.

My laughter echoes his at this bit of news. How could there not be a large buffet with Liponie involved. He adds that my mother has been giving cooking lessons. There is a whole section of pies and she is having the time of her life. Dad found individuals to weed their garden, but first he had to create the weeds!

Creating weeds is definitely an about face for my father. I know he had to pull a lot of weeds as he was growing up because his dad died when he was only twelve and he and his mom had a huge garden to support them. In his later years he spent a lot of time battling different kinds of weeds in our pasture. I know there would be no element of vindictiveness in the Fifth Realm. It must be that he just wanted to give other people a chance to experience that kind of labor.

"Has he got any cows to milk?"

"There are now cows and they are part of a new project. Your mother is teaching people to make bread. They must first plant the wheat and grow it. Then they must collect all the little seeds and mash them into the flour. Next, they milk the cow and gather eggs for the bread. Your mother even has individuals mining salt that goes into the bread. She is quite a character; she is the chip off of your block, my dear. This is a big project and the people are having a lot of fun. The Fifth Realm was a delightful place before, I am sure, but now it is an adventure!"

I am astonished by this view of my mother. I have to remind myself that she spent the equivalent of seventeen Earth years in the Master Academy. That must be what brought her out of her shell because she was never this outgoing when she was alive.

"Are there only humans involved in these projects?"

"Oh, no, there are individuals from many universes. I will say that the funniest of all of them are the dignitaries. Your father has them wearing bib overalls and straw hats and they are on their knees pulling weeds."

Again, I am gasping with laughter; this truly sounds exactly like something my dad would do.

"You have not lived, my dear, until you have seen Henry the 8th on a tractor."

My credulity has almost reached its limits but Liponie assures me he is not joking. He explains also that Dad has as many tractors as necessary, since they can be instantly manifested. It must be an amazing experience for a former farmer, like my dad, to think of a tractor and have it appear. They are John Deere tractors, of course.

Liponie laughs and says I started something that is a lot of fun for him. Mom and Dad define and create what they wish; he is simply giving them extra ideas.

Privately with Tonas:

His summary of the party is that there will be fireworks to Handel's music, then the dark sky will be revealed and he will turn the ship to the Sun. He reminds me, unnecessarily, that since *Music for the Royal Fireworks* was inspired by Liponie, hearing that will be very special for our genie. The food and gifts are in another room.

"We will sing 'Happy Birthday' when we roll the cake out. It will feed four billion."

I really can't imagine how big a cake would need to be to feed four billion. It has to fit inside the ship, though.

"All who have been assisted by Liponie are invited. It will be the largest party ever. My ship is not my ship anymore; it is now gargantuan."

He probably needed to make it that size so the cake would fit in it.

"Tonas, can you whisper to me tomorrow so I know what's happening?"

"I will blow in your ear, my dear." Before I can get too distracted by that thought, he adds, "Blow by blow account, of course."

He then tells me that Kee Kee has been presenting herself before Liponie to see if he will recognize her. I advise him to tell her to cool it. We'll definitely have a problem if Liponie gets suspicious. Tonas says he is not being a tale teller but that it is important for me to have "loop."

I thank him for keeping me in "loop" and bid him farewell.

CHAPTER FORTY

January 12, 2015

I am speaking with Esthra about the fact that I don't want to get this Joyce mixed up with the 10th dimensional Joy. He explains that the Joy that everyone knows at the council is reflecting my perfected version of self and everything I do enhances that other part of me.

I don't really understand what he just said. Joy seems very different from me. She seems naïve; Charlie let her win three bike races and she didn't pick up on that. She doesn't even like the same kind of orchids I do. I ask him if I become her. He replies no, and that does reassure me.

"You're always going to be the one. You will meet that other part of you, but this part of you is always going to override her. Tonas is in love with you; he's not in love with her."

That's hard for me to believe, but since there doesn't seem to be anything I can do about the situation now, I move to the Joy Council.

With the full council, I ask if the people in Equinox will experience any of the down sides to duality like aging, disease and dying. Charlie says they are in the honeymoon phase of this experience where they can eat all they want and have the sex. "They can do *everything* they desire. They will soon tire of this because there is more to stimulate their mind. Liponie has created for them a great opportunity for experiences that are evolutionary based, and, since they came from a non-dual environment, it will take very little time for them now that they have embodiments to feel and to sense."

I explain I was concerned that with the ability to manifest anything they want and not have to deal with the negative aspects of duality, they might want to stay in that reality forever. Charlie answers that they are having a higher experience because they are in the 5th dimension, not the 4th dimension. Also, he says Liponie gave them the *Oprah Winfrey Show* to watch. Liponie is such a genius!

Private meeting with Tonas, Aton, Charlie and Osiris:

Tonas says hello and comments that it has been a very full day with a great deal of trauma—for a moment he thought there would be no party at all. I am aware of the cause of the drama, me, and the instigator of the drama, Jill Marie, but I'm not exactly sure what she did. I was so down-hearted about the idea of having a measly circus for Liponie's birthday that I had a conference with her yesterday. She told me that she took some drastic action and everything will be perfect today. What a friend!

I share with the group that although I don't know what's going to happen, I am really relieved that we won't have to sit and watch a circus. Tonas says that none of them were impressed with the idea but they didn't want to tell Osiris that he had made a poor choice in Comahlee.

"I know that Jill Marie went to Liponie's future self to see what he would want so I'm sure we're going to have a great party."

"Her idea was magnificent and we came together to support her. She was very strong with Comahlee, perhaps even a little too strong."

"I wish I'd done it and not left it to her. I'm just kicking myself that I didn't speak up."

"She told him her idea and he would not comply."

Oh, oh, that means trouble ahead.

"Then she told him that she was going to fire him and he burst into flames right before us all."

Hearing this description helps to make it worth it that we had to change the party plans. Seeing him wreathed in flames would have been mind-blowing to experience in person but I really can vividly imagine it.

"It was very dramatic! He has not watched any television programs so he did not know what being fired means. She sent him to a room to think about it and told him that if he was not able to be a team player, he could take his shoddy tent and leave."

I'm able to laugh at the way she phrased her command, but I bet Comahlee was suitably shaken. You just don't mess with Jill Marie in her goddess mode. I don't know if I can ever repay her for saving the day, but I'm going to try.

It's time to start the party. I take a moment to do a quick SVH sweep because I'm nervous about messing something up. Then I say, "Hey, Liponie!"

Immediately, I hear his laughter along with a greeting. Trying to act natural, I tell him I've got some things I want his advice about and I'm going to gate us there. Before I can do it, he starts to protest that he can move to wherever it is. I explain that this is for me to do, grab his hand and move to the ship. The room must be dark as planned because I hear him ask me what's going on. Then I hear him say, "Aaah…"

Tonas begins to whisper to me that the music has begun quite softly, Handel is conducting and Liponie seems to recognize the music. "The fireworks begin above our crystalline ceiling and they are bursting in time with the music. I think Liponie still believes you want his opinion because he looks like he is judging it to strategize with you. Ah, he has just seen Handel. Oh, he is most excited; he is clapping his hands. Handel is dead, you know. (I love it when people remind me of that unimportant detail, death.) He is becoming one with the music and the fireworks. Now he is noticing that it is our darlings who are making the music. We are all impressed."

"Do they really sound good?"

"It is beautiful! Of course, if not, we would have made it so. Believe me."

"Charlie and the others really did get good playing the instruments?"

"They are expert; his idea of the collective was divine, of course."

"What instrument is he playing?"

"At this time he is playing viola. It is a flower."

This statement startles me as I imagine that Charlie has somehow created a flower you can play.

"Viola is a flower, you know, but he is playing an instrument. And now there are the final fireworks in the sky; it is the great culmination. The cake, not the one we will eat, is being rolled out, and Liponie now has put together the picture in his mind. He knows that this is a special occasion."

Tonas is still whispering and I've been giggling for some time as I picture Liponie observing all that is happening. "The drums are rolling; the Sun is now shining through the top of the ship onto the cake and out comes our beautiful Cory. Liponie is laughing; he is laughing; he is laughing. He is lifting her from the cake."

"What is she wearing?"

"She is wearing a beautiful sequined gown and it makes her look as if she is wearing a crystal dress. This is strategy to make her mother happy. I think it is important for you to offer your gifts now. Zeezzz is ready; she is wearing crystalline shoes and a crystalline gown similar to Cory's. She is beautiful and Marilyn taught her how to walk. She is ooh-la-la."

"Does she still have a tail?"

"Yes, it is quite nice. She is hidden among the group of people. When you announce the birthday you may give him your first gift. I have it in my hand now but we almost lost it when we thought everything was going up in flames. I leave this to you."

I call Liponie over. He is laughing as he tells me this is a great surprise. "Embracing everyone will have to come later because I have my beauty here."

"Here's my first present (the earring) for you, and happy birthday, Liponie."

"It is my very first birthday, and my very first party. I have never had a party for me."

"We had an extreme amount of difficulty because you are the supreme party planner."

"Well, I could not have done better. This is quite a surprise, my dear. I love this. Thank you, thank you, I will wear it always."

"We change our earrings; now you can do that, too."

"I will never take it off."

"Oh, Liponie, I love you so much, and I wanted it to be a really special day for you."

"It is, my dear. What could make this better?"

"There are a couple more things that might make it better. Here's another little present."

"Hmm, tell me of this."

"Is it red?"

"Yes."

"It's a Speedo swimsuit."

"Oh, you, naughty, naughty, I thought it was a handkerchief!"

Laughing, I comment that Cory couldn't resist him if he was standing on a diving board and wearing it. I have one more present but before I can tell Liponie about it he sees Lowmoeshee.

"It is my dear little boy! Cory, you must know my little boy who is now grown up. Lowmoeshee, I wish for you to meet the love of my heart, Cory. Embrace her, of course. Oh, what could be better than this?"

"Lowmoeshee, I know Liponie is going to want to chat with you, but I do have another person I would love for him to meet. I think this person is going to be someone who will be important in your life, Liponie. Would Zeezzz please step forward?"

The tone of her voice is cool as she greets Liponie. I introduce her to him as the lovely lady who is Cory's mother.

"Ah, Joy, you have brought me the greatest joy. Dear Mother…"

Zeezzz sounds neutral as she comments that Liponie has called her mother.

"Indeed, and I will now lean down upon my knee in your presence and ask for the hand in marriage of your daughter. Dear Cory, what could be better with your mother here. Will you be my bride? Will you be my everything forever? Will you spend the rest of existence beside me, living life with me, creating the destiny of the universes together with me as my partner? In heart, in my body and mind I am one with you now. Will you agree to be my forever?"

There is a pause before Cory speaks and there is supplication in her voice when she tells her mother that she loves Liponie more than anything.

"Please, will you give him a little piece of something for the ring so that we know that we have your heart?"

Zeezzz's voice has softened as she agrees to provide a piece from her crystal form for their ring. I'm breathing easier now that she's not going to refuse her daughter's request. She says that Cory is the light in her life and if Liponie makes her "pleasurous" then here is a ring for them.

Liponie asks Cory to look upon the ring that has been made from "the heart of her mother" and asks her if she will wear it.

"Always, always…"

Liponie says this is the best birthday and his only birthday. Then he asks, since everyone is here, if they should marry now.

I am finally able to laugh a little bit at this impetuous idea. I have *never* cried at any of the many human weddings I've attended or performed for, but with this special genie friend, I began sobbing during his proposal. If he asks me to conduct his wedding ceremony, I'm not sure I will be able to get through it.

Osiris clears his throat and agrees that he would love to see the wedding happen today, but perhaps another time would be better. "You know how the women like to plan. There are other imaginings afoot. We would like to bring into your presence a lovely woman named Kee Kee. She is someone I recommended who has assisted in creating a side party for others. It is a lovely circus and we are expecting to have the fountains of champagne. Kee Kee, I wish for you to show this dear one your true presence."

I hear Liponie gasp. Then he repeats Comahlee's name several times as he laughs and tells Comahlee that he did very well hiding. I thank Comahlee for keeping his identity hidden and for the work he did. Comahlee's only comment is that it has been interesting.

Osiris tells Liponie that there is another present from me and from Jill Marie. "I think the best way to offer this gift to you is to simply let the future self of Jill Marie begin the next phase of these party plans. She has a very interesting idea for you and so I will leave this to her."

Jill Marie's voice does sound somewhat like her, but perhaps a little smoother as she says, "Greetings, Liponie. I am the same person that you know, but a bit older and much wiser. In the time you are in now, I wished to offer you a great gift for your celebration. Nothing was shaping up to be good enough for you. All of us were in a position of struggle because the best party planner in all universes is you. It was impossible for us to consider bringing you into the loop, except that current self of me thought to bring you from the future into the loop. She, or I guess you could say I, had a conversation with you in the future. What I said to you was, 'Liponie, what do *you* desire more than anything in the worlds? What is the one thing?' You told me that you had the love of your life, that you had hundreds of children that were the gift of your heart, and that you had everything that you would ever dream of. In the moment of presence that we exist within now, there was only one thing that you would truly desire above all else. There was one focus of your mind, and that was to be everything for Joy. You said to me, 'If I can be everything for Joy, *give me that*, so that I may know that I have done all that I could do for her and for her passion and for our quest that we all join in heart.' These were your words to me.

I visited this part of me existing in the future, and asked myself how I could give you this gift. I wanted to show you, Liponie, that you have done it. My future self, the part of me speaking to you now, has seen that great vision. And so, Liponie and Joy and all of you in presence, I wish to show you in the night sky the culmative which is spurred by the collective. Liponie, you are a grand piece of the collective and the key stone of the work. I wish I could bring you the vision of the steps leading to this, but this is something that all of you must find on your own.

Those of you in witness, bring your eyes into the night sky and watch as the beautiful boundaries between universes erase. Watch as stars and moons and worlds in every universe quicken to their moments of completing, every sentience within each ascending and then the ascension of the actual stars and worlds. Look at the boundaries between the universes coming into their geometries as they merge upon one another into a great star. Watch as all of your passions and your works come into the final moments of the culmative.

Hear the voices of those whose hearts have met their match due to the focus of the matchmaker, Joy. Listen and feel the energy of the oneness, and feel Earth joining to be the last one to come into the geometries. See the star, ever so bright, that is created of those geometries, entering into what is called the Fifth Realm. You, Charlie, the gang and all of you working together took your hearts and caught onto the spirit of Joy's beautiful matchmaking. She has found love in the future, in the present and in the past and she is learning how to embrace and remember it. That has spurred her wish for all to experience it. As the culmative is being formed before your eyes and you watch as that grand star merges into the Fifth Realm, may you hear the endless voices, dear Liponie, that are spoken to Joy, for it is your desire to be in honor to Joy and that is your gift."

(I hope you will choose to step into this grand spectacle and open yourself to experiencing it at any level. I have been sobbing non-stop since Jill's future self revealed Liponie's wish.)

We hear a feminine voice say, "You saved my heart; you brought me the greatest joy. You helped me to find my beloved one."

Masculine voice: "You brought to my attention the star that was before me forever. I did not notice it because it was in my view always, and then when I watched it become so bright in its non-dual state, my attention was drawn to it and my heart opened to see the true love that this star became to my heart. I fell in love; I had the opportunity to be in a body because of you."

Feminine voice: "I felt the wonder of touch. I was a world that felt all of everything and yet I did not have other lips to kiss. You brought me those lips and when they met mine, the heart of my journey and experience became ever more."

"You, Joy, assisted me to find the moon that is my love."

"It is you who assisted me to bring the greatest joy to my everything. The people of my world enjoy the love that is a reflection of what I feel."

Feminine voice: "I am most excited to have a body because of you. To be a star is to be a great wonder, and yet to be embodied, as well as that presence, and to have joined the council and to have been an instrument of this that we witnessed is the gift you gave me."

Masculine voice: "You have changed our life, Joy. You have given us a meaning that never was known."

"You have given me the dream of my existence. I have a heart that beats and I have arms to wrap around my beloved."

"You have brought me the dream of my existence."

"Help is what you brought to me. I cried out for it and you brought me solace."

"The dream of my heart was not known because there was no thought of it. And then there was a vision of what could be, and I became one with a heart of a goddess."

Jill Marie continues now by saying, "This is all for you, Liponie, that you shall know that you have given Joy all that you wished. You said to me, 'All I want, because I have everything else, is to be everything for her.' Believe me that you are the one, that beside her, and working with the team, has with one thought created many incredible council presences. You have used your ingenuity and you have found ways to show other species how to come into an understanding of unity. Liponie, I wish for you to see now that this is your life and every being that you have touched and enriched will be singing your name forever. This, my dear, we have put into a necklace so that the song of it and their voices can always be felt by you. It is the same beautiful crystal that you wear only it is instilled with their voices. Joy, I'm giving this to you now so that you may present it to him."

I'm still crying too much to make any kind of creditable presentation so I just hand Liponie the necklace and tell him I love him.

"Joy, I cannot speak... You have given me my everything."

"That's OK, I can't speak either."

Zeezzz says that she can speak. "It is my great honor to give you my daughter. I could not imagine or wish for any other. You are my family now, and I accept you in any form you wish to be, Cory, and I bless your union."

Still crying, I manage to thank everyone. Tonas tells me he is overcome and that it is not often that he sheds tears. He asks Liponie if he can borrow his red handkerchief and then announces that there is cake and a fountain of champagne.

I am finally able to wish Liponie a happy birthday with all my love. Tonas echoes my wishes for a happy birthday and tells me that everyone is crying.

"They will cry into their champagne and they will cry into their cake. Oh, Comahlee has put a candle for every year of Liponie's life on the cake. How will he ever blow this out?" Then Tonas starts chanting Liponie's name and I join in. He reminds Liponie that he must blow out all the candles, and says that if anyone can do it, it is him.

Liponie laughs and says he is almost afraid to create such a wave. Then he reminds us that first he must have a wish. I remark that he could probably have more than one wish with all of those candles.

"My wish is granted…by you. You have given me a life."

"Liponie, I never want to plan another party without you. Never! If we have a party for you next year, you have to plan it!"

"Of course, my dear, Gogohsha may have given me life, but he did not give me a life. You have given me this life, you have given me purpose, and I am having the time of my life."

I hear him exclaim that he is going to extinguish the candles with one thought. Then, softly, he says the thought is great joy.

Taking control of his party, Liponie asks Comahlee to step aside, directs everyone to have a piece of pink cake and to put out their hand for a champagne glass. "We must have a toast and I cannot toast myself."

Taking that as a cue, I offer a toast to the joy that Liponie has brought to my life and add, "I wish a trillion fold of this joy for you, your family and all of your blue babies. If they're not blue, that's OK; I just want to hold one of them. Thank you, Zeezzz, for being so gracious."

"I am sold, my dear."

"I knew if you had a chance to get to know him you'd see how wonderful he is. I hope you get to taste the cake. I bet it's delicious."

Privately with Tonas:

He says that none of them ever thought they would see the culmative and that it is a great wonder to them that there will be "love in the stars."

He confirms that the different voices I heard at the end were from stars, planets, suns and moons that had embodied from every universe.

"What did it look like at the end when all the universes joined?"

"When it came together, it looked at first like what you call the Flower of Life. It compressed on itself and then it opened up to be the brightest of light. As I witnessed that, it was as if I could see myself somewhere in there. I could see us and the Earth. I could feel it, although it was only energy, and I knew that it was the folding upon folding upon folding of universes. When every single individual being with an essence ascends and then the world or the star ascends, at that point it is able to become part of the flow. I was watching to understand it more; it was quite amazing."

"What did the final form look like?"

"It looked simply like a particle of light."

"And then it moved into the Fifth Realm?"

"It did. It was our life's work. To witness what our works created is an affirmation of their worthiness. What a fellow that his only wish for a gift was to make you happy."

"He's the best friend ever."

"I must raise the bar on my adoration. It was the perfect gift."

"It was."

Mission Participation Directives:

Move into the chair reserved exclusively for you at one or both of the Joy Council tables (Councils are located on the 10th dimension of our Moon and in the center of the Earth.) and add your blessings, prayers, wishes and good intentions to the transmissions we send out. (These transmissions are also supported by the masters and angels overseeing the councils.) The easiest way to do this is to relax someplace comfortable and close your eyes intending to visit the council(s). Your intention automatically transports your consciousness there.

Another option is to choose a specific session to visit while you're sleeping. To enhance your enjoyment, set the intention that you will remember your visit upon awakening.

GLOSSARY

A special thanks to Jill Marie for her assistance in articulating the definitions in the glossary of terms.

Boomerang Stone: An SVH boomerang stone is a rock that has been selected to be instilled with codes and directives that engage the higher consciousness and soul of the implementer; to stretch a filament of their energy body to connect with specified areas of the world where the footprints of aspects of their soul lineage and the stones have been. When a connection is made between the implementer of a boomerang stone and the footprints of an aspect of the soul lineage, the Creator activates a series of elevating principles to support personal advancement for both parties. Depending on the focus of the boomerang, the higher principles can timelessly enhance sovereignty, alignment with soul purpose, freedom from drone mentality and the release of servitude, slavery and poverty imprinting. Some boomerangs connect with footprints of aspects of the soul lineage for reasons of anchoring higher energies and enhancing personal empowerment and lighting up paths to ascension.

Footprints: The use of the word footprints refers to energy imprints from aspects of our soul lineage that are timelessly registered on the Earth matrices, anywhere those individuals have been. The same is true for all of us; everywhere we have been on Earth holds an energy imprint that marks our presence there. When we step in to the footprint of an aspect of our soul lineage, a timeless connection occurs as both souls merge. In that union, both transmit life story data that can be energetically utilized to shift the consciousness of both.

Timeline: A timeline is a representation of one Earth cycle of experience. Timelines are typically representative of spans of 116 to 124-year increments.

Here's a little peek into what to expect in book 4…

PATHS OF FREEDOM

Other universes form Joy Councils, but it is touch and go until Liponie goes undercover to rescue a key figure in restoring peace and the team finally captures the mastermind (with supernatural powers) behind the plot to destroy all the Joy Councils. Even though the 3rd dimension left Earth in 2009, we discover and rescue 124,310 children stored in stasis there. Thankfully, there are many lighter moments, including: a chat with Lancelot (yes, very handsome); Gaia speaks about leprechauns; a pink crystalline spaceship, is unveiled and christened; precautions for time travel deemed necessary; celebrating the first anniversary of their meeting, Tonas gives Joy diamonds—she gives him a toaster; they might be engaged.

ABOUT THE AUTHOR

Joy has a Master's degree in music and is a professional violinist living in Bloomington, Indiana. She grows orchids as a hobby, enjoys walks in the woods and playing as well as listening to classical music.

Since 1990 she has been involved with Shaklee Corporation, a company whose philosophy of creating healthier lives matches that of her own. More information about Shaklee may be found at www.joyelaine.myshaklee.com.

She has studied and practiced SVH (Serenity Vibration Healing® and Enlightenment Technique) since 2003 and is a Master Practitioner and an Animal Healing Practitioner in that modality. She credits these studies with assisting her to bring forth the information in the Joy Chronicles. More information about SVH may be found at www.thejoyoflife.info.

cryptal of num - mt Shasta
SBT - space before time
chrome diopside

50327565R00267

Made in the USA
Columbia, SC
09 February 2019